TWENTIETH-CENTURY COV

The heart of the city

TWENTIETH-CENTURY COVENTRY

KENNETH RICHARDSON

The Lanchester Polytechnic, Coventry

ASSISTED BY

ELIZABETH HARRIS

CITY OF COVENTRY

First published 1972 by
THE CITY OF COVENTRY

SBN 333 13619 5 (paper cover)

Printed in Great Britain by
RICHARD CLAY (THE CHAUCER PRESS) LTD
Bungay, Suffolk

Contents

List of Illustrations

The authors and publishers wish to acknowledge the kindness of the following individuals and organisations in allowing us to use their photographs: Frontispiece, Aerofilms; 4. Jaguar cars; 6. Coombe Abbey; 7. A. C. Wickman; 8. Alfred Herbert's; 9. Standard Triumph International; 10. Coventry Climax Engines; 11. Mrs Bankes Price; 12 and 13. Hawker Siddeley; 14. G.E.C.–A.E.I. Telecommunications; 15 and 16. The Provost and Chapter of Coventry Cathedral (photographer, R. Sadley, A.I.I.P.); 17. Massey-Ferguson; 18. Courtaulds; 21. The Coventry and Warwickshire Collection (photographer, Stanley Jones); 23, 24 and 26. Coventry Corporation (photographers, P. W. & L. Thompson); 28 and 30. Coventry Corporation (photographer, Vivian Levett); 29. The Coventry and Warwickshire Collection (*Coventry Evening Telegraph* photographers).

All other photographs were taken by the Visual Aids Department of the Lanchester Polytechnic.

The maps were designed and executed by Philip Nicholls and 'Pip' at the Lanchester Polytechnic.

List of Maps

Preface

THIS book owes its existence to the patronage of Coventry City Council. When the suggestion was first made in 1966 that a history of modern Coventry should be written, the Estates and Parliamentary Committee sought the help of the Coventry branch of the Historical Association and the Lanchester Polytechnic to create a sub-committee which would give general guidance to the project. All members of that sub-committee have shown an active interest in the work, but two may be given particular mention. Alderman Harry Weston, senior member of the Council and a native of the city, has extended to this project his unvarying kindness and interest. Especially responsible for bringing the project to life has been Kenneth Turner, formerly Deputy Town Clerk, and unwearying in the help he has offered at every stage of the work. Also at this point should be mentioned the encouragement and assistance of the late Sir Charles Barratt, Town Clerk from 1946 to 1970, upon whom we could always call for guidance. Many other people have been good enough to read portions of the typescript and we have undoubtedly benefited from their advice.

The Coventry branch of the Historical Association has been closely identified with the progress of the work and has provided half the members of the controlling sub-committee. Among them should be mentioned John Short, Secretary of the branch, and Alan Dibben, City Archivist, who was one of those responsible for shaping the original scheme. He and his staff have also provided specialist help at every stage. We must also acknowledge the help and encouragement of Sir Alan Richmond, Director of the Polytechnic, and of its Library and technical staff. W. F. Gutteridge, formerly head of the Modern Studies Department, has been a valuable member of the sub-committee.

We must acknowledge our great indebtedness to Lord Iliffe, proprietor of the *Coventry Evening Telegraph* and a member of an old Coventry family. The Editor and Librarian of the paper have placed their files at our disposal and greatly facilitated our work.

The chief officers of the Corporation headed by Derek Hender, its Chief Executive Officer and Town Clerk, have been most helpful. Former chief officers, including A. H. Marshall, an ex-City Treasurer; Sir Donald Gibson and Professor Arthur Ling, both former City Architects; Walter Chinn, until recently Director of Education; and Cecil Dodson, the city's first Director of Housing, have all provided us with invaluable guidance. So have many other experienced public representatives, employees and ex-employees of the Council, one of whom was the late John Yates. We have had particular help from the staff of the Coventry and Warwickshire Collection which forms part of the city's Public Library Service, and from Vivian Levett, head of the Building Information Centre in the City Architect's Department.

Coventry's rich industrial life has provided us with ample material. We have received assistance from leading industrialists, among whom Sir Stanley Harley of Coventry Gauge and Tool, Sir Arnold Hall of Hawker Siddeley, Leonard Lee of Coventry Climax, J. J. Parkes of Alvis, Sir George Harriman and George Turnbull of British Leyland, and Alick Dick deserve special thanks. Lord Thomas of Remenham has placed his vast experience of the Nuffield organisation in Coventry at our disposal. We are also indebted to members of the staffs of Alfred Herbert's, Chrysler U.K., Courtaulds, G.E.C.–A.E.I., Massey-Ferguson, Rolls-Royce, Rover and Wimpey. Many with special knowledge of particular aspects of Coventry industry have helped us, including Sir Alan Cobham, F. M. Green, Walter Hassan, William Heynes, Jimmy Lloyd, W. S. D. Lockwood and the Honourable Ernest Siddeley.

Jack Jones, now General Secretary of the Transport and General Workers' Union, and Harry Irwin, his Assistant, were both formerly trade-union officials in Coventry and have given us much information. So have W. H. Stokes and Cyril Taylor, Bill Lapworth and Frank Chater, who between them have done much to shape the city's tradition of responsible trade-unionism.

Those leaders of the local community who have helped us will, it is hoped, not take it amiss if some names are omitted from this list. We would particularly like to acknowledge the help given us by Cecil Angel, George Moore, Alan Newsome, Sidney Penn, Sidney Snape and Patrick Twist; Dr Eric Kenderdine, John Mills, Mrs

Jagger, Mrs Mocatta, Dr Shulman, Mrs Sargent and Paul Stevenson.

The Right Honourable R. H. S. Crossman, M.P., senior member for the city, has given helpful advice, as have present and former members, including the Right Honourable Philip Noel-Baker and William Wilson. We have received help from the Home Office, the Treasury, the Board of Trade and the Ministries of Housing and Local Government and Technology, and we are particularly grateful to the local office of the Department of Employment and Productivity and to Major Bulman of the wartime Ministry of Aircraft Production.

We must not fail to refer to the help given by the Bishop of Coventry, the Right Reverend Cuthbert Bardsley; the Provost of Coventry Cathedral, the Very Reverend Harold Williams; Canon Stephen Berry, and Canon Proctor, Archdeacon of Warwick. The vicar of Holy Trinity, the Reverend Lawrence Jackson, and the minister of Queen's Road Baptist Church, the Reverend Richard Hamper, have been two among the many clergymen who have assisted us.

We must also thank the following institutes and societies which have searched their records and sent us much useful information: the Arts Council, the Horological Institute, the Institute of Mechanical Engineers, the Institute of Municipal Treasurers, the Royal Aeronautical Society, the Royal Institute of British Architects, the Town Planning Institute and the Association of Coventrians.

J. B. Priestley has kindly given us permission to quote in Chapter Ten a passage from his *English Journey*, published by Heinemann in 1934. In the same chapter we quote with permission from *Coventry New Architecture* published in 1969 by the authors, Grant Lewison and Rosalind Billingham.

Three typists have worked in succession on the preparation of this work, Mrs Pauline Harris, Mrs Mary Hunt and Mrs Joan Emanuel. We are deeply indebted to all three, and particularly to the last for her long service.

Mrs A. Mason, of the City of Coventry Library Service, has prepared the index with skill, scholarship and an endless patience.

Lanchester Polytechnic K.E.R.
June 1971 W.E.H.

CHAPTER ONE

The People and the Buildings

The Coventry of 'Middlemarch' and the Troughton drawings. A practical city, its freemen and its ancient schools. Apprenticeship. The enclosure of the Commons. Hillfields and silk. Chapelfields and watchmaking. The homes of the middle class; Stoke and Greyfriars Green. The social importance of Coundon Green. Cheylesmore and William Isaac Iliffe. The War Memorial Park and the Styvechale estate. J. G. Gray and Coombe Abbey.

I

Among the treasures which Coventry City Council has inherited from the middle of the last century are the Troughton drawings, executed by the solicitor who was then the city's part-time Town Clerk. These thousand drawings and watercolour sketches show a quiet Warwickshire town with streets of red brick and half-timbered houses surrounding the great sandstone churches and the Guild Hall of St Mary which survived from the mid-fourteenth century. Into these buildings in days of prosperity had gone part of the wealth of the medieval wool-merchants who drew their raw material from the near-by Cistercian houses of Coombe, Kenilworth and Stoneleigh. These same merchants also provided the city with a circuit of walls and, although very little more than two of the gates remained in the days of Troughton, houses had still not pushed far beyond that vanished circumference.

This is the city with its intimate links with the country, easygoing professional and manufacturing families and independent artisans which George Eliot described in 1871 under the name of 'Middlemarch'. She knew it well. As Mary Ann Evans, daughter of the agent to the Newdegates of Arbury, she had attended the school kept by the Misses Franklin, sisters of the Baptist minister at Cow Lane. The house now faces a trim municipal open space. It then fronted upon common land and was near the beginning of the great Lammas and Michaelmas meadows which were the main reason why the city's area had expanded so little.

A century later, despite enemy air raids and a vast increase in population, Coventry retains many of its medieval buildings. The Charterhouse on the London Road was a private residence until 1940 and is still as it was then. Near by, the house of the White-friars survives, with that magnificent upper room which, until recently, was one of the unseen gems in the city's still considerable collection. The churches of the Holy Trinity and St John, with the two sixteenth-century hospitals, Ford's and Bond's, remain. So does the fine Guild Hall of St Mary, the traditional centre of the town's government, now restored and cared for as carefully as it has ever been. The near-by Cathedral, formerly the parish church of St Michael, was burnt out in the raid of November 1940, but its walls still survive and its tower and spire, among the tallest in England, are preserved intact. The principal damage lies not in the great buildings, but in the small. The half-timbered houses, the top shops in which weavers and watchmakers once worked, many of these have now fallen victim to neglect, enemy action and the real necessities of replanning.

II

The visitor to Coventry today will find in Priory Row the scanty remains of the Abbey of St Mary around which, on a cliff overlooking the broad valley of the river Sherbourne, the first settlement grew. He will find that the lakes and pools which were once a feature of that valley have now, most of them, disappeared. The Swanswell Pool still exists, much altered and no longer the peaceful country retreat it once was. The pool which gave its name to Pool Meadow has gone, and the Bab Lake is remembered largely because it gave its name to one of the city's most famous schools. On the other hand, there is everywhere the evidence that Coventry is now a great centre of industrial production, above all in engineering. It has multiplied its population five times during this century and now

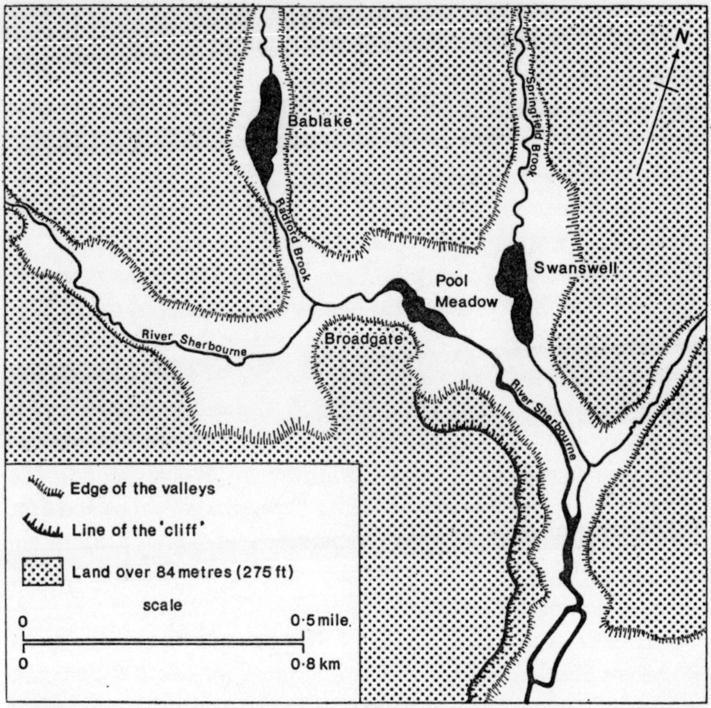

I The site of historic Coventry

ranks as the ninth city in the kingdom. The changes that this astonishing growth has brought about might be misleading, for Coventry today has more continuity with its past than is generally realised. Small place or large, Coventry has always been a practical, working town, rich in the skill, character and independence of its craftsmen. It has never contained a large leisured class, and nobility and gentry do not appear to have visited it regularly for the social season. No great merchant or banking families with wide international connections figure in its early business or social life. Its clergy have often been men of great character and learning with much influence on the life of the city, but it is only recently that Coventry has possessed a Cathedral Chapter with a number of full-time members free from parochial duty and able to make their full impact on the city's life.

The special position of the Freemen, with its traditional connection with apprenticeship, is perhaps the most significant consequence of the social composition of the city. One other should also be mentioned. Most citizens appear always to have had a special affection for schools which gave a practical education leading to a useful career,[1] and to have had little interest in classics, for a long time the only subject taught at the local grammar school. In consequence, the intellectual life of the city tended to be left in the hands of men who deserve the honourable title of self-taught.

Joseph Gutteridge, author of *Lights and Shadows in the Life of an Artisan*, admirably illustrates the best in the character of such men.[2] His book, which first appeared in serial form in the *Coventry Herald* during 1893, is a minor classic and won for its author praise and some help from Mr Gladstone himself. Gutteridge was a ribbon weaver, a quiet, decent man, whose love of nature was as great as his love of humanity. Possibly influenced by Holyoake, he once refused money which he badly needed because it would have meant making an avowal of religious beliefs which he did not possess. He built up a private museum in his home in Yardley Street and died, universally respected, in 1899.[3]

This tradition has not completely disappeared in our own day, as two recent lives show. J. H. Edwards (1891–1953) was a shoemaker, member of a trade which has always produced a large number of independent-minded men. He made himself an excellent antiquarian and was the first to excavate the neighbouring castles of Brandon and Baginton. He was made a Fellow of the Society of Antiquaries three years before his death in recognition of the expert professional approach which he had shown in all his work. J. B. Shelton (1875–1958) certainly never fell short of this same level of professionalism and he came to occupy in the city a position of respect which must

[1] For further illustration of this see the account of the Mechanics Institute and Technical College in Chapter Nine, page 244.

[2] *Master and Artisan in Victorian England*, ed. Valerie Chancellor: Evelyn, Adams & Mckay, 1969.

[3] Other men of the same tradition include W. G. Fretton (1829–1900), at one time a watchmaker and later a teacher at Katherine Bayley's Charity School in Little Park Street. He wrote a number of newspaper articles later collected as *Papers on Coventry History*. Benjamin Poole is another, an editor of the *Coventry Standard* who produced the classic local *History of Coventry* in 1870, which was printed by W. F. Taunton. Taunton had himself founded another local newspaper, the *Coventry Free Press*, which later merged with the *Coventry Herald*, then owned by Charles Bray.

have been remarkably similar to that earlier accorded to Joseph Gutteridge. He was the son of a farm labourer and came to Coventry from Nottinghamshire as a railway drayman. He built up his own haulage business and was soon able to devote more of his time to an exploration of the city's history, carefully watching every excavation during the period of redevelopment. He accepted the office of City Chamberlain in 1945, and the museum which he built up was handed over to the city before his death. J. B. Shelton is not forgotten today and an Annual Lecture is still held in his memory. He has named after him a square in the city centre and a school. While he lived, his acts of kindness to the less fortunate could not be numbered, and he made a great city into a friendly village when he walked about its streets.

Joseph Gutteridge himself had been educated at Baker, Billing and Crow's, one of the leading charity schools in the city. A charity school was intended to prepare sons or daughters of poor families for entry into a useful occupation. It was to be sharply distinguished from a grammar school, such as the Free Grammar School established in Coventry by John Hales in 1545.

The original hospital of St John, one of the few medieval hospital buildings left in this country, still stands at the foot of Bishop Street. Together with several other pieces of church property (including Whitefriars) it was purchased during the Reformation by John Hales, a Civil Servant in the Royal Household. This gifted and liberal-minded man, friend of Bishop Latimer and the Protector Somerset, converted the Whitefriars into his private residence and proceeded to found a school – a duty laid upon him by the conditions of sale. The old hospital building offered a very convenient schoolroom for his foundation, and here twelve children of Freemen were to be instructed, free, in the classics and music. The headmaster's house was constructed to the north of it and to the south lay a group of picturesque, half-timbered buildings, including the house of the assistant master and the library. This library, which contained volumes in Syriac, Hebrew and Welsh, as well as works on Egyptian hieroglyphics, must have been an object of wonderment rather than use in the city. It was swept away in 1794 as part of a street-widening scheme.

Most of the Freemen of Coventry, good, practical men, do not seem to have wanted their sons to enter the learned professions, but the school appears to have achieved some reputation in the early seventeenth century among the neighbouring county families and clergy. Its most illustrious headmaster was Dr Philemon Holland (1551–1636), translator of Livy and Suetonius. His successors, however, by no means equalled him in learning and the school's history soon became one of disputes and small numbers. Until its move to a new site on Warwick Road in 1885 and a period of reorganisation in the early part of this century, it appears to have enjoyed far less popular esteem and affection than Bablake.

The half-timbered buildings which originally housed Bablake School still stand, forming a pleasant courtyard with St John's Church and Bond's Hospital, one of the city's two surviving sixteenth-century almshouses. The buildings stand on land given in 1344 by Queen Isabella, widow of Edward II, who certainly had good reason for devoting herself to works of piety in her old age. There may well have been a school there before the Reformation. Certainly, in 1563, Thomas Wheatley gave money for a school which was to be very different from the Free School established not very far away by that gentleman from the Court, John Hales. Bablake was to be a charity school and, following the example of Christ's Hospital in London, was to educate poor boys and equip them for apprenticeship to an honest trade. A constant stream of benefactions from Coventry, men who knew and valued this school, shows how firmly it established itself in the city's heart. In 1890, when it moved to a new site to the north of the city centre, it was still a progressive school rendering good service to industry. It had been one of the first schools in the country to establish a laboratory in 1886. In 1908 it was said to be one of the best endowed schools of its kind in the country and His Majesty's Inspectors had already reported that it was beginning to give more attention to the literary side although 'substantial work has been done in science, mathematics and manual instruction'.

No less than six other charity schools came into existence in Coventry between the end of the seventeenth and the middle of the nineteenth centuries. Three were for girls; the Blue Coat School[4]

[4] The Blue Coat School has recently reopened on another site as a mixed comprehensive school.

whose Victorian home in Priory Row still exists, Southern and Craner's in Vicar Lane and the Freemen's Orphan Girls' School. There were three larger foundations all eventually confined to boys. These were Baker, Billing and Crow's in Cow Lane, Katherine Bayley's in Little Park Street and Fairfax's in Spon Street. All these schools took their pupils for two or three years, gave them a uniform, often boarded them for one year and took them to church or chapel on Sundays. The girls were trained for domestic service and the boys for apprenticeship with a small premium. Their charity school uniforms, black for Baker, Billing and Crow's, blue for Katherine Bayley's and green for Fairfax's, disappeared from the city when the three schools were amalgamated with Bablake between 1887 and 1901, but the names of their founders are perpetuated in those of Bablake Houses today.

III

Any apprentice in Coventry can receive the Freedom of the City, provided his name has been enrolled in the annual register of apprenticeships kept by the Lord Mayor of the city, and that, in time, it has been entered in the annual register of those completed. He will then be invited to attend a Freemen's Court to be sworn in before the Lord Mayor. Apprenticeship has, however, changed so much that perhaps another word now ought to be used to describe it. At one time an apprentice was bound for seven years to a single master who was also a working craftsman; now he is usually bound to a firm for four. That firm may well be part of a group apprenticeship scheme, intended to give its young men the widest possible experience within a number of co-operating factories. It will usually call upon the help of a local college and expect its apprentices to attend there for courses. In 1963 the Industrial Training Act strengthened and reinforced the old voluntary system by providing that each industry should create an Industrial Training Board, financed by a levy from the employers and responsible for supervising the efficiency of training within the industry as a whole. Things have moved a long way, but the Freemen's Courts still continue, and a great city still does honour through them to the pride of craft upon which its life depends.

Nowadays the status of Freeman is simply a recognition of a training but at one time it meant a great deal more. For many decades in the last century the Freemen were still the living heart of Coventry. The typical Freemen were the small masters in the city's two main industries, ribbon weaving and watchmaking. Friendly societies and city charities protected them in bad times, and their children might find a place in the city's charity schools. The Freeman had a Parliamentary vote which, for a long time, he treated as a piece of property which he had the right to sell to the highest bidder at election time. He would almost certainly be a commoner, having the right to keep animals on one of the city's many commons. Citizens still alive can remember the commoners' cows at pasture on Stoke Green, and the commoners' rights were not finally extinguished until 1927, when the conservators were swept away and the City Council took over the administration of the commons.

In one way or another, the commons which ring Coventry today have been given their place within the general pattern of the city's parks and open spaces. In the centre Greyfriars Green has become an ornamental walk and garden. So has Top Green, that little triumph of simple naturalism in landscape design. Further south the beautiful, unspoiled woodland of Styvechale Common still stands on either side of the Kenilworth Road. In October 1953 the Duke of Edinburgh opened the playing-fields which had been created on $33\frac{1}{2}$ acres of Whitley Common at the expense of Sir Billy Butlin, then at the height of his fame as a holiday camp proprietor. On the other commons and heaths, such as Hearsall Common to the west, the Corporation has itself provided opportunities for recreation on lands which were once a fiercely defended part of the livelihood of the city's Freemen.

The commons which remain today represent what is left of the wastes which once separated the ancient city from neighbouring communities such as Stoke and Styvechale. More important were the meadows, the Lammas and Michaelmas lands, which were also available for grazing after the proprietors had taken off the hay crop. In 1860, when all the commons were systematically surveyed, they were found to cover an area of 1400 acres. For one reason or another that total had declined in the years before the survey, but the 1817 estimate of 3000 acres is almost certainly exaggerated.

This broad belt of green was particularly impressive to the west and south, where the Lammas lands extended on both sides of the river Sherbourne. From Foleshill and Radford in the north they ran down the whole of the west side of the city until they touched the parklands of the Manor of Cheylesmore, owned until 1871 by the Marquess of Hertford.[5] Nobody in Coventry was very far from clean, fresh air but, as long as the commons remained, the city's expansion was impeded, one of the reasons why Coventry missed the Industrial Revolution. The number of Freemen actually using their grazing rights appears by the nineteenth century to have been small and land suitable for the building of houses and factories was standing unused.

It was only in 1857, after a fight which had gone on for twenty years, that the decision in favour of enclosure was taken. The Freemen gave the necessary two-thirds majority, and other opposition was overcome. The actual enclosures came under two Acts of 1860 and 1875, but the common lands which are left today are one proof of the public feeling which the controversy had aroused. Another was the creation of the Freemen's Trustees. Under each enclosure certain lands were set aside, so that their rents could be applied for the benefit of the Freemen as a whole. It was decided to apply the proceeds of these rents in two directions which were already familiar in Coventry charities. There already existed a Freemen's seniority fund which gave old-age pensions to a number of Freemen from money derived from earlier enclosures such as those for the Holyhead Road and the railway. This has now been broadened so that such payments are made weekly to 200 senior Freemen, although no longer on Saturday mornings in the centre of the city. Following the example set by Sir Thomas White's Charity,[6] the Freemen's Trustees also make available interest-free loans to young men who are anxious to start up in business on their own and who are expected to start repaying the money after nine years.

Many things have caused a diminution of the importance of the

[5] The third Marquess of Hertford (1777–1842), who was Recorder of Coventry, is said to appear twice in literature. He is regarded as the original Lord Steyne of Thackeray's *Vanity Fair*, and Lord Monmouth in Disraeli's *Conningsby*.

[6] For Sir Thomas White's Charity see note at the end of this chapter, page 32.

Freemen within the city. The interest-free loans and seniority payments once played an important part in giving city life a special character. They encouraged much useful initiative among the young and removed the threat of dire poverty from many of the old. Commercial borrowing is now very much more widely developed and the State has entered the field of social security, so that the seniority payment no longer makes the vital difference between independence and the workhouse. There have, therefore, been a number of complaints about apathy among Freemen with calls for some kind of an association which could bind them together. The first attempt at this came in 1937, when Provost Howard, then at the Cathedral, called the first meeting of a Guild of Freemen and Apprentices. It was intended that the Bishop of Coventry should be invited to become the Master and that meetings should be held in St Michael's School, conveniently near the city centre in Much Park Street. The war snuffed out whatever life had been breathed in this early Guild and it was not until 1946 that another attempt could be made. From this dates the present Freemen's Guild, with its annual banquet at which the loving-cup presented by the Lord Mayor of London in 1953 is still proudly circulated.

IV

Previous to the enclosures the city had tended to expand by developing separate manufacturing settlements on the far side of the commons. Hillfields had been begun in 1828 as a centre of ribbon weaving and the building of the two watchmaking villages of Chapelfields and Earlsdon started in 1847 and 1853 respectively.

The visitor today will find very little left of either the charm or the social cohesion of Hillfields. It appears to have been built on part of the estate of Primrose Hill House, one of the many country houses which has paid the penalty of being situated too near an expanding industrial city.[7] When the Church of England gave this detached settlement a vicar in 1843, it provided him with a vicarage fit for a scholar and gentleman, which still stands near the site of the

[7] After a chequered career, during which it was at one time a boarding-school and at others a private residence and municipal washhouse, the house has now been pulled down, but some of the grounds still form a public park.

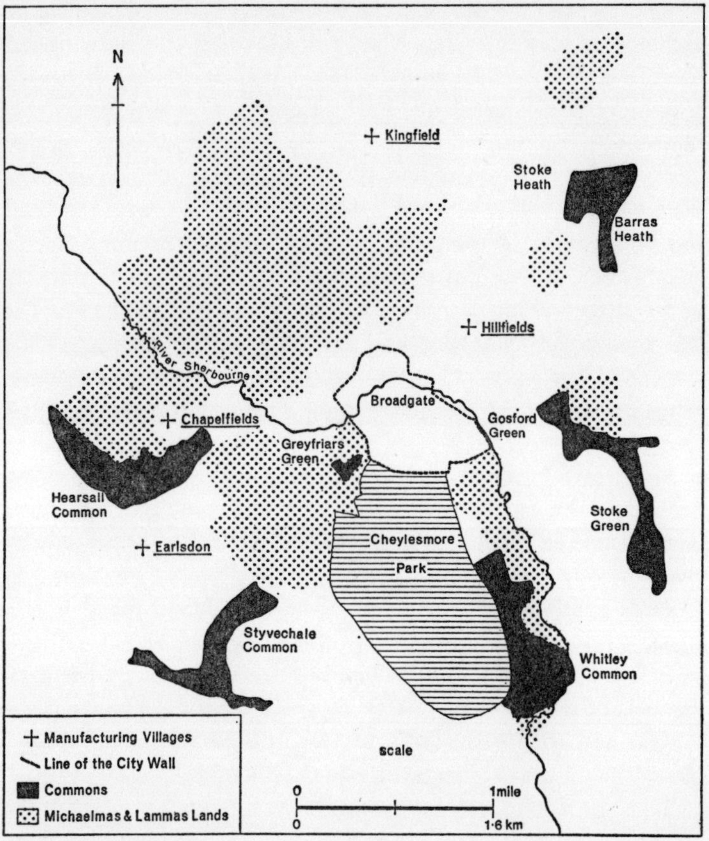

II Coventry's first green belt – commons, Lammas and Michaelmas lands and the Cheylesmore Estate

old house. Two distinguished Christian Socialist vicars, P. E. T. Widdrington and Paul Stacy, were to live there between 1906 and 1944, and serve in the austere red-brick church of St Peter. But the glory of Hillfields was always its independent ribbon weavers.

In the decade before the great days of the industry ended with the crash of 1860,[8] factories were getting an increasing hold in the centre

[8] On 11 February 1860, Gladstone announced in the House of Commons that the protective duty on foreign ribbons was to be removed immediately. This blow struck the Coventry weaving industry at a time when its position in the home market must already have been undermined by the serious industrial disputes of 1858 and 1859. A depression began with calamitous suddenness and the trade never recovered its previous position.

of the town and independent craftsmen tended to congregate more and more in Hillfields. Here it was that Eli Green, a wealthy ribbon manufacturer, launched an experiment, part of which can still be seen in Vernon Street. He erected a triangle of sixty-seven cottage homes with top shops for looms on the second floor taking power from a central steam-engine. Besides working on Eli Green's materials and selling him the finished ribbons, the weaver would pay him rent for the power he used. He would, therefore, have to start work when the power came on, but he was still not working in a factory and much of his cherished independence remained. It was an idea worthy of an industry with a strong co-operative tradition, and it had a greater chance of success than was often supposed, but it came too late. The first Vernon Street houses were not built until 1858.

Further out in the country, in the district known as Kingfield, the brothers, John and Joseph Cash, were trying to do the same thing. They planned to erect a settlement of one hundred cottage homes by the Coventry Canal, each of them provided with a top shop and furnished with power. The present row of buildings facing Cash's Lane, with their ornamental half-timbering and ample gardens, represent all that were built. The present Cash factory has been erected at the rear of this interesting social experiment which owed a great deal to the friendship of Joseph Cash and Charles Bray, himself at one time a manufacturer in the silk trade.[9]

Thus the ribbon weaving industry was based to the north of the city, with the most skilled men tending to live in Hillfields and the least skilled in the country districts from Foleshill to Nuneaton. The watchmaking areas, on the other hand, were to the south and west, running along the course of the river Sherbourne from Chapelfields to St John's Church and including the separate village of Earlsdon. The annual figures for enrolled apprentices show that, long before the ribbon trade went under in 1860, watchmaking was beginning to supplant it in the affections of young men who wished to acquire a skill. Until it declined in the early part of this century

[9] Charles Bray was the son of a wealthy Unitarian family of ribbon manufacturers. He became a radical and a reformer, a friend of George Eliot, Herbert Spencer and Robert Owen. He bought the *Coventry Herald* in 1846 and interested himself in many reforming movements such as the Coventry Labourers' and Artisans' Friendly Society of the 1840s.

under the impact of Swiss competition, this trade fed into the life of the city a breed of proud, independent and obstinate men whose memory still has its attractions. There were a few left after the First World War, but S. Alexander of Chapelfields was still describing himself as a watchmaker until his death in the early 1960s, and that stout Englishman, J. K. Newsome (1864–1947) attended his office in the Butts every evening until shortly before his death, although he had not sold a watch since 1904.

The district of Spon End is one of the few places in the city where buildings of the sixteenth and seventeenth centuries can still be found on their original sites. After it was discovered in 1966 that only thirty-four buildings constructed before 1700 were still in existence in the city, the Council adopted a policy of moving them into this area. These newcomers must be distinguished from such little masterpieces as the Windmill Public House, situated next to Rotherham's, the biggest single factor in the Coventry watch-making industry for over a century and a half. This firm has long since ceased to make watches and the Rotherham family is no longer concerned in it but a business associated with the names of Vale, Rotherham and others can be traced back to the mid-eighteenth century. From the first it appears to have gathered all its workers on one site, housing them in a series of adjacent workshops which were converted into a true factory in 1884, when John Rotherham (b. 1838), installed power.[10]

Five years later in the same street the Coventry Movement Company was established as a further attempt to make the local industry more competitive. Hitherto Rotherhams had been the one large establishment in the watch trade in Coventry. Organisation in the rest of the trade had been so complex that those who require a fuller description must look elsewhere. The metal parts of the Coventry watch appear, as a general rule, to have been made in rough in Lancashire. They were purchased by local manufacturers who employed specialists to finish and assemble the wide range of components in the completed watch which they eventually sold. It was the domestic system at its most complicated and long before the Coventry Movement Company came into existence there had been

[10] The workshops still exist and the old Rotherham family house, dating from the mid-nineteenth century, still forms the frontage on Spon Street.

a tendency to make it simpler. In 1817 there were specialist craftsmen engaged on no less than 102 separate processes. Towards the turn of the century the number of those still working in their own homes appears to have been drastically reduced for a number of reasons. Small factories had emerged such as that of Fred Lee in Dover Street and Errington's (later Williamson's), in Holyhead Road. One would like to know more of the Co-operative Watch Manufacturing Society which still existed in the Allesley Old Road in 1912 after a life of nearly thirty years. The Coventry Movement Company was itself part of this streamlining process. It consisted of a number of manufacturers who pooled their resources in order to establish a factory which would give them a complete movement to which they could add their own dials, hands and cases.

The Coventry handmade watch was never intended for the mass market, and its makers were proud of the fact. It gave quality to those who appreciated it, and there is still a touch of quality about old Chapelfields and Earlsdon today. The wives of ribbon weavers usually had to work to supplement the family income, those of watchmakers did not. They were therefore able to keep a neater home, with a trim little garden in front. In Craven Street or Upper Berkeley Road today it is still possible to distinguish the larger houses in which the masters lived alongside the men. Philip Cohen eventually took a house on Greyfriars Green, but it was rare for a master to move to another district.

The career of J. W. Player (1865–1956) admirably illustrates the virtues of the Coventry watchmaking industry, and equally admirably accounts for its decline. There were many Players in the business. In 1874 Craven Street, besides containing two Bands and three Lees, had Players at numbers 4, 6, 8, 9 and 10. (Number 9 was the home of William Player and not intended to be used as a workplace.) In the four houses on the other side of the road members of the family carried on related businesses as watch dial makers and painters. Other members of this family were to be found along the Butts and it appears to have been Joseph Player, watch manufacturer at number 24, who was J. W. Player's father.

Joseph Player was an intelligent man running an up-to-date business and wise enough to send his son to Switzerland for advanced technical training. There J. W. Player remained for some years, becoming something more than a fine craftsman and marrying a Swiss woman who was herself closely connected with the industry. He was to produce two revisions of Britten's *Watch and Clockmakers Handbook*, one of them finished in 1955 in his ninetieth year. His practical skill was shown by his completion in 1909 of the most complicated watch ever made in England, with perpetual calendar and a great deal of astronomical information which only the specialist was likely to want. It cost £1000 to make and perhaps it is not surprising that his Coventry business failed in the following year. He spent the rest of the time before his retirement working either in Switzerland or in England as agent for a Swiss company.

If J. W. Player's background was typical of many men from the Coventry watchmaking industry, A. E. Fridlander's (1840–1928) was not. There was a long tradition of Hebrew scholarship in the family. He himself talked about Jewish religion and history to George Eliot and probably had his influence on the writing of *Daniel Deronda*. He was certainly a good scientific watchmaker and remained in the trade until 1907, but he was always something more. Charles Bray knew him as a fellow intellectual and he was also a financier. As such he was concerned in the foundation of the Leigh Mills Company, formed in the city during the depression of the 1860s in order to alleviate some of the distress caused by the collapse of ribbon weaving. He was later on the Board of Triumph with Siegfried Bettmann and he took his part in the public life of the town, being particularly interested in education.

As the difficulties of the watchmaking industry increased towards the end of the century, the manufacturing families reacted in different ways. Fred Lee began to specialise in watch jewels and moved towards that position of importance in industrial jewels which made his little firm indispensable in the Second World War. The Williamsons tried to enter the field of the petrol-driven engine and manufactured motor-cycles and cars. A number of families moved over to the retail side of the business. Oliver Flinn, for instance, established a shop in Broadgate in 1884, and the same path was followed by the Gilberts and the Bands. In 1874 the Hattrells are found as watch compensation balance makers in Duke Street, Chapelfields, but W. H. Hattrell became an architect and estate developer and was largely responsible for those parts of Earlsdon built before the First World War.

The extraordinary growth of the city caused by the coming of the bicycle boom gave opportunities to some of the bolder young men from the watch industry, which had never lacked brains or initiative. Alick Hill (1847–1921) realised in 1896 that Coventry made everything for the bicycle except the chain. He, therefore, began to manufacture chains in a small way in Dale Street, near the city centre, sharing power from a small steam-engine with a carpet cleaning company next door. He invented nothing new, but his keen business sense rapidly carried the Coventry Chain Company out of its small workshop into the large factory where it still is. In the middle of the nineteenth century, Isaac Newsome had been bound apprentice to the watchmaking trade because his father saw that the heart was going out of ribbon weaving which had been the family's traditional centre of interest. A similar situation occurred about sixty years later when it became clear to Samuel Theo Newsome (1868–1930) that the watch trade was also nearing its end. He, therefore, made a bold move. Together with others, he put his money into the theatre and became the managing director of the Coventry Hippodrome, a field into which his son, Samuel, followed him.

V

Few buildings in Coventry survive from the late eighteenth century when those who had prospered were still content to build within the city. Two such are in Little Park Street, one being Kirby House, later the offices of Troughton, Lee and Kirby, the firm of solicitors of which the creator of the Troughton drawings was the senior partner. Along Priory Row, between Holy Trinity Church and the new Cathedral, stands all that is left of what was once a select residential quarter. Number 11, now known as Gorton House, still retains its original and very beautiful frontage although the remainder has been completely rebuilt.[11] It is now used mainly by the

[11] The pleasant area round it including the new Cathedral, Holy Trinity Church and St Mary's Hall is now protected by one of the seven Conservation Orders made to protect areas of particular beauty or interest within the city. Others cover Greyfriars Green, Kenilworth Road, Stoke Park, Allesley Village, Lady Herbert's Garden and Spon Street.

Cathedral, which naturally spreads its influence along the whole row. Even at the beginning of this century most of these houses were no longer homes. One of the last which survived as such was probably number 7 where, until his death in 1904, lived John Gulson, Quaker, liberal reformer, patron of public libraries and education and at one time Mayor of the city.

When the comfortably off began to move to within carriage distance of the city they first went in any considerable numbers into the rural parish of Stoke to the east. It is possible to understand even today what attracted them. Of the parish's two manor-houses, Stoke Hall had long since gone and Biggin Hall was a mere shell, but there was a pleasant church, plenty of good farm land and space around the Green to build attractive houses, many of which still exist. It was in this pleasant knot of buildings, with the trees and little National School that there lived, in 1880, William Herbert, elder brother of Sir Alfred, and, in 1892, Daniel Turrall, textile manufacturer. At a small farmhouse called 'The Hollies', the Reverend George Heaviside ran a school until Kevitt Rotherham took over the house in 1891. There he stayed until the building of the Humber factory near by in 1908 when he fled to Kenilworth.

Some of the houses built in Stoke by the Coventry middle class were larger and more isolated. William Hillman was later to build his motor-car factory in the grounds of his home, Abingdon House. Stoke House, now a children's home, was built on the farm lands between the Binley and Walsgrave Roads and Sir William Wyley was born there in 1851. Last and most spectacular of these larger residences was Copsewood Grange, an elaborate neo-Gothic mansion in which lived James Hart and later Sir Richard Moon. James Hart had come to Coventry from Lancashire in the 1850s to start a ribbon weaving factory. His intensive discipline and contempt for the easy-going methods earlier prevalent in the trade earned him great unpopularity. Sir Richard Moon was Chairman of the London and North-Western Railway between 1861 and 1891 and associated with Joseph Cash of the textile family in his attempt to produce a synthetic fibre.

This outward movement of the middle class was bound, sooner or later, to raise the question of the development of the Cheylesmore Estate immediately to the south of the old city centre. It is difficult for the visitor nowadays to realise that there ever was a manor of Cheylesmore. Much Park Street and Little Park Street, both formerly more important than they are now, are so named because they led to the park of that manor. The site of the Manor-House is marked by its gateway, which still survives much restored at the end of the street called Cheylesmore. Greyfriars Green, which was enclosed under the Act of 1875 and made into a pleasant little park, was once a triangular piece of common. Building had taken place on what was then a detached portion of the Cheylesmore Estate overlooking orchards which ran along the course of the River Sherbourne.

For many years the attractions of this view over open country made the houses in what is now Warwick Row the most sought-after in the city. In 1874 their occupants included Charles Bill, the silk broker, Dr Charles Webb Iliffe, Miss Rotherham, Samuel Vale and Frederick Browett. Samuel Vale lived at the most famous of these houses, number 29, at one time occupied by the Misses Franklin's school, attended by George Eliot. It is probably this house which figures in *Middlemarch* as that which Dr Lydgate took on his marriage to Rosamond Vincy.

On the far side of Warwick Road a terrace of houses bearing the fashionable name of the Quadrant had been completed by 1863. It was never quite as successful as its creators must have hoped. When the Quadrant was first built open country lay just behind it, but towards the end of the century the development of the Cheylesmore Estate seemed to push the countryside further away, and the building of tram-lines down Warwick Road brought the centre of the town a great deal nearer. The district became a favourite one for girls' private schools. The Quadrant itself had two; Miss Rolfe's was there in 1906, and the Quadrant School, under the direction of Miss Hales, continued until her death in 1923. Miss Ward's school in one of the neighbouring villas continued until the outbreak of the Second World War. Successive vicars of St Michael's found the district very convenient, and Provost Richard Howard lived there until he retired in 1958.

Most manufacturers and people of great substance still preferred to live out of town, although within easy reach. A rather special case was Charles Kingston Welch (b. 1861), inventor of the detachable pneumatic tyre, which he sold to the Dunlop Company. His royalties gave him an income which enabled him to pursue a range of interests so wide that they would have earned respect if found in a figure of the Italian Renaissance. He was interested in medicine, photography and telescopes. His working drawings were very exact, showing his natural artistic talent, and he had a passionate interest in music. He installed two pipe organs in the house, and they were still there when the property later passed into the hands of Leonard Lee, owner of Coventry Climax.

George Loveitt, the estate agent, and William Goate, the solicitor, were among the other professionals who found the Quadrant and district convenient. Doctors also lived there and in 1911, Dr Walter Brazil arrived from Lancashire to take over number 1 The Quadrant. He had a passionate interest in collecting and repairing old clocks about which he was to write a book in 1934. The household was soon completed by the arrival of his two sisters, Angela (1868–1947) and Amy (1863–1951). They had travelled widely together studying art and Amy soon became a leading figure in the Coventry and Warwickshire Society of Artists. Angela had published the first of a long line of girls' school stories – *A Terrible Tomboy* – in 1905. The family kept a holiday cottage at Polperro, filled their Coventry house with clocks, water-colour paintings and a valuable collection of old china and held musical evenings with their friends around them. One of these was Mary Dormer Harris (1867–1936), daughter of a Stoneleigh farmer who may have been an unusual man, since he sent his daughter to Lady Margaret Hall at Oxford. Later, while a member of the Brazil circle, she was to place the city in her debt in various ways. She and the Brazils became prominent members of the City Guild, formed in 1914, and she made an invaluable transcription of the Coventry Leet Book between 1907 and 1913.[12]

VI

Eastwards from the city of Coventry, through the parishes of Stoke, Binley and Walsgrave, the land gradually merges into the plains of Leicestershire. It is a pleasant landscape, but rather lacking in strength and we are grateful to successive earls of Craven for giving

[12] See also *Life in an Old English Town* (1898) and *The Story of Coventry* (1911).

it trees, a great lake and perspectives in their park at Coombe Abbey. To the south we are equally grateful to those who planted spinneys along the Kenilworth Road. To the north and west, the landscape is subtly different. The soil changes, the hills are more varied in their contours and memories of the great forests are nearer. By the late nineteenth century parishes such as Foleshill and Coundon with Keresley consisted of a number of scattered hamlets which had once been in forest clearings, and some woods of great beech trees were still in existence. Houses which had once contained George Eliot's friends were still there in plenty and great estates did not exist. It was for all these reasons that the social leaders of Coventry, when they moved from the city, tended to go to the north and particularly to Coundon Green, before development along the road to Kenilworth became possible during the late 1920s.

Photographs alone survive to give some imperfect idea of the charm of Rose Hill, that beautiful, comfortable villa near the top of Bishop Street where lived Charles Bray. The movement to the heights in the north which he had begun was to continue steadily over the next forty or fifty years, bringing Coventry business families among the local gentlemen and farmers, such as the Ortons of Foleshill, the Hollicks of Fillongley Grange and the Knowleses of Corley Hall. In 1874 Henry Rowbotham, silk broker, lived in Edgwick House, Charles Bill, another silk broker, on the Fillongley Road and John Cash at Coundon Vicarage. At this time Coventry, although it had recovered from the depression of the sixties, was still not enjoying the prosperity that was to come later, when, with the invention of the safety bicycle in 1884 followed by the patenting of the Dunlop pneumatic tyre in 1889, came the great bicycle boom which was to create an entirely new middle class, many of them coming from outside the city. The supply of existing properties was insufficient and the answer was found in new building along the Radford Road.

In 1902 two of the three brothers who owned the Riley Cycle Company were living there, William at Holly Bank and Basil at Middleborough House. The Rileys had been ribbon weavers and later manufacturers of textile machinery before turning to bicycles. Charles Hill, watchmaker, father of Alick and Chairman of Coventry Chain, lived near by in an enormous house at Elmfield. These were all Coventry-born men who had changed their trades, but J. K. Starley at Barr's Hill House on the other side of the road was not. Like his uncle, James Starley, the first man to make bicycles in Coventry, he had come from outside, bringing prosperity with his invention of the Rover Safety Bicycle. The Sturmeys, of the Sturmey-Archer three-speed gear, were living around the corner in Middleborough Road in 1904. The most imposing mansions of the new cycle kings, however, were Coundon Court and Keresley Hall, built by George Singer and William Hillman in the very exclusive district of Coundon Green.

The principal inhabitants there were a relatively small group of long-established professional and business families who were proud of their deep roots in the life of the city. Their social set included, at one time or another, the Rotherhams, Cashs, Jaggers, Iliffes, Twists and Browetts. The Rotherhams and Twists had always been Church of England, but the Cashs and Browetts had behind them a long Quaker ancestry. By the early twentieth century the social habits of the two sets of families had coincided. The older men gave a very real social leadership to the city through their work in the charities and their influence within the six surviving city companies, of which the Drapers' was by far the most important. The young men went to public school, often to Rugby, and introduced the game of Rugby football into the city by founding the Coventry Football Club in 1873. They became officers in the Yeomanry or the 7th Battalion Royal Warwickshires, and in the First World War four out of the fifteen members of the Coventry Old Rugbians Association were killed in battle.

This was the age of Soames Forsyte; the age which saw the emergence in every large town and city of an upper middle-class establishment consisting of respectable, educated men and women of position, strong in a sense of public duty and no longer looking for guidance to near-by members of the landed classes. The process has particular interest in Coventry because of the city's fivefold increase in population during the first half of this century, caused by the emergence of a series of new industries and the boom brought about by work for two world wars. Among the many consequences of this great urban revolution was the snapping of the city's links with the surrounding countryside. At one time local landed families had exercised influence within the city, but the Marquess of Hertford sold the Cheylesmore Estate in 1871. In 1923 the Craven family disposed of their great estate at Coombe Abbey, near Binley, and the Leighs of Stoneleigh ceased to play any conspicuous part in the public life of Coventry at about the same time. But the relatively few old upper-middle-class families were by no means to be left unchallenged, since new industries meant newcomers to the city, often with considerable money. During a period of great change, however, they provided a much-needed continuity, the value of which should not be forgotten.

For more than one generation the Twists and Browetts had stood as the twin pillars of the legal profession in Coventry. In the days when public business was not as crushing in volume as it is now, it was possible for a private solicitor to hold a public office part-time. Between 1843 and 1896 two generations of Twists had acted as Clerks to the Magistrates and between 1858 and 1893 Thomas Browett was Town Clerk to the city. When Harold Twist died on 15 April 1942 his family had been practising law in Coventry for four generations and had been clerks to the vestry of Holy Trinity Church since 1778. The Browetts had been later arrivals, but could claim a close relationship with John Bright, the Quaker and Liberal M.P. of the nineteenth century. One branch of the Browett family had been in silk manufacture but, as this became increasingly precarious towards the end of the century, more importance came to attach to the other branch of the family who were among the most respected solicitors in the city.

After his father's death, Walter Browett continued the firm until his own death in 1936. He belonged to clubs in both London and Bath, loved the theatre and knew both Fred Terry and Mathieson Lang. Perhaps he was happiest, however, when acting as host in his own home to fellow members of a city company at one of those annual feasts which always included a dish to show that these had once been bodies of poor people.[13] As the city grew greater and richer than ever before through the coming of the motor-car Walter Browett watched the process without enthusiasm. He was succeeded by his partner and son-in-law Arthur Jagger (1895–1962), who him-

[13] Beans and bacon were served to the Cappers and tripe and onions to the Worsted Weavers.

self had deep local roots. The Jagger family home was at Coundon Green and they had at one time owned a silk mill between Bedworth and Nuneaton, with an office in Old Palace Yard. After his retirement Arthur Jagger's father had become Chairman of the Singer Motor Company at the invitation of his near neighbour, George Singer. The company prospered under his guidance just as other companies were later to prosper under his son. He laid a firm foundation of respect for the family in the city and upon this his son was later to build.

By the beginning of the twentieth century the expansion of Coventry had broken asunder one green belt represented by the Commons and the Cheylesmore Estate. On the land made available were built factories and homes for their managers and immigrant workers. The connection of the two developments was symbolised in Queen Victoria Road, where the Cheylesmore Estate developers built factories on one side of the road and the Freemen's Trustees on the other. In size and comprehensiveness the Cheylesmore development dwarfed all others. In Godiva Street, to the east of the city, houses were built for George Singer's workers and in Queen Victoria Road and along Parkside factories arose which were to play a decisive part in the city's future development. The construction of Eaton Road opened up a new approach to the railway station around which was created a residential district which retained its importance until the Second World War changed the face of things in a way which could not be altered. The scale of the Cheylesmore development was perhaps characteristic of William Isaac Iliffe (1843–1917), who was very much concerned in it.

Iliffe's father, William, had kept a shop at the corner of Smithford Street and Vicar Lane among those narrow streets which were once part of the city's medieval ground plan and have now disappeared. He sold books, stationery and wallpaper and ran a growing jobbing printing business. In order to provide his son with wider opportunities he apprenticed him to the ribbon trade three years before the crash of 1860. Shortly afterwards William's brother, Francis, who had been a master in that trade, emigrated to Australia and William Isaac Iliffe returned to his father's printing business. But it was Coventry's growing bicycle industry together with journalism which was to point the way forward for him. Long before the arrival of the safety bicycle he had noticed that, whereas Coventry made the bicycles, London published the papers which were read by their riders. In 1878 he began *The Cyclist* in collaboration with Henry Sturmey and later, in 1895, he was to commence publication of the *Autocar*. *The Cyclist* was so successful that it absorbed two of its rivals and was soon being edited in London under the title of *The Bicycling News*. When Iliffe wanted an assistant editor in Coventry he engaged Alfred Harmsworth, later Lord Northcliffe and the creator of his own great newspaper empire.

W. I. Iliffe himself could hardly be described as a journalist; he was one of that new breed of newspaper proprietor called forth in an age where the mass of the people were beginning to have a better education and slightly more leisure than their parents. The technical journals which Iliffe had founded were to pass from the control of the family after the First World War. More lasting was to be his impact on the newspapers actually published in Coventry itself. He found the city dependent on two long-established weeklies, the *Coventry Standard* and the *Coventry Herald*, the first Conservative and the second Liberal. Neither looked very up to date to the shrewd, steady eyes of the man who was one day to employ Alfred Harmsworth. In order to give the city a taste of modern journalism he first purchased the *Coventry Times* in 1879, and twelve years later he brought out an evening paper, the *Midland Daily Telegraph*. The 1901 census gave the city a population of nearly 70,000, less than half what would be thought necessary today for starting a new evening paper.

The building on the Cheylesmore Estate had been preceded by development around Spencer Park, near the new King Henry VIII School and on the ridge overlooking the old city from the south. In 1886 two houses in Spencer Road were already occupied and within ten years the adjacent roads had been laid out and the district was becoming popular. In 1901 tenants included both the Town Clerk, Lewis Beard, and the City Engineer, Joseph Swindlehurst. Old-established Coventry families were represented by the Bushills, Charles Kirby, Thomas Daffern and Richard Caldicott, while among the men of the new age were Oscar Harmer, general manager to Alfred Herbert, John Starley and William Herbert, elder brother to the future Sir Alfred.

VII

As a result of development in Cheylesmore and in other areas such as that around Spencer Park, the city was brought nearer a second green belt represented by two great estates and two small ones. The two great estates were those of the Earl of Craven at Coombe Abbey and of Lord Leigh at Stoneleigh; the two small ones, those of the Bromley-Davenports at Baginton and the Gregory-Hoods at Styvechale. There was an obvious gap in this second green belt. No such estate existed to the north and west of the city and, therefore, much of the industrial development of the first twenty years of this century went into the parishes of Foleshill and Radford. Here were erected the Courtaulds' works in 1904, the Daimler works at Sandy Lane in 1908 and 1909, the munition factories of the First World War and the workers' housing that went with them. This abrupt change in what had hitherto been the most favoured part of

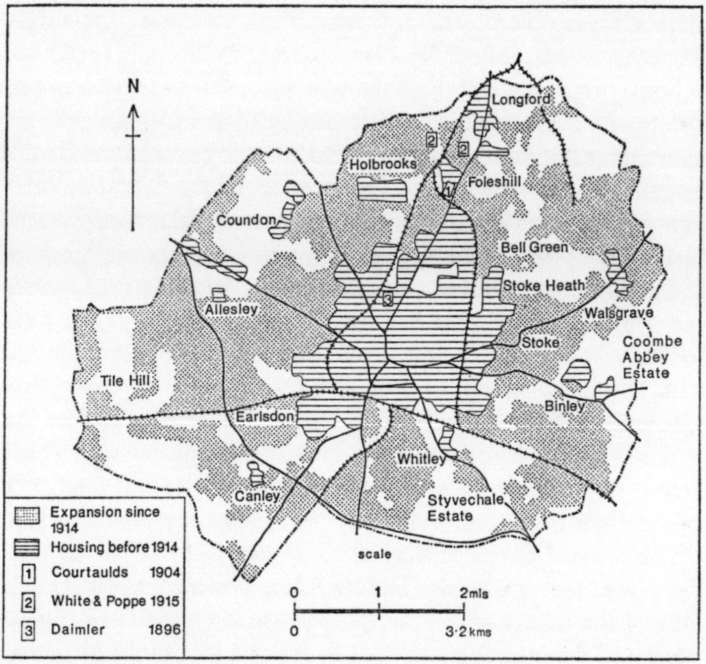

III The expansion of Coventry, 1900–51

the city was bound to result in a pressure for development to the south on the lands of the Styvechale Hall Estate. In 1920 this small but interesting country estate, near what is now the Coventry to Leamington road, was still held by the Gregory family, later to bear the name of Gregory-Hood.

The original manor-house had been Styvechale Grange, a fourteenth-century building which was later occupied by Reginald Hollick, who farmed the land around it from 1891 until just before his death in 1964. In the eighteenth century one of the Gregorys had built a small, rather cheerless Hall at the back of the little church. It was stone-built in the fashionable palladian style, but it appears to have been so extremely uncomfortable as a home that few of the family ever liked it and it has proved impossible to preserve. More to their taste was the Manor-House, now a girls' private school, a homely red-brick building. The Church, the Hall and the Manor-House were all on a little knoll approached by a footpath from the valley which contained the hamlet of Styvechale and the sixty odd acres of Styvechale Common. Coventry was very near; nearer than Baginton, where the Bromley-Davenports had sold out in 1918.

Some people can still recall the year 1920, when the quiet of the Kenilworth Road was barely disturbed by a bus which ran once an hour and green farmland filled in the triangle between the Kenilworth and Styvechale roads. The creation of the War Memorial Park, which began in the same year, can be regarded as the first stage in the development of the Styvechale Estate. Coventry City Council had decided that their war memorial should take the form of a park, and a public subscription had been launched. The £31,500 subscribed to it proved sufficient to purchase 120 acres of land together with the manorial rights over about sixty acres of Styvechale Common. The Honourable A. F. Gregory returned £2000 of the purchase price as his own contribution towards a project with which he was very much in sympathy. Very little was left in the fund after the land was purchased, and this appears to be the reason why part of the planned development had to be cancelled. Whatever may have been the case in the Middle Ages, Coventry today knows little of the beauty which can be found in large sheets of natural water and the intention had been to create a lake in the Memorial Park. This was to prove expensive and the times were against it.

The project had to be postponed and, although it has never been forgotten, it has not yet been carried out.

It was only after the Second World War that proposals were heard for adding to the pleasing, but unambitious layout of the park. In 1947 it was suggested that there should be a swimming baths and winter garden built on it, and there was some discussion in 1951 about buying the Dome of Discovery after the Festival of Britain had finished. In 1952 came something much more ambitious which it was intended should be built partly on the War Memorial Park and partly on Styvechale Common. There was to be an assembly hall capable of seating 2000 people or accommodating 1000 dancers. The hall would have had movable screens to allow open-air dancing in the summer and be the central feature around which would be grouped bars, two restaurants, a palm house and other greenhouses, together with ornamental ponds and car parks. It was an expensive project and a certain amount of unspoilt country would inevitably have disappeared. Coventry in those days was not over-blessed with restaurants or other amenities, but many people were convinced that this was not the right place in which to attempt to create them, particularly if it meant sacrificing some rather pleasant spinneys. The project has never been proceeded with and the park still remains much as it was.

The first portion of the Coventry by-pass, constructed in the mid-1930s, opened a further large area of the Styvechale Estate, at that time owned by Major Charles Gregory-Hood of Styvechale Hall. This became the concern of J. G. Gray, one of the most powerful personalities in the city at the time. He purchased part of the land, including Styvechale Hall, carefully developing the area including Leamington Road, Baginton Road, Armorial Road and Styvechale Croft. He was at great pains not to spoil the rural beauty of the Styvechale Hamlet, and it is largely due to his good taste that this is still preserved today. At a later stage Major Gregory-Hood himself became associated with J. G. Gray in the Gregory Land Company, formed for the purpose of developing practically all the rest of his land. Before the war their development consisted of the southern end of Green Lane, Anchorway Road, Crossway Road and Gretna Road. The war interrupted the development of this estate, but it was eventually resumed to a revised plan in the late forties, although in the early sixties the death of J. G. Gray caused the withdrawal of the Gray family from the venture.

A great deal of the success of the initial stages of the Styvechale development had been due to the sympathetic interest of Frederick Smith, then Town Clerk of the city. Coventry was his birthplace and he had never worked outside it in civilian life. He saw it growing into a large city, and wanted to help to make it a great one. Such planning legislation as there was would give the City Council little help in securing planned and harmonious growth, but there could be an alternative way of achieving this. As the Corporation's chief legal adviser, Frederick Smith was in favour of using the existing resources of the law of property in order to enable the city to plan effectively. He was in favour of the city's buying land in order to develop it properly. His most outstanding success was, perhaps, the purchases from the Stoneleigh Estate which led to development along the Kenilworth Road, and it is only now that the city is beginning to reap the full reward of the far-sighted action he took in 1937 over parts of the Coombe Abbey Estate on the eastern side of the city.

On the death of the fourth Earl of Craven in 1921 Coombe Abbey was the centre of a great estate containing seventy cottages and twenty-nine farms, extending in a broad band from Brinklow in the north to Willenhall in the south and including land now well within the city, such as the farms at Ernesford Grange and Lyng Hall. Its deer park and ninety-acre lake almost made one forget that the house itself was large and opulent rather than beautiful. 'Capability' Brown had been engaged to lay out the grounds in 1771, but no one master hand had built the house. Little remained of the old monastic buildings and nothing of the church. The west front of the house was designed by the architect who later was responsible for the original design of Buckingham House, now Buckingham Palace, but Coombe Abbey did not take its final shape as a nobleman's residence until the nineteenth century. In 1860 William Eden Nesfield demolished much of the early work and gave the house a Victorian wing which few nowadays seem inclined to defend.

The interior also contained examples of work from every period between the Tudors and the present day. There was an Inigo Jones frieze, a Grinling Gibbons overmantel, more than one Adam fireplace, and a main staircase built on the extensive scale considered suitable for a grandee's house in the seventeenth century. Paintings by Rubens, Cranach, Van Dyke, Lely and Poussin adorned the walls, together with needlework hangings originally created at St Cyr for Louis XIV. A priceless collection of Indian armour of the sixteenth and seventeenth centuries, Venetian glass, Dresden and Delft figures, Chippendale, Hepplewhite and Sheraton furniture were all part of the profusion of art in this great house. After the finest pieces had been taken elsewhere, the sale of the house in 1923 consisted of 2277 lots and the disposal of the books alone occupied two days.

Among the first owners of Coombe Abbey was Sir John Harrington who, for many years, had in his care Elizabeth, daughter of James I. In 1623 the estate was purchased by the widow of Sir William Craven, a City merchant and former Lord Mayor of London. The grandson of a Yorkshire dalesman, Craven had become one of the richest men of his time. The estate, which had remained for three hundred years in the family of one self-made man, was now to pass by various stages into the hands of another.[14] Shortly after the sale in August 1923 the house and its immediate grounds were purchased by J. G. Gray. After serving his apprenticeship as a carpenter in Lincoln he had walked to Coventry with his belongings in a bundle. The city was then in the middle of the cycle boom, and this forceful individual was practically bound to get ahead in a trade where individualism was favoured. He founded his own firm, built Courtauld's Main Works in 1904, and soon became the largest single building contractor in the city with the deserved reputation for high quality in his work.

Gray's commanding frame and piercing eyes showed that he was a man of exceptional distinction. He had a fine taste in pictures, an interest in good sculpture and a love of distinguished houses. Having lived at Rose Hill, he now intervened to save Coombe Abbey from being demolished. He stayed there until 1954, creating

[14] The estate as a whole was first purchased by a local syndicate which included Charles Band (see Chapter Two), and of which Samuel Gorton was the nominee. It was repurchased by John Todd, a retired auctioneer from Northallerton in Yorkshire, who broke it up for sale in various lots. Most of the farms and other properties were offered to the sitting tenants and a considerable number of them purchased their holdings at the sale in August 1923.

a herd of a thousand shorthorn cattle, besides working two other farms. His first care, however, was to modernise the house, which he did by pulling down the Victorian additions and some other parts, as well as selling off a great number of staircases, fireplaces and other fittings.[15] Some people were surprised, but he left Coombe Abbey a much more compact and manageable residence still containing many art treasures.

J. G. Gray himself certainly never intended to build on his part of the estate, and, until he left, the grounds looked very much as they had always done. W. N. Lindley and some other professional men had purchased other parts of the estate, mainly for the fishing and the quiet of the country which it would give them. They were not likely to let their hearts dictate to their heads, but were sympathetic to one of Frederick Smith's greatest dreams. Thanks to his tireless persistence, the City Council had never entirely abandoned the idea of acquiring this great estate as a public park. Resources at their disposal for such a long-term project were small, but they were able to achieve one substantial victory before the outbreak of the Second World War, thanks to the co-operation of some of the men who had purchased parts of the estate. The Town and Country Planning Act of 1932 had given the Corporation certain powers to prevent undesirable development in areas which were not already built upon. On 5 March 1938 the City Council at last concluded an agreement which would have the effect of preserving 218·2 acres of field, wood and lake as a private open space. It did this by paying compensation for the owner's development rights out of rate revenue, since a loan was impossible. At the same time an agreement was concluded to give the Corporation an option to purchase the land outright within three months of the deaths of the owners. It was the first step towards the Corporation's acquisition of the Coombe Abbey Estate and this was to be followed by many more.

For almost twenty years after the end of the Second World War the Corporation had to bide its time, purchasing portions of the land already covered by the 1938 agreement whenever they came on the market. In 1953 they acquired 16 acres and, in 1958, a further

[15] Some Jacobean panelling was purchased by the American newspaper proprietor, William Randolph Hearst, and later found its way into the home of Bing Crosby.

114–67 acres of the lake and 47 of woodland. Then, in 1964, came a great prize. After the departure of J. G. Gray from the Abbey, G.E.C. had taken it on lease as a hostel for their graduate apprentices. When they decided that their lease should terminate ten years later, Coventry Corporation stepped in and purchased the house and grounds. Now that they were the owners of the mansion and 279 acres of land and lake adjoining it they were faced with the question of how this great property could best be developed.

This debate has by no means been concluded, but it will certainly be greatly influenced by the passing of the Countryside Act of 1968 and the establishment of the Countryside Commission. In July 1970 the Commission recognised the Coombe Abbey Estate as a countryside park thus enabling the Corporation to receive additional government grants for further land purchases and the provision of certain types of development. This recognition will undoubtedly encourage development which will leave the countryside untouched. A children's playground and boating on the lake have already been provided and there have been other projects, such as that for an eighteen-hole golf course. There has been talk of a sports centre and a family play area and Coombe Abbey has occasionally been mentioned as a possible site for the winter garden which was not erected on the War Memorial Park. It is too early to say what exactly will happen to some of the ideas.

The creation of a great regional park drawing people from an area far wider than that of the city itself is an exciting undertaking, although there are many problems still to be solved. It has not yet been possible to decide on a final use for the Abbey itself, in which some of the Craven portraits are once more displayed on permanent loan from the family. Towards the end of 1963, when preparations for the building of the University of Warwick were in their earliest stages, the then City Architect suggested that Coombe Abbey would be an admirable site for it. He produced excellent arguments in support of this, but he produced them a little too late. Nor has it yet been possible to decide upon the proper place for cars in the Park. One day, it is hoped, they will be left on its extreme edge enabling walkers to enter the Coombe Abbey grounds at Clifford Bridge Road and follow an unspoiled nature trail to the great house. This has not yet happened but no doubt it will. The right time will always come, and a great local authority always contains men who are willing to wait for it.

NOTE: *The Charitable Tradition in Coventry*

In 1544, at a time of great social difficulty, Sir Thomas White, a London merchant, made an outright gift of £1400 to the Mayor and Commonalty of Coventry. Sir Thomas White's money was used for the purchase of church lands and, out of the revenue which this provided, pensions for one year were to be paid to twelve poor men and small loans were to be made to apprentices who wanted to set up in business on their own. His prudent charity was, in fact, an attempt to stimulate economic activity as well as to relieve distress. Its resources have grown with the growth of the city and the purposes to which they are devoted have been modified under the guidance of the Charity Commissioners. Payments are also made to four other towns, but the money spent in Coventry is principally applied to education. Sir Thomas White's Charity was not the first to be established in Coventry but it was certainly the most creative. Its two purposes were pursued over many centuries by an increasing number of other charities and long before the twentieth-century welfare state these did much to remove a great deal of the worst poverty from the city as well as to preserve its spirit of individual enterprise. It was announced on 24 March 1965 that the number of charities registered in Coventry under the Charities Act was ninety-seven.

CHAPTER TWO

The Growth of a Big City

The bicycle industry and large-scale production. Sir Alfred Herbert. The present economic and social pattern of the city. Silk. Pioneers in the motor-car industry. Volume production; William Morris and the Rootes brothers. Daimler. John Davenport Siddeley. Machine tools. Estate development; the Newcombe brothers, Charles Band and others.

I

In one sense, the most important historical relics destroyed in the air raids on Coventry were the old cycle factories; the original Coventry Machinists' Works in Cheylesmore, the Meteor Works of the Rover Company, the Triumph factory in Priory Street and others. Together with those which still survive, they would have reminded us that, at the end of the nineteenth century, there came into the life of this city, something new and decisive; the bicycle boom. This made the large factory the dominant production unit in Coventry because demand could be satisfied only by volume production, backed by heavy capital investment in equipment.

Factories had existed previously in the city. After the collapse of the ribbon trade in 1860 a number, such as Leigh Mills, had been established in an attempt to alleviate distress. Even in the two classic industries of ribbon weaving and watchmaking there had been factories such as the Cash's establishment in Kingfield and the Rotherham factory in Spon Street. It is true, nevertheless, that in both these skilled industries the most cherished unit had been the independent craftsman working on his own, probably with tools and equipment which he owned himself. Neither industry had required heavy capital investment of its masters, nor presented formidable problems of production control. Now all was to be changed, and it is not surprising that the city had to learn its new industrial habits from an influx of formidable newcomers.[1]

By far the most important man in this new and decisive phase of the city's development was Alfred, later Sir Alfred, Herbert (1866–1957). He was born into the comfortable middle class which the Industrial Revolution produced in Victorian England. His father had been a building contractor and had built many of the railway stations on the old Midland line from Rugby to Leicester. He had then bought a farm at Whetstone Gorse, near Lutterworth, and was able to educate his son at a good private school in Leicester. Alfred Herbert came to Coventry to join the firm of Coles and Matthews in the Butts and in 1887 his father was able to find £2000 to enable him to buy the firm in partnership with W. S. Hubbard. Two years later he was in sole control, running a general engineering business. The balance sheet for 1888 shows the firm hiring out steam-ploughs and a steam-roller, as well as making machine tools. An important step forward came when the firm won the agency for the sale of French weldless steel tubes in Britain. In three years, sales of these tubes were valued at £20,000, and in 1891 the profit of £5712 made from them was equal to almost three-quarters of that from his machine tool output in that year. In 1914 he had 2000 employees, making his the largest machine tool firm in England.

There was a long career still before him, and he was to continue to display all the virtues of the entrepreneur. In due course, he was to reap the traditional reward and become very rich, devoting a share of his wealth to the improvement of his adopted city like the responsible, kindly man he was. He gave two acres of land in the Butts for a park in a district badly in need of one and was also very generous to the Coventry and Warwickshire Hospital. As a memorial to his second wife he created Lady Herbert's Garden upon the

[1] Among these we must find a place for Ernest Terah Hooley (1858–1947). The demand for bicycles was there and growing, with the demand for power-operated cycle units and petrol-driven cars treading on its heels. Production of all these things in adequate volume required heavy investment and the law had not erected adequate safeguards against human fallibility. Hooley became a professional company promoter and had a lot to do with the Daimler and Rudge-Whitworth Companies in Coventry. In one sense, the Companies Act of 1908, which bolted a great many stable doors, is his monument.

site of the Chauntry and Rope Walk, some of the city's worst slums. Shortly before the outbreak of the Second World War he gave Town Thorns to Coventry Corporation as a Camp School for Coventry children, and later gave £200,000 towards the present Herbert Art Gallery and Museum. Like others of his type and generation, he valued individual skill and effort. In consequence he made the apprenticeship scheme in his firm a model for the city and a conspicuously large number of Alfred Herbert apprentices are to-day running their own firms in Coventry and throughout the world. For a long time he gave close personal supervision to his business, and when this became too much for him, chose carefully such men as Oscar Harmer (1850–1939).

Harmer was an American, like Charles Churchill who started the machine tool firm which still bears his name. After working for many years with American firms of high standing, at a time when American machine tool practice was becoming very important, he came to Britain and first met Alfred Herbert in 1897 at a lunch which was part of a bicycle show at the Crystal Palace. Herbert had then been in charge of a rapidly growing business for a number of years, but Harmer does not appear to have gone to work for him immediately. Shortly after this, however, he left Babcock and Wilcox to begin the career in Coventry which was to end in his becoming General Manager of Alfred Herbert's, a position he held until his death. Many stories about him still circulate; about his dignified presence accentuated by his beard, and his insistence on quality which sometimes led him to smash work with a sledge-hammer because it did not reach his high standards. He has many claims to rank as the first great name in Coventry's list of efficient production managers.

Not many of the cycle men were Coventry born. It is true that the Rileys were a Coventry family, who went from the manufacture of looms for ribbon weaving to cycles, motor-cycles and sports cars, but George Singer and the Starleys came from Sussex and William Hillman had qualified as an engineer at Greenwich. William Herbert, Hillman's partner and elder brother of Sir Alfred, had come from Leicestershire. Thomas Humber, a Nottingham moulder, and Daniel Rudge, a Wolverhampton publican, were both associated with famous bicycles made in Coventry. These are the men whose trade-names came to dominate the business, but they are perhaps less interesting to a later age than Siegfried Bettmann (1863–1951), who had come to the city from far afield and was to outlive them all.

Bettmann had been born in Nuremberg, where his father, Meyer Bettmann, was agent to a Bavarian landowner. The family were well-to-do, and Bettmann was obviously an educated man with quick and wide intellectual sympathies. He wrote a great deal throughout his life, and in his autobiography has described how he went via Paris to London in his twenties to set up in business, dealing in bicycles mainly for export. It was there that he established relations with a number of Coventry firms and had to choose his own trade-name to be stamped on the machines which he sent overseas. He chose that of Triumph, because it appeared in substantially the same form in so many European languages. The boom in the bicycle trade drew him to Coventry where, in 1890, he began manufacturing with the assistance of a fellow German, Mauritz Johann Schulte.

Bettmann tried very hard to identify himself with the life of the community of which he was now a member. From 1907 he sat on the Council as a Liberal, and was actually Mayor at the outbreak of war in 1914. He suffered in the anti-German hysteria of those years, being deprived of the Chairmanship of the Standard Motor Company, losing a great many social contacts, and being drawn steadily away from the Liberal Party towards Labour. He had long been friendly with two local Labour leaders, Hugh Farren, one of his foremen at Triumph, and George Poole. He now became a member of the Union of Democratic Control, and a friend of E. D. Morel, also cultivating the acquaintance of Ramsay MacDonald, afterwards first Labour Prime Minister. Perhaps the height of his sympathy with the Labour Party was reached in 1923, when he took the chair at a meeting in the Coventry Opera House for the Countess of Warwick, then engaged in fighting as a Labour candidate in the county against her nephew, Anthony Eden.

He remained active in his business which had done very well during the war. Because Triumph motor-cycles had proved so successful in the Army, Bettmann had been helped to increase his production from fifty to seventy a week. He quarrelled with

Schulte and in his place chose C. V. Holbrook, whom he had first met when the latter was a staff captain at the War Office. Bettmann, however, continued to exercise such direct control that he, personally, still opened all the letters each morning.

The Triumph factory in Priory Street consisted of two seven-storey buildings, one on each side of the road. It was completely unsuited to motor-car production, but Bettmann was determined to enter this most competitive of industries. It is said that he refused to buy out William Morris in the depths of the post-war depression, but he managed to build his own first car in 1923. Triumph produced an interesting family car in the Super 7 of 1928 and the very impressive Dolomite in 1937, but car production was always in difficulties and the firm was placed in the hands of the Receiver shortly before the outbreak of the Second World War. It had already proved difficult to keep the three sides of the Triumph business together, and the cycles had been sold to Raleigh of Nottingham who continued to make them in Coventry until 1954. The motor-cycles, which had been the real basis of the business for a long time, were separated from cars in 1936 and formed into an independent business, the Triumph Engineering Company, which was sold to B.S.A. This still exists on the Meriden Road and was to have a successful career under the control of John Sangster, assisted by one of the ablest in Coventry's long line of able production engineers – Albert Camwell (1883–1968).[2]

II

The new dynamism and purpose which the cycle boom brought into the city has never been completely lost. By the time the First World War began in 1914, a greatly increased population, which had been organised into large productive units in peace, could easily

[2] Camwell was the son of a small farmer and breeder of shire horses at Exhall, to the north of the city. He had left the land and worked for Humber when they made bicycles and later when they tried to make aircraft. He became shop foreman at Triumph, and was never really happy working under C. V. Holbrook, whose background was very different from his own. He himself was always a motor-cycle man and must have been rather glad when they became a separate concern.

be transferred to production in war. Countless stories circulated in polite drawing-rooms about high wages, extravagance and revolutionary tendencies among the men, and the way in which the 'Guinea Girls', employed in shell filling, squandered their money on grand pianos which they could not play. Far more important, and less commented upon, was the fact that the city was being endowed with a number of new and up-to-date factories which were to serve it well in the coming peace. A similar process was to happen after the Second World War; it is difficult to see how volume production in cars after 1945 could have made such progress in Coventry without the existence of shadow factories which, though originally built for aero-engines, could easily be adapted for something else.

In the early twenties it seemed that the West Midlands, which had benefited most from the war, would suffer most from the peace and the social stresses which came with it. In February 1921, the percentage of unemployed in engineering trades in the area stood at 21·9. This was then the highest figure in the country, and the rise continued. In June 1921 it reached a peak of 33·1 and even in December 1921 it had fallen only slightly to 32·8. After this came a steady decline, so that by December 1925 the percentage for the Midlands as a whole had fallen to 7·2.

Coventry at this time was becoming the centre for new industries which had no problems of technical obsolescence to overcome; a centre for the manufacture of motor-cars, machine tools, telephones and synthetic fibres. At the beginning of the twenties William Morris took over the Hotchkiss factory and later built a new one at Courthouse Green in order to bring Coventry within his scheme of car production. In 1928 William Lyons brought the Swallow Sidecar to Coventry and Courtaulds showed their continuing interest in the city by building a factory at Little Heath for the manufacture of rayon. The difficulties of the time themselves caused an expansion of machine tool production, shown by the move of Alfred Herbert's to a larger plant at Edgwick in 1928 and similar moves to larger premises at about the same time by Coventry Gauge and Tool and A. C. Wickman Limited. Then, in 1936, came the drive to re-arm and expand the Royal Air Force, with the building of the first shadow factories. The city, therefore, became more of a magnet than ever for young men from the older industrial areas such as South Wales and County Durham, where the Depression seemed deep and unending. For them Coventry meant work – and to Coventry they came.

Coventry has reached its present (1971) population of 335,230 by a series of rapid increases due to the emergence of new industries and the needs of war. Nevertheless, behind these sudden increases there is revealed an underlying continuity; an emergent social pattern which can be glimpsed as early as 1907.[3] An article in the *Economic Journal* of September of that year described the city at a time when watchmaking was beginning to yield its place to the cycle industry which was then in the middle of its greatest boom. It gave the following figures for the occupations carried on in the city:

TABLE 2.1 Occupations in Coventry 1907

Occupations	*Men*	*Women*	*Total*
All occupations	22,255	10,379	32,634
Building trades	2067	—	2067
Metal and machine-making trades, cycles and motors excluded	2992	—	2992
Cycle and motor manufacture, excluding dealers	5372	602	5974
Watchmaking, including dealers	1937	687	2624
Silk industry	506	1671	2177
Other textile industries, omitting dyers and dealers	224	833	1057

It shows the swing towards mechanical engineering already beginning and describes the city as enjoying a decent prosperity by the standards of those times, with remarkably little grievous poverty, due to the influence, in part, of the distribution of aid by the City Charities. It also speaks with satisfaction of the city's lack of building and labouring classes; a satisfaction which would not be shared today. Perhaps the special characteristics of the Coventry social pattern can best be seen when set against those of two other Midland cities, Leicester and Nottingham:

[3] For table of population see page 64.

TABLE 2·2 Total Insured Population in Three Midland Cities in 1956 and 1966

	Coventry				*Leicester*				*Nottingham*			
	1956 Numbers	%	*1966 Numbers*	%	*1956 Numbers*	%	*1966 Numbers*	%	*1956 Numbers*	%	*1966 Numbers*	%
Agriculture	796	1	439	—	1469	1	1452	½	1594	1	647	½
Mining	4137	2	1628	½	1551	1	325	—	19,203	8	4143	2
Chemicals	299	—	520	—	1110	1	1525	½	6599	3	1611	1
Engineering and Vehicles	114,391	64	123,458	61	34,615	19	45,263	22	41,263	18	21,318	11½
Textiles	7839	4	6120	3	34,537	19	33,453	16	27,863	12	22,873	12½
Clothing	299	—	90	—	21,861	12	15,544	7½	12,168	5	9246	5
Other manufactures	4640	3	5649	2½	16,550	9	20,570	10	22,583	9	21,937	12
Construction	8289	5	9187	5	12,058	7	12,712	6½	12,781	6	13,342	7
[8]Non-classified service industries	37,464	21	57,417	28	55,235	31	77,159	37	87,709	38	89,936	48½
Totals	178,154	100	204,508	100	178,986	100	208,003	100	231,763	100	185,053	100

By 1956 the enormous preponderance of workers engaged in vehicle construction and mechanical engineering had grown to 64 per cent of the total. This preponderance has remained and efforts to introduce diversification, though frequently discussed, have had very little success. There is perhaps something to be said for the view that the city should go on doing what it obviously does very well. The comparison with Leicester is very interesting. There we have the picture of an extremely stable city with its labour-force shared out in remarkably equal proportions between three industries and, consequently, immune from tremendous fluctuations in any one. A further comparison can be made with Nottingham, which is a regional capital. As such it provides services for most of Nottinghamshire, Derbyshire and south Lincolnshire. It, therefore, has always had a high proportion of professionals to man its hospitals and consultancy services, as well as its regional Civil Service departments. It possesses the wholesale and merchandising houses which have enabled it to provide an attractive shopping centre for a wide area. In the West Midlands, these are to be found in Birmingham. Coventry's shortages of doctors, hospital beds and quality shops are by no means only the result of air raids in 1940 and 1941. They were there before, had been there for a long time and we shall see later how efforts have been made to overcome them, and with what success.

A further feature of Coventry over the last seventy years has been the steady growth in the size of the productive unit. In 1884, when the Rotherhams mechanised their manufacture of watches, a labour-force of four hundred men and one hundred women was something to be commented upon. In 1907, the Rudge-Whitworth Cycle Factory, the largest industrial unit in the city, employed 1800 people. These are very much dwarfed nowadays by the 18,000 employed in three factories by the General and English Electric Company, the 14,000 at Standard, 10,000 at Massey-Ferguson, 7300 at Alfred Herbert's and 5000 at Wickmans.[4] Attention is so often concentrated on these large units that we are apt to forget the number of small ones in the city, a fact which is brought out in the following table:

[4] Figures given are for 1967.

TABLE 2·3 Number of Employers, 1969, arranged by size and industry

Size of firm	*5 to 10*	*11 to 50*	*51 to 200*	*201 to 500*	*501 to 1000*	*1001 to 2500*	*2501 to 4999*	*5000 and over*	*Total number of employees*	*Total number of firms*
Engineering and Electrical goods	40	90	37	9	3	7	1	2	40,300	189
Vehicles and Aircraft	3	10	10	4	2	4	2	6	66,125	41
Metal manufacture	15	31	14	1	1	1	—	—	4925	63
Totals	58	131	61	14	6	12	3	8	111,350	293

III

As late as 1927, 7000 workers were still employed in the narrow weave textile industry in Coventry by thirty independent firms. John Bill, Dresser and Company and E. O. French, who had begun as silk importers, still managed to keep themselves in business, and there was at least one manufacturer of textile machinery still working in the city. In 1935 the number of firms had been reduced to thirteen and that of workers to 5000. With the exception of Courtaulds, which will receive special treatment later, there is now very little left and the reason is not difficult to discover. Capital investment in engineering and vehicle production in the city has been so enormous and the consequent reduction in costs so dramatic, that these industries have been able to afford a rate of wages which the much smaller textile factories have not. It is always a pity when long-established names are lost from the business life of the city, as when in 1963, William Franklin, probably its longest established business, moved to Northern Ireland. Almost as old is the firm of J. and J. Cash, which still operates its historic works at Kingfield. After the crash of 1860 even this distinguished family of Quaker philanthropists had had to consider hard realities and the firm survived only by discovering various specialities, first bed frillings, then name tapes and, finally, woven trade labels.

Thomas Stevens, who established his own business in 1869, had a hard struggle to find specialist lines from which he could make a living. Among other things, the firm manufactured blue bands bearing names of warships to be worn around sailor hats by little boys. He even managed to keep silk weaving alive by producing bookmarks with pictures on them, for prayer-books and Sunday School prizes. Similar and larger pictures were produced for sale, and the man is still alive whose father sold them from a stall in the Winter Gardens at Blackpool. Stevengraph pictures have now become valuable collectors' items, but in November 1940, when the Stevens' factory in Cox Street was destroyed in the great raid, its cellars were full of pictures which could not be sold because there was no demand for them. The raid put an end to the working of Thomas Stevens' firm in Coventry and after the war it did not return, although the name was kept before the public in association with a textile firm at Leek until 1962.

IV

It is impossible to exaggerate the immense self-confidence with which the young men working in Coventry approached the making of motor-cars in the years before 1914. Some worked on their own account in backyard workshops, others in quality firms such as Daimler, where it was difficult to persuade anyone that real motor-cars were being made anywhere else. They were an astonishing social cross-section, army and public school men mixing freely with former cycle workers, all united by a common enthusiasm. Young apprentices worked at Daimler, Siddeley-Deasy or some other factory during the day and argued about cars all evening in the relatively few hotel lounges which this overcrowded city possessed. The work of Henry Ford in America they regarded as not worthy of the name of engineering. When someone like Charles Friswell, the sales concessionaire for Standard, talked about volume production of cars which could actually be driven by ordinary, inexpert people, they felt that he did not know what he was talking about. For them, a motor-car was something which should be placed only in the hands of an informed enthusiast.

No one can be quite certain that he has compiled a complete list of motor-cars manufactured in Coventry in those very early days. Few have heard of the Priory or Hamilton Motor Companies which existed in Dale Street near the city centre in 1901 and 1910 respectively. The same applies to the Academy, produced by E. J. West on the Foleshill Road in 1908, and the Lotis, manufactured in Widdrington Road, Radford.[5] The attempt to provide petrol-driven transport took many forms. Various Coventry firms, such as Progress and Triumph, were by 1900 fitting small petrol-driven engines to their bicycles. A Beeston Tricycle of 1½ h.p. made in

[5] The Lotis was one of the products of the restless energy of Henry Sturmey (b. 1857). He was born in Somerset and became a schoolmaster. His first job in Coventry was as the proprietor of a private school in King Street. He had already entered the field of cycling journalism and the manufacture of bicycles before he met W. I. Iliffe (see Chapter One, page 23), who, in 1877, became his partner in *The Cyclist*. He was later to invent the Sturmey-Archer three-speed gear and to study motor-car manufacture in the United States. In 1902 he began making the American Duryea motor-car in this country with Willans and Robinson of Rugby building the engine. The name of the car was changed first to Sturmey and then to Lotis.

Coventry, took part in the first London to Brighton run in 1896, and there were twenty-two motor-cycle manufacturers in Coventry in 1905. In 1909 Triumph sold over 3000 machines, and the Rover Company in 1914 produced 1435.

The number of car manufacturers in Coventry was to increase after the First World War. It was then that many ex-officers, of whom the most celebrated nationally was Walter Bentley, put their gratuities into the motor-car business and set out to conquer the market.[6] They usually failed through lack of money, and though there were still eleven separate car-producing firms in Coventry in 1931, a further forty had entered the business and retired defeated since 1918. Among the cars which came and went were the Cooper, Emms, Wigan-Barlow, Omega, Stoneleigh and Warwick, the last being the product of S. H. Newsome, a local man and an experienced racing motorist. The Cluley was produced for a time by the old cycle firm of Clarke, Cluley and Company. Another cycle firm, Calcott's, which at one time occupied a large factory in Gosford Street, failed in 1926 and the premises were taken over by Singer.

It was natural that the larger cycle companies, with their experience of volume production, often including motor-cycles, should wish to enter this new field where so many hazards were to be overcome and problems solved. Rudge-Whitworth, largest of them all, appears to have been the most unadventurous, content to produce in 1912 a cycle-car which was on the market for one year only. Humber and Singer, both among the largest firms, displayed a greater enterprise. The Swift, the oldest Coventry cycle company, had begun as the Coventry Machinists in 1867 with James Starley as its first foreman. It was he who took the company into the manufacture of the early bicycle, and the firm later changed its name after its success with the Swift safety bicycle. It followed the usual path into motor-cycles and then into motor-cars; and in the 1920s it was moving towards the production of a relatively cheap car, the Cadet, but moving too late. Its resources did not enable it to compete with the growing Morris organisation, and this is probably why it failed in 1931.

[6] In 1920, fifty-nine new motor manufacturing firms came into being in England.

The Rover Company, with its fine pioneering tradition, had experimented with an electric tricar in 1889, produced its first car in 1904, and in 1923 took the bold decision to close cycle manufacture altogether. At first it does not appear to have been sure which public it wished to attract and faced many difficulties. These began to give way in 1932 when Spencer Wilks, with the help of his brother Maurice, guided the company towards that quality market which it still holds. Wilks was so successful that the company was soon suffering from a shortage of factory space to which the rearmament programme was to provide an answer.

Two other cycle companies which achieved considerable reputations in motor-car manufacture were Lea Francis and Riley. The Lea Francis company made no less than four attempts to enter the field, the first at the quality level in 1904, the second in 1920, the third in 1937 and the last in 1960. It was still producing good cars after the Second World War and could be regarded as a competitor with the Alvis. The Leaf-Lynx, developed in 1960, never reached the production stage, and the company is no longer involved in car manufacture. In 1938 the Riley Company lost its independence to the Nuffield Organisation. The great inventive gifts of Percy Riley had enabled the firm to establish a fine reputation in the sports car field. There were, however, five Riley brothers and this was a charge which the firm could not easily bear.

Considerable interest attaches to the career of J. W. F. Crouch, a Daimler-trained motor engineer and a very good one indeed. He was able to remain in business until 1928, manufacturing a total of over 3000 cars and having his own body works on part of the site now occupied by Lady Herbert's Garden near the Cook Street Gate. The cars built up a considerable racing reputation and both Stirling Moss's father and James Cocker of Clyno drove them.

T. G. John (1880–1946) came to Siddeley-Deasy from Vickers at Barrow, where he is said to have designed naval monitors and to have held a position of some responsibility. He was charming, shrewd, optimistic and always ready to bite off rather more than he could chew. His abilities were real, but never as extensive as he seems to have imagined. After the war, when optimism was essential for starting and remaining in business, he began T. G. John Limited by buying the business of Holley Brothers, an American-owned carburettor firm operating in Coventry. From this time he owed a great deal to ideas which others had started. The Alvis 10/30 car, which was very successful, originated with G. P. H. de Freville, who also seems to have given John the name of Alvis for his firm. J. F. Buckingham had manufactured cycle-cars in Coventry before the war and came back to the industry with his officer's gratuity and money from a tracer bullet he had invented. He produced the design for the Buckingham car which was manufactured by John until it was eliminated from the market by the Austin Seven.

From 1922 T. G. John had the formidable help of George Smith-Clarke (1884–1960), an A.I.D. Captain stationed in the district during the war. He had spent three years with Daimler and had designed several scooters, in particular the Kenilworth, before becoming a director and chief engineer of Alvis. A gifted and opinionated man, he did not take disagreement lightly and not everyone liked him. On the other hand he achieved much in the fields of astronomy and medical technology. In the first, he built his own 18 in. reflector telescope, now at Jodrell Bank, and was asked to give advice on the 100 in. Newton reflector at Herstmonceux; in the second he designed and built a machine for the X-ray examination of the heart, the first in the country, and improved the iron lung at a time when the danger of polio was causing great concern.

Far more colourful was Captain D. M. K. Marendaz. He had been an apprentice at Siddeley-Deasy and there met John. Going into business on his own account with his gratuity as capital, he found himself caught up in the production of the Emscote, a cycle-car which had been designed by Marlowe, Works Manager of the Standard, and a Dane called Seelhaft. The Emscote was very short-lived and Marendaz found himself with 260 gear-boxes on his hands. He therefore went into partnership with Seelhaft to produce the Marseel, which John manufactured for them. It failed after a few years, and Marendaz left Coventry. After a short period on the Stock Exchange, about which one would like to know more, we find him running a car-testing business in an arch of a railway viaduct at Putney. Between 1932 and 1936 he ran a factory at Maidenhead where he produced a series of Marendaz Specials, attractive, low-hung sports cars which had a remarkably good performance. He finally emigrated to South Africa and established a factory for the manufacture of stationary diesel engines in the Transvaal, not without success.

V

These men belonged to the heroic age of the motor-car, along with the makers of the great limousines for royalty and maharajahs and the gifted London distributors, of whom the greatest was Charles Rolls, de Freville another, and Ernest Instone from Coventry a third. J. W. F. Crouch, Percy Riley, Buckingham, Marendaz and the rest were engineers first and businessmen second. They built cars to race against each other at Brooklands in the days of such drivers as Henry Segrave, Malcolm Campbell and Woolf Barnato. The passing of an age was symbolised when, in 1931, Walter Bentley sold out to Rolls-Royce. Since none of the sports-car firms ever had enough money, they could never produce at an economic rate. When T. G. John began the business which later became Alvis, he had a capital of something like £4200, partly his own savings, and partly the result of borrowing from friends in Pembroke. It was not much, and he was probably better off than many. The Crouch car in its best days was probably produced at the rate of eighteen a week and the Buckingham at never more than fifteen. The whole industry was waiting for someone of an entirely different kind; practical businessman first and engineer second, one who could produce a cheap car in which the average man could take his family motoring.

As early as 1911 Henry Ford had produced the Model T, the car within the reach of the American working man. Its construction was so simplified and so sound that practically anyone could drive it. He had taken the process of production, broken it down into the simplest possible form and sunk heavy capital investment in machinery capable of reinforcing the labour of human hands. This had enabled him to produce so many cars that their price had come crashing down. It was Ford's methods of production which were adopted in Britain by William Morris (1877–1963).

Coventry was to play an essential part in the organisation which he created. When he came to Coventry in December 1936 to receive the Honorary Freedom of the City, he had already gone very far.

He had been made a Baronet in 1927 and was raised to the peerage as Lord Nuffield seven years later. His achievements had brought him great wealth, and he had already begun honourably to recognise his social responsibilities. He saw that wealth which the community had helped to create was something in which the community should share. As early as 1927 he had made a substantial contribution to the Coventry and Warwickshire Hospital, and his name is preserved to this day in that of an Oxford College and a great educational research foundation. His donations were already considerable by 1936, but few can then have had any conception of the heights to which they would ultimately rise. It was already clear, even then, that he had wide social interests, since he had already been active in trying to solve the intractable problems of the distressed areas. He certainly realised in the 1930s that economic problems have political solutions, and still remains to us a rather baffling figure. He was a shy, diffident man, and there is perhaps still much to be discovered of how he would have liked to see the problems of the economy dealt with in this troubled decade.

Nuffield's generosity to the Coventry and Warwickshire Hospital was not the only reason why the City Council had resolved to honour him. He had also given employment to Coventry during a particularly difficult period when, as we have seen, the percentage of unemployed in the West Midlands was almost the highest in the country. In 1921 he had taken over the lease of the government factory in Gosford Street, in which the Hotchkiss Company had made its medium machine-gun during the war. Later, Morris Motor Engines Branch built a special factory at Courthouse Green, so that the two factories together could produce the engines which were assembled in completed cars at Cowley. In 1923 the Gosford Street factory produced a total of 22,144 complete engine units, almost certainly greater than the numbers produced in the rest of the city.[7]

[7] The increases in production in 1922–3 and 1926–7 after the opening of the two Coventry factories is very clearly reflected in the following figures of cars sold by the Morris organisation in the 1920s:

1919 – 387	1925 – 55,582
1921 – 3076	1926 – 48,330
1922 – 6956	1927 – 61,632
1923 – 20,648	1928 – 55,480
1924 – 32,918	1929 – 63,522

In 1929, with the opening of Courthouse Green, annual production rose to 50,000, while the share capital of Morris Engines trebled and now stood at £1,195,000.

One of the reasons for this outstanding achievement was the uncanny flair Morris showed in picking the men to manage this great investment. The young Miles (now Lord) Thomas (b. 1897), was an ex-officer of the Motor Machine Gun Corps who had become a journalist with the Iliffes in Coventry. His shrewdness and good judgement made him an invaluable advisor to Morris, particularly on the commercial side. Leonard Lord (1896–1967), afterwards first Lord Lambury, was the son of the Coventry Baths Superintendent and an old Bablake boy. An apprentice at Courtaulds before joining Morris Engines, he was to complete his career by becoming Managing Director of the British Motor Corporation after it was created in 1952 from a merger of the Morris and Austin interests.[8] The ablest man attracted to this new venture was probably Frank Woollard, (1883–1957). His use of linked transfer machines made the Gosford Street factory a model of low cost and efficient production in the early 1920s and gave him the right later to speak as a pioneer of enlightened management methods.

In 1926 the various companies which Morris had formed were swept together into the broad framework of Morris Motors (1926) Limited in order to enable the streamlining of production to be carried further. A great landmark, however, in Morris's attempt to bring low-cost motoring within the reach of the average family was the appearance of the Mark I Morris Minor in 1929 at a sale price of £125 and with petrol consumption of 50 miles per gallon. He did not rest there. In the following year he produced a new mark of the Minor for which the sale price of the two-seater version was cut to £100. His was a familiar story; he did not succeed because of his engineering gifts, considerable though they were, he succeeded because he had an uncanny sense of the market and a capacity to convince people that he could be safely trusted with their money.

The Clyno Company of Wolverhampton, which waged a price-

[8] George Harriman, senior, Works Superintendent at Courthouse Green, was the father of the present (1970) President of the British Leyland Motor Corporation, and a very able production engineer.

cutting war against Morris until it failed in 1929, had sold its cars through a firm of distributors owned by the two Rootes brothers, William and Reginald. Reginald (b. 1896), the elder, was an accountant who had worked as a Civil Servant during the war and was a quiet, self-effacing man with an admirable accountant's brain. William himself (1898–1964), a much more colourful figure, had actually served an apprenticeship in Coventry at the Singer factory. He was attracted there because his father had been an agent for Singer cars. During the war he had been an R.N.V.R. officer and as such had gained experience in the handling of engines and vehicles, without being a considerable engineer. He was above all a salesman, resplendent, self-confident and immensely shrewd. His flair for selling, together with his brother's sound knowledge of finance, led to a rapid expansion of their company, Rootes Limited, particularly in the late twenties and early thirties when there were properties to be acquired at very reasonable cost. In 1927 Rootes Limited took their first step towards acquiring manufacturing capacity when they took over the Hillman Motor Company, then in the hands of John Black and Spencer Wilks as joint managing directors. Within two years Rootes had merged Hillman with Humber which already owned Commer Cars.

The Humber Company, like Daimler, had at one time been drawn under the spell of Harry J. Lawson. It had originally been a cycle firm, with headquarters at Beeston, near Nottingham, and for a time it manufactured tricars and quadricars at its factories in both Coventry and Beeston, until the latter was closed in 1908. The company had an adventurous manufacturing policy and its efforts to enter the aircraft industry are dealt with later. The Rootes brothers left the company with a considerable degree of autonomy after becoming its largest single shareholders; Colonel Cole, the Chairman of the Company, was left undisturbed until after the Second World War. Under the new control the Humber marque became identified with quality cars such as the Pullman, the Super Snipe and the Hawk and appears to have secured the services of a number of eminent engineers; both W. O. Bentley and Alec (now Sir Alec) Issigonis served with them for some years. The company was also noteworthy for the high quality of its management, and the names of E. W. Hancock and Horace Pryor are entitled to a leading place among those of production managers in the city.[9]

The brothers were too shrewd to rest content with this expansion. They realised that there were many other things that were essential if the Group was to be truly independent, and these they proceeded to acquire. They needed distribution outlets, and had already bought two chains of garages, George Heath in Birmingham and Tom Garner in Manchester. They needed to control their own body-making so, in 1932, they acquired control of Thrupp and Maberly, who had originally made coaches for George III. To all this was added, in the same year, British Light Steel Pressings at Acton, later to prove one of the most difficult parts of the Group's inheritance. By 1935 the Rootes Group had arrived as a significant factor in the British motor-car industry.

The final addition to the Group came as late as 1956 when Rootes bought Singer, thus ending the independence of what had at one time been one of the biggest motor-car manufacturing companies in the country. After the death of George Singer, cycle manufacturer and original founder of the firm, the guiding hand had been that of W. E. Bullock who was with the company from 1909 until 1956. In 1927 the firm produced the Junior, a very successful baby car selling at £148 and by 1928 it was the third largest producer of cars in this country next to Morris and Austin. Unfortunately, the company had made an unsound investment in the previous year. Their original premises in Coventry's Canterbury Street had long been inadequate, so they purchased an old B.S.A. factory on the Coventry Road in Birmingham. This had been built during the First World War for the production of small arms and was five storeys high. It was not in the least suitable for the production of motor-cars, and this alone must have had its effect upon the company's subsequent fortunes. In 1935 Singer's suffered a severe blow when all the company's entries were eliminated from the T.T. race by spectacular

[9] The Group also acquired the S.T.D. (Sunbeam, Talbot, Darracq) interests in the 1920s. The Sunbeam Company was made famous through the work of Louis Coatalen (1879–1962) who joined it in 1909. He had been in Coventry for eighteen years before this, first at Humber and then at Hillman. His racing engines continued to be successful in the 1920s and he was also responsible for the design of engines for Short seaplanes and the first transatlantic airships.

steering failures and from then on, things did not go well. The firm was not able to join in the Shadow Factory Scheme, and after the war its absorption by another company was only a matter of time. In its last years, most interest probably attaches to its attempt to produce a steam-car.

The headquarters of the Rootes Group was in Devonshire House in London and it was there that William was mainly to be found when he was in this country. After the Second World War he became Chairman of the Dollar Export Council and something of an industrial statesman. Many of his qualities admirably fitted him for this work. He had a rare love of people, and that equally rare gift of persuading anyone he met that that person was the man he had been waiting to meet all day. This dangerous gift, together with his ability to read people at a glance, made him a formidable chairman of committee and he rarely failed to get his own way. In 1959 he became Lord Rootes and shortly before he died was designated prospective Chancellor of the newly formed University of Warwick in Coventry, a city which he had come to know and for which he had a very great affection.

VI

The name of Gottlieb Daimler became attached to an English car company in 1893. A London engineer, F. R. Simms (d. 1944), who knew him well, acquired the licence to manufacture his car in the United Kingdom. Unfortunately, in 1896 he sold out and the Daimler Company fell among financiers. The chief of these was Harry J. Lawson, who had several technical improvements to his credit in the bicycle industry, but who for the past few years had been devoting himself to company finance. In 1896 he moved the company to Coventry where he had taken over an old cotton mill on the Foleshill Road. The next six years were far from happy, but a turn for the better came in 1902 with the appointment of a new management which included Ernest Instone, Edward, later Sir Edward, Manville and Percy Martin.

It had been an odd beginning for what was to become undoubtedly the most respected car firm in the city. The company was the first to sell a British limousine to the Royal Family, with the result that many other exalted people began to take the British motor-car much more seriously than they had previously, and to waver in their allegiance to the French. The consequent demand for impeccable workmanship meant that the Daimler labour-force contained no one who was not a skilled man. It also meant that such valuable men had to be carefully looked after, and the Daimler Company set an enviable example in arranging its work so that, when the demand for fine cars slackened, the same men could be employed on buses and commercial vehicles. The demands of Indian maharajahs were not active all the year round, and bread and butter there had to be. This golden age, born of the connection with B.S.A. which became complete in 1910, closed only with the end of the Second World War. After the war Daimler was still producing good cars, but a certain lack of direction brought to nothing the efforts of its designers. Plans for reorganisation were being made in 1956 but four years later came a merger with Jaguar.

Besides enjoying a reputation for producing fine cars, the company also produced highly trained engineers. At one time or another it employed F. M. Green;[10] Pelham Lee, afterwards founder of Coventry Climax; J. W. F. Crouch, perhaps the best of the small independent car manufacturers of the twenties; and F. R. W. England, now of Jaguar. As a result of talks begun in 1906 by Edward Manville, the company purchased the sleeve valve engine from C. Y. Knight, but much had to be done to make Knight's design a commercial reality. The company, therefore, turned to F. W. Lanchester (1868–1946), owner of a car manufacturing business in Birmingham, who had already faced and overcome similar problems with his own first silent-running car of 1901. He was an intellectual aristocrat among the technologists of his time, a product of the Royal College of Science, and eminent in many other fields besides that of motor engineering. His two volumes on Aerial Flight, published in 1907 and 1908, have not lost their value even today, and in 1927, in the field of radio, he produced a loudspeaker much superior to the others of his time. Lanchester remained consulting engineer at Daimler for twenty years, between 1910 and 1930, while still producing his own cars in Birmingham. When, in 1931, the Daimler Company took over the Lanchester factory, it continued to produce cars under this famous name until 1956.

[10] See Chapter Five, page 128.

Four years later a further name which had always ranked high in quality production came to an end when, in the summer of 1960, the last Armstrong-Siddeley Sapphire emerged from the works at Parkside. Although the company had made one attempt to produce a small car, the three-seater Stoneleigh, in 1922, the general run of Armstrong-Siddeley models was large limousines, comfortable, easy to drive and produced with superb craftsmanship by a highly trained work-force. For years they had secured and maintained their own rather special public. Some Indian rulers bought them, but the company relied largely on the patronage of colonial governors and other high administrators; the men of quiet good taste who had run the Empire. In a way it was fitting that production of the car should cease at a time when its buying public was disappearing. The firm had produced the Siddeley Special Sports in 1933, but probably the hard core of their buying public was found among an older generation.

The Armstrong-Siddeley car had been one of the creations of John Davenport Siddeley, afterwards first Lord Kenilworth (1866–1953). He belonged to the same generation as Sir Alfred Herbert and had many things in common with him including a long tradition of personal management which could only have been built up by immense hard work. Even in the days shortly before his retirement, when he was often away from Coventry, he would still be about the place, asking junior draughtsmen what they were doing and remembering the Christian names of his long-service employees. He could then look back on one of the most diverse lives of any British industrialist.

Speaking at a dinner given for him after he had been created Lord Kenilworth, Siddeley looked back to the beginning of his working life as a shirtcutter in the garment trade in Manchester. He had then entered the bicycle industry, first as a draughtsman in the Humber Works at Beeston, and afterwards as a salesman for the Clipper Tyre Company in Belfast. By 1902 he had developed an interest in cars and was selling a Siddeley car from premises in London. How much of it he made is not quite clear, since he certainly bought a Peugeot chassis and, equally certainly, put on his own radiator. His enterprise attracted the attention of the Wolseley Company, which had a showroom on the opposite side of the road. He worked for them in

Birmingham and Crayford in Kent, and it was actually in Crayford that he quarrelled with Douglas Vickers, son of the famous family owning the firm, and decided to move. In 1909 he accepted an offer from the Deasy Motor Company in Coventry where Captain H. H. P. Deasy, an eminent racing driver, needed help in design. Very soon the firm became the Siddeley-Deasy and as such it remained until 1919.

It was during the First World War that Siddeley took his firm into the aircraft industry and stayed there. In 1919 he looked north for additional reinforcement, and linked himself with the Armstrong-Whitworth Group, forming his Coventry interests into Sir W. G. Armstrong-Whitworth Aircraft and Armstrong-Siddeley Motors. The first had its headquarters at Whitley, an old R.A.F. airfield which he had bought at the end of the war. The second was based on his premises in Parkside. Here Siddeley experimented with many things in order to maintain employment. In the early twenties he produced an excellent cinema projector and in 1935 a pneumatic-tyred, light-weight diesel rail-car.

The very way in which he had acquired his training in engineering imposed limitations on what he could be expected to achieve. In the designing of car engines and still more when he entered the aircraft industry, he was bound to be dependent to a very large extent on others. Here his debt to F. R. Smith (d. 1930) was always immeasurable. Siddeley himself was really an entrepreneur, with a cool brain and an instinct for a profitable purchase which never seemed to desert him. He had shown this in 1919, when he linked himself with the Armstrong-Whitworth interests on Tyneside, and again in 1926 when he broke that link. He was to show it still more in the series of purchases which marked his contribution to the creation of the Hawker Siddeley Group.[11]

VII

Large or small, British motor-car manufacturers have usually found it more convenient to buy components from outside firms rather than manufacture them themselves. Many firms such as White and Poppe and the Alpha Motor Company in Gosford Street made engines

[11] See Chapter Five, page 131.

which went under the bonnets of cars bearing the names of a number of different manufacturers. Armstrong-Siddeley made its own bodies in the Burlington Coach Works at Parkside and Daimler also kept most of its body-building to itself. It sent the rest out to Charlesworth of Much Park Street, one of the many specialist body-builders in the city. Charlesworth also did work for Morris, as did Hollick and Pratt of Mile Lane, a company bought out by Morris in 1925. In 1911 the traditional Coventry coachbuilding firm of Thomas Pass was still in business, but ten years later it, like Hollick and Pratt, had disappeared and its premises in West Orchard were taken over by Bobby Jones, a former Daimler workman who had branched out on his own to establish the firm of Carbodies. In 1928 Jones was able to open the company's present factory on the Holyhead Road, having realised that the development of light steel pressings for car bodies was inevitable.

A similar picture of accessories firms clustering around main manufacturers had been presented earlier by the cycle industry. One of the most important of these firms had then been Dunlop, manufacturers of the most successful patent for pneumatic tyres. J. B. Dunlop himself had been a Scottish veterinary surgeon practising in Belfast, and he probably did not realise the full commercial possibilities of his own invention. Its actual exploitation appears to have been due to his friends, the two Du Cros. For a short time after its incorporation in 1900 the Dunlop Company set up its works in Coventry, but soon moved to Fort Dunlop on the edge of Birmingham. It returned to Coventry in 1906, after acquiring a rim and wheel company in the city. Since then Dunlop has enlarged its interests so much that, at the present day, the city is the headquarters of the Dunlop Aviation and Engineering Divisions as well as of the original Rim and Wheel Company itself.

Like the various accessories trades, the machine tool industry benefited from the development of motor-car production in the 1920s. In a curious way some industries can be helped by a depression in trade. The early 1920s were years of political and social disturbance, culminating in the General Strike and the National Coal Strike of 1926. The remainder of the decade was a brief respite, but we should not now regard it as a Golden Age, as some did at the time. It was followed by the grim years of the early thirties, and manufacturers who wished to survive had to reduce their costs. The installation of new and improved machine tools was one way of increasing production without increasing labour costs. 'For several years past, the position and prospects of the machine tool trade have been steadily improving', wrote Sir Alfred Herbert in December 1929: 'The volume of work going through the shops has increased, and in many instances overtime and night shifts are running.' Manufacturers, however, did have their problems; the country's export of machine tools in 1931 was less than half what it had been two years earlier, such was the intensity of the Depression. Herbert's own firm, nevertheless, was able to move from its old premises in the Butts to the present large factory at Edgwick. Two other machine tool manufacturers, both owing much to Alfred Herbert, showed the same tendency to expand in this same critical period.

Harry Harley (1878–1951) was created Sir Harry in 1950. He was the son of a watchmaker and had risen from being the first apprentice at Herberts to being Works Manager. In 1913 he decided to go into partnership with his brother-in-law to create a specialist firm producing gauges and small tools. They started business in a weaving shed at the back of Earlsdon House and later took over the White watchmaking factory next door. They further extended their premises in 1920 by buying Earlsdon House. In 1928, they converted their firm into a public company to attract additional capital for further extensions. In consequence, they were able two years later to move into part of the Meteor works owned by the Rover Company and in March 1936, with the beginning of rearmament, Oscar Harmer laid the foundation stone of the Coventry Gauge and Tool's large new premises on Fletchamstead Highway. As long as men who love their craft are respected the legends about Harry Harley will continue to circulate; about his abrupt manner, his many acts of sudden kindness, and his ability to do the job of any man in his shop better than that man himself.

The year 1926, which saw the Gauge and Tool open a second extension, also saw the foundation of the firm of A. C. Wickman. Axel Wickman was a Swede who knew something of the astonishing re-equipment of German industry after the First World War, having been trained at Krupps. He made two great contributions to technology in this country. In 1927 he introduced tungsten carbide, that tremendously hardened steel which is the basis of modern machine production. Later, he introduced the multi-spindle automatic lathe which was one of the most important factors in enabling the motor-car industry to cut its costs of production. Wickman was a very able man and soon his small premises at the Charterhouse Works on the London Road were inadequate for the business he brought in. After three years in Queen Victoria Road, he too was able to think in terms of a new factory. In 1937 he acquired the company's present Banner Lane site, and two years later opened 42,300 square feet of model factory. This had doubled before the end of the war. The firm has now become part of the John Brown Group and the total Wickman factory space throughout the United Kingdom amounts to over one million square feet.

VIII

This exuberant and purposeful economic activity which has made Coventry the ninth largest city in England could not have begun without the spending of vast sums of money on the often unnoticed services, which alone could keep the factories going, and guarantee that the people who worked there would be provided with the means of a healthy and tolerable environment. In Coventry, as in other great cities, this responsibility fell first upon the City Council. The magnitude of its problems was never quite matched by the means it had at its disposal to solve them, but the increase in its area and the coming of new factories brought an increase in rateable value from £811,563 in 1929 to £1,559,805 in 1939. The use made of this money, and of government grants, is perhaps best indicated by the steady rise in the total of the city's loan debt. This had stood at £8,864,655 in 1939 and after the war was to climb steadily until it reached the figure of £77,839,074 in 1967. Against this background of vast public expenditure must be set the story of private housing and other development in Coventry. Like so many other things, it starts with the boom in the cycle trade which was beginning to build up at the end of the nineteenth century and which led to the first stage in the development of the Cheylesmore Estate.

Long before this was completed the prospects for development in

Coventry had attracted the attention of the two brothers Newcombe. They became professional estate developers at a time when local authorities did not yet possess powers to house working-class or other families who were not actually living in slums. The Newcombes, who came from Market Harborough, bought land on the edge of various rapidly growing towns. Newcombe Road, their first development in Coventry, was completed in 1905, four years before the first Act of Parliament which allowed a local authority to build working-class houses for other purposes than slum-clearance. After completing this estate, which joins the two historic watchmaking villages of Earlsdon and Chapelfields, they proceeded to develop the Highfield Estate near the Coventry City Football Ground. Between 1905 and 1930 the company developed almost 291 acres in the city. A lot of the Newcombes' work is still there in the streets of decent red-brick working-class houses near Hearsall Common and Highfield Road. They often open direct on to the street, and originally had no bathrooms since they were built in days when bathrooms were rare even in much greater houses. They are not great architecture but they are soundly constructed and people still find them sufficiently attractive that they are willing to buy them in order to do a little modernisation. They will be there for a long time, for the builders, such as the much respected Storer, knew their craft and had reason to be proud of what they did.

When the Newcombes first began their work it was the practice of the estate developer to purchase the land, lay out the roads, and install the services, and then sell the land to one or more builders who would actually erect the houses. The builders would then dispose of them to landlords, who might finance themselves in one of many different ways. In this city of comfortably-off craftsmen, many houses were sold in twos or very small numbers, to men who would live in one house themselves and rent the others as an investment. This is a very interesting social pattern about which rather more ought to be known, but it had changed completely by the 1930s.

In 1930 the Newcombes began to co-operate with the Whitmore Park Estate Company, a local firm incorporated in 1928, principally to acquire from the War Department the National Filling Factory and other premises in Holbrook Lane. Among its directors were

Harry Gillitt (Chairman), J. G. Gray and W. H. Jones, the largest building contractors in the city, and T. D. Griffiths, the able architect, who had, for some years, been connected with the Newcombes' developments.

The accompanying table of houses built in Coventry in the 1930s shows how heavy the pressure for accommodation had become, severely taxing the capacity of the building industry. This made it correspondingly difficult for any estate developer to produce really satisfactory results. Even though additional builders were attracted into the city, not every one of them was a Storer, and some were working with very slender resources. Many might easily have failed and the appearance of estates would not have suffered very much if they had. Nevertheless, there were good national reasons why failures should be prevented as far as possible. Builders and building societies alike saw that it was their business to alleviate the Depression rather than make it worse. They, therefore, established a tacit working understanding. Between 1929 and 1936 the number of building societies based outside the city which had offices or agents within it rose from five to sixteen. This was in addition to the four societies (now three) which had their headquarters in Coventry.

TABLE 2.4 Numbers of Houses Completed in Coventry between 1931 and 1939[12]

Year ended 30 Nov	*Houses completed*
1931	1095
1932	1362
1933	1559
1934	2211
1935	2606
1936	3841
1937	4510
1938	4634
1939	3683

Many of these societies had begun in a small way in the last century in order to provide careful and abstemious men with the

[12] Comparable figures are:

	Financial years 1935/6	*Financial years 1936/7*
Liverpool	3675	3274
Newcastle	2516	2537

opportunity of buying their own homes. The Westbourne Park Society, like many others, had been associated with the chapel. The Temperance Building Society had begun in connection with the Teetotal Movement. The Coventry Provident Society had originally been connected with the Provident Dispensary so that people coming to the Dispensary every Friday night could, if they wished, also pay something into the Building Society. Of the local societies none showed a more remarkable advance between 1920 and 1935 than the Coventry Permanent Economic Building Society (now Coventry Economic Building Society). Founded in 1884 by Thomas Mason Daffern, it had slowly developed until, in 1920, its total assets were a mere £350,000. During the next fifteen years its growth was phenomenal. In 1935 the amount advanced on mortgage was twelve times the amount advanced in 1920 and its assets at the end of 1935 amounted to £3,500,000.[13] In the 1930s it was these societies and the savings which they attracted which did a great deal to pull Britain out of the worst of the Depression of the period 1930–2.

The building industry in Coventry during the 1930s was so competitive that many small men did not survive. Those who were best able to hold their ground were the large contractors whose principal concern was industrial building rather than housing. Two firms were created by men coming from outside the city, while a third had been established within it for two generations. This last was the firm of Garlick's founded in 1862. Besides doing work for Humber, they had a long-standing connection with the Standard Motor Company for which they built the Canley factory during the First World War and the shadow factories in 1936–40. Two men of strongly contrasting character who came to the city as woodworkers and rose to be heads of large contractor's businesses were J. G. Gray (who has already been mentioned) and W. H. Jones (1878–1947).

W. H. Jones was born on the edge of the city in the village of Longford, also the birthplace of Tom Mann. He had no desire to follow his father in the tailoring trade and so was apprenticed as a joiner in the building firm of Kelley and Son of Foleshill. In 1906 he

[13] Daffern (d. 1930) was himself a man of real and quiet importance in the city, secretary of more than one company, stockbroker and insurance broker. He was a Quaker and a friend of the Cadburys.

left to form a partnership with James Bacon. After his partner's death he continued the business under his own name. During the next forty years his reputation for efficiency and hard work steadily grew; for the local authority he built houses, schools and the Whitley Isolation Hospital, which he completed in about eighteen months. Business firms of standing, including Morris Motors and Wickmans, made use of his services for factory extensions, and private estate developers called on him for road-building in, among others, the Radford area. He appears to have been a happy man, content in the success which his efforts had brought and never forgetting that he had travelled a long road.

Among the solicitors who played their part in the development of the city, Charles James Band (1874–1961) is a figure of particular importance. He was born of a solid middle-class Coventry family, his father having been an Alderman on the City Council and his grandfather a watchmaker. He attended the local Grammar School (now King Henry VIII School), and among the deepest feelings of this kindly, reticent man was an intimate understanding of the history and traditions of his native city. The firm of Band, Hatton, which he founded, first specialised in property development, and was actively concerned in some of the estates we have already mentioned. A new dimension was added to his activities through his great friendship with E. J. Corbett, who had come to Coventry in 1913 as Chief Clerk at the local branch of Barclays Bank and had soon become its Manager, a position he was to occupy until his death in 1951. Corbett, a very good banker indeed, brought into the city's life some of the atmosphere of the old private banking days. Many people banked at his branch because they trusted him personally. We are told that this included most of the local publicans, although he himself was known to be a total abstainer. It also included some very important companies such as the Standard Motor Company in the days of Reginald Maudslay.

In 1920 Standard required help from the bank and one condition of that help being given was that the bank should have representatives on the Board. Corbett became a member, together with Band as chairman, a position he was to occupy until 1953. As such he was responsible for appointing as managing director the young John Black, who had left the Hillman Motor Company when the latter was taken over by the Rootes brothers. Black's character was the last which one would have expected this careful man to appreciate, but in fact the two worked very well together. Band must claim his share of the credit for a rapid improvement in the company's fortunes. Unlike Corbett, he was never elected to the City Council but confined his public work to Sir Thomas White's Charities where his influence was very great. Owing to his close friendship with Frederick Smith, then Town Clerk, he was able to give active help in the three purchases which the Corporation made from the Stoneleigh Estate in the 1920s. At that time, if a local authority wished to plan an area, it had to become the landlord. This no longer applies, but the City Council was to continue this policy of large-scale land purchase, though for somewhat different reasons.

TABLE 2.5 Growth of Population 1901–64

Year	*Total population*
1901	69,978
1911	106,349
1921	128,159
[Boundary extensions 1928 and 1931]	
1931	168,900
1936	194,100
1937	204,700
1938	213,000
1939	220,000
1940	229,500
1941	192,470
1946	232,850
1951	258,245
1956	267,300
1961	305,521
1964	315,670
1971	335,230

CHAPTER THREE

The City at War

The shadow factories. War production. The National Emergency Committee and Civil Defence. Other civilian services. The air raids. The aftermath. Dispersal. Civilian life in wartime; hostels and C.E.M.A. Work of the City Council. The Anglo-Soviet Committee.

I

On 23 July 1936 Sir Alfred Herbert attended a very important meeting in Whitehall with Sir Thomas Inskip, Minister for the Co-ordination of Defence, in the chair. The Service Chiefs attending placed on the table estimates showing that their departments would need a total of 17,650 machine tools at an average price of £400 each. Herbert thought that the bill would be nearer £10,000,000, and he knew as well as anyone else what the orders were for – rearmament was beginning. Stanley Baldwin, Prime Minister of the National Government, had already announced in the Commons that it was now Britain's aim to achieve air parity with Germany, and as early as February 1936 the Cabinet had accepted 'Scheme F'. This provided for the expansion of the R.A.F. to a total of 8000 front-line planes and for its re-equipment with new types of aircraft which were just beginning to emerge from the design stage.

The Service Chiefs had realised that this would entail the creation of new sources of production and they had already found an answer to the question of where these were to come from. In May 1936 their scheme had been put to a meeting of Midland motor-car manufacturers, including Lord Austin, Spencer Wilks of Rover, John Black of Standard and William Rootes. Sir Geoffrey Burton of Daimler was also there, but Lord Nuffield, who had been invited, was not. He later firmly announced that he would have nothing to do with the scheme. Lord Swinton, Secretary of State for Air, took the chair and announced what was, in fact, the beginning of the first Shadow Factory Scheme. It was proposed that those around the table should go into the aero-engine business.[1] The Government would build and equip special new factories, and pay the manufacturers a management fee for controlling production. Their operation would be kept rigidly apart from that of the existing private companies. There would be government auditors at each factory, but they would not intervene in day-to-day running. The factories were to produce fifty engines a week, each making a part of the engine, with the assembly being completed either by Austin of Birmingham or by the parent Bristol Company at Filton.

The engines were to be first the Mercury, and later the Pegasus for the lightweight Blenheim bomber, and under this scheme four factories were built in Coventry during 1936 and 1937. On the Fletchamstead Highway, within the Standard perimeter, were constructed the Standard No. 1 Shadow Factory and a separate shop for the manufacture of the Hobson Carburettor. The Daimler No. 1 Shadow Factory was built near the parent works at Capmartin Road and the Rootes Group opened their Shadow Factory at Stoke Aldermoor, near the works of the Humber Motor Company. Factories were built as rapidly as the construction technology of those days would permit, but full production could not be expected to start at once. A new labour-force had to be recruited, key skilled men were not easy to find and production was only beginning to get into its stride by the early months of 1938.

The table opposite shows how the occupation pattern of Coventry between 1932 and 1938 had begun to change significantly in the direction of rearmament production. Nevertheless, 'Scheme F' was not going well. It had been expected to produce 8000 front-line aircraft in three years and had actually produced only a little over half of that total in two. To some extent the Service Chiefs had

[1] Of all the men present, Spencer Wilks of Rover was the best qualified engineer, and soon won the deepest respect of the Ministry for his technical gifts and personal qualities. He was later to play a great part in the work done by the Rover Company during the production stage of the Whittle jet.

created their own early difficulties. They could have rearmed and expanded the R.A.F. very much more quickly if they had been willing to sanction the building of aircraft which they knew were already becoming obsolescent. Instead they were determined to have new designs, the Hurricane, Spitfire, Blenheim and Whitley among them, and in consequence they had to wait for results. By the spring of 1938 there was still only one Spitfire squadron in existence and five others in the process of being equipped with Hurricanes. The lights of Europe were not yet out, but they would obviously not last much longer. 'Scheme F' was, therefore, scrapped and replaced by 'Plan L' which, among other things, removed financial curbs in an effort to secure a dramatic speed-up.

TABLE 3.1 Selected Change in Occupations between 1932 and 1938

Industry	*1932*	*1938*
Engineering	4165	8937
Iron Founding	1420	1989
Electrical Manufacturing	4935	3093
Vehicles and Aircraft	29,658	41,825
Electrical Communications	41	6376
Metal Industries	4932	5919

It was only in May 1939 that the Service Chiefs realised that the R.A.F. was heading for serious trouble, even though production from the shadow factories was now beginning to flow. New designs for heavy bombers such as the Stirling and Lancaster were becoming available and there was a serious possibility that there would be no engine capable of powering them, since the Mercury and Pegasus were for the much lighter Blenheim. To disrupt existing production of Blenheims at the shadow factories seemed impossible. The logical answer was an entirely new series of factories. Much to their surprise the manufacturers, already managing one factory each, were offered a second over the telephone. Rover were asked to build another three times as big as, and next to, the one they already had at Solihull. Daimler wanted their No. 2 Factory to be in a different town altogether, but were told it had to be within five miles of the Standard No. 2 which was being sited on the edge of Coventry at Banner Lane. The Rootes No. 2, the last to be planned and built, was at Ryton-on-Dunsmore, to the south of the city. The second

Shadow Scheme was for the Hercules engine and was constructed on a slightly different basis from the first. Daimler and Standard each made halves of the same engine and worked together, as did Rootes and Rover.

The actual outbreak of war between Britain and Germany came on 3 September 1939 with the Banner Lane factory still unfinished. Work on the site had begun so hurriedly that the farmer had sown his fields in the previous spring, expecting nothing of what was to come. When the contractors took over, their first operation was to use steam traction-engines with steel winches to grub up hedges, destroy crops and convert eighty-eight acres of some of the best Warwickshire farmland into a site in which excavators could work. Then – a proof of the technical revolution which was overtaking the building industry – fourteen excavators on caterpillar tracks were sent in to excavate the factory site to a depth of ten to fourteen feet. After this, between 1000 and 1200 building workers were brought in to put up the largest shadow factory in the city, a work which they did at speed within twelve months. They worked from left to right across the site, building behind the office block, which fronted the road, three parallel machine shops, each spanned by a roof 250 feet wide. At one time machines were coming in at one end of the shops while construction continued at the other. In the depths of the winter of 1939/40, in order to keep ahead of the delivery of machines, the subcontractor responsible for concreting decided to lay a floor under the open sky, without waiting for the roof to be placed in position. He was risking the ruin of his work in a sudden frost or rainstorm; however, he was still paid because, in such an emergency, this was a reasonable action. So the work went on, handled by men working seven days a week, anxious because they knew that they were working against time.

When the shadow factories were fully extended during 1943 and 1944, they were producing 800 engines a month, four times what had originally been expected from the first scheme of 1936. The workers they employed had become a significant proportion of the city's labour-force as the following figures show. Nevertheless, it was to be expected that the greatest contribution to the R.A.F. should come from those factories which had been making aircraft before the war began. Half the aircraft flown from this country during the war were actually produced by the two firms of Vickers Armstrong and Hawker Siddeley, and the latter was significantly present in Coventry.

TABLE 3.2 Workers Employed in Shadow Factories, 13 August 1943

Parent factory	*Location*	*Number of employees*
Daimler No. 1	Capmartin Road	2584
Daimler No. 2	Browns Lane	5321
Hobson Aero Components	Holbrook Lane	590
Rootes No. 1	Aldemoor Lane	Figures not available
Rootes No. 2	Ryton-on-Dunsmore	5528
Standard No. 1	Fletchampstead Highway	4323
Standard No. 2	Banner Lane	6064

The Group had three Coventry factories: Parkside (the oldest), Whitley, built on a First World War airfield, and Baginton, the largest and newest. Their wartime contribution was to lie in the production of bombers; the Whitley had been one of the new aircraft selected, along with the Hurricane, Spitfire and Blenheim, for the great re-equipment designed to begin in 1936. The first Whitley was produced in that year, at a time when the Group had a labour-force in Coventry of just over 2300. Three years later that force had risen to nearly 6000, and the number of Whitleys built to 121. Then the production run really began, with 427 aircraft in 1941 and 596 in 1942. Production ceased in 1943, by which time the Group had produced 1824 of this useful and dogged aircraft, with its tremendous resistance to enemy punishment. Meanwhile the Coventry factories had been formed into what was called the Manchester Group by the Ministry of Aircraft Production. This had a design centre at the A. V. Roe Works in Manchester and it was from there that the design came for the Lancaster bomber, to which the Coventry factories were diverted during 1943. In 1944, at the height of their effort, with a labour-force of over 10,000, the three Coventry factories were responsible for producing 550 Lancasters and 106 Stirlings. It was a formidable record, and to it must be added the production of the Cheetah engine for the Avro Anson and Airspeed Oxford trainers.[2] This continued for the duration of the war in many

[2] The Cheetah was first produced in 1932 and its manufacture ceased as late as 1964. The figure quoted above is, therefore, only part of its total production during an abnormally long life.

places throughout the country and numbers reached the astonishing total of over 36,000.

J. D. Siddeley had early seen what might happen, and had got in with his plans for expansion in the building of Baginton. T. G. John of Alvis had his own reasons for wanting to break into the aircraft industry, since competition was becoming keener for the Alvis car in the quality market. Certainly no later than 1935, he saw Service Chiefs and announced his intention of establishing an aero division in order to manufacture Gnome-Rhône engines under licence. He was told that if he did so he would get no Service orders. The French company was a very reputable one with strong English connections, but it would certainly be willing to allow only its older and almost obsolescent engines to be manufactured elsewhere. These would be useless for the R.A.F. at a time when it was waiting for new British designs which were known to be ahead of anything else in the field. Nevertheless, John went ahead and George Smith-Clarke, his Chief Engineer, who recognised quality when he saw it, bought nothing but the best equipment for the new factory. The Air Ministry was as good as its word; no orders came for the French engines, although one, the Leonides, proved very useful for helicopters when the war was over. John seemed to have new troubles but he also had a very good new factory and this was to prove invaluable when the war came. He virtually became a subcontractor for Rolls-Royce, stripping, reconditioning and repairing the Kestrel and Merlin engines which had been damaged or had reached the end of their mileage life. At the end of the war Alvis had twenty factories engaged on this work, dispersed throughout the country. They were responsible for making, repairing and reconditioning nearly 18,000 aero-engines, together with an enormous production of spare-parts.

Years of worrying and planning, of calamity and triumph, were to go by before the British war effort was to rise to its greatest heights of achievement. In June 1939 government plans were revealed for the new shadow factory at Banner Lane, but Coventry City Council protested at its siting because it would conflict with its planning policy of maintaining the green belt between Coventry and Birmingham. In the issue of the *Machine Tool Review* for March/April 1940 Sir Alfred Herbert wrote critically of the pace at which his own industry was moving. He himself knew well what was coming, and had had his factory blacked out and a night-shift working since the Munich crisis of September 1938. Nevertheless, that night-shift was using only just over half his machines. He had succeeded in recruiting 310 women of whom 58 worked on night-shift due to the wartime relaxation of the statutory prohibition contained in the Factory Act of 1937.

This is not the place in which to examine the curious mood in which the British people, in 1939, slipped into the greatest war in their history. There was no great rush into the forces; there was not even a great rush into the factories, and there were still over a million unemployed in the spring of 1940. Memories of the First World War, a sense of detachment from the Continent, all played their part together with many other things. Even when the war began the sense of unreality continued. There was a black-out, the evacuation of schoolchildren and the rationing of butter, but no enemy appeared. It was only in May and June 1940, when the German victory in the West brought them to the Channel, that England seemed, at last, to face the dangers of invasion and attack from the air. In the next twelve months, Coventry was to face almost forty enemy air raids. Three of these were very serious indeed, those of 14/15 November 1940 and of 8 and 10 April 1941. Each produced moves from the Government to protect Coventry's war industries by dispersing them into the surrounding countryside in emergency premises of all kinds. Coventry still remained a great centre of production in its own right, but a proportion of what its firms achieved was done in premises requisitioned outside the city.

Not all this production was for the R.A.F. Climax built 25,000 trailer pumps for the National Fire Service as well as generators used for emergency lighting on landing fields. Daimler built a scout car of such quality that Rommel, when he captured one in the Western Desert, was so satisfied with it that he used it for the rest of the war. Dunlop Rim and Wheel made tyres, wheels, barrage balloons, anti-gas clothing and underwater swimming suits. The three great machine tool firms of Herberts, Wickmans and Coventry Gauge and Tool greatly expanded their production. Between September 1939 and November 1944 Herberts had delivered over 65,000 machine tools; Wickmans, who had produced and installed

300 machine tools in 1935, had raised their total to over ten times that number by 1940. From Gauge and Tool came three-quarters of the gauges required for the country's armaments as well as a large number of specialist tools. Standard, as well as making the airframe of the Mosquito trainer, produced 2800 light-armoured cars.

Nevertheless, it is true that Coventry's main effort related to the R.A.F. The then B.T.H. factory in Ford Street was extended and produced no less than 500,000 magnetos for aircraft. The firm of Fred Lee, which had been founded for watchmaking in 1900 and moved into industrial jewels as the watch trade declined, now assumed a tremendous importance. On the outbreak of war importation of these jewels had ceased. This one firm, therefore, played a major part in the manufacture of the industrial jewels required to give accuracy in the bearings of compasses for the use of the Services. But perhaps one of the major achievements within the city was the VHF Radio Link, developed and produced by G.E.C. in its Copsewood Works. This enabled a squadron leader in flight to communicate with all his aircraft, to give instructions to them and to receive orders direct from base. It is said that, when the G.E.C. works were severely damaged during the air raids of April 1941, the dispersal of work on this invention was the only matter concerning Coventry's war industry ever brought to the personal attention of the Prime Minister, Winston Churchill.

II

Such a smithy of war was bound to be in peril once the Germans had decided to use their strength in the air against British cities. Under the Air Raid Precautions Act of 1937, Coventry City Council had taken the responsibility for guarding it against damage and loss of life. Together with other large authorities, it was to work under the supervision of the Home Office to set up an organisation which could give protection against such dangers as were already being revealed in the air raids of the Spanish Civil War. The peaceful and humane men who were members of the city's first Air Raid Precautions Committee now had to build up an organisation for which there was no precedent against a danger in which they probably still only half believed.

In peacetime the new organisation was to be run by the Town Clerk. He was assisted by four of the city's Chief Officers, acting as Chief Directors of particular services. Ernest Ford, the City Engineer, was to be in charge of the Emergency Engineering Service since his men were the natural nucleus for demolition, decontamination and rescue squads. W. G. Cartwright, the head of the city's Fire Brigade, was responsible for fire precautions and, as the Transport Engineer, R. A. Fearnley was given the duty of providing the other services with the transport which they might need. The casualty services were under the control of the Medical Officer of Health, Dr Arthur Massey, who was the man best able to build up the casualty services by drawing upon the doctors in the city, the nurses at its hospitals, and the help of such voluntary bodies as the Red Cross and St John's Ambulance. In the event, much was to depend upon the Executive Officer and Chief Air Raid Warden, who was directly responsible to the Chief Controller for the handling of all matters of recruitment and equipment. Between 1941 and 1947 this post was to be held by Captain Norman Thurston (1897–1968), who came to work in Coventry from the Regional Commissioner's Office immediately after the raid of 14/15 November 1940.[3]

For the purposes of the scheme the city was divided into six zones, each of them under a Zone Controller who was appointed by the Chief Controller. At this level there would be Zone Directors of all the services already mentioned, together with squads organised for the purpose of restoring water, gas and electricity. Each zone had a headquarters, and all the services were expected to build themselves up within this framework. This broad plan of services and zones was sound enough, as far as it went, and lasted in essentials throughout the raids. Early difficulties were to arise, less from weaknesses of organisation, than from slowness in the recruitment of volunteers. By the end of 1937 Coventry's services still had only 44·86 per cent of its authorised establishment.

Most people did not want to believe that there could be another war or that Britain might be involved. Rearmament was, perhaps,

[3] Captain Thurston was a Londoner educated at Dulwich College. He had been commissioned, decorated twice and mentioned in despatches once during the First World War. His later services to the city will be found in Chapter Six.

beginning to be reluctantly accepted, but the Home Office plans for A.R.P. were often criticised as offering insufficient protection against the wrong dangers.[4] Then, in September 1938, came the Munich Crisis and war suddenly seemed very near. Trenches were dug on open spaces, gas-masks were hurriedly distributed and a trial evacuation of schoolchildren was carried out. Things could never be the same again, and the smell of danger was now in the air; danger coming from more than one direction.[5] At the beginning of March 1939 Coventry received its War Orders from the Home Office, as did all other large local authorities. The seals on that envelope were broken within six months, at the end of August 1939, when the armies of Germany invaded Poland. Then, in days of crisis and confusion, of blackout and evacuation, the entire Civil Defence Service was transferred to the Chief Constable. The Council's Policy Advisory Committee proceeded to operate an earlier decision to transform itself into a National Emergency Committee in what was expected to be a swift and dreadful war.

By that time a new link had been added to the chain of responsibility. The Cabinet had decided upon the creation of Regional Commissioners, who would take over the functions of government in their particular area if enemy attack should disrupt the operation of central government altogether. The choice of Commissioner for the West Midlands had fallen upon the Earl of Dudley. When they had lived at Dudley Castle the Ward family, from which he came, had played a great part in the economic development of South Staffordshire, living much in the world of business and driving shrewd bargains with iron masters and coal-owners. No family had been more deeply involved in the industrial life of the West Midlands. It was, perhaps, this involvement which enabled Lord Dudley (1894–1969) to become so liked and respected in Coventry by such vigorous and uncompromising personalities as Alderman William Halliwell, then the strongest man on the City Council, and Mrs Pearl Hyde.

[4] Cf. the leaflet of 16 August 1937 issued by the National Peace Council and Peace Pledge Union – 'Poison gas is the least of all dangers according to expert spokesmen . . . [the Government's plans] constitute a further stage in the organisation of the whole country on a militarised basis'.

[5] For the activities of the I.R.A. in Coventry between February and November 1939, see page 97.

The men at the Home Office who guided the work of local councils, approved Civil Defence Schemes, issued instructions and wrote training manuals, did not have our advantage of knowing exactly what was going to happen. They could make use of contemporary experience. The Italians had used aircraft against the civilian population of Abyssinia, and there were reports that they had sprayed mustard gas. It would have been very difficult to neglect the possibility that gas might be used again, particularly in view of the horror aroused by the limited use of this most uncontrollable of weapons in the First World War. Perhaps this sense of horror accounts for the fact that the first Civil Defence leaflet, issued by the Home Office in July 1939, devotes a large proportion of space to anti-gas instruction. It says very little about the danger of fire since incendiaries had not been used in Abyssinia, nor in the more recent Civil War in Spain.[6]

Steps were, however, being taken to increase the national capacity for fire-fighting, although time and events were to show that what was achieved did not fully match the extent of the danger. By March 1939 the Home Office had approved the construction of a main between Birmingham and Coventry to give each city access to the other's water supply. Coventry Canal, coming into the city from the north, was regarded by the local Fire Brigade as the principal source of water in an emergency. On the outbreak of war, temporary dams, later replaced by permanent sluice gates, were built on the river Sherbourne to convert it into a series of static water tanks. These measures seemed insufficient to the Home Office, which in April 1940 recommended the construction, in all high-risk areas, of batteries of steel dams[7] to provide storage accommodation for from 100,000 to 200,000 gallons. The Chief Fire Officer did not think that such batteries were necessary, but instead recommended the construction in residential areas of twelve additional dams holding 5000 gallons.

In the spring of 1938 an Auxiliary Fire Service was created to

[6] 'An air attack may bring numbers of small incendiary bombs . . . water is the best means of putting out a fire started by an incendiary bomb. Have some buckets handy'.

[7] The word 'dam' as used by the Home Office appears to have had two distinct meanings. In the text above it is used to describe a steel-framed storage tank.

bring additional men and equipment to the work of fire-fighting. Its establishment in Coventry was fixed at 434 in October 1939, although only 110 had been recruited to man the six zonal fire-stations and their area substations. There was also general understanding of the value of voluntary fire-watching in streets or at places of work, and the owners of premises were expected to take all reasonable precautions through parties of fire-watchers. An incendiary bomb could do comparatively little damage if smothered with sand or extinguished with water from a stirrup-pump in the moment after impact. Unfortunately, while a great deal of voluntary effort was undoubtedly applied in this, conscription was not. This meant that many residential streets, in particular, were not covered by adequate fire-watching arrangements, and serious consequences were to follow from this.

An example of untiring diligence was set from the first by G. W. Clitheroe (1883–1968), Vicar of the Church of the Holy Trinity, who at once took the emergency seriously. The stained glass from his church, like that from St Mary's Hall and the Cathedral, was promptly moved to a place of safety. Clitheroe distinguished himself above all others by the excellence of his fire-fighting and fire-watching arrangements. He equipped the church with modern fire hydrants, had a roster of fire-watchers so that every one of his nine roofs was patrolled, and placed ladders against the outside of the building so that, if the Fire Brigade had to come to his help, they could get to the scene of the trouble with the minimum of delay. He increased the number of taps in the church and installed a field telephone system linking the various fire-watchers' posts to his own command post by the camp-bed where he slept. There, like a twentieth-century Odo of Bayeux sleeping in his cloak on the battle-field, this veteran fighter lay down every night to protect his church.

If what was happening in Spain caused Britain seriously to underestimate the danger of fire in air raids, the same thing cannot be said of the need for shelters. Unfortunately, the question of shelters was to become entangled with politics on the one hand and war logistics on the other. In 1938 two very distinguished scientists, J. B. S. Haldane and J. D. Bernal, launched a public campaign for the construction of deep bomb-proof shelters for the civilian population. This campaign had connections with the Communist Party, of which the two men were members, but it certainly had great influence. In Coventry Alderman William Halliwell does not appear to have been moved by it, but Ernest Ford produced a design for an underground car park which could be used as a bomb-proof shelter. The A.R.P. Committee wanted to build two of these, but the Home Office refused to approve them in June 1939.[8]

There was one real difficulty; in the event of war, great numbers of factories would have to be built, and these would use precisely the same resources which would be required for deep bomb-proof shelters. It was a difficult decision to take, but the Home Office appears to have chosen to look in other directions for its shelter policy. Under the Civil Defence Act of 1939 it went some way towards meeting the Haldane–Bernal case by empowering local authorities to designate, and later to requisition, suitable existing basements as shelters. They were also given wide powers to construct shelters underground and on highways. These were in addition to the Anderson shelters of sheet steel which householders could erect in their own gardens and the trenches in open spaces still preserved from the time of the Munich crisis.

In the spring of 1940 came yet another change in the Home Office shelter policy. The unreal calm which had followed the declaration of war was, much to everybody's surprise, beginning to break. The German armies were on the move at last. Steel would soon become a very precious commodity, far too precious to be used in Anderson shelters the issue of which was stopped.[9] The Home Office, therefore, produced four designs for shelters which could be erected in streets or on vacant plots of land, in order to accommodate groups of neighbouring families. The best design, with a flat concrete roof, could not be widely used because of a shortage of cement and steel reinforcement. This threw the National Emergency Committee back upon the second design, which had an arched roof of brick. Ernest

[8] H. H. Harley of Coventry Gauge and Tool built deep shelters for his workpeople outside the factory perimeter. These shelters were sunk into the ground and anyone in them had several feet of concrete above his head. They were rather far from the factory buildings, but were so safe that in March 1941 he was able to offer them as shelter for 2000 schoolchildren.

[9] A survey made in Coventry in March 1940 revealed that 102,096 places in public and domestic shelters still had to be provided.

Ford felt that this was unsafe. The arched roof would exert an outward pressure, particularly if inferior materials were used. He believed that it should at least be erected on a concrete foundation, but this was overruled. The Home Office felt, on their side, that speed was essential and every builder who offered to construct shelters had his offer accepted.

In 1941 the condition of the Coventry shelters gave rise to serious concern in the city and at the Home Office. Some had fallen down, others had been pushed down by the householders who were supposed to occupy them, but regarded them as a danger to the lives of children at play. They were dirty, with little control and regarded as breeding-grounds for disease. Most of them were unlit and, since Coventry had a large floating population during the war, there were fears of what might be going on in them at night. On 13 February 1941 Lord Horder, Chairman of a committee set up to investigate conditions in shelters, came to Coventry to see for himself. On 9 June 1941, after two further heavy raids, the Emergency Committee was reported to be considering a project to provide tunnelled shelter under Corley Rocks to the north of the city. But it appears to have been the cessation of the raids, rather than any other factor, which put this problem to rest.

III

Many other civilian services, as well as Civil Defence, had to be established to guard the city and these also called forward respectable owners of businesses, professional men, housewives and industrial workers. Many gave leadership to the various cadet forces such as the Air Training Corps; others were drawn into the Royal Observer Corps, Women's Voluntary Service and Home Guard. In all these Services the general tendency was towards increasing central control, often combined with closer links with the armed forces. This process may have led to increased efficiency, but it also often led to the rather unwilling retirement of local enthusiasts who had given generously of their spare time. One such was Horace Garlick, (1891–1960). This kindly man, with many unobtrusive acts of charity to his credit and head of one of the city's largest construction firms, had been a Special Constable since 1920. Captain Hector, the Chief Constable, recognised his quality and asked him, in the spring of 1938, to become Controller of the Coventry Centre of the Royal Observer Corps. When Garlick started his work the Centre consisted of thirty part-time volunteers; on the outbreak of war it had grown to 180. These figures are, in themselves, a tribute to him, as was the operational efficiency of his Centre which was put out of action only once, and then for little more than an hour. Increasing control by the R.A.F. led to national pressure for full-time controllers, and this brought about Garlick's retirement in 1943.

The Royal Observer Corps had originally been formed in the south of England as a voluntary organisation for aircraft spotting. The new No. 5 Group, which had its Centre at the General Post Office in Coventry, covered an area running from the Severn Valley to within thirty miles of the Wash. Their Central Control Room was linked by land-lines to thirty-five observation posts, where duty observers identified and immediately reported enemy aircraft, whose flight was plotted for interception by the R.A.F. In October 1940 a second and equally important duty was added. Production had been lost in the early days of the war because many factories had stopped work on the sounding of an alert to send their people to the shelters. This had often proved unnecessary as no enemy aircraft actually appeared overhead. Coventry factories and the No. 5 Group R.O.C. played a prominent part in initiating a system of factory spotters. From observation posts on their own roofs they gave the signal to the workers below when danger was imminent and it was actually necessary to take cover. No fewer than 150 of these factory spotters' posts eventually came into existence in Coventry, and it has been estimated that eleven million man hours had been saved through this system by the end of the war.

In May and June 1940, with France obviously collapsing, various people here and there began to form themselves into the nuclei of local forces intended to harass an invading enemy. An unknown higher authority gave to this movement the name of the Local Defence Volunteers. An even higher authority, proud of his use of the English language, rapidly substituted the magnificent simplicity of the phrase 'Home Guard'. The invasion did not come, but in Coventry, as everywhere else, men who, for one reason or another, were not in the services hastily formed themselves into companies, trained and did patrols. Norman Pugh, the City Water Engineer, was one of the first and most devoted enthusiasts. He was to become a full colonel and Commandant of the Coventry Garrison of the Home Guard long after the War Office had come to control it and many posts were occupied by full-time regular officers. In July 1942 conscription for all men of military age not otherwise engaged in war work was brought in to swell the ranks. The Coventry Garrison in 1944 had eight battalions, six based on the various works in the city and two open battalions for general recruitment. Regular officers had been brought in to command many of them and the total garrison strength in September 1944 was 12,350. With the turning of the tide of war and the opening up of the Second Front it became vitally necessary to release every possible soldier for active service. The Home Guard, therefore, was trained to take over and operate the rocket-firing anti-aircraft batteries on the War Memorial Park.

From June 1940, long before the Home Guard had appealed for women voluntary helpers nationally, the Coventry units were already receiving help from that admirable body – the Women's Voluntary Service. This had been formed two years earlier on an initiative from the Home Office, which had asked the Dowager Marchioness of Reading to form a women's organisation to carry out a number of welfare duties which certainly would have to be done in a national emergency, but which were not allocated to anyone else. The Coventry W.V.S. ran a permanent canteen at the railway station for the benefit of service personnel in transit. It provided a further canteen in the Council House for the benefit of the staff on duty at the Civil Defence Central Control, as well as others at various times during the raids. It provided drivers, saw to the reclothing and temporary housing of families whose homes had been destroyed, helped with the care of women war workers in the city, and was spurred on in everything it did by the personality of its local organiser, Councillor Mrs Pearl Hyde (1904–63).

She was large, blonde and the daughter of a publican. When she came to Coventry she soon fell under the influence of that gentle pioneer of the Labour Movement, Emily Smith, who brought her into the Labour Party, and ultimately to a seat on the City Council.

She was a daughter of the people, but in the W.V.S. she was to show that she could exercise an incomparable authority, because everyone knew that she would never ask anyone to do anything which she was not prepared to do herself. Later, in 1957/58, she was to become a very successful Lord Mayor, and her warm humanity appears to have made her remembered with a real affection by three generations of the Royal Family.

IV

At three o'clock in the morning of 10 May 1940, the German army moved into action on the Western Front. All military leave in Britain was cancelled and Civil Defence services were placed on permanent alert, but still massive air raids on cities did not come. It was not until the night of 25 June that a small force of German raiders came near Coventry, bombing the airfield at Ansty. Throughout that radiant summer enemy pressures slowly increased, and on Sunday 25 August the new Rootes Shadow Factory at Ryton, still not in full production, was ringed by incendiaries and the contractor's yard set alight. No damage was done to the factory, but, in the same raid, the empty Rex Cinema in Corporation Street was destroyed, and fires were started elsewhere. One of these early raids was in broad daylight and conducted with such daring that it caused admiration, even in Coventry itself. About 5.30 in the afternoon of 26 September a single raider, flying low through the cables of the barrage balloons, bombed the Standard factory at Canley. His target was the Hobson Carburettor Shop and he only narrowly missed it, scoring three hits on the paint shop near by. He then hedge-hopped away.

Then, from 21 October, the really grim business began. Raids were still small, but very frequent. Many moved out of the city and commuted into work every day. Private operators began to run coaches out into the country every evening. To the south, the local authorities at Warwick, Leamington and Kenilworth opened halls so that people from Coventry could get a night's sleep. Many slept in their cars in secluded roads around Stoneleigh Abbey, and others at Corley Rocks in the north. On the night of 24 October pressure on local trains from Coventry Station was so great that hundreds were turned away and had to seek refuge in shelters on Greyfriars Green. Then, on the night of 14 November 1940, came the greatest raid so far directed against an English provincial city.

That night was clear, cold and beautiful and the four men fire-watching on the roof of the old Cathedral could see the frost white in the moonlight. The raid followed a pattern which was to become all too familiar. First, to light up the target area, flares were dropped by parachute; this was followed by incendiary bombs with explosive charges, and then by attack with high explosive bombs. The Central Control at Coventry received the yellow warning at seven o'clock, the red warning ten minutes later and fourteen minutes after that the first fires in the city were reported. By the time the 'raiders passed' signal was received at 6.16 on the following morning, 400 enemy aircraft had appeared over the city. They had dropped 500 tons of bombs and landmines and 30,000 incendiaries, which proved in many ways the most dangerous weapon of all. The raiders had not been halted by anti-aircraft fire, although mobile guns were rushed to the city and used from Broadgate and Pool Meadow. No one actually engaged on the ground knew what was happening to anybody else. There was so much danger that, for some, danger ceased to matter. It was a grim, confused business, interspersed with sudden, brief moments of great and unexpected beauty – one local Fire Officer in the middle of the danger was suddenly aware of the sight of a cluster of four landmines in the air, their parachutes glowing like haloes from the light of the fires beneath.

Raids on this scale were new, and there were people who lacked the discipline which ought to have kept them at their duty on the streets and many houses burned because householders were in their shelters. On the other hand, ordinary people discovered within themselves new reserves of strength and courage. Two Wyken Air Raid Wardens, Hubert Jones and Percy Barham, dug with their hands in spells of ten minutes at a time, to release people trapped when three houses were destroyed. Gilbert Griffiths returned through the raids to his post at the switchboard at the top of the General Post Office and managed to keep some communication open throughout the night. When a landmine fell on Coundon, Bill Lewis commandeered a Corporation double-decker bus and drove 300 casualties out to Allesley, making many journeys and never being able to take the same route twice. Charles Turner-Hughes and Eric Greenwood, first and second test-pilots for the Whitley bomber, drove all night through burning streets in cars loaded with petrol to keep fire-engines and ambulances going. There were many others, such as the lads of sixteen who kept communications open after land-lines had been destroyed, riding bicycles which soon had their tyres cut to pieces by glass on the roads.

In that terrible night many things which intelligent men had hitherto regarded as perfectly satisfactory crumbled and broke under the hard test of practical experience. Within twenty-five minutes of the sirens going fifty fires were being dealt with by the Fire Service and every appliance in the city was in use. It soon became clear that local resources alone could not possibly cope with the situation. The National Fire Service was not yet in existence, but Fire Brigades in each region were expected to help one another when asked. Brigades came from as far afield as Stoke-on-Trent and Nottingham but the best use could not always be made of them. Fire-fighting equipment had not yet been standardised and many hoses brought into the city that night would not work from the Coventry fire hydrants. For the purpose of fire-fighting, Coventry depended upon three sources of water; the trunk mains, Coventry Canal, coming into the city from the north, and the Swanswell Pool. All the trunk mains were broken within two hours of the sirens sounding, the only storm-water culvert under the Canal capable of draining it over a six-mile stretch was hit, as later was one of the three ducts which could drain the Swanswell. Even when water was available, those on duty might not be able to make use of it as incendiaries burned hoses and rubble covered hydrants. The Stoke-on-Trent crew were all killed and their pumping unit destroyed as they attempted to lay overland pipes from the Swanswell and one landmine on Mattersons put out of action the eight pumps working in Smithford Street.

As the raiders withdrew and the weary men and women on the ground savoured the rare pleasure of being still alive, the work began of assessing the damage and doing something about it. In terms of human life 554 people had been killed and 865 seriously injured. These numbers included 26 firemen killed and 200 injured while on duty. The historic Cathedral of St Michael's was a gutted ruin with only its great tower and spire intact. According to a later estimate of Lord Rootes, nearly 75 per cent of the city's industry had been seriously damaged and so had over 46,000 houses. Of these, over 2000 had been damaged so seriously that they were uninhabitable. The city's tram-cars were unusable since the tracks had been destroyed. Of the total bus fleet of 181, 156 had been wrecked or damaged. The city lacked telephones and water, as it lacked shops and essential food.

On the afternoon of 15 November the Ministry of Home Security issued a communiqué which, for the first time, mentioned the name of a raided city. That evening, the centre of Coventry seemed to belong to the dead. Over the neighbouring three counties, rest centres were opened for those moving out of Coventry at night. Marshals were sent out to find people and get them under cover, but many preferred to remain in the open air. Coventry Railway Station had itself been hit and was immobilised, but it was possible to get to the north from Tile Hill, and to the south from Brandon, and undoubtedly many did. Some never came back, others returned after a few days' rest with friends or relations. Many factories were forced to stop work completely and unemployment relief for 15,500 people was hastily organised at an emergency exchange. Angela Brazil had been on duty all day at the Y.W.C.A. Headquarters at Hertford Place, making arrangements to help girls here on war work to get home. Lord Dudley had received news of the raid at Himley Hall. He knew his duty, immediately ordered his car and was at the Central Control in Coventry shortly after the end of the raid. Early in the morning he had gone into one factory which was busily at work with the machines open to the sky. In the middle of the High Street, E. J. Corbett, the best-known bank manager in the city, was seen selling off the stock of chocolate from a ruined shop near by. He was making what he could for its owner, a young girl, who stood beside him. On 16 November the King arrived without consulting anyone, visited the ruined Cathedral, spoke to the principal helpers and lunched off cold food in a candlelit council house.

No local authority could have coped unaided with all this and help was already coming in on 15 November. Lord Beaverbrook, Minister of Aircraft Production, had a special interest in getting the city working again. He arrived inconspicuously that day with Sir Peter Bennett, head of the Emergency Services Organisation at the Ministry. They took William Rootes back with them to London. That same evening Beaverbrook telephoned Lord Dudley and demanded that he should take control of the local authority. This he wisely refused to do. However, the job of getting the city's industries back into business was given by Lord Beaverbrook to a special Coventry Industrial Reconstruction and Co-ordinating Committee, meeting at Ryton under the chairmanship of William Rootes. The committee was composed mainly of Service Chiefs and Regional Civil Servants, with one representative of Beaverbrook himself. Local people who attended the meetings were John Varley, a solicitor and Secretary of the Engineering Employers' Association, Cyril Taylor, a leading local trade-unionist, and Alderman William Halliwell, then Chairman of the National Emergency Committee of the City Council. Nominally none of these men was actually a member of the Committee, but in practice this distinction cannot have counted for much. The National Emergency Committee was in daily session at the Council House where the Service Chiefs and Regional Civil Servants also had offices. The business of the two Committees was bound to overlap a great deal since by far the most serious obstacle to the restarting of industry was the lack of services, of gas, water and, above all, electricity.[10] These were Corporation responsibilities. Questions of who had the right to give instructions to whom were wisely left on one side and over the next fortnight order gradually emerged.

On 15 November six hundred soldiers were drafted into the city to help with the work of demolishing unsafe buildings, clearing the streets and keeping order.[11] Soon this number was doubled and, in addition, 1200 slaters and other building workers were released from the Army to help make the city's houses and other damaged premises weatherproof before the worst of the winter. These men were quartered in a large camp erected on the Stoneleigh Estate at Prince-

[10] For an excellent account of problems involved in reconstructing the gas undertaking see *Sent to Coventry* by George Hodgkinson, who was Chairman of the Gas Committee at the time, page 164.

[11] It is said that at the time the demolition of the tower and spire of the old Cathedral was seriously considered.

thorpe. Their value was stressed in the final report of the Industrial Co-ordinating Committee, which was sent to the Cabinet at the end of December. This report came out heavily in favour of regionalising all assistance likely to be required as the result of air-raid damage. Nevertheless, local initiative had played a worthy part. The City Architect, Donald Gibson, was placed in charge of emergency housing repairs and the city was divided into thirty-four areas with a Clerk of Works and dumps of material in each. The most spectacular achievement, however, was probably that of the then Chairman of the Housing Committee, Councillor Harry Weston, supported by his Vice-Chairman, Annie Corrie. They had very little time for Civil Service forms and procedures, realising that there were 30,000 houses which needed weatherproofing fairly rapidly. Knowing of a Service dump near by which contained approximately that number of tarpaulins, they commandeered these on their own authority. Later, Councillor Weston was the centre of a fine little storm when auditors began asking who had stolen the tarpaulins. By that time, many of them had in fact disappeared, but an amicable write-off was eventually achieved.

It was equally important to get the people fed. Plenty of food existed in the city, but much of it had to be salvaged by the military from the 180 food shops which were closed through damage or for other reasons. The rest simply could not be distributed because seven out of nine wholesalers had had their premises damaged, and the system for distributing food had completely broken down. Nothing could have replaced the army field kitchens which came in immediately after the raid, but these were later supplemented by several mobile canteens supervised by the W.V.S. Meanwhile, the normal machinery of distribution was slowly being re-started. An oil-fuelled bakery on the outskirts was the first to begin baking bread. Road milk tankers were despatched to other towns to draw supplies. Birmingham and Leicester wholesalers brought in additional food and for the first ten days those shops which were still open were asked to keep their sales close to normal but not to insist on seeing ration-books. Then, by a great effort, the local Food Office prepared 20,000 new ration-books within a few days, enabling rationing to be restored.

Immediately after the raid there was neither water, gas nor electricity and, therefore, the means of cooking meals did not exist in many homes. Fish supplies on their way to the city were diverted since they could not be used, but a special issue of tinned corned beef was released from store by the Ministry of Food. After a week the National Emergency Committee was able to organise a Communal Feeding Centre in the dining-room at the Technical College. Two weeks later this was moved to the Rover sports pavilion a short distance away, but the same pattern of service was followed. In this one centre, two hundred soldiers were fed twice a day, 2000 school meals prepared and sent out, general service offered to the public who came to eat on the premises and a cash and carry meal provided for those who brought their own basins in which to take food away. They could have stew or something similar for *6d* and a pudding for *2d* extra; the food was hot, sustaining and off the ration. Council members and officers personally visited places like Stoke-on-Trent to find the cups and cutlery required. The speed with which they tried to get things done would not have been effective, however, but for the devotion of the women who worked cheerfully and swiftly seven days a week in order to keep the place open.

V

No other raid upon Coventry was to haunt the imagination like that of 14 November 1940, but two others were to challenge comparison with it for the damage and casualties they caused. On 8, 9 and 10 April 1941 the whole effective strength of the German Air Force seemed to be thrown against the West Midlands. On the night of 8 April came a heavy attack upon Coventry to be succeeded by one on Birmingham during the night that followed. On 10 April the attack was first directed against Birmingham, but from midnight onwards the enemy diverted his strength to a short, intensive attack upon Coventry, which was probably the most concentrated that the city ever had to endure.

Historic buildings such as St Mary's Hall, churches such as Christ Church, St John's and St Mark's, were burned or damaged and the attacks upon industry were more effective than they had been in the previous November. Courtauld's was severely damaged by fire,

Armstrong-Siddeley was attacked and fifteen acres of buildings at the main Daimler plant and No. 1 shadow factory were destroyed on the night of 8 April. Two nights later, the enemy turned his attack to the G.E.C. works at Copsewood, where a V.H.F. radio link with automatic changes of wavelength was being produced. This was so important for the operational efficiency of the R.A.F. that its production was already being dispersed into the more remote parts of the West Riding before the raid actually came. Now, in a serious attack with oil bombs, a third of the Copsewood plant was destroyed, and production suffered a severe blow.

In terms of human calamity the great tragedy of these raids was the virtual destruction of the Coventry and Warwickshire Hospital on the night of 8 April. This hospital still stands in the Stoney Stanton Road, near the centre of the city. Its importance in the provision of medical and surgical services in a community never well endowed with them was then paramount. Many people, besides those who were air-raid casualties would need to use it during the war, but it had been designated in the Civil Defence Scheme as the Base Hospital to take cases too serious to be dealt with in the network of First-Aid Posts and Casualty Clearing Stations. The use of the Coventry and Warwickshire had caused some misgivings from the first. During the November raid it had been damaged and its evacuation was already being considered in December of that year. In January 1941 the doctors attached to First-Aid Posts came out in favour of moving the Base Hospital; but this did not necessarily involve moving the Coventry and Warwickshire as the everyday work of the hospital had to continue. There was a genuine conflict of principle here, which events themselves were to resolve.

On the night of 8 April the hospital received no less than ten direct hits and was rendered virtually unusable, except for the Out-Patients' Department. Two doctors and seven nurses were killed, as well as twenty-one patients, while twenty-four others had not been accounted for a fortnight later. Three George Medals were afterwards awarded: to Miss Burton the Matron, Cecil Hill the House Governor, and Staff Nurse Horne, for their courage and example at a time when panic could easily have ensued. They kept up the morale of patients, fought fires, carried out rescues from bombed wards and brought men out from collapsed basement tunnels; but there were many others who remained at their posts amid the darkness, the splintering glass and the crashing concrete.

This determined the immediate future of the Coventry and Warwickshire. Only an Out-Patients' Department could remain in the city. Very rapidly additional premises were found in Kenilworth and at Keresley Hall for other departments. In the grounds of Keresley Hall were erected two large buildings, each provided with its own heating and services and capable of carrying on independently. Great banks of earth protected them against blast and it was intended that here future casualties from raids and other in-patients from the hospital should be tended throughout the remainder of the war.

A solution of one other important Civil Defence problem was also precipitated by the two April raids. As a result of what had happened in every bombed city, the Government finally decided to merge the regular and auxiliary fire services in one organisation completely under central control. When the change was announced, it was noticed that the Coventry services would be controlled from Birmingham and that the Chief Fire Officer, who had hitherto been in charge of the Corporation Fire Brigade, would be posted elsewhere. There had long been much bitterness behind the scenes. On 25 June 1941 five of the six Divisional Officers of the A.F.S. had sent to the Press an open letter addressed to the Mayor and City Council protesting about conditions in the service. They were at once suspended for indiscipline.

In one further respect the local authority was overruled by the central government. In January 1941 the Emergency Committee had already put forward a plan for a city-wide fire-watching service which would require the recruitment of no less than 2000 full-time paid fire-watchers. This was certainly one way of dealing with the problem, though perhaps an expensive one. The solution which was eventually worked out between August and October 1941 was the compulsory organisation of householders into parties of fireguards. These parties were made responsible for blocks of streets and a number of full-time firemen were appointed to train and supervise them. It worked, in that Coventry, like every other large city, was soon completely covered by a network of fire-watching parties. That their effectiveness never had to be tested was due to the change in the course of the war.

VI

After the major German air raid on Birmingham on 16 May 1941, enemy air activity was drastically reduced. Some knew why, and Winston Churchill sent a warning to Stalin which was disregarded. Then, at dawn on Sunday, 22 June, the main strength of the German Army and Air Force was thrown into an attack on the Soviet Union which was calculated to bring victory within six weeks. In a short time the face of the war had dramatically changed. Japan joined Germany, and the United States brought all its resources to the aid of Great Britain and the Soviet Union. The successes of Germany appeared at first to be more imposing than before and, until the end of 1942, it seemed as if her armies would soon control the valleys of the Volga and the Nile. Only a full-scale mobilisation of the vast resources of the United States could defeat her, and that would, inevitably, take some time.

Over the years 1942 and 1943, therefore, the significance of the British Isles in the general scheme of the war began to change. German invasion had ceased to be practicable and there were no longer effective air raids on ports and arms centres. Immediately after the raid of 14 November 1940 an urgent conference of Ministry of Aircraft Production officials had been held in Leicester to consider the dispersal of Coventry industry, in case of similar attacks in the future. At least one Leicester man spent several harassed weeks hurriedly finding alternative premises for several Coventry firms, Alvis and Coventry Climax in particular. Some dispersal was still being continued after the raids in April 1941, but, by 1942, government departments had other preoccupations as the total mobilisation of the country's resources was reaching its height. City councils, including that of Coventry, gradually found that Civil Defence now absorbed less attention and they could begin to concentrate more on their other wartime responsibilities, which were, perhaps, less dramatic but equally important.

One of the most heartening results of the war was the increased sense of social responsibility which it brought. Rationing was becoming stricter, supplies of everything were becoming shorter and many things would have to be sacrificed but great efforts were made by the Ministry of Health, in partnership with local authorities, to make sure that these sacrifices would not include the health and well-being of children. In July 1940 the National Milk Scheme had begun operation, entitling expectant mothers and children under five to one pint of milk a day for 2*d*, or free in cases of need. From August, dried milk was provided for babies under twelve months for whom liquid milk was unsuitable. From July 1941 the Ministry of Health was becoming seriously worried by the danger of rickets due to the absence of fresh fruit. By December 1942 cod-liver oil and free concentrated orange juice from the United States were made available to all expectant mothers and children under five.

The distribution of welfare foods was not the only matter in which Coventry City Council found itself working under the guidance of the Ministry of Health. Campaigns were conducted against disease with immunisation against typhoid and diphtheria and the provision of mass radiography for the detection of tuberculosis. The national campaign against diphtheria was so successful that the number of cases in 1945 was half what it had been before the war. Coventry City Council did not warm to the suggestion that it should maintain a register of home minders. These were the women who looked after young children whose mothers worked in the factories, and some might well be unsatisfactory. The Council proved more interested in the establishment of day nurseries and by the end of 1942 it had established nine. They were open for as many as fifteen hours a day, providing meals and milk and the chance of regular sleep and baths for children under school age.

The tireless energies of the W.V.S. had first been directed towards salvage drives by Lord Beaverbrook in the summer of 1940. Bauxite was necessary for aircraft and the only European source of it, Yugoslavia, was too near the enemy to be regarded with equanimity. Bauxite was also used in aluminium saucepans and kettles, and thousands were sent to be melted down as a result of this energetic campaign. There were to be many later salvage drives in order to save shipping space during the Battle of the Atlantic in 1942. The W.V.S. and other voluntary organisations became involved in the collection of paper salvage, milk-bottle tops and old books for repulping. The local authority removed railings from its parks as well as from private houses. Collections of pig swill were carried out to help home agriculture and a 'Dig for Victory' campaign was set on foot to increase the home production of food.

The growing concentration of American troops in Britain during 1943 foreshadowed the time when there would inevitably be an invasion of the Continent. When that time would come no one knew, but it would necessarily come suddenly and during good weather. It would obviously be a good idea to keep civilian traffic off rail and trunk roads as much as possible during the summer. The action of local authorities could play a valuable part in helping to achieve this. There was also much to be said for anything which economised in the use of petrol and prevented people from visiting seaside resorts which were, many of them, out of use. During each summer between 1942 and 1944, therefore, Coventry City Council organised a varied programme for 'stay at home' holidays. There were football matches, concert parties, open-air dancing and baby shows. A Drama Festival was held which was to found a permanent post-war tradition, in 1943 a troupe of Russian Cossacks came and in 1944 a visit by the Halle Orchestra attracted over 1200 people.

VII

To assess the mood of a great city in wartime is almost impossible. The atmosphere during the grim years of 1940 and 1941 was very different from that of 1943 when the tension was beginning to slacken, and of 1944 when victory was in sight. Civil Defence workers waiting for an emergency which seemed less and less likely to happen would see things in a different light from the men and women working in the factories, and being very well paid for doing so. To many the war must have meant black-out, boredom, plenty of money and nothing in the shops to spend it on. To some at least the disturbance of normal life brought a new awareness, a new sense of community and a new interest in the arts.

Many intelligent men and women had more spare time than they could use, and this led to the development of discussion groups in air-raid shelters, First-Aid Posts, wartime hostels and other unlikely places. A most significant event in Coventry was the formation of the Guild of Citizens as the result of a meeting at the Council House on 8 May 1943. The Guild included many Civil Defence workers and was intended to help them to organise their discussions in a constructive way. When its first Annual Report was issued in the autumn of 1944, the Guild had secured over six hundred members divided into twenty-six groups. They met regularly in various parts of the city and often dealt with the question of replanning, thus helping to create a public opinion in favour of a dignified and exciting rebuilding.

As early as January 1940 the Government had provided money for the establishment and running of C.E.M.A., the Council for the Encouragement of Music and the Arts, and from this has grown the Arts Council. In 1944 C.E.M.A. reported that it had organised 3169 factory concerts, some of which were held in Coventry. Concerts were also given in the Technical College Theatre and Central Hall. The bombing of London had virtually transferred the theatrical capital of the country to the North-West and many great artists, such as Sybil Thorndike, found responsive audiences in Lancashire cotton towns, mining villages in South Wales and Midland industrial cities. Work of this kind in Coventry centred on the Technical College Theatre and from it was to arise the Midland Theatre Company after the war.[12] A company headed by Walter Hudd and Wendy Hiller produced *Twelfth Night* there in 1943. Like other companies later, they toured the district, using Coventry as a base, being quartered at Tile Hill in one of the hostels built to house war workers.

These hostels belonged to the National Service Hostels Corporation which had been formed in May 1941 to bring the problem of housing war workers under central control and to make the best use of available building labour and materials. They were built to a common pattern, consisting of a number of blocks of bedrooms erected according to the most austere wartime standards and a communal block which provided a large dining-room and recreational facilities. The bricks of which they were built provided a shelter from wind and weather and the roofs were of felt, cheap and

[12] Coventry's present civic theatre has grown from this company. See Chapter Eleven, page 317.

easy to erect. They were not pleasing in appearance, being rather like the army camps which were being built by the same contractors at the same time. The hostels provided accommodation that was a good deal cheaper and cleaner than could be found elsewhere, good food and rooms in which games could be played, letters written home, a book read, or the radio listened to. We look a little wryly now at talk of the hostels as a great experiment in communal living which would help to break down the barriers between classes, but this was not entirely unfounded. People who had never before been drawn into organised activities now found themselves joining table-tennis teams, playing billiard matches or taking part in discussion groups. All these activities did exist in the hostels, although they were the activities of the minority.

The total number of hostels built in the Coventry area by the National Service Hostels Corporation was fifteen to sixteen, from Exhall in the north to Baginton Fields in the south; from Clifford Bridge Road in the east to Kirby Corner Road in the west. They each held about five hundred people. At first the City Council does not appear to have welcomed them. It was inclined to object when a particular project was in conflict with its own post-war schemes for a green belt round the city and it appears to have halted the erection of at least one of the projected hostels. It was probably in order to bury old scores and bring all concerned together in a spirit of harmony that a lunch was held at the Baginton Fields Hostel on 26 June 1943. It was presided over by Lord Rushcliffe, Chairman of the National Service Hostels Corporation. A representative of the City Council was present and a great deal was said about the essential value of collaboration between the Corporation and the local authority in enabling the work of the hostels to be done.

VIII

By the autumn of 1941 it was becoming clear that while the Russians would not easily be defeated, they would not easily be victorious. No less than three humanitarian appeals were launched under the patronage of names well known from the Spanish Civil War days; Hewlett Johnson, Dean of Canterbury, appealed for medical stores and field ambulances for the Russian front, Sybil Thorndike for comforts for women and children in Russia and the Duchess of Atholl for comforts for the Red Army. In addition, a network of committees arose to support the Russian cause through education and propaganda. On 1 November 1941 the Coventry Anglo-Soviet Unity Committee was formed on the initiative of three leaders of the Labour Party – Aldermen Sidney Stringer, George Briggs and George Hodgkinson. Although few equalled the tireless attendance of the local Communist Party at its meetings, the Committee received a broad measure of general public support. The Conservative, Liberal and Labour parties sent members to its meetings. Representatives of the Engineering Employers' Association and of the Chamber of Commerce attended occasionally, as did the city's leading wartime trade-union leaders, W. H. Stokes and J. L. Jones. The Workers' Educational Association and the local branch of the British Medical Association gave some support. Nine councillors attended the meetings in their personal capacity, and for four years the Committee was under the Presidency of the Mayor of the city. When it became obvious that the tide of war had turned, the Committee's activities declined since many people felt that there was no longer any need for them. By 1944 many important people, who had once attended its meetings, sent apologies instead.

The really effective work of the Committee was accomplished in the two and a half years between the end of 1941 and the landings in France in June 1944. Despite many difficulties, the Committee organised a speakers' service for schools, and found managements willing to allow them to send speakers to address workers in their canteens at lunch time. In January 1942 it organised an Anglo-Soviet Week with a civic parade and service, an exhibition on life in the Soviet Union and a concert given by the London Philharmonic Orchestra with Sir Malcolm Sargent conducting. In addition the Committee raised £15,000 for medical relief. When, at the end of 1942, the German Army was at last halted after it had all but overwhelmed the city of Stalingrad on the Volga, people began to link the names of Coventry and Stalingrad as two cities which had suffered in the hands of the common enemy. The Committee was, therefore, made responsible for organising an exhibition in Coventry of the sword forged in London and presented to Stalingrad by King

George VI. Coventry also received a book of greetings containing 30,000 signatures from the women of Stalingrad, as a salute from one city to another. These two acts helped to lay the foundations of an international friendship which endures to this day.

This educational and humanitarian work was not the only campaign into which the small but tireless Communist Party threw its enthusiasm. Many who were not Communists were inclined to feel that there was an undue disparity between the Soviet and British military commitments in 1942 and 1943. Whether the national campaign for the immediate opening of a Second Front actually did anything to advance the Normandy landings is very much open to question. Nevertheless, meetings such as that addressed by Harry Pollitt in Coventry on 6 June 1942, demanding an all-out war effort as well as a Second Front, undoubtedly influenced public opinion. They also brought many new recruits into the Communist Party itself. It is said that the Coventry Communist Party increased its membership from 70 to 1500 with such speed that the local organiser had to stop counting. In many ways this sudden increase was to be expected.

The workers who came to man the war factories in Coventry must be taken as they are found. Many of them had known long spells of unemployment. They had been directed into the city, worked long hours, earned good money and had the benefit of strong trade-union organisation since a great trade-union General Secretary, Ernest Bevin, was Minister of Labour from May 1940. Many of them took little interest in the war until after June 1941. The local Labour Party had a majority on the City Council, but its organisation was not well adapted to attract men who, living in hostels, had struck no deep roots in the city. The leadership to which they looked was that of the shop-stewards in the factories, and many of the leading shop-stewards tended more and more to look towards the Communist Party. This certainly did not mean that the Party's influence would be permanent and there were signs that it was shrinking even before the end of the war.

In the latter part of 1944 it became increasingly clear that the war could not last much longer. Industry was already beginning to lay off some men and the Civil Defence services were being gradually run down. Life at the Nuffield Factory in Gosford Street, at Baginton, Banner Lane and elsewhere had been good while it lasted. Peace was now coming and it seemed incredible to men who remembered the 1920s that expanded war industries could continue production at the same level. In particular, what would happen to the shadow factories, all of which were government-owned? Nobody knew, but rumours began to supply an answer. The word got around that they would simply become storage places for government surplus of all kinds, and as such would require only a very small number of storekeepers. Unemployment seemed to be waiting for the rest.

NOTE: *The I.R.A. in Coventry, February–November 1939*

On Friday, 25 August 1939, five people were killed and many others injured when explosives, which had been placed in the basket of a tradesman's bicycle, blew up in Broadgate. Coventry had been the scene of a number of much smaller incidents since the previous February and these had been, in their turn, part of a countrywide campaign conducted by the Irish Republican Army. Irish organisations in the city hastened to disassociate themselves from the action of 25 August but strong anti-Irish feeling was, nevertheless, aroused. Strikes were threatened in protest against the employment of Irishmen in Coventry factories and 2000 aircraft workers from the Armstrong-Whitworth plant at Baginton marched into the city to attend a meeting addressed by their chief shop-steward. Many Irish undoubtedly left the city for a time, although it must be remembered that war against Germany was declared on the following Sunday, 3 September.

CHAPTER FOUR

The Age of the Individualists

'Boom Town'. Sir John Black and Standard. Harry Ferguson and the light tractor. Massey-Ferguson. Trade Unions. Strikes, piecework and the gang system. The later years of Lord Rootes. Sir William Lyons and Jaguar. The Lees and Coventry Climax.

I

On 10 September 1950 a national Sunday newspaper published an article under the headline 'Blitz Town has become Boom Town'. It did not, by any means, ignore the post-war difficulties of life in Coventry; the centre of the city was still almost as the enemy had left it and prices in the shops were appreciably higher than those in neighbouring towns; a shanty-town of derelict railway coaches and homes made from corrugated-iron sheeting had grown up almost in the centre, and wartime hostels and army camps were still occupied by squatters. The article, however, concentrated on the large number of jobs that were going begging at £15 a week and, in the next fortnight, 1700 applications by letter were received at the Coventry Employment Exchange. Hundreds came personally to the city, most of them only to return home disappointed, but this was certainly not the depression which some had foreseen in 1944. There were many reasons for this continuing prosperity. Full employment was now accepted as an objective by both political parties and the devaluation of September 1949 was beginning to have its effect. The local trade-union movement, which had acquired great strength during the war, was anxious to maintain the wartime level of wages as far as possible, and the Korean War was bringing fresh armament contracts into the city. Among these many factors, however, something can be attributed to the drive, ambition and self-destroying energy of Sir John Black (1895–1965), then Managing Director of the Standard Motor Company.

Like many others, the young John Black had come to the West Midlands after the First World War with his officer's gratuity in his pocket. He had been demobilised with the rank of captain from the Royal Tank Regiment, and Clough Williams-Ellis, his former C.O. and the official historian of the R.T.R., remembers him with respect as an intelligent and able officer. Black had no formal engineering qualifications, but had obvious gifts of command and sufficient knowledge of petrol-driven engines to make him worth a job on the sales side of any car firm. He was, therefore, recruited by William Hillman in 1919, and two years later he married one of the six Hillman daughters. Two other daughters were also to marry young men fresh from the wars; one, Captain Spencer Wilks, and the other, Major Sydney Dick, who had been one of those leading the first tanks into action by walking in front of them.

A time of decision came to all three men when, in 1927 and 1929, the Rootes Group broke into manufacturing by acquiring control of first the Hillman, and later the Humber Company. All three left; Sydney Dick to become Chairman of Auto Machinery Limited. Spencer Wilks to save Rover from extinction, and John Black to join the Standard Motor Company, where Reginald Maudslay, founder of the firm, was still Chairman and Managing Director.[1] Standard had been founded in a small way in 1903, and had run into the early troubles which beset so many car firms. There appear also to have been differences between Maudslay and Charles (later Sir Charles) Friswell, the concessionaire who handled all Standard's sales. Friswell, who shipped seventy Standard cars to India in 1911 after obtaining the contract for providing transport for the Imperial Durbar, probably had interesting ideas concerning volume production. Charles Band and Siegfried Bettmann later helped to buy him out, and in the 1920s the company was, despite troubles with the banks like everyone else, a respectable producer of useful cars.

[1] The Maudslays, like the Whitworths and Armstrongs, were of the unofficial engineering aristocracy, and made a contribution to more than one firm in Coventry. The Maudslay Motor Company, now at Alcester, was making heavy goods vehicles at Parkside until after the Second World War.

When Maudslay died in 1934 John Black was appointed sole Managing Director.

Black could well see that immense prizes were still to be won in Britain through volume production of cars for the ordinary family. The useful Standard Nine, introduced in 1927 before he joined the company, was supplemented by a whole range of models known as Flying Standards. In 1938 the cheapest of these, the open tourer version of the Eight, sold at £125, and the most expensive, the Twenty, at £325. Production totals were small compared with those of today, but Standard was already using a track with subdivision of jobs in the thirties. Much of this was due to Frank Salter, an excellent planning engineer who had come with Black from Hillman. Black's expansionist policy brought its rewards; bank debts were paid off, and by 1937 the company's dividend was running at the rate of over 20 per cent each year and Black had been invited to take part in the first Shadow Factory Scheme.

His imperious military manner and flamboyant personal spending were apt to disguise the fact that, almost to the end, Black was a very prudent Managing Director. He was in advance of his time in paying proper attention to safety, and to the cleanliness and appearance of his factory. He always dressed impeccably himself and had the old army officer's liking for white lines, combined with the artist's eye for bright colours. In 1936 he introduced a non-contributory pension scheme for men on the shop-floor, long before he thought of one for executives. He took on student apprentices with a higher standard of education than was average in the thirties and, after the war, sent some to university. He appears to have kept the number of executives down to an absolute minimum and always took pride in moving around the factory personally, so that he might see for himself what was going on. At first sight John Black appears the last man to justify the description of Victorian, but his belief in personal oversight was in direct line from Sir Alfred Herbert, one of the many people who did not like him. In any balanced judgement of his achievements, these things are more important than the complexities of his personal character.

He was actually the son of a Civil Servant, keeper of a section in the Public Record Office. He received the good grammar school education of those days but nothing more, and was already articled to a solicitor when the war came in 1914. The Blacks were an artistic and intelligent family of the professional middle class in Kingston upon Thames, but those who knew him later in Coventry would never have guessed at these comparatively modest origins. He often gave the impression of playing the part of the aristocrat and old military man. He always wished to excel in everything, taking lessons in sports and working hard to ensure that he could not be outshone. A Coventry businessman once recalled how, on being advised by his doctor to give up tennis, he was invited by Sir John Black to play a last foursome. He was surprised to find that their partners were to be Fred Perry and Dan Maskell. On one occasion Black is said to have asked how to get a really good education quickly, and on another to have claimed that his father was a university professor. From these and other incidents one can only guess at the tensions, the deep sense of inferiority and the overwhelming desire for compensation which must have lain behind that resplendent exterior.

Black, nevertheless, had great gifts of leadership and able men were to feel themselves fulfilled in working for him. One such was Frank Wilde, the designer of the Flying Standards of the thirties. Another was Harold Weale, who had joined Standard as a boy long before Sir John Black came. He was to become Works Manager and to handle all the detailed negotiations for the Standard-Union agreement of 22 November 1948. A shrewd, tough, likeable man, he was to retire from Standard shortly before his death in 1969, and was one of that select band of outstanding production men whose personal qualities go far to explain the success of Coventry industry. Others came and went. These included Frank Lord, Frank Salter and Edward Grinham, who was to become Sir John Black's deputy. Grinham, who was a fully trained engineer, had been with de Havilland's before he went to Humber, and was to return to the former company during the war to reorganise the production of the Mosquito. He possessed the technical training which Sir John Black lacked and was well aware of his own great share in Standard's success. There was, therefore, often a certain tension between the two men. Their relationship was by no means uninterrupted, but they appear to have needed each other, and Grinham was back on the Board in January 1954 when Sir John Black retired.

With this small but able team around him, Black decided to allay much speculation and many fears in the spring of 1945. He announced that the Standard Company would take the lease of the Government's shadow factory at Banner Lane, using it for the development of car production. This would obviously help to solve the city's post-war employment problem, but it gave Standard problems of its own. Steel was still rationed, but the company had already developed a number of ideas which would be economical in its use. In 1943 they had gone some way towards developing a Jeep-type cross-country vehicle called the Stag, and followed this with the 'Jungle Bug' which was so light that it could be picked up and carried by two men in difficult terrain. They also had plans for producing a mechanised farm cart. Other companies, such as Rover, were thinking along the same lines at the time, but Standard suddenly changed its mind when another prospect came into view. It appeared that Harry Ferguson was seeking manufacturing capacity for his tractor in the United Kingdom after quarrelling with the Ford Company in the United States.

II

Circumstances at the time favoured an expansion of tractor production in Britain. The country's supply of suitable factories was now greater than it had ever been and during the war many of these had been operated by car firms which had thus immensely enriched their experience of large-scale production. They had worked on tanks, gun carriers and other vehicles designed to operate in rough country and could not at present look to an immediate return to car production since steel was still rationed. On the other hand, they could look forward to government help if they kept their factories open for the production of vehicles which were economical in their use of steel. The Land Rover was one such vehicle, the Stag another. The Nuffield interests, however, were considering the making of tractors and this was a field in which Henry Ford I and Harry Ferguson had already been operating for a long time.

Harry Ferguson had been interested in tractors since 1916, when the government of Ireland had brought him into the 'Grow More

Food' campaign. He had been connected with the land since his birth as the fourth of eleven children on one of those hill farms of County Down where strong character grows as easily as good grass in the fields. The Fergusons were not poor and their father was able to find the money when Harry and one other brother left the farm to start a garage business which still exists in Belfast. He was not, perhaps, the great inventor which some have claimed, but he had an enormous capacity for organising the gifts of other men and welding their contributions together into something in which his was really the greater and more creative part. His countryman's appearance and the direct gaze of his blue eyes were among the things which made Henry Ford instantly like him. Another was his genuine idealism about the way in which the tractor could help to raise the world's supply of food and banish poverty from areas which had known it too long.

Ferguson was not the first man to build a tractor but he certainly saw more deeply than most the implications of the technological revolution in agriculture which he was helping forward. With the horse-drawn plough the farmer walked behind to guide the ploughshare while the horse took the strain on its shoulders. The earliest tractors were very heavy and the man driving had to raise and lower the plough by using a rather cumbersome set of levers. The Ferguson tractor revised the whole structure of the machine by a novel hitch system which made it possible for the tractor to be built much lighter. The tractor was only part of the Ferguson system, and for every Ferguson tractor there had to be a plough so designed that it could lock together with the tractor and become an integral part of it. Other agricultural implements designed by the Ferguson team could be locked into position behind the tractor in the same way.

When Harry Ferguson returned to England in May 1945 it was with the intention of finding a centre for the production of his light tractor. One agent had already preceded him and at least four firms appear to have been considered. Two, one in Sheffield and another in Cardiff, were rejected at a very early stage because they were too small. Lord Nuffield, whom his Managing Director, Miles Thomas, was trying to interest in tractor production, heard of the arrival of Harry Ferguson and met him twice. At the second interview Nuffield was perceptibly less interested than he had been at the first. In the middle of what was providing a rather awkward discussion Miles Thomas received a telephone call from Sir John Black, who already knew of Ferguson's arrival and was anxious to meet him.

It is practically impossible to say who first told Black about Ferguson. George Cummings, the London advertising agent who handled Standard business, had certainly known of him for some time. So had Colonel Hanson, a Standard director who was living in Westmorland keeping an eye on a small Standard factory near Kendal. He appears to have been told about Ferguson by Thomas Hoggarth, owner of an agricultural machinery business in Kendal, but when he telephoned Black, the latter already knew of Ferguson. Hanson appears to have played a useful part by persuading Black to sacrifice a little pride and go to London instead of expecting Ferguson to come to Coventry. Once this was done the matter was arranged very rapidly, and at a dinner party at Claridges in the autumn of 1945 the two principals came to an agreement which was embodied in nothing more formal than a few lines written on a menu. Also signing were Henry Tiarks of Schroders, at that time the Standard merchant bankers, Oliver Lucas and Robert Sinclair. Everything seemed to be set for a long, useful and prosperous collaboration.

However, it was not all going to be plain sailing. The Standard team knew that the Ferguson tractor had been using a Ford engine which would now no longer be available. Before volume production could begin there were things to do, and not merely at the technical level. Ferguson and Black had to see Hugh Dalton, Chancellor of the Exchequer, in order to obtain the necessary dollars to buy the 25,000 Continental engines needed to power the tractor before the Standard engine was ready. They also had to get money to import American specialist machine tools already on the market, as British substitutes would take a long time to manufacture. All this was arranged on condition that the expenditure of dollars would eventually be balanced by sales in the American market. Sir Stafford Cripps, then President of the Board of Trade, also knew both men and he and Dalton were sympathetic and helpful.

The output of tractors from Banner Lane appears to have faithfully kept pace with the national trend in economic activity. In 1949, which was a year of recession, Fergusons had over 3000 unsold tractors on their hands and the production schedule was cut from 350 to 150 a day. In 1951, which was a good year following devaluation, output rose to 73,623.

Both Sir John Black and Harry Ferguson were men of such strength of character that probably no factory in the country was big enough to hold them both, and no agreement between them capable of functioning without personal stresses. Of course they quarrelled magnificently according to the fashion of an older generation. The ways of men are not always easy to interpret, and they probably retained a real respect for each other, although they would never have acknowledged this. There was also an inherent difficulty present from the start. Ferguson was designing a tractor which John Black was producing at Banner Lane in order to sell to Ferguson as his sole customer. Ferguson, who was thus on both sides of John Black, could hardly have avoided actions which looked as if he was interfering in the actual process of manufacture. On their side, the Standard men could claim to have made a contribution towards the design of the tractor by providing it with a remarkably efficient engine (which was afterwards used for the Vanguard car).

Ferguson, that creative idealist, seems often to have found it difficult to work with his equals. His pre-war collaboration with David Brown of Huddersfield had run into trouble and his association with Henry Ford I in the United States had lasted a long time simply because that great man had recognised in the other much of a character which matched his own. After Henry's retirement and Edsel's death Henry Ford II took over and the connection soon ended in a lawsuit which Harry Ferguson won. Some people found him devious,[2] but he was well within his rights when, in the summer of 1953, he departed for the United States to take certain decisions about the future of his American company, Harry Ferguson Incorporated, which was causing him some concern. In July 1953 he decided to merge his American interests with Massey-Harris, a Canadian tractor manufacturing company which also owned two

[2] Shortly after becoming associated with Standard he appears to have wanted to bring in Sir Miles Thomas as Chairman in order to counterbalance Sir John Black.

factories in Britain, one at Kilmarnock and the other at Manchester. Their distributive outlets would provide him with the sales facilities he needed in the Western Hemisphere. Had the agreement stopped there, there would probably have been few objections.

Then, on 4 August 1953, at his home in the Cotswolds, he made a surprise proposition to James Duncan, President of Massey-Harris. Massey-Harris themselves were in some financial difficulty since, as a Canadian firm, most of their production had to be paid for in dollars, which were not readily available on the international market. James Duncan was now offered all Ferguson's tractor interests through the world, including, of course, the disposal of the whole production of Banner Lane. Ferguson stipulated that his own name should appear in that of the projected company and that he should be given a place of honour on the Board which two of his associates should also join. He wished to retain control of the design of Ferguson equipment, but explicitly stated that he was anxious to be rid of anything to do with the commercial side. Standard, which had begun with one single customer for its tractor, was now faced without warning with another. The Standard men were furious and Sir John Black's persistence in signing a new ten-year agreement with Duncan may, perhaps, have been one of the reasons for his departure from the managing directorship of Standard in January 1954.[3]

III

The great new combine of Massey-Harris-Ferguson[4] was soon to part company with the man who had brought it so much, and who had trodden out many of the paths in which the company still walks. No one who really knew Harry Ferguson could have expected him to accept the self-denying ordinance which he had imposed upon himself at the Abottswood conference in August 1953. His new colleagues soon began to feel that he was interfering in precisely those matters from which he had pledged himself to abstain. Within a year he had left the company in order to devote himself com-

[3] He had also earlier been involved in a serious accident during the test run of a new Standard sports model in the factory grounds.

[4] The name of Massey-Ferguson was not adopted until 1958.

pletely, through the firm of Harry Ferguson Research, to the development of his interest in cars.

His remarkable capacity for gathering able men around him, kindling their enthusiasm and co-ordinating their inventions, had enabled him to produce a number of interesting and useful ideas for the development of the motor-car. Harry Ferguson had been designing tractors for most of his working life, he knew all there was to know about them and his opinions naturally carried great weight. He came to the motor-car industry as a stranger, faced by established manufacturers who saw their own products as more sophisticated than the tractor and who were convinced that they knew their own business very much better than did Harry Ferguson. When they discovered that he did not mean to build his own vehicle, but to allow existing manufacturers to use his inventions on licence, their reserve deepened, and he had made little progress when he died in 1960.

The relationship between Massey-Harris-Ferguson and Standard did not long outlast the departure of Harry Ferguson. Friction arose in 1958, when Standard purchased the Birmingham bodybuilding firm of Mulliners on terms which Massey-Harris-Ferguson felt diminished the value of their own shareholding. Standard had originally used bodies from Fisher and Ludlow, also of Birmingham, and it was the Standard order which had caused that interesting firm to establish a Coventry factory at Tile Hill before the war.[5] Fisher and Ludlow had merged with B.M.C. in 1953 and Standard, therefore, had to find another bodybuilder if they wished to preserve their independence. It was becoming increasingly clear that independence was not a thing which Standard could expect to enjoy forever. At one time it seemed likely that it might merge with Massey-Ferguson but the latter company did not find the arrangement attractive. This was followed by the outright sale of the Banner Lane premises to Massey-Ferguson in 1959, and by the eventual

[5] The original Fisher had set up a small Birmingham business making tin spouts for the kettles sold by travelling tinkers, and had gone into partnership with James Ludlow in 1849. The contract which the firm gained during the Boer War for making mess tins for the army was a step up in the world, and another followed in 1920 when it began to make motor-car bodies. It was eventually to merge with Pressed Steel to form the present firm of Pressed Steel-Fisher.

merger of Standard itself with Leyland Motors (as it was then) in 1960.

Under the ownership of Massey-Ferguson Banner Lane has become the largest factory in Europe devoted solely to the production of tractors. In a tower block within its perimeter is housed the headquarters of the export division which controls the exports of Massey-Ferguson from its factories throughout the world. Most of these exports come from Great Britain and it has been estimated that Europe is still the greatest market, taking 38 per cent of Massey-Ferguson's total exports, thus slightly exceeding the 37 per cent sold to the North American continent. A further 4 per cent goes to the Republic of South Africa. This represents a total of almost 80 per cent of Massey-Ferguson's exports flowing through normal commercial channels via distributors in the importing countries to farmers who do not represent any kind of credit risk. It is a different matter with some of the remaining 20 per cent which includes 3 per cent to the rest of Africa and 4 per cent to Asia. There, the tractor plays a part in an attack on world primary poverty such as Harry Ferguson himself envisaged in his speech to the International Food Conference at Bethesda, Maryland, on 5 June 1943.

The problem is perhaps greater than he then imagined. There are areas of the world where mechanisation of agriculture would merely lead to unemployment among the peasantry. There are other developing countries which have their own native-born distributors, but where much also depends upon the assistance provided by the country's government. With this portion of the Massey-Ferguson export traffic, government export credits and the work of such agencies as the Colombo Plan gain great importance.

Export and technical training must go together, since it is useless to supply tractors to people who cannot use and maintain them properly. As early as 1947 Harry Ferguson had started a tractor training school in the grounds of Packington Hall, near Meriden. Two years later it was moved to the Stoneleigh Abbey estate of Lord Leigh, where there existed a wartime camp which proved admirable for the purpose. There it has remained ever since, the principal change being in the increasing range of countries from which its students are drawn. A recent course included students from Portugal, Tanzania, Zambia, Pakistan, the Cameroons,

Gambia, Borneo, Uganda and Nigeria with the addition of one English student sponsored by the British Council. One is a distributor's son, another an estate manager, a third a farmer, but most are either employed or about to be employed by a government which will use their training to train in turn the men who actually work the fields. The company also maintains two mobile schools. One moves around agricultural colleges in the United Kingdom but the overseas school has a much more colourful existence. It visits farm institutes wherever they exist, but also spends days giving advice and information in market places. One recent tour began in Bombay, travelled north through India and Pakistan to Afghanistan via the Khyber Pass, moved into Iran and finished in Yugoslavia by a route which is not quite clear to those who sent it there.

VI

Compared with employers in other industries, car manufacturers have never paid badly even in the 1930s, when many of their workers were compelled to face at least three months' seasonal unemployment owing to the nature of demand. They were powerfully represented in the Coventry Engineering Association which had been established before the war to represent the collective interests of all employers, large and small, particularly in their relations with the trade unions. It was to owe much in the difficult post-war years to the wise guidance of Christopher Oliver (d. 1959).[6]

For their part, the trade unions with large numbers of members in engineering were combined for negotiating purposes in the Confederation of Shipbuilding and Engineering Workers. The

[6] The memorial service to Christopher Oliver at St Barbara's Church, Earlsdon, on 27 February 1959 was attended by such leading trade-unionists as Cyril Taylor and Charles Gallagher, as well as by such leading industrialists as Sir William Lyons. Oliver had been an elder statesman among engineering employers for many years, having served on the management board of the Engineering Employers' Federation since 1939 and as Chairman of the Central Conference Committee since 1953. He had come to Coventry in 1921 as a foreman at Humber, succeeded Sir John Siddeley as Managing Director of Armstrong-Siddeley and was Chairman of Rotherhams for some time after the war.

Coventry District Committee included a number of skilled craft unions such as the Metal Mechanics, the Birmingham and Midland Sheet Metal Workers, founded in 1859, and the Vehicle Builders, whose members had at one time been coachbuilders and upholsterers. The Transport and General Workers had inherited the strength of the Workers' Union, with which they had merged in 1929, but the heart of the trade-union movement in Coventry had, in many ways, been the group of skilled unions which was eventually to amalgamate and form the A.E.U. in 1921.[7] These included the Toolmakers, the Steam Engine Makers, who claimed to have been founded in 1826, and the Amalgamated Society of Engineers itself, founded in 1851. This group of classic unions had given the local Labour movement most of its leadership, and their total strength stood at 11,000 on the eve of the great dispute of 1922. This dispute, which was over the question of the employers' right to decide when overtime should be worked, was disastrous in its outcome. In the following few years the strength of the engineers melted away, so that by 1931 the District Committee exercised its jurisdiction over 2400 members only. The beginning of rearmament caused membership to rise and organisation to improve[8] and, at the outbreak of war, membership of the District had returned to something like the 1922 level with shop-stewards appointed at such key trade-union strongholds as A.W.A. Baginton. Since 1937, however, one of the principal assets of the Engineers was, perhaps, the negotiating skill of their Divisional Organiser, W. H. Stokes.[9] Stokes became District Secretary of the A.E.U. in 1931, at a low point in its fortunes. His appointment as Divisional Organiser six years later in-

[7] The A.E.U. rejoined the Confederation nationally in 1946 after a long absence owing to differences with other unions.

[8] One consequence of this was the gradual abandonment of dismissal by the foreman. Questions of dismissal had to be reserved for higher management as trade-union membership grew.

[9] Stokes had been born in Earlsdon in 1894, the son of a watch finisher who worked at Rotherhams. The family were decent, self-respecting working people, and although the home had little money, it had a great deal of kindness, love and discipline. At the age of twelve. Stokes left school for a job painting rims in a cycle factory. After the First World War he worked at Daimler and there became a shop-steward, meeting such other leaders of the Labour movement as George Hodgkinson and Robert Thompson. He was among the leaders of the 1922 dispute and became a member of the Minority Movement and a strong critic of the trade-union establishment of the day.

evitably took him away from Coventry a great deal but inter-union difficulties would, in any case, have prevented him from becoming Secretary of the newly formed District Committee of the Confederation of Shipbuilding and Engineering Workers.

The first occupant of this new post was J. L. Jones (b. 1913), now (1971) General Secretary of the Transport and General Workers' Union. He was born in Liverpool into a family of the militant left of the Labour movement. He wanted to become an engineer, but his indentures were broken by the firm in the depths of the Depression. His father sympathised with Connolly and Larkin of the Irish Citizen Army, and Jones himself served on the Republican side for part of the Spanish Civil War. Shortly after taking up his new post as District Secretary to the Transport and General Workers' Union in Coventry he found himself immersed in the intricate problems which beset the full-time officials giving leadership to the trade-union movement during the war.

The collaboration of trade unions in solving problems of war-time production was particularly important in such a great engineering centre as Coventry and it took many forms. The Production Defence (later Production Control) Committee, upon which the principal trade-union officials sat, helped to work out the industrial warning system which prevented the loss of many hours of production through workers being sent to their shelters unnecessarily.[10] Joint Production Committees were established in the main factories and committee members from the aircraft factory at Baginton were particularly active in visiting their suppliers in order to eliminate production difficulties down the line. But perhaps the most enduring example of trade-union responsibility was shown in the Toolroom Agreement of January 1941, framed in accordance with a Ministry of Labour directive of the year before. This was originally an attempt to conserve scarce supplies of skilled manpower at a very difficult time. Trained engineering workers were hard to come by and their proper distribution was being threatened in two ways. Some were taking jobs as production workers where they could get a great deal more money, and others were being attracted in excessive numbers to factories offering particularly high wages. The Agreement, which applied to the Coventry district only, provided

[10] See Chapter Three, page 79.

toolroom workers in each factory with an hourly rate not less than the average hourly rate paid to production workers in nine selected factories throughout the city. This rate was to be calculated afresh every month.

This agreement, now in process of being drastically modified has proved as decisive in peace as it was in war. With the exception of a brief period of hesitation during the early uncertainties of peace, the general tendency of these wage rates has been to move steadily upwards. They have been surprisingly unaffected by periods of limited short-time working, since production workers during such periods tend to work harder in order to meet their fixed domestic commitments, such as mortgages and hire-purchase payments. The Toolroom Agreement proved to be the first of the two pillars upon which Coventry's reputation as a high-wage engineering centre was to stand. The second was the separate agreement between Sir John Black of Standard and the Coventry engineering unions in 1948. But before this was achieved there intervened a period of bitterness and conflict.

The twelve months following the end of the war in Europe were a period of great uncertainty in Coventry. Many employers had greatly extended their commitments during the war. Though anxious to maintain them at the new level in peace, they were not at all sure that they could continue to pay overtime rates once they entered on a peacetime market with difficulties and complexities which had yet to be discovered. Workers in engineering had also greatly improved their position. Seasonal unemployment had passed into history and their unions were organised as never before. It was perhaps natural that they should see behind the employers' attempts to reassess the wages position a deliberate move to attack a recently won high standard of living. Like the employers, they too had memories of peacetime depression. Only wise leadership on both sides prevented the conflict from becoming very much greater than, in fact, it was. Shop-stewards at Nuffield Mechanisations in Gosford Street, which had paid the best wages in the city during the war, tried to insist that these should not be diminished now that peace had come. The factory had been damaged during the war and was marginal to the Nuffield requirement. It was, therefore, simply closed down. On 21 January 1946 a strike began at Daimler when the company tried to reduce piecework rates. These were, however, dwarfed by the four weeks strike which began at Humber on 23 February 1946.

The Humber complex at Stoke had consisted during the war of three separate elements: the Rootes No. 1 Shadow Factory making aero-engines, the old Hillman factory repairing them, and the old Humber factory engaged on the manufacture of tank engines and tracks. Piecework rates at the last had been by far the lowest and this had led to discontent and low productivity for a number of years, particularly after the temporary departure in 1942 of the wise E. W. Hancock, then Works Manager. It was to be expected that the shop-stewards should try to improve the position under the leadership of Pat Brogan, Charles Gallagher and Howard Millerchip. The installation of a new and highly efficient mechanised foundry, with its possible threat to many jobs added to the tensions of an already difficult situation, and the growing discontent led, after the war, to an organised go-slow campaign. At one time in early 1946 the Humber factory was producing one car per week. Rootes' management retaliated by bringing in the Ministry of Labour under the wartime procedure which still prevailed and declaring 550 men redundant. It was this which precipitated the strike and during the following four weeks there was a serious risk of a city-wide engineering strike. Feelings were running high, but restraint prevailed on both sides. The Rootes Group drew back, the local unions did not rush forward, and calm ultimately returned.

These events must have played an important part in inducing Sir John Black to reconsider Standard's position in relation to the trade-union movement. An employer who wanted the best workers – and Black always wanted the best of everything – would have to tempt them by inducement. He would have to pay them well, probably a great deal more than the smaller engineering employers in the Association could afford. This would mean a separate agreement and brought Sir John Black face to face with two features of West Midlands' industrial practice which had existed long before modern trade unions. These were piecework and the gang system.

Piecework is an inheritance from the domestic system when the worker drew materials from his employer, worked on them in his own home and returned them at the end of the week. Since he was left to decide his own hours of work, he could be paid only according to the number of jobs completed. Masters in the same trade and in the same area would pay according to an agreed price list, and when trade was good and demand stable the system worked well. Many workers in engineering like it still. They point out that it contains an obvious incentive to greater productivity, since the more the worker produces the more he earns. Employers are not always so sure. As far as they are concerned, they have to maintain extra supervisory staff to fix piecework prices, which is not an easy procedure. If prices are fixed too low the firm may find it difficult to get workers, if they are fixed too high they may often fail to lead to any increase in production. Many workers who know their weekly commitments find it easy under piecework to work until they have met them and then stop. To save himself a lot of trouble over individual piece-rates and, at the same time, retain an incentive to higher production, Black looked, in 1948, to the gang system.

When the history of human work comes at last to be written the gang system, as evolved in some Coventry engineering factories will, undoubtedly, find a respectable place in it. Gangs had existed elsewhere in many industries, and still do. They had dug canals, built railways and worked coal faces under the control of a ganger who was, in fact, a petty capitalist who paid them out of the contract price which he received from the main employer. In Coventry the element of democratic co-operation from below appears to have been particularly prominent, and that of petty capitalism from above almost completely absent; and one would like to know more about the methods of working in parts of the watchmaking industry and in the small specialist cycle firms. The fully-fledged gang system, however, seems to have emerged in the aircraft industry, at A.W.A. Baginton, where the work was peculiarly suitable. Each aircraft produced at A.W.A. had a team working on it for a very long time. Each team, therefore, was recognised by the management as a gang. By 1938 each gang was allowed to elect its own ganger, who was often the trade-union shop-steward, and in practice took over many of the functions usually associated with the foreman. The foreman himself tended to become a technical adviser, which, since the production of an aircraft requires ten thousand drawings, still left him with a great deal to do. This system passed to the Standard works at Canley when that factory began to build the Mosquito airframe during the Second World War, with key labour transferred from Baginton. These men took the gang system, with the principle of elected gangers, to Canley, and Black, therefore, knew of it during the post-war period.

What Black wanted to do was essentially simple. He wished to treat all the men working at Canley as belonging to one gang and those working at Banner Lane as belonging to another. On top of his basic wage, each man would be paid a further incentive bonus dependent upon the number of tractors or cars actually leaving the gates of the factory each week. In practice, Black had to yield ground on the number of gangs allowed in each factory, but this retained the very substantial innovation that indirect workers were, for the first time, to be included within the gangs. Other employers in the city would almost certainly have had to pay as highly as did Black for production workers, whether or not the Standard agreement had been signed but a lot of his subsequent unpopularity arose from the fact that now they also had to pay highly for maintenance men, storekeepers, pattern-makers and similar grades. In more ways than one, the agreement was a landmark. It accepted the working week of $42\frac{1}{2}$ hours and contained one clause from which all might have benefited if it had been framed a little more rigorously and observed more exactly. That clause stated that every effort should be made by management and workers to eliminate overtime, and that the required weekly output should be obtained in five normal working days.

From the point of view of the Standard management their agreement with the unions appears to have paid off handsomely for a number of years. Trading profits continued to be good and in some years, such as 1951, very good indeed. But it was for jobs only indirectly concerned with production that Standard was particularly attractive, and over a long period the result was not invariably in the company's favour. This was particularly true because of the responsibilities which the trade unions accepted for the recruitment of labour. For many years the way to get a job at Standard was through a trade-union office and, in the larger unions, the hard-pressed officials soon found that, while they could always fill a vacancy, they could not always guarantee to fill it well. Even in the last few years of Sir John Black's managing directorship the operation of the Agreement was not always bringing to Standard the type of men whom he had wished to attract and even if his unique personal ascendancy over the shop-floor had not been removed early in 1954 a time of testing might well soon have come.

This time actually began to develop in that very year, when Standard were considering the necessary preparations for producing for Massey-Harris-Ferguson a new and heavier tractor, the F.E. 35. In order to get the maximum flow of production on the new vehicle Standard proposed re-equipping Banner Lane with machines which would take at least two years to build. When they were delivered, the plant would be closed down and all the men temporarily laid off. It would then be replanned and when production started again the men would be taken back. All this was explained to a works conference of shop-stewards in March 1955. The union representatives stressed that, during the re-equipping, all labour should be transferred to car production. The management agreed to this, although they had already received one reminder of the uncertainties of business life in 1955 when their contract for the manufacture of the Avon jet engine for Rolls-Royce was cancelled. In 1956 they found car sales falling, largely due to a government credit squeeze. Their previous undertaking that all labour at Banner Lane would be transferred to car production could, therefore, no longer be kept.

On 26 April 1956 the powerful shop-steward machines at Banner Lane and Canley brought the two factories out in an unofficial but highly organised strike. It lasted a fortnight and never gained national recognition from any of the unions concerned. The national officials examined the situation at a meeting in London; a meeting which was one of the first engagements of Frank Cousins as General Secretary of the Transport and General Workers' Union. Cousins found himself in the same room as Frank Foulkes of the Electrical Trades and Joe Scott of the Amalgamated Engineers. They referred the problem back to local level, and the credit for the ultimate settlement goes to Jack Jones and Cyril Taylor as much as to anyone. The strike had its importance within the trade-union movement in the development of thinking about redundancy. The strikers were putting forward the traditional British trade-union view, that redundancy should not happen and that, if work was short, it should be shared equally among everyone concerned. There was an instinct of comradeship behind this which deserved respect, but some of the more far-sighted permanent officials were already growing unhappy about it. They saw that, pushed to its logical conclusion, it was a demand that no man's job should ever disappear, and that the industrial pattern of the country should be frozen. The newer American unions, such as the United Automobile Workers of America, had long accepted the view that, if redundancy was inevitable, it was their job to negotiate the best terms for their members when it occurred. Redundancy agreements are now becoming common practice in British industry, and the Standard strike may well have played its part in securing this change of thinking.

V

The two labour disputes already mentioned were not the only ones to take place in the city during the post-war period. They have been selected for attention because they were fought over fundamental principles. In the Humber strike of February/March 1946 both sides believed their action to be necessary if a return to inter-war depression was to be avoided. In the Standard strike of 1956 the men put forward their traditional demand that no one should be dismissed in times of bad trade, but that all available work should be shared. A third dispute of decisive importance for the motor industry as a whole lasted over two years at the Rootes Group's Ryton factory. Between 1967 and 1969 management and men were divided over an attempt by the new American owners of the Group to replace piece-work by the measured day.

The acquisition of Singer in 1956 was intended to improve the Rootes Group's spares and service side rather than to increase its manufacturing capacity and, when the Macmillan government initiated a plan for the expansion of motor-car production in 1959, the Group agreed to take over a factory at Linwood in western Scotland. This involved them in many early difficulties and did not lead to an improvement in their position against their European rivals. Their prospects were further clouded by a prolonged strike at their Acton subsidiary, British Light Steel Pressings, so that in 1961/2 the Group made a loss of £1½ million. It became clear over the next few years that it could retrieve its fortunes only by a fresh injection of capital and the most probable source of this was the United States.

American investment in the British motor industry was, of course, not new. As early as 1919 the Ford plant at Trafford Park, Manchester, was the largest single producer of motor vehicles in the British Isles. A second American company, General Motors, had acquired a stake in Britain by the purchase of Vauxhall Motors of Luton in the depths of the Depression. In the post-war period both these giants had increased their investment in Britain, as well as expanding their subsidiaries in other European countries. A third great American car company, Chrysler, was now following in the wake of the other two. In June 1964, six months before the death of the first Lord Rootes, Chrysler acquired 30 per cent of Rootes ordinary voting shares, plus 50 per cent of the non-voting shares. This represented an investment of over £12 million.

However, trading losses continued even after this first injection of American capital. In the twelve months to July 1966 Rootes lost £3 million, and in the following six months a further £4¾ million. In January 1967 the Government at last reconciled itself to the impossibility of retaining the Group under British control and the Treasury gave the necessary sanctions for Chrysler to acquire a controlling interest. The workers employed in the Group's factories were naturally very concerned with the effect the new owners' plans for reorganisation would have on their livelihood. These plans proved bold enough. The Thrupp and Maberley plant at Cricklewood was closed down, and bodybuilding moved to Coventry, where no less than £20 million was to be spent on a completely new layout. Two assembly tracks would be replaced by one with a productive capacity of thirty-seven cars an hour. The Ryton factory would be one of the most up-to-date assembly plants in Europe, fed by engines from the Humber factory at Stoke. Although schemes of reorganisation were also announced for Dunstable in Bedfordshire and for Linwood, it did not seem that Coventry was going to be downgraded in importance as far as the Chrysler Corporation was concerned.

The new executives wanted to look afresh at the functions of management as they inherited them. They were accustomed to the practices of the United States and looked askance at the hold which the big gang system had acquired at the Ryton factory. There, a succession of able and intelligent shop-stewards, working together with remarkable unity and paying little attention to inter-union differences, negotiated keenly with management over piecework prices, decided the speed of the track and settled many matters of labour loading as they emerged. They always maintained that management got value for money in return, and that no other system of work could be quite so productive nor so cheap in management overheads. The new owners for their part felt that their proper functions were being usurped and that the factory floor had been converted into something like a self-governing republic.

Between early 1967 and March 1969 the men at Ryton, supported by their colleagues at Stoke, fought a long battle to retain the big gang system as they had known it. The dispute was not primarily about money. The company made three cash offers, each better than the other, and the Ryton men finally emerged with a settlement which left them among the highest paid workers in the car industry. The leaders on both sides respected each other, but had principles upon which they felt they could not yield. The management felt that piecework was wasteful and wanted to replace it by the system of time payment known as the measured day. The men were firm in declaring that man assignment, track speeds and labour loading had to be decided by mutual negotiation between management and shop-stewards rather than by management alone. The final decision appears to have gone in favour of the management, but the tradition of the gang system in Coventry dies hard.[11]

VI

The same forces which had already caused the Rootes Group to seek new strength across the Atlantic were beginning to have their effect upon the rest of the British motor-car industry. Home sales could be expanded and prices maintained at a reasonable level only by progressively greater investment in new machinery, and this was

[11] The adoption of the measured day is, nevertheless, steadily continuing throughout the British car industry.

making it progressively more difficult for the smaller non-specialist manufacturer to remain independent. The large European concerns, such as Fiat, Volkswagen and Renault, were becoming increasingly important competitors in various export markets upon which the British had previously relied. British manufacturers knew only too well by the end of the fifties that competition from the Continent was much more intensive, that West European car manufacturers were beginning to draw advantages from the Treaty of Rome and that they themselves would have to improve their performance in sales and service if they were to hold their position. Above all, they would have to combine, and the end of Standard as an independent producer has already been noticed. The same movement towards amalgamation did not spare one of the most interesting firms in the quality car market, the Coventry-based firm of Jaguar.

In 1922 William Lyons had gone into partnership with a young friend, William Walmsley, in order to manufacture a sidecar of their own design. Walmsley, son of a Cheshire coal-merchant, was one of the many young men who, after the war, hoped to make a living by reconditioning and selling motor bicycles. Lyons, besides being a gifted designer of bodywork, appears to have been the commercial brain of the partnership from the first. In 1927 he turned his attention to the unattractive bodywork of the sturdy, reliable Austin Seven, which had then been on the market for five years. Many people, he thought, might be willing to pay more for that excellent chassis and engine if they could have them combined with a more stylish body. He, therefore, concluded an agreement with Herbert Austin whereby he took chassis into his little factory in Blackpool, built new bodies for them and sold them. That factory had begun by employing three men and a boy and was still very small, but soon the goods yard at Blackpool North Station was full of the chassis which the factory could not store, and Lyons decided that the firm would have to follow its manifest destiny and move to larger premises. These he found in the Midlands.

He came to Coventry in 1928 and took a lease on part of an old shell-filling factory in Lockhurst Lane. Here he continued the manufacture of what had now become the Austin Swallow, the first of several similar ventures. He took the chassis and engines from a number of manufacturers, fitted them with a stylish body of his own design and sold them to customers who wanted style, but did not always have the money to pay for it. By 1929 Lyons had also developed links with Fiat and Swift and was exhibiting their models with his own coachbuilt bodywork at Olympia. Far more extensive was his connection with Standard and its new managing director, John Black.

Until the outbreak of war in 1939 collaboration between the two firms was very close. The first S.S. car, which appeared in 1932, had many close links with the Standard Sixteen. The first S.S. Jaguar appeared in 1936 with a redesigned engine still capable of being built in the Standard machine shop. One thing which had worried Lyons was the question of the name his cars should bear. They had been carrying the letters S.S. and no one now can say exactly what these initials had been intended to represent. In the late thirties with the Nazis in power in Germany, they were beginning to suggest something not very pleasant. Lyons was on the lookout for a new name when someone reminded him of one of the aero-engines produced by Sir John Siddeley in the 1920s – the Jaguar. Though the letters S.S. did not disappear until 1945, Jaguar cars they were from then on. Sidecars were by now forgotten. His partner retired from the company in 1935 and Lyons was on his own.

After the war when all car manufacturers were at last able to resume their peacetime business, Sir John Black took yet another decision which was to influence the future of Jaguar. He had his own plans for volume production and thought that his pre-war commitment to the production of the Jaguar engine would only stand in his way. He therefore offered to sell Lyons the plant used in manufacturing the engine, quoting such a reasonable price that the offer was immediately accepted. Lyons sent transport and a cheque to get hold of the machines straightaway and politely turned a deaf ear when Black some months later changed his mind and wanted them back. The two firms were also in some danger of competing for the assets of the Triumph Motor Company which Black eventually bought because it would give him an improved trade name. Even then Black seems to have wanted to renew his old connection with Jaguar, but Lyons was now determined to become a completely independent car manufacturer.

The XK 120, which appeared with such effect in the London

Motor Show in 1948, was the first car wholly designed and manufactured by Jaguar. The number contained in its name was an estimate of its speed which later proved to be rather on the modest side. In 1951 the 'C' type, a competition model based on the XK 120, brought Britain the first victory for fifteen years in the Le Mans Twenty-four Hour Race, and in the eight-year period following Jaguar repeated this success five times, besides gaining many other awards. It was a remarkable achievement, the basis of the firm's reputation in the export field, and much of it was due to William M. Heynes,[12] with the team he had gathered around him to design the XK engine. In one particularly successful year the firm exported over 80 per cent of its products and its export total rarely, if ever, fell below half. The firm soon gained a foothold in both the North American and European markets. The American market is vast but all European manufacturers together take only 13 per cent of it. Jaguar has kept its footing, even though it has had to use the smaller dealers for its sales. In Switzerland at one time a Mercedes dealer was expected to sell ten Mercedes for every one Jaguar: that number has now been reduced to three to one. Production was rising so successfully as the result of the 1948 début that the company was soon in need of extra factory space, and in 1951 it took over the government-owned former Daimler shadow factory in Browns Lane.

After the war the Daimler company had failed to find a use for the million square feet of this building. At one time they had intended to use it for the manufacture of construction equipment, but this had not been proceeded with, and the company had entered a rather unhappy phase of its history. Jaguar was able to buy the freehold of this factory and during the Korean War they manufactured the Rolls-Royce Merlin tank engine in part of its space. This they did for two years, after which they were able to use the entire factory for the expansion of car production. Even the great fire of February 1957, which rendered a quarter of the factory space unusable, could not halt Jaguar's progress. On the contrary, it was the occasion of a remarkable demonstration of loyalty by workers, executives and customers alike. On the night of the fire workers, management,

[12] Heynes had taken over complete responsibility for engineering when the company was made public in 1935.

typists and cleaners drove or pushed as many cars as they could out of reach of the flames and on the following morning the office was inundated with offers of help from competitors, customers and dealers. Although for a few days 2000 were idle on the production line, 2500 others were able to continue work; it was a long way from the £40 a week wage bill of 1924.

At the beginning of the 1960s Sir William Lyons was once again searching for additional factory space and there were many reasons why he should again look to the Daimler company for this. The latter still possessed a fine name but was obviously falling behind in a race which was becoming increasingly competitive. Although there were still good engineers at Daimler the great days from Percy Martin to L. H. Pomeroy were over, and the company had been unable to use either of its two shadow factories after the end of the war. Jaguar, therefore, bought the firm in 1960, preserving the name on part of what is, in fact, the Jaguar range of cars.

By this merger Jaguar were widening their interests by going outside the field of car production. For a long time Daimler had manufactured buses and the Ferret, a useful scout car for the Army, as well as high-quality cars. Jaguar put fresh heart into the production of the Daimler bus, so that the company is now the largest single manufacturer of double-decker, rear-engined buses in Britain. The purchase of Guy Motors of Wolverhampton in 1961 gave Jaguar an interest in the heavy goods vehicle field and by acquiring Henry Meadows, whose factory was next to that of Guy, it obtained additional machine shop capacity as well as a range of marine gearboxes. The Meadows' company had great experience in this field although at one time they had thought of car production and had actually produced an interesting precursor of the Mini which they called the Frisky. Guy Motors and the bus interests of Daimler have now become successful constituents of the British Leyland Truck and Bus Division.

The acquisition of Coventry Climax in 1963 gave Jaguar an old-established firm with a fine reputation in engine manufacture. H. Pelham Lee (1877–1953), its founder and the son of a London architect, was a public school man who had wanted to be an electrical engineer. After serving in the Boer War he came to work at Daimler in Coventry because he had become convinced of the great future ahead for the internal-combustion engine. In partnership with a Dane, Rudolph Stroyer, he established his first factory in East Street in 1903; but their attempt to produce the Lee-Stroyer car was not a success. After Stroyer left, the company changed its name to Coventry Simplex and became a manufacturer of engines only. Sir Ernest Shackleton used Simplex 4 engines for his snow tractors in his 1914 Imperial Trans-Antarctic Expedition. Between the wars the company, now known as Coventry Climax, devoted itself mainly to the development of light car engines, and the list of firms to which they were supplied included many honoured names, such as Swift, Crouch, Clyno and Morgan.

For some time before the war Pelham Lee had been gradually handing over to his son, Leonard. He had never pretended to have much in common with the other Coventry manufacturers and had taken no part in social activities within the city. He could still recall the details of the family home at Putney, with a father who had been a gifted amateur painter and an aunt who had kept her own carriage with two Dalmatians to run beside it as she drove out.[13] He now decided to devote his time to his art collection and to give advice on the business only when asked. At the age of twenty-one Leonard had already felt it necessary to give up all hopes of a career as a painter. Instead he became increasingly immersed in the details of engineering.

Before the war Leonard Lee's original and creative mind had become fascinated by Harry Ferguson's plans for the tractor. Even in the 1930s Ferguson was a visionary, possessed by his own awareness of the good which large-scale tractor production could do for world agriculture. He was apt to talk in terms of 5000 engines at a time but orders on this scale never seemed to materialise. When Ferguson left David Brown and went to America the two men corresponded, and in 1943 Leonard Lee crossed the Atlantic in order to inquire into Ferguson's plans for returning to the British market once the war was over. Coventry Climax could have been the firm to manufacture the Ferguson tractor if it had been large enough. It certainly had the first offer but, as the discussions went on, Leonard Lee found himself suggesting other names whose re-

[13] When the carriage reached the old wooden Putney bridge, the dogs always swam across the river and the carriage waited for them at the other side.

sources might be more equal to what Harry Ferguson had in mind. This was not the only adventurous idea which this interesting firm has considered, but it was probably wise to leave this opportunity to Sir John Black and Standard.

During the First World War Coventry Simplex had made generators for searchlights and, during the Second, it produced an excellent fire pump which became standard Home Office and Service equipment. In the 1950s Leonard Lee and his chief engineer, Walter Hassan, found to their disquiet that the firm's early reputation as a maker of quality engines was being forgotten. They resolved to retrieve this situation by entering the field of motor-racing where they proceeded between 1958 and 1965 to build up a magnificent record of achievements. During this period Climax engines won forty Grand Prix races, twenty-four in Lotus, fourteen in Cooper and two in Brabham cars. This represented victory in over half the total number of races held, and far surpassed the fourteen successes of Ferrari, the second engine manufacturer in the list. Jack Brabham won the World Championship in a Cooper-Climax in 1959 and 1960 and Jim Clark won in 1963 and 1965 with a Lotus-Climax. It was magnificent, but it would not continue for ever. In 1965 the international formula was changed to three litres and Climax decided that their commercial work, which was already being hampered, would be seriously damaged if they developed engines to the new formula. They therefore decided to concentrate on such profitable products as their fork-lift truck. However, this fine record of achievement in racing had done much to make their alliance with Jaguar creditable to both parties.

CHAPTER FIVE

The Age of the Giants

Aviation and Coventry. Major R. F. Moore, W. A. Weaver and Frederick Lanchester. John Davenport Siddeley. Sir Frank Whittle and the jet. The Hawker Siddeley Group. The contribution of Baginton and its closure. The Lord Mayor's Conferences of 1968. The new Corporations; G.E.C., Courtaulds.

I

Coventry's contribution to aviation began as early as 1890 in Dale Street, one of those streets with a mixture of small houses and factories which have played such an important part in the city's industrial development.[1] In the factory of John Shaw, hollow fork manufacturer in the cycle trade, attempts were made for several years to bring to reality the idea of Major R. F. Moore, R.E. Ross Franklin Moore (d. 1923) was one of a small group of R.E. officers who were interested in experiments with kites, spherical balloons and aircraft towards the end of the nineteenth century. He had had a long army career in India and came home on leave in 1889, retiring from the Service altogether in 1892. It must have been during this time that he established contact with John Shaw, one of those small manufacturers which were and are the salt of the Coventry earth. Shaw appears to have begun his own accessories business after working for many years with Singer's. It must have taken some courage to tackle Moore's idea for the construction of an ornithopter, an aircraft which flies by imitating the motion of birds. The machine had

[1] Dale Street, which was near the city centre, has now disappeared and its site is occupied by the Central Swimming Baths. The Priory and Hamilton motor companies were housed in its little factories at different times and after the First World War the Triumph factory occupied most of the street.

two enormous oscillating wings, which were intended to imitate the flight of the bat,[2] and was designed to be powered by electricity which would be produced by either a generator or batteries on board, or by a generator on the ground linked to the ornithopter by a power line.

Major Moore was an Army officer, a member of the Royal Aeronautical Society and part of the established world of aviation of his day. W. A. Weaver (b. 1888) was an individualist working on his own account, paying scant attention to anyone else and having the pioneer's obsession with his own ideas. He was born in Peterborough but spent many years in and near Manchester, where he had become a friend of John Siddeley. If he had come into contact when young with someone such as the elder du Cros, the world would probably have heard a great deal more of him, since he produced ideas as a catherine wheel throws out sparks. He was known to sketch out projects on the dining-room tablecloth, and for some time he kept a drawing-board at his bedside so that he should not lose ideas that came to him in the night. He did interesting work in his early days on a steam-car and a farm tractor, and later founded the firm of Coventry Victor, which produced sturdy motor-cycles as well as high-speed diesel engines in its factory near Pool Meadow. Between 1905 and 1910 he appears to have given most of his attention to the problem of flight. Like Moore, he constructed an ornithopter and the Mark I, now lost, appears to have been produced in 1905, although whether it ever flew is uncertain. In the following year a Mark II with rigid wings is said to have risen to a height of fifty feet over the Hampton-in-Arden golf course. A third machine with a great deal of aluminium in its construction and an aluminium propeller was tested in the same place on 17 May 1910 and flew steadily for about a quarter of a mile.

During these years many doors opened which had hitherto been closed. On the theoretical level, Frederick Lanchester published his significant work on aerial flight in 1907 and 1908.[3] On the practical

[2] These wings were manufactured by Spencer and Sons in London, and presumably Shaw was asked to make the body.

[3] Lanchester's work was quickly adopted and developed in a more advanced mathematical form by the outstanding German aerodynamicist, Ludwig Prandtl. Like many other original thinkers, Lanchester had had his ideas rejected ten years earlier by the learned societies, although in defence of these

level, the flight of Blériot across the Channel in 1909 awakened many to the fact that flight in heavier-than-air machines over quite considerable distance was at last technically possible. Flight was still a sport for the young and daring, and much of the early development appears to have been in France rather than in England. Nevertheless, there were Humber entries in rallies at Cairo in February 1910 and at Allahabad in India in 1911. In 1910 Humber had established in their Coventry factory an aeronautic department for the manufacture of monoplanes and biplanes to the designs of Captain Lovelace and a Frenchman named Le Blon. The company appears to have been anxious to manufacture on a fairly considerable scale, but found that the market was, as yet, too small.

The Coventry Ordnance Works was also building aircraft at this time. After taking over the Warwick Wright concern and its factory under the arches of Battersea railway bridge, the Works built two biplanes which were flown by T. O. M. Sopwith in the Military Trials of 1912. In August 1914 came the war, and the aeroplane at last had plenty to do. As the Western Front hardened into two systems of trenches, the general staffs on both sides sought for new weapons with which to break the deadlock. One of these was the tank, another was the fighter aircraft. Until 1916 all aero-engines required by the Services could be built at the Royal Aircraft Factory (later the Royal Aircraft Establishment) at Farnborough. In that year a successful Press campaign made sure that the R.A.E. would henceforth be confined purely to research and that actual manufacture of aircraft and their engines would be handed over to engineering firms with useful production experience. Car manufacturers were obvious choices and two Coventry firms became involved in aircraft production. Daimler agreed to manufacture a 70-h.p. Renault engine and an 80-h.p. Gnome engine. An even greater responsibility was taken by John Siddeley at the Siddeley-Deasy works at Parkside. He began to manufacture the 200-h.p. B.H.P. (Beardmore-Halford-Pollinger) engine, and employed three people from Farnborough to help him in this. The first was Major F. M. Green, who was mainly responsible for redesigning the engine

societies it must be said that Lanchester, working in isolation, tended to express his ideas in unorthodox, difficult terminology and in rather rudimentary mathematical form.

which afterwards became the famous Puma. He brought with him two very able young men, S. D. Heron and J. L. Lloyd.

John Siddeley was an excellent businessman and financier who knew most of what there was to know about the production of engines through his experience as a motor-car manufacturer. He had never flown and never belonged to that select brotherhood which included Handley Page, de Havilland and A. V. Roe.[4] As soon as the war was over, Daimler decided to leave the unaccustomed field of aircraft production, but Siddeley did not. His production of the Puma had been so successful that, after the war, he was embarrassed by the problem of disposal. Pumas were sold all over Europe to the infant airlines then coming into being. He also had on the drawing-board at the end of the war a very useful fighter, the Siskin, first flown at Radford aerodrome in Coventry in 1919. The Air Ministry, faced by the task of keeping some kind of aircraft industry in being in the bleak days of peace, found it useful to get several other firms, such as Vickers, to manufacture the Siskin on sub-contract. For this reason and because of the continuing demand for spare parts Siddeley probably found that he could not leave the aviation industry even if he had wanted to.

Siddeley needed more money and for this he looked north to Tyneside, where Armstrong-Whitworth were one of two powerful armament firms. He concluded an agreement with them, transferred their aeronautical work to Coventry and established the firm of Sir W. G. Armstrong-Whitworth Aircraft in a large corrugated iron shed which still (1970) exists on the London Road. A.W.A. took

[4] Frederick Handley Page (1885–1962), Geoffrey de Havilland (1882–1965) and Alliott Verdon-Roe (1877–1958) were all practised engineers, building and flying aircraft before the First World War. Handley Page had trained as an electrical engineer, and this may have accounted for his submitting, with Major Moore, a paper to the Royal Aeronautical Society in 1909. He began his own factory at Barking in 1908, built bombers during the First World War and, in 1918, was given a contract for 255 four-engined bombers to attack Berlin. De Havilland had his own company by 1920 and built the Moths, of which the Gipsy Moth, flown by the young Francis Chichester, is probably the most famous. He was not much interested in business and never bothered to become more than technical director in his own company. A. V. Roe can claim to have been the first man to fly an all-English aircraft from English soil in 1908. He had travelled widely as a marine engineer, an apprentice in a railway workshop and a draughtsman in a motor works before starting to make aircraft. All three were knighted for their services to aviation.

over the old design department in which J. L. Lloyd had designed the Siskin and which occupied the top floor of the Charlesworth Works in Much Park Street. In 1923, Siddeley transferred all his aircraft work to an old R.A.F. airfield at Whitley, which he had acquired for £5000. A year later A.W.A. had a total work-force of 351 men and women. The times ahead were going to be difficult, but no one could have been keener in the search for business or more alive to the value of publicity than was Sir John Siddeley. This is best illustrated by his characteristically frugal help to the pioneering work of Alan, now Sir Alan, Cobham.

In 1924, when Sir Sefton Brancker, then Director of Civil Aviation at the Air Ministry, wanted to survey the projected airship route to India, the cost of the return sea passage by P. & O. was £750. Lord Thomson, then Air Minister, offered that sum and no more to the young Alan Cobham, who thought it more fitting for Sir Sefton to fly and had, therefore, approached the Government for help. Their austere patronage forced him to make the rounds of the spares manufacturers, petrol companies and aero-engine makers in order to raise the extra £750 which would make the journey by air possible. One of those he approached was Sir John Siddeley, who well understood his own interests as a manufacturer in the expansion of air transport. He gave Cobham a Puma engine. Cobham flew not merely to India, but to Rangoon and back, and later Siddeley gave him the same kind of help, always nicely calculated and controlled, on his flights around the Mediterranean, between Cairo and the Cape and back in 1925 and from London to Australia and back in the following year. On one of these flights, that around the Mediterranean, Cobham's mechanic was H. M. Woodhams, who had begun work at de Havilland's and then transferred to Siddeley's and was finally to become Managing Director of Armstrong-Whitworth Aircraft.

Sir Alan Cobham (b. 1894) was a gentleman explorer in the old tradition, costing the Government practically nothing and relying mainly upon himself. He came of a Worcestershire farming family and had transferred from the Veterinary to the Flying Corps during the war. Later he had flown in the de Havilland Air Taxi Service and had then set out to explore the air as Burton, Speake and Livingstone had opened up central Africa. Along the paths which he travelled were later to come the great airliners, although they were to come all too slowly for manufacturers such as Siddeley who had factories to keep going and men to employ. It was not until 1926 that the Whitley factory was able to produce the first Argosy, which went into service with Imperial Airways Silver Wings on the London to Paris route.

The twenties were, nevertheless, years of expansion for the Siddeley interests. In 1926 he managed to rid himself of the connection with Armstrong-Whitworth and two years later brought off one of those shrewd and carefully calculated bargains for which he was famous. He purchased the Crossley Motor Company for £30,000 in collaboration with Charles Sweeney, and acquired with it the aeronautics firm of A. V. Roe. Roe himself, a former Lancashire and Yorkshire Railway apprentice, was one of those fertile, inventive brains which really ought never to be in business on their own. His talents extended far beyond the field of aeronautics and at the time of the takeover he was experimenting with a washing-up machine, building a scooter remarkably like the Lambretta, and developing many other ideas which were far ahead of his time. It was with this purchase that Siddeley acquired the services of Roy, later Sir Roy, Dobson and the experimental factory at Hamble in Hampshire to which he was able to move his air training school from Whitley.[5] This was the herald of further expansion in the thirties, when High Duty Alloys at Slough was purchased.

It was characteristic of Siddeley that he should never reveal to anyone his intention of retiring. By the mid-thirties, his business interests had grown considerably. He had also been in contact with Sir Thomas Sopwith, who had been flying before the First World War and had named his own company after his friend and test-pilot, Hawker. Sopwith himself had been extending his interests and in 1935 the two men met. Out of their discussions came the Hawker Siddeley Group. Siddeley himself suddenly retired after disposing

[5] Siddeley had shown an early understanding of the importance which attached to the training of pilots as a reserve for a possible expansion of the R.A.F. His school for reserve pilots at Whitley was one of four which existed in the 1920s and in 1931 it was transferred to the former A. V. Roe works at Hamble under the title of Air Service Training. In 1960 the Hamble School became a College of Air Training for B.E.A. and B.O.A.C. pilots. An early chairman of Air Training was Air Vice-Marshal Sir John Higgins, who had retired from the R.A.F. in 1930 for this purpose.

of all his interests in the Group. He said good-bye to no one, and few people realised it when he left his office for the last time.

II

If Siddeley's touch as a financial organiser had never been better or sharper than it was in the ten years or so before his retirement, the same cannot always be said for his judgement in matters of aeronautical engineering. Between 1922 and 1926 Armstrong Siddeley was, without question, the dominant British manufacturer of air-cooled engines. By 1926, however, the development of the Bristol Jupiter began to show that the company was being overtaken. The Jupiter had a normal output of 450 h.p., the Jaguar, designed by F. M. Green and S. M. Viale, only 385. Siddeley had excellent men around him, but he was too ready to prefer his own ideas and F. R. Smith, his chief engineer, was too conservative to oppose him. In the thirties there were more signs that the growing technical revolution in the air was outdistancing him. In particular, the Air Ministry and others were beginning to prefer Rolls-Royce aero-engines to his. In 1932 the Atalanta, which was supplied to Imperial Airways for their African route, had to have its Siddeley engines replaced before it could operate successfully. In 1934 the Scimitar failed to become the new R.A.F. fighter, because the Air Ministry preferred the Gloster Gauntlet with its Rolls-Royce engines. The Whitley bomber, one of the most successful of Armstrong-Whitworth's achievements, had to have its Tiger engines replaced by Rolls-Royce Merlins before it could operate with complete success.

As the technical revolution progressed Siddeley saw that aircraft would soon be unable to fly from Whitley, and he arranged for the building of a much larger factory at Baginton with a convenient municipal airfield near by.[6] There were other things which he found less easy to appreciate and much of the strength and many of the weaknesses in Siddeley's methods were inherited by the men he had trained, men who remained at Baginton until the factory closed in 1965. These weaknesses and strengths were often two sides of the same coin. His frugality in management led to an increasingly

[6] For the development of Baginton airport see Chapter Eight, page 240.

serious underestimate of the amount of money which had to be spent on research and, until the end, the outlook which was dominant at Baginton tended to be that of the good production engineer.

The technical revolution in aircraft during the thirties took many forms. The first A.W.A. Argosy in 1926 looked remarkably like one of the wartime bombers, such as that in which Brown and Alcock flew the Atlantic in 1919. It was a biplane of wood and steel, looked rather like a box kite and had engines developing 1155 h.p., a range of 522 miles and a maximum speed of 110 m.p.h. In the Mark I form it carried twenty passengers and in the Mark II version only eight more. Aircraft such as the Whitley bomber, produced in prototype in 1934, and that fine civil airliner, the Ensign, were completely different. The steel and wood had disappeared from the construction of their hulls to be replaced by aluminium alloys. They were monoplanes, and the Ensign had twice the range and over twice the speed of the Argosy. Even more dazzling achievements were foreshadowed, for a few men in each advanced country were beginning to see that the piston engine with propeller was not far from reaching the limit of its speed. It had helped forward a great increase in airspeed; it would soon make it impossible to increase that speed any further. In 1937 the R.A.F. allowed Frank, now Sir Frank, Whittle to start work in his special unit on the development of a gas-turbine engine.

III

On 15 May 1941 came the first flight of a British, jet-propelled aircraft, the Gloster-Whittle E 28/39, powered by a turbojet engine designed by Flight Lieutenant Frank Whittle and manufactured by the B.T.-H. Company at Rugby.[7] The Germans too were successfully developing the turbojet aircraft and in 1939, four days before the invasion of Poland, a Heinkel aircraft powered by the Ohain turbojet engine achieved a ten-minute flight, but apparently did not

[7] In jet-propulsion the aircraft is propelled by a high-speed jet of gas issuing rearwards from a propelling nozzle, and in a turbojet this gas is supplied by a gas-turbine engine. In a turboprop engine the gas turbine drives a propeller, (airscrew). Rockets, ramjets and pulse-jets (e.g. the German V1) are other forms of jet-propulsion which were developed at about the same time.

fly again. Later other German turbojets were developed and, like the Whittle engine, were in production and operation by the end of the war. The Whittle engine was superior in both reliability and performance.

The significance of the British achievement was quickly realised in the U.S.A. where, as late as 1940, an influential committee had advised against the development of the aircraft gas-turbine engine. General H. H. Arnold, Commandant General of the U.S. Air Force, who had initiated work on rocket-assisted take-offs in 1938, now asked that drawings, a Whittle engine and a team of advisers be flown across the Atlantic. A year later came the first flight of a Bell aircraft powered by the General Electric Company's version of the Whittle engine, but there, as elsewhere, quantity production was not achieved until 1944, when the main issue of the war had been decided.

At the time of that first flight Frank Whittle was thirty-four. He had been born in Coventry at 72 Newcombe Road, in one of the sober, well-built, red-brick houses which had filled in the gap between Earlsdon and Chapelfields in the early years of the twentieth century. His father, of whom the son always spoke with affectionate respect, was a man of considerable mechanical talents, and might himself have gone far had he been given the opportunity. At the age of nine Frank Whittle moved to Leamington, where his father opened his own general engineering business. There he developed his natural gifts by helping in the workshop. He became a scholarship boy at Leamington College and later tried to join the R.A.F. At his first attempt he was turned down because he was undersized and underweight according to Service Regulations. It was only at the third attempt that he was accepted, sent to Cranwell and, at the end of his training, passed out as the Second Cadet of his year.

The R.A.F. appears to have quickly realised that it had an exceptionally gifted young man on its hands and in 1931 it sent him to Felixstowe, where he could work among seaplanes and had a chance to develop his project of a new form of propulsion. In 1934 it sent him to Cambridge University where he was a fellow undergraduate of Arnold, now Sir Arnold, Hall, and where he was encouraged by Professor Sir Bennett Melvill Jones. Whittle not only obtained a first-class degree in mechanical sciences in the short time of two years, he was also fulfilling some R.A.F. duties and was perfecting the design of his turbojet engine at the same time.

It was at this time, shortly before his University examination in 1936, that he achieved some recognition for his ideas. In 1930, as a twenty-two-year-old pilot officer, he had privately patented his engine design, but for years had been unable to interest either the Air Ministry or industry. But now his two friends, R. D. Williams, now Sir Rolf Dudley-Williams, and J. B. Tinling, who had been invalided out of the R.A.F., managed to form the company of Power Jets Limited, with modest financial backing from the London investment bankers, O. T. Falk and Partners, whose representatives, Sir Maurice Bonham Carter and Lancelot L. White, became directors of the new company, together with Williams and Tinling. By special permission of the Air Ministry Frank Whittle became Honorary Chief Engineer and Technical Consultant to the company, and was given a postgraduate year at Cambridge, during which his first experimental engine was made by the B.T.-H. Company at Rugby and tested on 12 April 1937.

With this success Whittle was posted to special duties with Power Jets, and progress was rapid, though not without its difficulties. Finances were precarious and Whittle's health was deteriorating through continuous overwork. At the request of B.T.-H., the work was transferred from Rugby to part of a small disused foundry, the Ladywood Works, at Lutterworth, and Whittle set up his office at Brownsover Hall, near Rugby. The Air Ministry placed contracts for the Gloster-Whittle E 28/39 experimental aircraft in 1939 and for quantity production of the Gloster Meteor in 1940. Power Jets was not equipped for such work and soon many Midland firms were drawn into the development and production of the engines, including B.T.-H., the Rover Company, Joseph Lucas and Rolls-Royce. Activities were co-ordinated by the Gas Turbine Collaboration Committee set up in 1941 under Dr H. Roxbee Cox, now Lord Kings Norton. The Government now made a massive contribution to the development of Power Jets by building a large new factory at Whetstone, six miles south of Leicester. But there were anomalies in the situation, for the Government was now supporting two separate gas-turbine teams, the second being at the Royal Aircraft Establishment under, first, Dr A. A. Griffith and, later, Hayne

Constant. Unlike Whittle, who was using the centrifugal compressor, they were slowly developing the more complicated, but potentially more rewarding, axial-flow compressor which is now used in all the larger engines. Since 1938 engines based on their designs had been developed by the Metropolitan Vickers Electrical Company, under Dr D. M. Smith.[8]

Clearly there was much duplication of staff and facilities and in 1944 Power Jets and the Gas Turbine Section of the R.A.E. were merged to become Power Jets (Research and Development) Limited with Dr Roxbee Cox heading its board of high-ranking industrial and government representatives. Within two years this new company was transformed into the National Gas Turbine Establishment and quickly grew into one of the world's leading research centres. (The Whetstone factory was vacated in the 1950s.) Several factors had contributed to this transformation. Sir Stafford Cripps, then Minister of Aircraft Production in Churchill's wartime government, favoured the creation of a national research establishment, as did the R.A.E. staff, and Whittle himself had proposed the complete nationalisation of the aircraft gas-turbine industry. But probably the most powerful factor was the opposition of the established firms to the idea of a government-subsidised company competing with them in the manufacture of engines. The prospect of never again being allowed to build a complete engine was quite alien to Frank Whittle's concepts and, together with some of his gifted team, he resigned. Paradoxically, only a few of them moved to the aircraft engine companies.

Air Commodore Whittle declined to claim anything for his inventions on the grounds that he owed his career to the R.A.F. and indeed, the R.A.F. emerges as the one authority which had consistently encouraged him in the days when he was struggling for

[8] Armstrong Siddeley also appear to have displayed some early interest in the gas turbine, having employed two men, Paravacini and Heppner, on engine research before the war. This does not seem to have led to any practical conclusion. They remained manufacturers of jets as long as the firm itself continued in existence, and the work was retained when, in 1959, it became a constituent part of Bristol Siddeley. Its most successful achievement was the Sapphire, which has claims to be considered one of the most widely used gas-turbine engines in the world. Its success in this country was far surpassed by that in the United States where 20,000 were manufactured on licence by Curtiss Wright.

recognition. The established firms had offered him little encouragement, though they were willing later to take advantage of his pioneer work. In 1948 he received a knighthood and was awarded £100,000 by the Royal Commission on Awards to Inventors, and since then very many other honours have been bestowed upon him, including an Award of Merit by the City of Coventry in 1966 and the Honorary Degree of Doctor of Science by the University of Warwick in 1967. Retirement from practical engineering did not come easily to Sir Frank, and after a period as adviser to the Government and B.O.A.C., he turned his inventive mind to the problem of developing powerful turbo-drills in conjunction with Bristol Siddeley Engines and other firms.

IV

Coventry's contribution to the post-war aero industry includes that of the Dunlop Aviation Division, established in the city in 1945. The Dunlop Company's interest in the air goes back to 1910, when it produced its first catalogue of aircraft tyres and rims. Since the First World War it had maintained a leadership in the manufacture of braking and de-icing systems. In the post-1945 period it has developed disc brakes, electrical de-icing and anti-skid units, and its products have been incorporated in both the Concorde and the Harrier. Although this work continues, it is natural that a greater interest should be aroused by the less fortunate history of the two A.W.A. factories at Whitley and Baginton.

After the war the original home of A.W.A. at Whitley had been virtually abandoned, but H. M. Woodhams was sufficiently far-sighted to resist all pressure to sell it. He had his reward in 1949 when he was able to reoccupy it with a team brought together for missile development. This early work on the Seaslug, a ship-to-air missile, led to the opening of an Australian Division at Woomera in 1953. Two years later came a grant of £1 million from the Government for a more ambitious programme of development, and it was the increasing importance of this work which led to the transfer of Whitley to the newly created Hawker Siddeley Dynamics in 1960. This was not the only thing being done at Whitley. An interest in space flight had existed there before the launching of the first Russian Sputnik in 1957, and a small research team appears to have given some thought to the problems of satellite design and re-entry. All this was very expensive and was entirely dependent upon government patronage. It was therefore a serious matter for Whitley when the expected large-scale government interest in space did not materialise, and even more serious when missile expenditure was finally reduced. It was lack of government support which ultimately led to the closing of Whitley in the summer of 1968.

Perhaps Whitley's greatest success lay in a project which was closely linked with its missile programme. During the war A.W.A. had accumulated a research fund of £100,000 and it was decided after the war that this should be spent on the construction of a supersonic wind tunnel. The actual work of construction took about three years and, during that time, costs rose so that the projected total was, in fact, exceeded. Nevertheless, the wind tunnel, once it began work, proved to be an excellent investment. The team of six or eight people, working under Dr William Hilton, decided that the tunnel should be linked with a Ferranti Pegasus computer, in order to enable the readings to be delivered as rapidly as possible, a point of great importance since it has been known for readings from computerised wind tunnels to be available only after six months. The computer used at Whitley was the largest and best available at that time, and enabled Whitley to offer facilities to all aviation manufacturers. In that tunnel, for a number of years, tests were carried out on missiles and aircraft for almost the whole industry, and the results were available with a speed and accuracy which has probably never been surpassed.

V

After the war Baginton remained a factory with one of the highest reputations in the country for production knowhow. Its designers were still to produce some complete aircraft and to have one important research initiative to their credit, the A.W. 52 Flying Wing, which first flew in 1947. The highest decisions in planning and policy were, nevertheless, being taken elsewhere, although H. M. Woodhams was undoubtedly one of the most respected men in the industry. A further source of difficulty lay in the fact that the near-by

Baginton Airport lacked concrete runways, which the City Council were not permitted to provide. Hawker Siddeley, therefore, had to spend a great deal of money buying Bitteswell, with its airfield and concrete runway, for the flight testing of aircraft which Baginton could not take. More important than these local difficulties in determining the fate of Baginton, however, were the national problems which faced the aero industry in the post-war period.

For many reasons, it was generally accepted that the country would require a very much bigger aircraft industry after the Second World War than it had after the First. The nation's armed forces would remain much larger, and the R.A.F. would have a much more important role within them. The flow of Service orders would certainly be considerable, as would government money for research and development. It was equally necessary for the Government to take steps to provide the industry with other customers by securing the development of civil aircraft. It was for this purpose that the Brabazon Committee was established. This committee, like the great aircraft which it favoured, was perhaps a little ahead of opinion at the time. Besides the Brabazon itself, the seating capacity of which (272) would cause little surprise nowadays, it recommended that help should be given to the development of two other aircraft. At one time it seemed probable that these two aircraft would be the Vickers Viscount and the A.W.A. Apollo, designed and built at Baginton.

The Apollo was to prove one of the two great disappointments of Baginton in the post-war period. Its maiden flight was a year later than that of the Viscount, and its normal cruising speed proved to be almost 50 m.p.h. slower. The Viscount had Rolls-Royce Dart Engines, the Apollo did not; it carried about fifty passengers and the Apollo only thirty-one. When the Government super-priority scheme for civil aircraft was launched in 1952, the Apollo had no place in it and resources were given to the Viscount, the Bristol Britannia and the de Havilland Comet (the first British pure jet airliner in service). During the 1950s Baginton was occupied on the manufacture of service aircraft which it had not designed, such as the Meteor, Seahawk, Hunter and Javelin. From 1957 onwards an increasing proportion of its time appears to have been taken up by repairs and modifications.

A good managing director such as Woodhams could see the writing on the wall. Baginton would have to find a successful aircraft of its own or it would be closed down, and 10,000 people would lose their jobs. He therefore took a bold decision; the passenger field was virtually closed to him, but he foresaw great possibilities for the transport of freight by air. He obtained an allocation of money from the Hawker Siddeley Group and proceeded to plan and build civil and military versions of a new plane to be called the Argosy without any orders having been received. The civilian version of the Argosy first flew in January 1959 at a time when jet-powered aircraft, produced mainly by the American industry, were sweeping all before them. British manufacturers were discovering that their delay in adopting the jet had cost them their technical superiority over their American rivals. They began hastily to convert their unsold turbo-prop machines for freight, since their sale as passenger aircraft was no longer possible. As a new plane, the Argosy was rather expensive and it had two doors front and rear. These hasty conversions had one cut in the side and sold more cheaply. A dozen or so Argosys were sold, but there were no more, and a promising initiative was brought to an early halt.

Then, in the sixties, came a period of almost continuous crisis which was dramatically to affect the aircraft industry in Coventry. In 1960 most British aircraft firms were amalgamated under government influence into two large groups, the British Aircraft Corporation and Hawker Siddeley. Bristol Siddeley Engines was formed as an amalgamation of the engine interests of those two great companies, in order to compete with the increasingly important firm of Rolls-Royce. Then, at the end of 1964, came a change of government and of policy. Two service projects, the H.S. 681 and the Hawker P1164, both at an advanced stage of development, were cancelled in February 1965. This was followed two months later by the cancellation of the T.S.R.2. The industry had now to face problems of reorganisation which had been calling for attention for some years but which had been masked by the succession of orders from the Government. In August 1966 Bristol Siddeley amalgamated with Rolls-Royce, thus producing one major British maker of aero-engines. In Coventry, Bristol Siddeley had two factories, one out of town at Ansty Aerodrome and the other in Parkside, near the city centre. Parkside, a monument to the success of extensions to John Siddeley's original factory, has received little in the way of new buildings since the 1920s, but still continues in full production. At the time of the merger it was transferred to Rolls-Royce's Bristol Engines Division while Ansty became part of its Industrial and Marine Gas Turbine Division. More was to follow. One of the aircraft cancelled by the Government, the H.S. 681, had been allocated for production at Baginton. The Group, therefore, pursued its normal policy of closing factories from which work had been withdrawn, and, at the end of July 1965, the Baginton factory finally closed its doors as a production unit.

VI

The closing of Baginton on 31 July 1965 was only one of a number of similar happenings which caused concern over Coventry's employment prospects during the next few years. The former A.E.I. factory in Ford Street was closed when the company was absorbed into the new G.E.C. being created by Arnold Weinstock. At the end of 1967 Smith's Stamping Works at Stoke ceased production and Albion Drop Forgings closed down a year later. In July 1968 the Hawker Siddeley Dynamics factory at Whitley was closed and many of its skilled and graduate workers transferred out of the city. There seemed to be good reason for leaders of opinion in Coventry to become seriously worried about the city's future. In October 1968 it was reported that the aircraft industry in the city had lost 11,000 jobs in the five-year period from the middle of 1962. It was true that during the same period the motor industry had created 4400 new ones and that, in March 1968, Coventry's percentage of unemployed males was no greater than the national average.[9] There were, nevertheless, good reasons for disquiet. The aircraft industry, which ought to have had abundant prospects for growth to offer the city, was obviously leaving it and Coventry's dependence on motor vehicle manufacture would inevitably be increased.

[9] 3·3 per cent. Two months earlier the percentage of unemployed persons in Coventry had been double the national average (7 per cent as against 3·5 per cent). Included in the Coventry figure were 5210 males classified as temporarily suspended.

It was for this reason that five Lord Mayor's Conferences on Industry were held in the period between 6 March and 11 October 1968. At these meetings political leaders and chief officers from the City Council met with Members of Parliament, representatives of industry and trade-union leaders. They appear to have achieved little in concrete terms, but the conferences were undoubtedly a useful exercise in clarification for those who attended.

At the time when the conferences were held, three currents appeared to be washing at the foundations of the city's economic life. The first was the Government's policy towards the aircraft industry and the second its additional measures of aid to development areas, such as the Regional Employment Premium introduced at the end of 1967. Third came the increasing pace of national reorganisation in British industry which was drastically changing the old industrial landscape. Of these, the second, which was not unconnected with the first, was to prove the most intractable problem.

Between the two wars, Coventry, with its cars, aircraft and other new industries, had enjoyed a relative prosperity which the Greater London area alone had rivalled. Very different was the position in such classic areas as the north-east coast and South Wales, Lanarkshire and Lancashire. The prosperity of their exporting industries was destroyed by the loss of overseas markets and people were compelled to move elsewhere if they wished to avoid the risk of almost permanent unemployment. This disparity had long disturbed the nation's conscience and had come to be regarded as the inevitable result of unchecked individual enterprise. It was felt that the location of industry after the war should be planned with regard to the national interest. The Barlow Report of 1940 had spotlighted the problem and the Distribution of Industry Acts of 1945 and 1952 had placed in the hands of the Board of Trade wide powers to control industrial location by offering grants to tempt prospective employers to the Development Area. The Local Employment Act of 1960 had systematised the powers the Board already possessed for the licensing of the building of new, or extensions to old, factories. It gave to these licences the name of Industrial Development Certificates.

It was natural that I.D.C.s should be discussed at the Lord

Mayor's Conferences and that some speakers should feel that the national policy of deflecting industry away from Coventry was not in the economic interest of the city. The Board of Trade had certainly refused to give any guarantee that industries planned out of the centre of Coventry would necessarily be relocated within the city boundaries. On the other hand, most of them remained near by, at Exhall and Kenilworth, and usually continued to employ the same workers. The Board of Trade stated that no I.D.C.s applied for by firms anxious to establish themselves in Coventry had ever been refused.[10] This was of course true, but they certainly do not seem to have been encouraged. The Board's officers were well aware of their responsibilities to other parts of the country. There were those at the conferences who argued that the I.D.C. should be abolished and that the matter should be left in the hands of the local planning authority, which, of course, would have removed it entirely from the sphere of national policy. This was refused by Peter Shore, Minister of Economic Affairs, when he spoke in the city on 25 October 1968.[11]

The conferences did, however, reveal two related problems which are still very much with Coventry; its ageing factory buildings and the low level of employment offered to office workers. Some Coventry factories date back to the days of the cycle trade and in their very structure make the planning of modern production more than usually difficult. Even the shadow factories, built for the Second World War and once the pride of the city, are now over thirty years old. The increasing age of the city's stock of factory buildings was rightly seen at the conferences as a serious long-term problem which would be bound to make it progressively more difficult to attract new industries with a heavy scientific content. It was also felt that attempts should be made to increase the city's proportion of office workers and executives in order to decrease its dependence on manufacturing. The electrified railway line now gave rapid

10 The Rootes Group, one of the largest employers already in the city, had applied for and had been granted a very substantial I.D.C. This was later withdrawn when the Group's needs were satisfied when they took over the former Hawker Siddeley factory at Whitley.

11 According to some, new industries were being kept out of the city by its reputation for high wages and bad industrial relations. On the other hand, the premises left vacant by Smith's Stamping Works, Albion Drop Forgings and Hawker Siddeley were easily let as trading estates.

communication with London and it was not unreasonable to feel that head offices might well come to Coventry in order to avoid the difficulties presented by an overcrowded metropolis.

Of all the problems which Coventry was facing, that presented by the national reorganisation of industry into great corporations has so far proved the least substantial. There was a curious symbolism about the memorial service to Sir John Black, held in Coventry Cathedral on 18 January 1966. Black had died on the previous Christmas Eve after living for twelve years in North Wales, seeing few people and never revisiting Coventry. The organisers of his memorial service were as surprised as everyone when about seven hundred people, mainly from the shop-floor at Standard, attended to pay a last tribute to an able but puzzling man. Black had never taken part in the public life of Coventry and had shown scant sympathy for those who did. He had, nevertheless, been one of that band of great individualists which began with Sir Alfred Herbert and Sir John Siddeley, and which was now beginning to disappear. The age of the buccaneer was over; the great corporation, administered by self-effacing executives, who regarded themselves as the servants of their shareholders, was now arriving.

When the young Alfred Herbert first assumed the responsibilities of marriage and ownership of a business he lived in a modest, stucco-fronted villa near the railway goods yard and not far from his works. Shortly afterwards, he moved across the track to the newly built Spencer Road, conveniently near a pleasant park, and on an estate especially planned for the new businessmen of a booming city. Later he went to Kenilworth, then to Barford and still farther afield, but he always retained a flat at his factory and occupied it for a part of every week. John Siddeley lived at Meriden before moving to Crackley Hall, Kenilworth, now St Joseph's Convent. His son, Cyril, later the second Lord Kenilworth, lived for some time at Boston Lodge in Earlsdon, just around the corner from Harry Harley, founder of Coventry Gauge and Tool. As time went on, they had all tended to live near the city rather than actually in it, but they were part of its life, at their offices most days, taking decisions and often influencing the city's life in other ways as well. Siddeley and Harry Harley both served terms on the City Council and, although Sir Alfred Herbert was never actually a councillor, he was intimately concerned in the city's development. They were all around for a long time and even Lord Nuffield and Lord Rootes, who really did not visit Coventry very often, became, nevertheless, part of the city's folklore.

Their disappearance has undoubtedly caused a change, but we must be very careful in defining exactly what this change has been. The new executives who replaced the individualists are professional managers, much better trained than their predecessors, and certainly not less able. There are two obvious reasons for their failure to make an equal impact. They are usually not here long enough, and they have inherited a tradition of self-effacement which the first Lord Rootes, to take an obvious example, would have found incomprehensible. As far as the power of taking decisions is concerned, one has to avoid the obvious pitfalls of exaggerating the real independence of the individual and the size of the decisions which they had to take. In practice, they usually relied a great deal on their London merchant bankers, who must often have brought to their affairs a caution and realism which would otherwise have been lacking. We must also never forget that the decisions which are taken today by British Leyland or Massey-Ferguson are infinitely greater than any which ever faced Sir John Black.

It is likewise easy to ignore the fact that the process of industrial reorganisation over the last ten years has actually increased the importance of Coventry rather than diminished it. The disappearance of the Hawker Siddeley Group is the one major exception to this rule. The great machine tool firm of Herbert's has expanded its interests outside the city by buying the machine tool firms formerly owned by B.S.A. and has been reorganised in consequence into a number of operating divisions co-ordinated by a holding company. That holding company and most of the operating divisions have their headquarters in Coventry. Massey-Ferguson, although controlled immediately from London and ultimately from Toronto, has made Coventry the centre of its tractor production, and the place from which its world export trade is organised. Additional plant for the motor industry has been opened during the 1960s in various parts of the country, but both British Leyland and Chrysler still regard Coventry as a substantial centre of quality production. When the dust settled after Arnold Weinstock's creation of the new

G.E.C., Coventry remained as the headquarters of the most important telecommunications division, with employment prospects substantially better than they had been for some time.

VII

In 1916 a subsidiary of the General Electric Company, Conner Magneto Ignition, opened a works for the production of magnetos near the city in the grounds of Copsewood Grange. In 1920 they began building a larger factory on the same site for the production of telephone equipment, and this started manufacture as the Peel-Conner Telephone Works in 1921. This beginning led to a lasting slant towards telecommunications in the city's contribution within G.E.C. It was a favoured industry coming to a favoured city, with the likelihood that the production of signals equipment for the war would be followed by steady orders from the Government for telephone equipment in the peace. Nor was this to be all. Wireless telegraphy had been known before the First World War and the development of sound radio would be one of the greatest advances in technology during the period which followed it.

The firm could trace its origins to the small business created in London during the 1880s by Hugo, later Lord, Hirst (1861–1942) and Gustav Byng. In 1887 they published the world's first electrical catalogue, which included telephone equipment. Hirst founded no family dynasty and, after his death, one of the most important men in the company was Sir William Noble (1861–1943), Managing Director of the Coventry Works. Sir William had entered the Post Office as a telegraphist at the age of sixteen and retired as its chief engineer in 1922. He was Chairman of the first Broadcasting Committee which led to the foundation of the British Broadcasting Company of which he was later a Director.

G.E.C. added to its telephone exchange production that of transmission equipment for trunk circuits and crystal, later valved, radio-sets, with such success that between 1921 and 1938 the Copsewood factory more than doubled its area. In addition it had taken over the Ford Street factory of Lea Francis and the Queen Victoria Road factory of A. C. Wickman's, while in 1939 production of radio-sets and the planned production of television receivers was transferred to a factory in Spon Street which had been taken over from Rudge-Whitworth.[12]

After the end of the Second World War the company continued to expand. It was taken for granted that the sale of radio-sets would diminish over a period, but great things were expected from the new demand for television, since the B.B.C. announced that it would resume transmission from November 1946. However, it was not going to be quite such plain sailing. At intervals of about four years after 1949 successive governments have been obliged to move into the economy to check an increase in consumption and reduce government expenditure in order to rectify our international balance of payments. In the field of public expenditure the reduction or holding back of the Post Office's programme of capital investment in new telephones was a first and obvious target. In the field of domestic consumption hire-purchase restrictions upon consumer durables, such as refrigerators and television-sets, became as customary as increases in the hire-purchase charges for cars. By 1960 the great electrical companies were beginning to find their trading position unsatisfactory and their minds were turning towards merger. This was true of G.E.C., with important interests in Coventry, as it was of A.E.I. at Rugby and English Electric, with its great factory at Stafford. In 1961, therefore, G.E.C. acted by taking over Radio and Allied Industries and bringing on to their own board that firm's brilliant young accountant, Arnold, now Sir Arnold, Weinstock.

Then began two years of fundamental change which was to leave no aspect of the G.E.C. organisation untouched. The production of radio- and television-sets was transferred from Coventry to the South Wales factories of Radio and Allied and the Spon Street factory had turned to electronics, particularly the manufacture of computers, mobile radio-telephone equipment and defence projects before being absorbed into the telecommunications group in 1969. The productive capacity of G.E.C. was now divided between five and later six separate companies, each of which was made fully responsible for the production and sale of its own range of products. Into the company's new and smaller headquarters in Stanhope Gate flowed monthly reports from production chiefs who soon found

[12] For G.E.C.'s wartime activities see Chapter Three, page 72.

that, if they clearly knew what they were doing, they were left remarkably free to get on with it.

As a piece of administrative reorganisation it was an interesting rehearsal for the great mergers with A.E.I. and English Electric which came in 1967 and 1968 respectively. From these two mergers has come the General Electric and English Electric Companies, the fourth largest electrical concentration in the world, the other three being American. This has tended, if anything, to emphasise rather than diminish the importance of Coventry in the company's scheme of things. The merger with A.E.I. had the immediate effect of practically doubling G.E.C.'s telecommunications business. Under a new title, G.E.C.–A.E.I. Telecommunications, the original Telephone Works at Copsewood became the headquarters of a vast manufacturing complex employing 30,000 people in seven factories in Coventry, seven in the development regions and two others at Rugby and Wellingborough. The Copsewood headquarters has grown continually through the years and the seven Coventry factories now (1970) employ 14,595 people, making G.E.C. the largest industrial employer in the city.

These years of fundamental change in the organisation of G.E.C. have also seen technological progress which can be only briefly indicated here. A development programme to apply electronic techniques to automatic switching had its first success in 1958 when G.E.C.'s electronic register translators provided the first subscriber trunk dialling service in Britain. The first step towards full automation of trunk telephone calls was taken when the Queen opened the first S.T.D. exchange in Bristol. This now covers practically the whole country and deals with over 80 per cent of all trunk calls. More recently, G.E.C. became the first British company to develop and manufacture powerful on-line multi-processor computers for the control of telephone exchange switching equipment. It is still the only British manufacturer of this very advanced equipment, known as Stored-Programme Control (S.P.C.). Telephone exchanges, with their masses of switching equipment, form the heart of all telecommunications networks. It is not surprising, therefore, that the Telephone Switching Group is by far the largest division of G.E.C. Telecommunications.

The transmission business has grown at a phenomenal rate since the end of the war. The first microwave radio link in the United Kingdom was designed in Coventry and installed in 1949 to carry television signals from London to the regional television transmitter at Sutton Coldfield. Other routes were then added to form a nation-wide television network, which was later expanded to carry multi-channel telephony. By 1970 G.E.C. had supplied the bulk of the Post Office network of microwave links including one of the most heavily loaded routes in the world, London–Birmingham–Manchester, with fifty radio channels giving a total capacity of 27,000 telephone circuits and nine television programmes. Another achievement in this field was the first microwave link across the Swiss Alps. Installed in 1954, it connected Germany and Italy in the Eurovision television network.

In 1966 the company received the Queen's Award to Industry for the introduction of a range of completely semi-conductored systems which opened up many new overseas markets. The company has exported equipment since its earliest days but never to the extent it has since the end of the Second World War when world demands for communications accelerated, particularly in the developing countries. For instance, during the 1967/70 period 75 per cent of G.E.C.'s output of microwave systems was exported to thirty countries with a total radio channel route of 90,000 miles. These include some of the largest civil installations in the world such as the 1500-mile-long system across the southern seaboard of Australia. Opened in 1970, this system carried via its chain of fifty-eight repeater stations telephone circuits and occasional television programmes between Perth and Adelaide. In the same year installations began of a vast 2500-mile-long network of radio links which will connect all the large centres of population in Nigeria. This £10 million project is a turnkey contract in which G.E.C. is responsible for all aspects of the job including surveying, planning and all civil engineering works.

Telephone exchange switching equipment has been installed all over the world with particularly large concentrations in the Far East, New Zealand, the Middle East, Canada and South Africa. A contract received from Guyana is typical of G.E.C.'s ability to provide a complete telecommunications service. The contract is a turnkey one, shared with another G.E.C. Company, Telephone

Cables, and will provide the expansion of existing public telephone exchanges and the building of fifteen new exchanges, an international switchboard, 200 miles of radio transmission systems, expansion of the underground telephone cable network and subscribers' telephone instruments.

VIII

The tide of reorganisation and merger which swept through the electrical industry was also to affect the man-made fibres firm of Courtaulds which had been established in Coventry in 1904. In May 1957 the proposed terms of a merger were announced between Courtaulds and its greatest rival, British Celanese, a firm with main works at Spondon, near Derby. The two firms had been keen competitors for a long time but, rather to the surprise of some, these terms were accepted within a month. It was found in the subsequent rationalisation that a great deal of duplication of resources could now be eliminated. Within a year the total labour-force of the new concern was reduced by 7000 people. What did not disappear was the name of British Celanese itself, a name with a considerable lustre of its own. It was still regarded as a separate company with its own headquarters, and the Courtaulds works at Little Heath in Foleshill was transferred to the new company. This merger was by no means the only way in which Courtaulds was expanding during the 1950s. The company was also diversifying its interests by branching out into lines which sometimes had little obvious connection with man-made fibres. Their holdings in 1959 included companies manufacturing paints, cans, wax cartons, foil bottle-tops and foundation garments. Two new Courtaulds groups were formed in North America and the company took half share in a pulp mill established in Swaziland by the Colonial Development Corporation.

In 1961 and 1962 it seemed that even greater things could be expected when proposals were first put forward for a union between Courtaulds and Imperial Chemical Industries.[13] I.C.I. and Cour-

[13] The man who had founded it in 1926, Alfred Mond, first Lord Melchett, had been one of the great liberal capitalists in the Europe of his day. His ideas on productivity, a high-wage economy and industrial co-operation were remarkably similar to those which are heard of so much today. He founded no family controlling the business, since his son has chosen to look elsewhere.

taulds were bound to become steadily more aware of each other and they had established some sort of understanding as early as 1928. After the Second World War the interests of these two giant companies were tending more and more to overlap. Such a colossal merger would certainly have social implications, but there seemed to be no real reason why it could not happen. Nevertheless, it did not take place, and after negotiations were broken off the two firms drew apart, I.C.I. disposing of its 38 per cent shareholding in Courtaulds and the latter relinquishing its share in the previously jointly-owned firm of British Nylon Spinners.

Courtaulds had established the Main Works in 1904, between the Foleshill Road and the Coventry Canal on the edge of the city, not very far from the coal mines at Bedworth and Nuneaton. The firm then stood at the turning-point of its fortunes. The Courtaulds, originally French Huguenot silk throwsters, were affected by the difficulties in the silk trade towards the end of the nineteenth century when their speciality, the manufacture of crape, lost its profitability as funerals became simpler. The firm was, therefore, seeking additional lines, and had already undertaken the manufacture of *crêpe de Chine* when it became caught up in the great search for man-made fibres which was consuming so much energy and capital in the last twenty years of the nineteenth century.

That search itself was due to the great strides already made in chemistry in the 1840s and 1850s. It had then been shown in laboratories that cellulose was a common constituent of plant cells and that from it a great many diverse substances could be made. Peaceful application of this discovery had to wait until the end of the century when a number of developments appeared simultaneously and set afoot a widespread search for synthetic fibres. In Britain the incandescent gas mantle and the electric filament lamp were being developed to give light in many homes which had earlier possessed only oil lamps. Men and women, having a little more money than they had previously had, wanted to increase the amount of clothes in their wardrobes, but could still not afford dresses or shirts of natural materials. A fortune was waiting for the firm which could produce a yarn capable of satisfying these needs.

Two Englishmen who were successful in producing a viscose process for a man-made fibre were C. F. Cross and C. H. Stearn, who established the Viscose Spinning Syndicate in 1898. They disposed of the Continental rights to a mainly German company and accepted an offer from Courtaulds for the British rights in 1904.[14] In order to keep this rather speculative line rigidly separate from their existing business, Courtaulds decided to produce it at an entirely new plant. The Coventry site had many advantages; there was coal near by, communications were good, markets could be easily reached in any direction and labour was abundant. It is tempting to add something about Coventry's ribbon-weaving tradition and the great manual skill of its watchmakers, but, in fact, most of these weavers and watchmakers had been men, and the great majority of those who worked at Courtaulds in the early days were miners' daughters, most of whom came from outside the city in such numbers that a special tram station was built inside the works. Courtaulds' indebtedness to the watchmaking industry, though real, came from a different direction. The multi-hole platinum jets for extrusion of the synthetic fibres were first drilled by Rotherhams, Coventry's leading watchmakers, and John Criggal, one of that firm's most skilled craftsmen, later moved to Courtaulds to work.

The Coventry Works were the creation of Henry Greenwood Tetley (d. 1921), one of the first outside general managers to find a place inside what had been an exclusively family business. He had been brought into the manufacturing side in Essex in 1893 in order to train for responsibility and he was probably exactly the man that a difficult situation needed, arrogant, tremendously self-confident and with inexhaustible drive. At the beginning things did not go well at Coventry, and its first manager, Alexander Guthrie, a Glasgow chemist, broke down in 1906. He was replaced by Harry Johnson (1866–1938), who deserves a high place in Coventry's list of fine production managers. He was the son of a Macclesfield silk throwster and after some years of experience with Courtaulds in Essex, he was sent to Coventry to support Guthrie, who was gradually being overwhelmed by the difficulties which came upon him. After Guthrie retired Johnson took over, and achieved a break-

[14] Another of the men who engaged in the search for an artificial silk, as it was frequently called, was Joseph Cash, a member of the Coventry textile family. He established the Artificial Silk Company in a factory at Wolston, just outside the city, and was by no means the only man to fail in his attempt.

through in 1907 by producing a viscose yarn which could be sent to Essex to be successfully woven.[15] The product from the Main Works soon became by far the most valuable part of the Courtaulds business, and was used as a weft by many different fabric manufacturers. Courtaulds themselves used it with a cotton yarn to produce 'Luvisca', but they also had many important customers in the weaving industry. It was at the same time being used for trimmings on garments, in gas mantles and electric lamp filaments, and, shortly before the outbreak of war in 1914, it was being used in the first attempt to produce artificial silk stockings.

Just as the Main Works was created to produce rayon by one process, so the Little Heath Works, also in Coventry, arose to produce it by another. The 1920s saw a widening market for man-made fibres in women's stockings and underwear, but the cellulose acetate process, as developed by Courtaulds at Little Heath, was not a success. It tended to be expensive and in 1931 its production was only a tenth in value of that of the British Celanese Works at Spondon. There, a very much better article was being produced based on a greater awareness of the needs of the consumer.

A third man-made fibre process, the manufacture of nylon, was much more successful. It was first produced commercially by Du Pont in the United States in 1936, and it was I.C.I. rather than Courtaulds which first acquired the rights of manufacture in this country. Arrangements were made shortly before the war to establish a Courtaulds/I.C.I. joint subsidiary, British Nylon Spinners, to begin the spinning of nylon yarn in Lockhurst Lane, Coventry. The outbreak of war caused this development to assume a new importance. The R.A.F. became tremendously interested in the use of the new fabric for barrage balloons and parachutes and, after the war began, the importation of the necessary machinery became much easier.

There seemed at one time to be a possibility that the British Nylon Spinners' factory might be permanently established in Coventry, further increasing the textile interest in the city, but in fact the factory was directed by the Board of Trade to a development area. Courtaulds is one of the few firms where recent changes have diminished, rather than increased, the importance of Coventry in its organisation.

[15] Success finally came in 1911 when zinc sulphate was added to the bath of liquid into which the yarn was dipped in order to make it spinnable.

CHAPTER SIX

Coventry Cathedral and the Churches

The new men of the 1930s. Provost Richard Howard and his influence. William Temple and the Religion and Life Movement. The Christian Socialists of St Peter's, Hillfields. The rebuilding of the Cathedral. Bishop Neville Gorton. The life and work of the new Cathedral. The contribution of other denominations.

I

In the ten years or so before the outbreak of the Second World War, many of the Coventry churches were enjoying the last golden age in the traditional pattern of church going. The city had survived the difficulties of the early 1920s and now was prosperous by the standard of those times. Population was increasing and property values were rising, with an obvious effect on the income of independent churches which controlled their own endowments. The Churches nationally were beginning to feel that here was an industrial city with a special challenge, and ordained men of ability were coming along to take up that challenge. In the 1930s the two Anglican churches of St Michael's and Holy Trinity received new men, as did the Queen's Road Baptists and the Warwick Road Congregationalists. G. W. Clitheroe of Holy Trinity, a scholar and perhaps a mystic, but certainly no liberal in theology, is dealt with elsewhere.[1] The other three men were to become warm personal friends, at a time when friendship between Anglican and Nonconformist was not as common as it is today. A great deal was to spring from that deeply-rooted friendship.

When Ingli James (1889–1956) succeeded to a long line of Bap-

[1] See Chapter Three, page 76. He was Vicar of Holy Trinity, 1931–64.

tist men of learning[2] at Queen's Road in 1931, he was at the height of his powers. Eloquence was part of his birthright, for he was a Welshman and a son of the manse. Experience at two previous churches had made him a fine preacher and now he was to stay at Queen's Road for twelve years. His sensitive mind was deeply troubled by the problems of the times; by unemployment at home and the challenge of Soviet Communism abroad. It had a breadth that perhaps Queen's Road had lacked for some years, and the young people rose to him as to one whose sensitivity clearly matched their own, and whose rare charm inspired feelings for which perhaps loyalty is too light a word.

The congregation at Queen's Road was a large one, and for many years he made it larger still.[3] Ingli James had a great hold on the young and the aware, on the degree men and women coming into the city's industry and its schools. He taught them to think and feel, and out of his efforts came such organisations at the church as 'Pathfinders for Peace' and 'Christian Action', memories of which have not yet faded. Unfortunately, the congregation did not consist entirely of young people. The rather staid, decent old Coventry families,[4] which had been accustomed to exercise great influence in the Church, he antagonised and ultimately lost.

It was the coming of war which finally revealed that this gifted man of unquestionable sincerity had not come to bring peace to Queen's Road. Ingli James was a pacifist as well as a socialist. Unlike many others, he had not changed his mind because of the growing German danger. When National Service came he gave whole-hearted support to those of his young men who became

[2] Dr Arthur Dakin, 1914–19, President of the Bristol Baptist College and President of the Baptist Union, 1945; Rev. L. H. Marshall, 1920–4, President of Rawdon College, Yorkshire; Rev. F. Townley Lord, 1926–30, Minister of the Central Baptist Church, Bloomsbury, President of the Baptist Union, 1947, and President of the Baptist World Alliance.

[3] The membership, which had been reported as 695 in 1933, rose to a height of 761 two years later. By 1939 it had already fallen to 699. This was still a considerable figure, and the Sunday School, with 160 members, was 40 stronger than it had been five years earlier. The present Sunday School buildings at Queen's Road were built in Ingli James's time.

[4] Such as Sidney Peirson, J.P. (1865–1952), auditor to the Corporation for thirty years, Secretary of the Coventry Movement Company, first President of the Coventry Free Church Federal Council, Vice-Chairman of the Coventry Savings Association and a Sunday School Superintendent.

conscientious objectors. This step caused even greater controversy in the congregation with the coming of war. When Ingli James left Queen's Road in 1943 to become a General Superintendent, that great fellowship was in disarray – a disarray which the wartime black-out and call-up alone cannot completely explain.

Undoubtedly Ingli James lacked that ability to compromise with opinions he disliked, which some people call statesmanship. He was unmethodical, not a good organiser, and had little success as a General Superintendent where both these gifts are very much required. The Queen's Road congregation has, nevertheless, been rebuilt, and rebuilt very much as Ingli James would have wanted it. It is still a church of the young, with a tremendous hold among the teaching and other professions in the city. Between 1955 and 1961 they rallied to Gordon Hastings as once they had rallied to Ingli James. The church's tradition of interest in social questions had been resumed.

Anyone who dropped out of the congregation of Queen's Road was likely to make the short journey to Warwick Road Congregational Church near by. Both churches were, and are, deeply rooted in the heart of old Coventry. Their forms of government are practically the same, their teaching, except on one point, not vastly different. In the 1880s the Cow Lane Baptists, the congregation which George Eliot had attended as a girl, moved out of the old town to Queen's Road, then almost on the edge of the country. Shortly afterwards, in 1891, the Congregational chapel at Vicar Lane, with the pulpit from which John Sibree had thundered against Anglicanism, Owenite Socialism and capital punishment, was closed. The congregation moved to a new building facing Greyfriars Green, and it was this church which, from 1924 onwards, was to enjoy a period of great and deserved influence under two successive ministers of exceptional gifts, Maurice Watts (b. 1892) and Leslie Cooke (1908–67).

It is tempting to compare Warwick Road, Coventry during this time with the great Carr's Lane Chapel in Birmingham in the days of Robert Dale, a friend of Joseph Chamberlain. Dale was, of course, an avowed party man, a thing which neither Maurice Watts nor Leslie Cooke would have thought desirable. Their sympathies were on the liberal side, nevertheless, and they fostered in their church, with its predominantly middle-class congregation, a spirit of service to the community which was to make Warwick Road a powerful influence for good. Oliver Flinn, a leading Liberal on the City Council in the 1930s, is a good example of the best type of Warwick Road layman.

Maurice Watts was born at Bishop's Stortford, in a land where Independency had flourished since before the Civil War and where seventeenth-century dissenting meeting-houses still stand alongside the great, civilised churches built by the capitalists of the wool industry. He was tall, handsome and commanding; so intelligent and such a good preacher that success was bound to come easily to him in the ministry. While still in his twenties he was called to follow Sylvester Horne, that embodiment of liberal non-conformity, at Whitefield's Tabernacle in the Tottenham Court Road. In 1924 he came to Warwick Road, and was to remain there for thirteen years. The Sibree Hall and the present Sunday School buildings were all created in his time, and so was the new Manse. Nor was it through building alone that he helped to give Warwick Road Church the stamp which it still retains. He joined with Provost Howard of the Cathedral to found the Christian Social Council, of which he was the first Secretary, thus helping to build one of the earliest frail bridges between Anglicans and Non-Conformists in the city. He established a club for the unemployed in part of the church premises and spoke once a week on the old Market Square to those who, he knew, would never be seen inside any church. He was readily accepted in this varied fellowship of eager questioners, for open-air speaking was then still an art, and Maurice Watts lived up to its high standards.

In 1937, when he left for other churches and greater honours to come,[5] he was succeeded by Leslie Cooke, a man of comparable ability. Some were rather inclined to see in him only the good talker, the keen golfer and the lover of good living, but one of those who saw deepest into this nature was Richard Howard, the Provost of the Cathedral, twenty years older and a man of rare understanding. The two men were virtually co-authors of the twin ideas of the

[5] Chairman, Congregational Union of England and Wales, 1948; Moderator, Free Church Federal Council, 1949; Vice-Chairman, British Council of Churches, 1951–3; Moderator, International Congregational Council, 1953–8.

Chapel of Unity and the Christian Service Centre which were intended, in the dark war years, to make Coventry Cathedral a beacon for the future. Leslie Cooke was a careful and methodical pastoral worker. He did not make the mistake of thinking that all that was required of him was the delivery of sermons, although he preached regularly and very well. His sermons were thoughtful and carefully structured and those hearing them were always inspired by his beautiful voice and fine presence.

Coventry was bound, sooner or later, to lose such a man and in 1948 he was invited to follow Dr Sidney Berry as General Secretary of the Congregational Union. It was a rare honour and a dangerous one, since it would take him away from the things he knew best and put him into an office. Seven years later he resigned and went to Geneva in order to take charge of Inter-Church Aid, one of the largest divisions of the World Council of Churches. This was merely to exchange one set of offices for another, and towards the end of his life there is some reason to believe that he knew he had lost his way. He was known to talk longingly of wanting to return to pastoral work where his true genius lay. At last, in 1967, while on a visit to Canada he was struck down with cancer and died in hospital in New York. Nature had finally taken a terrible revenge upon a man who had striven for years to force his talents in a way they were not intended to go.[6]

II

The Church of England had begun to recognise the importance of Coventry early in the twentieth century. In 1908 the great church of St Michael was constituted a Collegiate church with its vicar as sub-Dean. The diocese of Worcester had already been divided in 1904, when the see of Birmingham was taken from it. Nobody was much surprised when, in 1918, the remainder of Warwickshire was taken away to form the Diocese of Coventry. Charles Gore, the great Christian Socialist, had been Bishop of Worcester at the time of the first division, and had regarded it as his duty to go to Birming-

[6] Hugh Jones, who succeeded Leslie Cooke in 1948 and stayed until 1961, continued his policy of associating the Free Churches with the Chapel of Unity and the work of rebuilding the Cathedral. He is now Moderator of the West Midland division of the Congregational Church.

ham. It was perhaps a little surprising that Bishop Yeatman Biggs,[7] his successor at Worcester, should regard it equally his duty to move to Coventry in 1918. He was a very old man when he did, and he died in 1922. After the nine years' episcopate of Bishop Lisle Carr, translated to Hereford in 1931, Coventry received as its third Bishop a man obviously destined for great distinction in the Church.

Archbishop Randall Davidson, that unerring judge of high quality in men, had taken Mervyn Haigh (1887–1962) into Lambeth Palace as his principal chaplain and secretary and given him several years' diplomatic experience in the chancery of the Church of England. The appointment had been a very great compliment, for he had succeeded George Bell, who had gone to be Dean of Canterbury and was later to be Bishop of Chichester. Mervyn Haigh came from Lambeth as a prince of the Church in the making, distinguished and fastidious, with fine manners and trained in high administration. He was unmarried, aloof, so shy, according to some, that he walked with his eyes on the ground for fear of recognising people. Nobody was surprised when, in 1942, he was translated to the Bishopric of Winchester, the fifth highest position in the Church of England. During his time in Coventry he had made himself liked by the great Anglican industrialists such as the Siddeleys and Sir Alfred Herbert, and their help had been of value in building churches for an expanding city. But perhaps the wisest thing he did was to appoint Richard Howard as Provost of the Cathedral in 1933.

Howard (b. 1884) was to remain in many ways the most important churchman in Coventry until he retired in 1958 in order to allow new men to take over the new Cathedral which he had done so much to create. His previous life seemed to have fitted him admirably for his new appointment. For four years he had been Vicar of Luton, a town with many of the problems which were to be found on a larger scale in Coventry. Before that, for ten years he had been Principal of St Aidan's Theological College, Birkenhead, and there he had met William Temple and come into contact with the work of the Christian Social Councils of Birkenhead and Wallasey. He

[7] Bishop Yeatman Biggs (1845–1922) appears to have been a bishop of the eighteenth- rather than the twentieth-century tradition. He had married a daughter of the fourth Earl of Dartmouth, his brother was a general, and he had assumed the name of Biggs so that he could succeed to his mother's estates in Wiltshire.

had spent five years in India, where he had seen a poverty which added to his natural compassion. He had been at Cambridge, and had been a rowing man at that greatest of all rowing colleges, Jesus. He had then gone straight into the Church taking with him first-class honours degrees in mathematics and theology.

In fact, though he himself would be the last to say so, he was an intellectual. He was widely read and deeply troubled by the problems of the thirties and knew both Hewlett Johnson and Sir Richard Acland. Perhaps his principal characteristic was his capacity for enduring friendship. It was this which enabled him to draw Maurice Watts, Leslie Cooke and Ingli James into the work of the Christian Social Council and create bonds between Anglican and Free Churchman which seem hardly to have existed previously in Coventry.

Until the war the achievements of the Christian Social Council probably did not amount to very much. Then came black-out, the call-up of members of church congregations and the destruction of church buildings in enemy air raids. The Congregationalists lost three churches in or near the city centre, the Baptists two. The Anglicans lost two parish churches, one in the centre, Christchurch, and one along the Foleshill Road, St Paul's, as well as the great cathedral of St Michael itself. Common difficulties tended to draw the churches closer together and the Christian Social Council received a wide response when, in January 1942, it set out to organise a 'Religion and Life Week' as part of the great national movement inspired by William Temple.

Cosmo Gordon Lang, who retired as Archbishop of Canterbury in 1942, had long been aware that he was not the man to lead the Church of England in the new and more democratic age which would follow the end of the war. Among his possible successors one name stood out above all others; William Temple, Archbishop of York, the greatest living Christian Socialist and the man on whom the mantle of Charles Gore had most visibly fallen. Temple had always been a maker of movements to bring home to Christians their social responsibilities. In 1908 he had been one of the founders of the Workers' Educational Association and, after the First World War, he had led the Life and Liberty Movement to emancipate the Church from State control. He had been a moving spirit behind the Copec Conference of 1924 on the Christian attitude to society. Now, at a time of great national danger, he had launched his new movement intended to bring home to all churchmen their social responsibilities. Undoubtedly the height of the Coventry Religion and Life Week was his own speech at the end of the week. It causes no excitement now, so much has what he said become part of our thinking. At the time it made men new, for such a speech had never before been heard in Coventry from an Archbishop of Canterbury. The fact that we now accept it all is in itself an indication of the tremendous influence of this very great man.

The Week was to prove of great significance to the church life of Coventry. It began on 26 April 1942, and speakers, in addition to Temple, included Dr Richard Livingstone, President of Corpus Christi College, Oxford; Dr J. H. Oldham, Editor of the *Christian News Letter*; Dr Herbert Gray, the Presbyterian Minister of the St John's Wood Church, London, and Miss Dorothy Sayers. On 29 May 1942 the follow-up meeting was held at Warwick Road Church, a meeting with the widest possible composition. It is significant that new lines of thought were evident in the resolution which finally emerged, and in the suggestion for further action which came from the meeting. Further work in education and in industry, with the appointment of chaplains in factories, was suggested and it was clear that some of those present were beginning to move beyond regarding their work as simply that of getting people to go to church. In this spirit the Coventry Council of Christian Churches was shortly to be established.

III

The tradition of Christian Socialist thought inside the Church of England in the twentieth century divides itself into two streams, of which that already mentioned was undoubtedly the broader. It sprang from the Christian Social Union associated with Charles Gore. Canon Masterman, Vicar of St Michael's between 1907 and 1912 and later Suffragan Bishop of Plymouth, was one of the contemporaries influenced by Gore. His true heir, however, as we have seen, was William Temple, and Richard Howard may find his place in this stream of the tradition. The other stream was associated in the nineteenth century with the Guild of St Matthew and in the twentieth with the Christian Socialist League. Few clergymen were like Scott Holland, who read the burial service at the funeral of Alfred Linnell, the people's martyr in the unemployed riots of 1887. Those few usually tended to be of the High Church, and for forty years in the twentieth century the living of St Peter's, Hillfields, was held by two of them in succession.

When the simple brick church of St Peter had been begun in 1840, Hillfields had been an industrial village, separated from Coventry by a stretch of common and open fields. By the beginning of the twentieth century, those fields had long since disappeared and a great new industrial housing estate was about to be built on the other side, where once Primrose Hill House and St Peter's Vicarage had looked out over open country. Canon Beaumont, Vicar of Holy Trinity, who had the gift of the living of St Peter's, did not try to pretend that it was a particularly attractive parish when he offered it to P. E. T. Widdrington (1873–1959) in 1903.

Widdrington had some family connection with Coventry, for his uncle had been Vicar of St Michael's at the time of the weavers' strike of 1860 and had earned a wide reputation as a radical for his sympathy with the strikers. His nephew was to remain here for fifteen years, until, in 1918, he accepted a gift of the living of Great Easton[8] from Evelyn, Countess of Warwick, and moved into an entirely different world. He may well have been happiest in Coventry where St Peter's Vicarage became the home of the Fabian Society, the centre of the St Peter's Fellowship and the light to which most people in the city looked if they had any sympathy whatever with the aspirations of the new Labour movement. In those days, political appointments inside the Church were not unknown. Ramsay MacDonald became Prime Minister of the first Labour government in 1924 but, although he took Donaldson to Westminster Abbey and sent Hewlett Johnson as Dean to Manchester, for reasons best known to himself he left Widdrington where he was.

[8] Great Easton was one of the three livings in the north-west corner of Essex which were in the gift of one of the most remarkable women of the early twentieth century, a Socialist sympathiser who surrounded herself with socialist intellectuals such as H. G. Wells, Gustav Holst and Dame Ethel Smythe.

In 1913 Widdrington had been one of the prime movers in the formation of the Christian Socialist League, the other being Conrad Noel, Vicar of Thaxted in Essex, a great patrician democrat related to two dukes. Although the two men were to become near neighbours they tended to draw further apart in doctrine. Conrad Noel became more and more interested in Marxism, until he eventually founded the Catholic Crusade and became a prominent supporter of the Communist Party in the 1930s. Widdrington himself was the leader of a move in 1923 to reconstitute the Christian Socialist League under the title of the 'League of the Kingdom of God', with a doctrine which looked in a different direction.[9] That the Church ought to take again its authority in economic matters was bound to be an attractive idea to any High Church priest. That it had used this authority to protect all other classes, particularly the common people, against the power of money and financiers was disputable, but not beyond maintaining. It had attractions in the twentieth century for Christian Socialists who were anxious to argue that a social revolution was unnecessary, and that changes in the monetary system were all that was required. Through this open doorway, the influence of Social Credit was to walk into the Christian Socialist movement in England.

Its influence was to be particularly marked in the career of Paul Stacy (1870–1960), Widdrington's successor as Vicar of St Peter's, who was to remain through the worst of the war until his retirement in 1944. The social position of the Stacy family is a difficult one to estimate. Enid, Paul's sister, had been Widdrington's first wife, and his father, Henry Stacy, who died in 1915, is described as a well-known artist in the Bristol and Weston-super-Mare districts. His mother, who died in 1929 having lived at St Peter's Vicarage for the last eleven years of her life, was certainly a gifted pianist and appears to have been the daughter of a Birmingham merchant. She nagged her son unmercifully, but it cannot have been easy to keep house for a saint with a tendency to give away the clothes from off his back.

A saint Stacy undoubtedly was, and a very active one, completely

[9] 'The League is a band of Churchmen and Churchwomen who believe that the Catholic faith demands a challenge to the world by the repudiation of capitalist plutocracy and the wage system, and stands for a social order in which the means of life subserve the commonweal' (Stacy, Paul, *The League of the Kingdom of God, what it is and what it stands for*).

without gloom. Most people appear to have felt that he was not as they were, but they could hear him speaking every week on the old Market Square and at one time St Peter's Vicarage was used as the organising headquarters of an important part of the Social Credit movement.[10] He certainly held himself aloof from other clergy, and does not appear to have gone much even to Thaxted. He seems to have been much in demand as a witty after-dinner speaker at the dinners of the Bristol firm of wine merchants where he had once worked. His compassion was so limitless and his charity so abounding that he was frequently imposed upon, particularly by people who would never have dreamed of coming to his church. His congregation was, in fact, very small, but as an old man of seventy he was still visiting his people in the air-raid shelters and risking his life along with theirs, until at last he could risk no more and had to move to less exacting duties in scenes which were nearer those of his boyhood.[11]

IV

Two years before Paul Stacy left St Peter's preparations had begun for the rebuilding of the Cathedral, destroyed in the air raid of 14 November 1940. The decision to rebuild was first announced on 16 May 1942, and the completed building was consecrated on 25 May 1962. During those twenty years the gigantic enterprise had come to dominate the lives of two Bishops and two Provosts. Others worked alongside them, meeting rebuffs, disappointments, opposition and delay. There was the tireless Captain Thurston, who had come to the city as Chief A.R.P. Officer during the war and stayed

[10] Robert Scrutton lived there while organising the United Christian Petition Movement which presented a petition containing 60,000 signatures to the Home Office on 29 October 1938. A special train took the demonstrators from Coventry to London where a procession was formed led by Paul Stacy and the then Mayor of Coventry, Alice Arnold.

[11] Paul Stacy was to live for a further sixteen years in the south-west, mainly at Glastonbury and Tavistock, serving as an assistant priest. He took no further part in the Christian Socialist Movement, and appears to have devoted himself mainly to a study of the local legend that Joseph of Arimathea and, indeed, Jesus Christ himself, came to Britain. He is still remembered as a withdrawn, but pleasant, indeed rather merry old man.

to be secretary of the Cathedral Reconstruction Committee. There were the local men who sat on the Cathedral Reconstruction Committee from 1948, particularly such chairmen as E. H. Ford and Sir Fordham Flower of Stratford-upon-Avon. Perhaps they made wrong decisions; certainly they must have sometimes have felt sadly at sea on the artistic matters which came before them. They were not experts in the arts, but they knew all that there was to know about keeping their tempers in committee and getting a decision on the matter in front of them. Coventry Cathedral today is as much a tribute to these dogged and fallible men as it is to the vision of the architect who conceived it and the workers in glass, stone and metal who adorned it.

Those who are looking for a guide to the art and architecture of Coventry Cathedral will not find one here. This was the building which first revealed the true stature of Basil, now Sir Basil, Spence and his story has been told.[12] Above all, Coventry Cathedral is perfectly capable of speaking for itself. Those who approach the Cathedral by the steps from Priory Street find it dominated by the great bronze statue of St Michael overcoming the Devil, the last work executed by Sir Jacob Epstein before his death in 1959. This work of a genius who had long outlived the rebellion of his youth is fittingly matched by the great tapestry by Graham Sutherland behind the high altar. The mosaic floor of the Chapel of Unity represents the contribution of the Swedish artist, Einar Forseth. John Hutton, who had already worked on the R.A.F. memorial at Runnymede, was commissioned to execute the etchings of angels on the great west screen and John Piper still dazzles us with the splendid yellows and blues of the Baptistery window. The five pairs of windows in the nave, which only become visible on looking back from the altar, are perhaps the best example of discriminating patronage in the buildings, since the collective contract for them was given to the Royal College of Art and the work executed by its students.

All this is very impressive, but is perhaps not as important as what the Cathedral is trying to do. The Church of England may have hesitated a little too long in asking itself what it wants its cathedrals for. Good men have lived in cathedral closes and regarded

[12] Spence, Sir Basil, *Phoenix at Coventry* (Geoffrey Bless, 1962; Fontana Books, 1964).

them as refuges from the world, but from the first Coventry Cathedral was intended to look outwards. It had its Chapel of Unity and the idea of a Christian Service Centre. It has endeavoured to foster international understanding, to look into the problems of its own community, to foster the arts, work among men and women of other races and show the Church's concern with the pattern of industry.

V

The Bishopric of Coventry was not going to be an easy one to fill after the translation of Mervyn Haigh to Winchester in 1942. The city from which it took its name was grim, busy and industrial, with factories working night and day for the war effort, a burnt-out cathedral and a devastated centre. It required a man of special and unusual quality to accept this challenge, to continue the work of the diocese as best he might until the war should be over, and then to face the inevitable tension between rebuilding the Cathedral on the one hand and the needs of a largely rural diocese on the other.

Neville Gorton (1888–1955) was such a man. Of his predecessors, Lisle Carr had been vicar of a large parish, that of St Nicholas at Yarmouth, and Mervyn Haigh had come from the Secretariat of the Archbishop of Canterbury. Gorton himself had been at Oxford, and had held fellowships at Balliol and All Souls. At the time of his election, he was headmaster of Blundell's School in Devon, but the diocese was soon to find that, although many headmasters had become bishops, none had been quite like Gorton.[13] A bishop who disliked both preaching and administration was a little unusual; one who forgot appointments, rode about on a bicycle and spoke to anyone with his own air of complete informality and academic distinction was not what Coventry had been accustomed to.

Bishop Gorton became a legend in his own lifetime. He was working with few resources at a time of great difficulty, and was trying to do what very few bishops had tried to do before him. He was one of the first to see that the Church should be alongside ordi-

[13] They included William Temple, the then Archbishop of Canterbury, and Geoffrey Fisher, who was to succeed him in 1944. Both had been headmasters of Repton.

nary people, participating in their daily lives, rather than in a position of authority over them. He appointed Canon Moore Darling to lay the foundations of what we should nowadays call industrial chaplaincy, but he made it his own business to know trade-union leaders and shop-stewards, and they invariably liked him. He was ahead of his time in appreciating the significance of higher education in technology, and made various attempts to interest the world in creating a major Institute of Technology in Coventry.

The decision to rebuild the Cathedral had been taken nine months before his enthronement on 20 February 1943, and it had been announced that Sir Giles Gilbert Scott would be approached to prepare designs.[14] Scott was one of the great establishment architects. His work, as in the new Bodleian Library at Oxford, was beginning to look a little tired, but at the age of twenty-one he had won the competition for the new Anglican Cathedral in Liverpool with a design so daring that the assessors had felt themselves unable to award the first place to him unless he agreed to be associated with G. F. Bodley. Himself a devout Roman Catholic, he had a sympathy and understanding of Gothic architecture. With Liverpool Cathedral he had shown that he could handle the Gothic manner with freshness and something like majesty, and he had also shown, in the new Waterloo Bridge, that he could bring a massive dignity to concrete. It must have seemed as if the problem of design for the new Coventry Cathedral was already solved.

Before taking action on the rebuilding, the Coventry Diocese was careful to consult the Central Council for the Care of Churches and the resolution of 16 May 1942 embodied the advice which it received. The graceful tower and spire, which had survived the raid, were to be preserved and not overwhelmed by the scale of the new building, which should be sited as far from them as possible. The remaining walls of the old building were to be kept as far as they could be. The new building should not be out of harmony with the old, and should be faced in a similar sandstone. The Bishop and Provost, in conversation with Sir Giles, had requested a central

[14] Provost Howard had been working under great difficulties since the raid. On the first Sunday he held morning service in his own front room. The small Wyley Crypt Chapel was later cleared and used, but until the end of the war he owed much to the hospitality of the near-by Vicar of Holy Trinity.

altar. One point was to give trouble later, no new land was to be acquired.

The Scott design preserved the outer walls of old St Michael's as part of a cloister garth which should run between the tower and spire on the one side and the new Cathedral on the other. Those who entered the new building from the cloister garth would descend by one of two flights of steps to a floor level which was, in fact, that of the old crypt. As they entered, the central altar would be facing them, and behind it would rise the old five-sided apse with the choir and the Bishop's throne. The total effect of those great walls and arches of concrete might well have been a little bleak and Byzantine, but nobody in 1944 really knew what the future style of architecture was going to be and the Cathedral authorities seemed to have every reason for regarding the design as decided and prepared to launch the Rebuilding Appeal. Previous objections seemed to have been successfully overcome. In 1942, some had complained that Sir Giles Gilbert Scott was too old and too much of a traditionalist; in 1944 there had been people in Coventry who wanted to see the restoration of the old St Michael's and there were always those who felt that the rebuilding of the Cathedral should take second place to the building of houses, schools and hospitals, but they raised no active opposition during the next two years.

In 1946 an appeal was launched for the rebuilding of Coventry Cathedral, with subscriptions from the King and Queen at the head of the list. Then two extraordinary things happened. The Scott design had included sites for the Chapel of Unity and Christian Service Centre, both of which had their critics within the Church of England. A week after the appeal was launched it was decided in the Convocation of Canterbury to appoint a Joint Committee of both houses to examine the project. This came a little late, but even more strange was the intervention of the Royal Fine Art Commission which announced that it would be unable to approve the Gilbert Scott design. Sir Giles behaved with great dignity and placed his resignation in the hands of the Cathedral Council, which now had to begin all over again.

This time, it was decided, the whole question should be placed in the hands of an independent committee under a chairman of great standing, Lord Harlech, formerly David Ormsby-Gore and a

Cabinet Minister. The report of the Harlech Commission, published in 1948, made two recommendations which were to prove of the greatest value. The first was that the detailed supervision of the rebuilding should be placed in the hands of a Building Committee, which eventually became the Cathedral Reconstruction Committee under a series of able lay chairmen. The second was that the design for the new Cathedral should be obtained as the result of an open competition, to be organised by the newly chartered Royal Institute of British Architects. It was the assessors of this competition who, in the summer of 1951, awarded first place to the design of Basil Spence.

The Commission also sifted with shrewdness all the suggestions for alternative sites.[15] and dealt in particular with the question of Holy Trinity. Holy Trinity was an older church than St Michael's and had many fine features, including a beautifully painted roof and a seventeenth-century spire. The Commission examined two suggestions put forward for making Holy Trinity capable of holding the large congregations which a Cathedral requires on special occasions. The first was to build an octagon at the east end to contain the High Altar, the second, an even more ambitious scheme, was simply to drive a new cathedral nave across the nave of the old church. If either of these suggestions had been adopted, the result would have been that Coventry, having lost one historic church, would, in fact, also lose another. The recommendations of the Commission in other respects were also not quite happy. It was suggested that the Cathedral should be built in the Gothic style, an opinion so contrary to that of most young architects and many others that the Cathedral Council were unable to accept it; it was also suggested that the walls of old St Michael's, though not the tower and spire, should be pulled down, but the Council decided instead to make additional land available from St Michael's graveyard and to build the new Cathedral outside the walls of the old.

Even in 1951 the climate was not favourable for cathedral building. The allocation of building materials still lay with the Ministry

[15] Including Spencer Park, to the south of the city, and the Canal Basin site to the north on the heights at the top of Bishop Street. It also did not favour a suggestion from the town of Warwick that the great church of St Mary's at Warwick should be declared the pro-Cathedral until the new Cathedral of Coventry was built.

of Works and the Town and Country Planning Act of 1947 obliged any owner who wished to develop his property first to obtain the permission of the local Planning Authority. The Planning Authority for the Cathedral was Coventry City Council, most of whose members at that time felt that houses were far more important than cathedrals. It is true that general planning permission was obtained. Alderman George Hodgkinson, the most important member of the Planning and Redevelopment Committee, was a friend of the project, but it was soon to be made clear that he by no means represented the general feeling of the Council.

On the evening of 4 November 1951 the Council held its usual monthly meeting. The minutes of the Planning and Redevelopment Committee recorded the receipt of a copy of the Bill which the Cathedral Reconstruction Committee proposed to submit to Parliament, and Alderman Sidney Stringer, Leader of the Council, rose to speak. He was careful to make it clear that the Council would not in any way oppose the Bill, since buildings of dignity and beauty were an essential part of the life of a civilised city. On the other hand, in view of other demands for building resources, he felt that the Planning Committee should make it clear to the authorities responsible that the rebuilding of the Cathedral should not be proceeded with for ten years.

The opinion of the City Council mattered a great deal to the Cathedral Reconstruction Committee. In 1948, when they began the long process of promoting the Parliamentary Bill which was necessary to enable them to carry out some of the recommendations of the Harlech Commission, they had obtained that goodwill readily enough. The aim of the Bill was to enable the projected Cathedral to be built where it now is, and the City Council readily agreed to the closing of Priory Street and did not question the other changes in the use of property involved. They showed no interest whatever in the Chapel of Unity and Christian Service Centre. It was in London, in the House of Commons and particularly in the Church Assembly, that these new features caused so much disquiet. The Bill had to be amended a great deal in order to conciliate opposition in the Commons, and in the Church Assembly there was actually a motion proposed in February 1953 to prohibit Chapels of Unity in this or any other future projected cathedral.

Meanwhile the move towards rebuilding was beginning to gather momentum. The Spence design had been accepted in August 1951, and the Cathedral Reconstruction Committee naturally wanted to see something on the ground. As early as June 1952 a licence for £10,000 worth of work was obtained for making the old ruins safe. At the end of 1953, when the Reconstruction Committee informed the Planning and Redevelopment Committee of the City Council of its intention to try to proceed with the major work, the response was not unfriendly. Nevertheless, on 2 February 1954 the Council carried a resolution declaring specifically that the building of the Cathedral at that time was not opportune. Building licences were normally granted by the Regional Officers of the Ministry of Works, but no Regional Officer could ignore such an explicit resolution from the Council of the city in which the Cathedral was to be built. The matter would now have to go for the personal attention of the Minister of Works himself, then David (later Lord) Eccles. He invited the City Council to send a deputation to discuss their objections with him, and gave them a very full hearing, but on 22 April, in a closely reasoned letter to the Lord Mayor, he announced that he proposed to grant the necessary licences to enable the building to go forward.

In actual fact, many of the arguments that the Council had been using for some time had begun to lose their force. It had never been easy to maintain that the building of Coventry Cathedral would directly hold up the housing drive, since houses and cathedrals do not require the same kind of labour or materials. Things were getting easier generally and this meant that financial allocations of building resources for various types of work were becoming less rigid. This in turn meant that the rebuilding of Coventry Cathedral would not automatically draw resources away from the rebuilding of the shopping centre, the Belgrade Theatre, the new College of Art and all those other projects upon which the City Council had set its heart. The letter was obviously conclusive, and had a Cabinet Committee behind it. It was not long before the actual building licence, dated 6 May 1954, arrived on the desk of the Secretary of the Cathedral Reconstruction Committee for the value of work not exceeding £985,000. Within a few weeks building licences were in any case to be abolished but the arrival of the small buff form was oddly symbolic of the end of a long struggle, always carried on with mutual respect and now forgotten.

The journey to the Consecration was to take another eight years and Bishop Neville Gorton was not to see the end of it. He died suddenly in 1955, the year before the Queen laid the foundation stone of the new building. It is unfair to say that his successor, Cuthbert Bardsley, took over at a time when things were getting easier. Positive opposition to the new cathedral had certainly disappeared, both inside and outside the church, resources were very much greater and national scarcities could no longer be used as a reason for holding up the work. The very extent of these new resources, however, was to bring new problems, but Cuthbert Bardsley was to prove himself shrewd in the selection of men. He had been curate to P. T. B. Clayton, founder of 'Toc H', at All Hallows, Barking, and afterwards had been Suffragan Bishop of Croydon; and he brought to his new diocese a genuine desire to understand the industrial worker.

VI

Among church people in North America and western Europe the destruction of Coventry Cathedral was to retain a special significance. The inscription 'Father, forgive', which Howard had placed in front of the ruined altar in old St Michael's, showed that he was aware of the need to restore international brotherhood after the end of the war. In 1947 he had the courage to visit Kiel on a mission of reconciliation which proved to be the beginning of a strong link between the two towns. When, after being Provost for twenty-five years, this wise man decided to retire in August 1958, the rebuilding of the Cathedral was beginning to make progress and its future mission was already clearly defined; it was to be one of international friendship and understanding.

A particularly heavy responsibility would rest upon Howard's successor, a gifted South African, H. C. N. Williams. He had been Rector of St Mary's, Southampton, for four years before his appointment to Coventry, and while there Williams had seen the completion of the rebuilding of his church. He had also acquired a wider understanding of the problems of an industrial community by extending his care to Southampton Docks, mixing with dockers, union leaders and management alike. In a television interview shortly after his appointment to Coventry he explained why he had been ordained and had taken on this significant new responsibility. 'The Church is irrelevant to the community if it doesn't give the impression of being a coherent society within an incoherent community. The Church has not only got to be the pattern of the unity of society but it has also got to be the means of expressing that unity when it is discovered. This involves the Church mixing itself up with the community a great deal more than it does, involving itself in the tensions and cross-currents of society, understanding them, and meeting society on the vast area of common ground that exists between them.'

Such a man would understand the spirit in which his predecessor had begun the Cathedral's work for international reconciliation and would continue it with the greater resources which were to his hand. Sixteen young Germans came in October 1961 to help to build the International Centre in the undercroft of old St Michael's, and Willi Brandt, then Burgomaster of West Berlin, has been among the many distinguished West Europeans to visit the Cathedral. Another was Archbishop Cardinale, Papal representative in England, who paid a private visit in 1965, two years before a much more resplendent occasion which will be mentioned later. The Cathedral has attracted parties of students from many different countries and now has its own international youth hostel, John F. Kennedy House.

The Arts Festival which followed the consecration was marked by the first performance of Benjamin Britten's 'War Requiem'. It was an outstanding event in the city's cultural life, and equally valuable has been the Cathedral's yearly programme of visits by great international musicians, such as Yehudi Menuhin, and orchestras, such as the Berlin Philharmonic. Medieval Coventry had created one of the best-known cycles of mystery plays so that it was natural that the Cathedral should try to refashion the links between church and drama. One of its experiments has all the informality of the mystery plays themselves. The great porch at the top of St Michael's steps, by the west door of the Cathedral, is used each summer for short plays dealing briefly with a particular social situation and lasting about twenty minutes. The audience stands and watches while the rest of the world passes by.

The Christian Service Centre is only now beginning to come into existence although its constitution was approved as early as 1944 when rebuilding first seemed imminent. Gorton House, one of the pleasant Georgian houses along Priory Row, is its headquarters, but the work it was intended to do has been done for many years by the Cathedral itself. It has appointed a Youth Officer, has a Department for Education and when, in 1964, the problem of immigration was clearly becoming important, the Bishop appointed Peter Berry his Chaplain for Race Relations and attached him to the Cathedral staff. The first clergyman to become aware of the nature and extent of the immigrant problem had been a young Methodist, Garth Rogers, Minister of the Stoney Stanton Road Church which the Methodists regard as a training ground for probationers. It also happened to be a district into which increasing numbers of Indians and Pakistanis were moving, and he soon found that he was living in a new and intricate social problem. He tried to do something about it and when he left the city much of his work fell upon Peter Berry. Perhaps the best illustration of Coventry Cathedral in action in the social field was the People and Cities Conference opened by the Duke of Edinburgh in the spring of 1968 and attended by delegates from all over the world.

If the Christian Service Centre has yet to emerge completely, the Chapel of Unity may require a little rethinking, so rapidly has the ecumenical movement developed over the last few years. Christian unity had appeared very remote when the idea of the Chapel was first put forward to be greeted with hostility by many within the Church of England itself. Even in 1962 when the Chapel of Unity was consecrated, adjacent to the Cathedral but administered by a separate Trust, John XXIII was on the Papal Throne and change already in the air. Five years later Archbishop Cardinale was received in the Cathedral itself in a great service which in its pageantry challenged that of the consecration. Great occasions such as this must naturally be rare. They are more conspicuous, but perhaps less important than the continuing daily ministry of the Cathedral. It has always responded sympathetically to important occasions in the life of the community such as the centenary of Coventry Co-operative Society, commemorated in a special service on 19 March 1967. When Sidney Stringer, leader of the Coventry Labour Party, died in 1969 the Bishop preached at his memorial service.

The Cathedral has also exerted continuous influence in the field of industrial chaplaincy. Edward Wickham, now Suffragan Bishop of Middleton, ran the successful Sheffield Industrial Mission in 1944 and it is from this that industrial chaplaincy is usually dated. His book, *Church and People in an Industrial City* (first published in 1957), gives the best available statement of the theory which has been built up around this most interesting movement. That theory does not necessarily have to be accepted as a whole, but it does call attention to the serious failure of the Church of England and several other large religious bodies to deal with the problem of the great new urban communities of the nineteenth and twentieth centuries.

The Church of England's traditional parochial organisation had never been completely successful even in country districts, where each parish represented a village community. In the poorer districts of new towns, where churches were inconspicuous, livings never attractive and suitable clergy difficult to find, the problem was insoluble and the majority of the working class did not go to church. As the Methodists were finding in Manchester in the middle of the last century, they did not go to chapel either. The devoted Christian Socialists, who have already been mentioned, toiled with very little reward in their parishes and came up with no answer to the problem. Industrial chaplaincy does not mean that clergy are now going into factories in order to save souls. They would, perhaps, say that they are going to learn rather than to teach, and to discover God's purpose in industry, that significant aspect of modern life.

One of the first effective industrial chaplains in Coventry was Lincoln Minshull, the Methodist minister of the Central Hall, who was invited to be chaplain of the Gauge and Tool works by Sir Stanley Harley, himself a leading Anglican. When Bishop Neville Gorton first revealed his own intense interest in industry, he met with very little enthusiasm and his first appointments in this field, G. L. Bennett and Canon Moore Darling, did not make much impression. The fact that industrial chaplains are now accepted by industrialists and trade-union leaders alike is mainly due to Simon

Phipps, now Suffragan Bishop of Horsham in Sussex. When he was appointed Bishop Bardsley's industrial chaplain in 1958, the Cathedral and Chapel of Industry were still far from completion. Ten years later, when he left for his new post in the diocese of Southwark, he left behind him a respected and organised industrial mission which included clergy of many denominations.

VII

The frail bridge which had been constructed between the churches in Coventry as a result of the Religion and Life Week of 1942 was to collapse three years later when the war ended, a common danger no longer threatened and a common resistance no longer united. In 1948 the Council of Churches was re-established, as part of the nationwide initiative which had seen the creation of the British Council of Churches in the previous year, but it was not until 1958 that the local Council of Churches was reorganised under a lay secretary and its work given a direction which it still retains.

A change in the emphasis of the Council's work was first perceptible in May 1942, when representatives of the churches met to consider what to do after the Religion and Life Week. Since then evangelism has tended to be emphasised less and social action to be emphasised more. Every year the Council acts as the organiser of Christian Aid Week, which raises money for Inter-Church Aid. The money raised is nowadays spent upon particular projects intended to make selected communities in underdeveloped countries more capable of standing on their own feet. The Council has also established the Coventry Churches' Housing Association in order to buy, refurnish and let at a cheap rate older houses which might otherwise fall into the hands of undesirable landlords. Young church workers do much towards the necessary cleaning and repair work and the project was partly intended to remove immigrant grievances. In 1960 the Council had accepted an invitation to join a Home Office conference to develop work for the rehabilitation of young offenders and the result has been Murray Lodge, a hostel for fifteen young people between the ages of eighteen and twenty-two. The body to which the Council looks as a model is the Christian Rehabilitation Trust, which established Langley House for this type of work and now has four Langley Houses in various parts of the country.

In September 1964 the British Council of Churches summoned a Faith and Order Conference at Nottingham to consider in what fields its member churches could work together. The most important suggestion made in its resolutions was that Councils of Churches might designate areas of ecumenical experiment in their own localities where a number of denominations could provide and use common premises. The most obvious areas for ecumenical experiments of this kind are in large new housing estates, and the Coventry Council of Churches has approved one such at Willenhall Wood. This may be slow progress, but it will surprise only those who are not familiar with the difficulties which have to be overcome. The churches in Coventry have a right to be proud of their separate traditions and this is particularly true of the Old Dissent – the Congregationalists, Baptists, Unitarians and Quakers – which can trace their roots to that great seed-time of democratic experiment, the middle of the seventeenth century. In all these churches the emphasis is laid upon the self-governing powers of the individual congregation. In all but one of them, the congregation chooses its minister. In that one, the Society of Friends or Quakers, there are no ministers at all.

VIII

The mainstream of Coventry Dissent takes its rise from the year 1662 when the vicars of St Michael's and Holy Trinity refused to accept the Religious Settlement of Charles II and resigned their livings. The history of their congregations is naturally not easy to trace in the difficult times which followed, but after the Toleration Act of 1689 we find a Meeting House in existence in Smithford Street.[16] The congregation which met there was Presbyterian, for the Presbyterians had been the heart of middle-class Dissent during the Commonwealth. A leather-covered book of the early eighteenth-

[16] '... of their Magistrates and Companyes the majority of the heads are now in sober men's hands, so its esteem'd a Fanatick town; there is indeed the largest Chapple and the greatest number of people I have ever seen of the Presbiterian way, there is another meeting place in the town of the Independents which is not so bigg ...'. (Morris, Christopher (ed.), *The Journeys of Cecilia Fiennes* (1947).) Cecilia Fiennes' visit to Coventry was made in 1697.

century, which gives a list of pew rents at this Meeting, shows that they were so still. Some of the families came with their servants and were obviously people of modest substance. Many old Coventry names appear, such as the Sodens, the Fulleyloves, the Eburnes of Allesley and Wyken and the ancestors of Charles Bray.

In that same tolerant century this respectable and substantial congregation was to split and split again. Toleration had brought free thought, and the advanced spirits among the Presbyterians were beginning to question accepted doctrines, in particular the doctrine of the Trinity. In Coventry, as elsewhere, those who remained with the original congregation became Unitarians, and the more orthodox split away, finally establishing the Vicar Lane Independent Chapel in the 1720s. This was to split in its turn, for reasons which are not quite clear, and out of this second split came the West Orchard congregation which was to exist in the centre of the town until the Second World War. These are the beginnings in Coventry of what we now call Congregationalism. Its flowering in the twentieth century has already been described.[17]

The Unitarians were to remain at the original Meeting House until 1935 when they left a crowded and valuable site near the city centre to move later to their present premises along the Holyhead Road. They have always remained a small group as Coventry did not have its industrial revolution at the time when Unitarianism was in the ascendant among the new manufacturers. To some extent, the Coventry meeting shared in the Unitarian tradition of an intellectual ministry with George Heaviside at the turn of the century, but its most distinguished contribution to the public life of the city was undoubtedly Richard Lee (1873–1950), who came to Coventry in 1938 and stayed here until his death. A widely read man and a lover of education, he was a supporter of the Labour Party, became one of its leaders on the Council and Mayor of the city.

A Meeting House of the Society of Friends, or Quakers, existed

[17] There are now eleven Congregational churches in the city of Coventry. The West Orchard congregation removed from the centre to the new suburb of Styvechale after its original building was destroyed in the war. The two working-class congregations in Well Street and Vine Street, Hillfields, having both lost their chapels in the war, are now combined in the church on Holyhead Road. An interesting tradition of mission work among the miners in old Wyken is represented by the small congregation at Potters Green.

in Hill Street, just outside the city walls, at the end of the seventeenth century. Until about 1849 the meeting was a large one. It then declined and has remained small ever since. A great change came nationally in the 1880s when the Friends became more anxious to share in social service than they had earlier. At this time we find the Cashs, then the principal Quaker family in Coventry, promoting Adult Schools and deeply interested in animal welfare.

The Coventry Central Hall, opened in 1932, was the last of the Methodist Central Halls, as that in Manchester was the first. They all represented a great Methodist revival known as the 'Forward Movement', associated with the names of Samuel Collier and Hugh Price Hughes. The year 1932 also saw the achievement of Methodist unity when Wesleyans, Primitives and United Methodists came together in one Methodist church. The importance of Methodism in Coventry has been difficult to judge because of one of the virtues of the Methodist organisation. At one time their circuit system and the central posting of ministers probably made the most effective use of clergy in any denomination. Nevertheless, the practice of moving ministers every three years gave them very little time to settle down. Only when these rules began to change, and Lincoln Minshull was able to stay at the Central Hall for ten years, did a Methodist minister play a part in the life of the town worthy of his own talents and of his denomination.

That great, untaught, religious genius, General William Booth, began the work of the Salvation Army in Coventry in 1878 by sending two women there from London, just as later, in their turn, Mr and Mrs Shirley from Coventry began the work of the Salvation Army in the United States. The Army, as Booth began it, was more than a great religious revival, with its uniforms, banners and silver bands, of which that of Coventry has always been among the best. It had a social purpose as well. Booth organised work schemes for the unemployed and formed Slum and Gutter Brigades of women to bring practical help to slum housewives who found that they could not cope. This tradition of social work still goes on in Coventry; tracing missing persons, giving help to discharged prisoners and maintaining a hostel of 146 beds in an interesting old building on the London Road. At the beginning of the Second World War the Army was without a building, since it had grown out of various premises and was in the process of finding new ones. Throughout the war it existed in temporary wooden huts, but it was a proud day when, on 12 October 1959, its new Citadel was opened by Lady Herbert in the presence of the Lord Mayor and General Kitching, the General of the Army.

In 1845 the Roman Catholic Church of St Osburg was consecrated in Coventry, and the mightiest of all Christian denominations at last came out into the open light of day. The congregation can be traced back to 1766. Fifty years after the consecration of St Osburg's a second church was formed in the Raglan Street area. Today, there are fifteen churches in the Roman Catholic Rural Deanery of Coventry; two are foreign, one Polish and the other Ukrainian. The remainder are ordinary parish churches, now using the English language and ministered to by parochial clergy whose attitude to their flocks might sometimes be a little paternal but is never socially aloof. For each church the community has striven to provide a Primary School, and it has also now created Roman Catholic Secondary Schools, the first of which was appropriately named after Bishop Ullathorne, first Vicar of St Osburg's and later Archbishop of Birmingham. In 1968 the city chose its first Roman Catholic Lord Mayor, Alderman Leonard Lamb. This entry into public life had been so long delayed for many reasons. For one thing, memories of old disabilities and suspicion die hard and for another, many members of the faith in Coventry, particularly those who are Irish, have perhaps only recently come to regard themselves as having a permanent home in the city.

There are religious orders at work in Catholic churches in Coventry and the church of St Osburg itself is served from a Benedictine Abbey in Gloucestershire. Of the two orders, the Jesuits and the Dominicans, which have been most responsible for the intellectual ferment in the Roman Church today, the first have recently arrived in the city. On the whole, Catholicism in Coventry has tended to move only after movement has been perceptible in Rome itself. That movement showed itself at the election of John XXIII in 1958. Even now, the Catholic Church has not joined the World Council of Churches, and only in February 1969 did the individual Roman Catholic parishes become full members of the Council of Churches in Coventry.

NOTE A: *The Coventry Jewish Community and its Synagogue*

The continuous records of the modern Jewish community in Coventry begin in 1775, when Isaac Cohen apparently came to the city. He is believed to have died at an immense age in 1835 and the watchmaker, Philip Cohen (see Chapter One, page 14), who died in 1898, was probably his grandson. Jews were certainly in Coventry in the Middle Ages, and a synagogue may have existed, but the first place of worship of which we have any certain knowledge was in Isaac Cohen's old house in Little Butcher Row. The present synagogue was opened in Barras Lane in 1870, and has been able to maintain an almost continuous existence until the present day. The community was never large. Among its most prominent members can be mentioned Alfred Fridlander (see Chapter One, page 15), Emmanuel Kalker and Maurice Angel. Siegfried Bettmann (see Chapter Two, page 36), the most prominent member of the Jewish community in Coventry, was never associated with the synagogue.

NOTE B: *St Faith's Shelter*

St Faith's Shelter can trace its origin to the rescue work of Alice Bourne. She took prostitutes and other friendless girls into her own home and, in 1895, formed a Coventry Branch of the Association for the Care of Friendless Girls. From that day the work of St Faith's has faithfully reflected the changing attitudes of our times (at one time it was ruled that no applicant should be refused admission unless she was hopelessly drunk). After moving about the city St Faith's has settled in a large house on Warwick Road and is an important part of the social provision for unmarried mothers and other girls in need. Miss Margaret Paton, who became Superintendent in 1934, remained for thirty-seven years but the Home also owes its continued life to E. J. Corbett, who managed its finances for thirty-five years until his death in 1951.

CHAPTER SEVEN

Men, Women and Elections

The old Council. The beginnings of the Labour Party. Parliamentary elections. Personalities; Alice Arnold, William Halliwell, George Hodgkinson, Sidney Stringer, Officers of the Council. Co-ordination in a large local authority.

I

At the census of 1901 the administrative area controlled by Coventry City Council contained a population of 69,877. The watchmaking village of Earlsdon and the built-up area along the Stoney Stanton Road in the north had been brought within its boundaries two years earlier. The cycle boom was rising to its height, the first motorcycles and motor-cars were being made in small factories and workshops by enthusiastic and dedicated men. The composition of the City Council at that time seems, however, to reflect the social pattern which was passing away, rather than that which was just beginning to emerge. Among the aldermen were several patriarchs, some of whom could remember the first Reform Act. The revered Quaker manufacturer, John Gulson, born in 1813, had helped as a young Radical Liberal in the 1830s to establish the Mechanics Institute; Joseph Banks, born in 1822, could remember the riots which had marked the campaign for reform in 1832 and Albert Tomson had started work in the ribbon weaving industry in 1844 at the age of twelve. He was later to take the lead, as a prominent Nonconformist, in the campaign to end the Vicar's Rate in Holy Trinity Parish and, as a manufacturer, he called the first meeting to promote the city's Technical Institute. William Andrews, whose published diary still repays reading, had been a somewhat unsympathetic manager at Cash's before setting up a textile business of his own. He appears to have played a part in changing the easy going customs of the ribbon weaving industry and to have brought to Coventry the industrial attitudes of the north.

Grouped around these venerable figures were others, most of them respectable small tradesmen, such as Frederick Bird the chemist and James Maycock, a draper in Hay Lane, or manufacturers in the city's two traditional industries of ribbon weaving and watchmaking. It is difficult to be precise about the occupational background of members of the Council in the days when a councillor who had retired on a modest annuity could be described as a gentleman and an alderman in the same position as an esquire but, between 1901 and 1911, at least sixteen councillors and aldermen appear to have had some connection with either ribbon weaving or watchmaking. As late as 1930 three senior aldermen, Alfred Drinkwater, Fred Lee and William Grant, and two councillors, Alec Turner and Frederick Yeomans, still represented these ancient interests.

Perhaps the virtues of the old Coventry Council were best embodied in the life and character of one who was neither ribbon manufacturer nor watchmaker, but a chemist. Sir William Wyley (1852–1940) came of a family which had, at one time, owned a little retail chemist's business in Hertford Street. They had long moved beyond this when William Wyley was born in the pleasant suburb of Stoke. He was educated at Rugby and in Guernsey and his family was able to maintain him in Paris where he learned business method so that he could return to the family firm of which he ultimately became managing director. He was to end his life at the Charterhouse, a mansion made out of the guesthouse of an old Carthusian Monastery along the London Road. Like many others he took an interest, first in the Volunteer movement, and later in the Territorials, which gave him a military rank and in 1938 he was knighted as a recognition of many years work for the Church and on the City Council.

When he first joined the Council in 1876 he was one of the rising young men deeply influenced by the contemporary interest in public health questions and with a very good record of concern in sanitary matters. He advocated purchase of the gasworks, secured the appointment of a Public Analyst for the city and helped forward the establishment of the Swanswell Park and the extension of the Isolation Hospital. He was a useful and progressive councillor for twelve years before he retired in 1888. There were many other spheres of public life in which he remained active but his early connection with the Council had been almost forgotten when, in 1911, he was invited to accept the Mayoralty. He was the last person elected to the position of alderman from outside the Council, a position he retained until his death while the Council changed around him. He gave the city the old Cook Street Gate in 1913 and for many years he was willing to help forward any project to create a museum. He was naturally one of the founders of the City Guild and Museum Society in 1914 and stayed with it as its Chairman in the 1920s. Upon his death it was found that he had crowned his benefactions by leaving to the city his home and lands at the Charterhouse.

The contribution of the watchmaking industry to the Council was considerable. Alexander Sargeant Hill, elected to the Council in 1902, was the founder of Coventry Chain, and came from one of the most important of the Chapelfields watchmaking families. Among others, James Band, jeweller and son of a watchmaker,[1] Henry Mander, watch material manufacturer, and Richard Steynes, gold-watch case-maker, were all serving on the Council in 1911, which appears to have been the height of the watchmakers' influence. They were followed in 1917 by Oliver Flinn, a member of another Chapelfields family which was moving from manufacture into retail trade. The length of service of all these men was much surpassed by Alfred Henry Drinkwater's forty-five years on the Council. He had been born in Gloucester in 1851 and did not serve an apprenticeship in Coventry. This meant that, unlike many other manufacturers, he was not a Freeman of the city, although in 1927 he was made an Honorary Freeman in recognition of his many years of public service. On the Council he was concerned with the obtaining of additional water supplies from Birmingham, thus saving the city much difficulty in the early days of this century. Outside the Council he was interested in many charities, raising money for the unemployed, organising boot funds for poor children and working hard on behalf

[1] For Charles James Band, his son, see page 63.

of the Royal National Lifeboat Institution. Drinkwater died an alderman in 1934, after a busy and creditable life. However, he and the other councillors and aldermen from the watchmaking industry were outshone in their contribution to the life of the city by Vincent Wyles (1876–1952).

Wyles came from the heart of the Coventry working class, son of a watchmaker and grandson of a ribbon weaver. His father had been a Volunteer and died when the boy was aged only six after contracting pneumonia while attending a camp in Stoneleigh Park. His mother, with four young children on her hands, had only one way in which she could keep the family together – she would have to marry again. Her second husband, a publican, treated her so badly that, within five years, she too was dead and Vincent Wyles was an orphan. After a short period of happiness with relations in Staffordshire, he was brought back to Coventry and apprenticed to a butcher. In those days cattle were walked through the streets every evening from the market or the railway station and the butchers themselves did the slaughtering at the backs of their shops when the rest of the day's work was done. It was a rough beginning for a gifted young man, despite the fact that he knew that his young employer and his wife valued his skill. Their young son so adored Wyles that he often had to wipe the blood from his hands in the evening in order to carry the boy to bed.

Because he was apprenticed in Coventry, Wyles became a Freeman of the city and was able to borrow £100 to set up in his own business.[2] Also at this time he married Marie Rolfe, a well-connected Belgian teaching at a private school in Coventry. His enormous energy drove him to public life and in November 1908 he was elected to the City Council as a Conservative. He was to prove himself one of those Conservative radicals with a sincere interest in social reform who have been rather more numerous than is often realised. He was never afraid to vote against his party and, at the beginning of his local government career, he joined with the Labour members to vote against a recommendation that the city should take six places in a tuberculosis sanatorium near Bath. It had recently been shown that the city contained two-hundred such cases and the idea that they should be dealt with at the rate of six a year appeared

[2] See page 32 for the benefits available to Freemen of Coventry.

to many to be somewhat long-term. It was, in many ways, fitting that Wyles should open the new Isolation Hospital at Whitley when he became Mayor in 1932.

As early as 1910 he had produced a plan for a street along the line of the present Trinity Street. This was defeated at the time by a Town Poll but it was eventually realised in 1937. He was one of the principal advocates of the Technical College which was opened in the Butts in 1936 and a year later he again supported the Labour Party when they moved for a minimum wage of £3 a week for all Corporation employees. Perhaps the triumph which gratified him most, however, was the building of the municipal abattoir, which he also opened during his year of office as Mayor. He had not been the only man to work for it, he had probably done rather less than George Poole, pioneer of the Labour Party, but unlike Poole he had had to face the opposition of his fellow tradesmen. In 1921 he had become an alderman and in 1937, together with all other Conservative and Liberal aldermen due for re-election in that year, he was axed by the controlling Labour group. In the following year he was re-elected as councillor and in 1939 he was again created an alderman. Although he remained on the Council until his death, age was now taking its toll and his activity and enthusiasm dimmed.

When Alec Turner (1873–1960) retired from the Council in 1956, he had completed thirty-one years of service as councillor and alderman. As a young man he had entered the watchmaking business with his brother in Craven Street, Chapelfields. They patented a rather complex but very serviceable clock for use in pigeon racing and it was widely manufactured, particularly in Switzerland. His business left him time for public work and he had been connected with the General Charities and Freemen's Trust long before he joined the Council.[3] He was also Chairman of the Coventry Provident Building Society and one of the acknowledged leaders of the local Conservatives after the death of Fred Lee. While Turner remains a slightly aloof figure with many depths to his character, Fred Lee was a very different type of man.

The Lees had long been manufacturers of watch jewels in their factory in Dover Street and Fred Lee himself was such a shrewd

[3] His work for Sir Thomas White's Charity has been recognised by the establishment of an Alec Turner Scholarship Fund.

businessman that this same small factory was to play a tremendous part during the Second World War.[4] He was a member of Holy Trinity Church, connected with the Charities for many years and interested in city politics as a Conservative. There were many reasons why he came to occupy a unique position as a manager of men. He was always accessible, always cheerful and anything he promised was always done. Many people had moved from work with the charities to service on the City Council but only Fred Lee combined this connection with another. For many years he was Secretary of the local Licensed Victuallers Association and this gave him a close contact with the city's publicans and their many opportunities for influencing public opinion.

The licensed victuallers themselves have undergone a great change in their social position during the course of the twentieth century. At its beginning many of them still owned their own premises and even brewed their own beer. Since their midday trade was not too heavy, many could find time for outside interests and some went on the Council. Perhaps the best known of these was Alderman Arthur Sage, landlord of the White Lion at Gosford Green. There are no publican councillors now and the same sort of change has overtaken the position of doctors.

In 1901 there were no less than five doctors on the Council. Charles Webb Iliffe had been born in Coventry in 1921, travelled widely in North and South America and learned to speak some of the languages of the American Indians. He returned to the city to be the Poor Law doctor and Coroner and lived in a large imitation Tudor mansion, the Chace, on the London Road. In 1901 a Quaker, Charles Webb Fowler (1861–1922), already had a record of achievement in public health matters. He had worked for the acquisition of Whitley waterworks, taken an active interest in drainage and sewage and helped to bring about the creation of an efficient fire service in the city. The retirement in 1945 of Thomas Soden, the last doctor to serve on the Council, was followed one year later by that of J. C. Lee Gordon (1887–1968). He was the son of a Scots doctor and was Clerk, first to the Coventry Insurance Committee and then to the Executive Council under the National Health Service Act. He joined the Council in 1928 when it was becoming less essential to have been

[4] See Chapter One, page 15.

born inside the city. His retirement from public life was not completed until he resigned from his post with the Coventry Executive Council in 1952.

Solicitors have rarely been present on the City Council in any considerable numbers. One is there now (1971) and in 1901 there were only two, Richard Rotherham and William Goate. The thin, piping voice and straggling grey beard of Alderman Goate made him a distinctive figure for many years and those who met him when he was an alderman in the early thirties were bound to revere a man who had first joined the Council in 1895. Perhaps the most effective solicitor to sit on the Council was Malcolm Pridmore (1869–1945). Like the Rotherhams, the Pridmores were one of the old Coventry families, accustomed to educate their sons at Rugby, see them enter the city's companies and often give service in its public life. Pridmore became a councillor in 1905 and remained on the Council until 1934. He helped to establish the old Electricity Department on a sound footing and perhaps this was the work most to be expected from this dry, austere and meticulous man. However, he also took a great interest in slum-clearance and in his early days had found himself in association on occasions with George Poole. He had, at one time, formed a small, non-profit-making trust which bought slum property to re-sell to the Council at the same price in an effort to speed the progress of slum-clearance.

This dominant group of respectable shopkeepers, professional men and traditional manufacturers was not as unaware of the changes in the city's pattern as may appear on the surface. Joseph Banks, for instance, had been one of the original subscribers to, and James Maycock later became a director of, the Coventry Machinists Company, one of the factories started in the late 1860s to repair some of the damage caused by the collapse of the ribbon weaving industry. It was this firm which manufactured the first bicycles in the city and was later known as the Swift. The cycle boom had already brought some of the men of the new industry to the City Council and George Singer had been Mayor as early as 1891. Siegfried Bettmann of Triumph was on the Council in 1911 and so was Vernon Pugh, then manager of Rudge-Whitworth and an associate of Lanchester in the infant car industry. From that same industry had already come Ernest Instone of Daimler, who was to be followed by W. E. Bullock of Singer Motors in 1919 and John Siddeley of Armstrong-Siddeley in the mid-1920s. Harry, later Sir Harry, Harley, creator of the Coventry Gauge and Tool, was elected to the Council in 1949, only two years before his death and W. H. Malcolm, manager of the G.E.C. Telephone Works at Copsewood, joined in 1928 and became Mayor in 1948. E. J. Corbett, who joined the Council in 1941, was manager of the local Barclays Bank, where a number of important firms had their business.[5] He probably has more claim than most to be considered the councillor with the closest contact with the city's leading industries in the 1940s.

There was actually to be no great influx to the Council of the major new manufacturers of the thirties for various reasons. Men like Lord Nuffield and Lord Rootes came to the city very rarely, and even those manufacturers who lived near by found that they had many other things to do. They also became increasingly unwilling to entangle themselves in local politics as party began to dominate municipal government. Several directors associated with smaller engineering companies are on the Council at present (1971) but the greatest influx from engineering has been from inspectors, draughtsmen and workers on the shop-floor.[6] This has been helped forward by the emergence of the Labour Party which has also been responsible for two other significant changes in the composition of the Council; it has brought on a number of members connected with the Co-operative movement at a time when private retail traders have virtually disappeared from it and it has also been responsible for the coming of women on to the Council.

II

Perhaps the greatest change which was to mark the conduct of the City Council in the period between the two world wars was the new emphasis on party. The members of the old Council described themselves as either Conservative or Liberal, the dividing line

[5] For E. J. Corbett, see also page 63.

[6] In 1967/8 the Council had thirty-seven members who were connected with engineering as executives, storekeepers, inspectors and shop-floor workers.

between the two corresponding very often to that other dividing line between those who went to church and those who went to chapel. In the early days the Drinkwaters, Manders and Iliffes had all attended West Orchard, the Flinns, Warwick Road and the Snapes, Well Street Congregational churches. Webb Fowler was a Quaker and Charles Payne a member of the Salvation Army. During the 1920s the working-class vote from the chapels which had once been Radical Liberal moved to the Labour Party. The two traditional parties, therefore, began to form an election alliance to which, in 1936, they gave the name of the Progressive Party. This pact, which finally disappeared in 1949, did not succeed in its aims and Labour duly gained its majority in November 1937.

When the Labour Party first gained its majority in the City Council there stretched behind the Coventry Borough Labour Party a long road reaching back over thirty-five years. A small meeting had been held at the Alexandra Coffee Tavern on 6 December 1902 in order to found a Coventry Labour Representation Committee.[7] It had been called by the Coventry Trades Council which was to be the effective organiser of Labour activity until after the First World War. Progress at first was very slow but from 1910, when the Labour Party had been represented in Parliament for four years, the Coventry Trades Council had two competent secretaries in succession, John Chater and J. C. Tyson. Under their guidance the Council engaged in an extraordinary wide range of activities. It protested against political trials in Japan, received a visitor from Dusseldorf, who spoke of the united action of the workers preventing an imperialist war, and took a positive attitude on the subject of trade-union amalgamation trying to bring this about by frequent conferences. It protested against the contributory basis of the 1911 Insurance Act and lobbied D. M. Mason, the city's M.P., to try to get this removed.

Coventry Trades Council's attention, however, was naturally mainly devoted to local issues and in this field some of its campaigns were models of their kind. It roused public opinion on the subject of the tramways, which had hitherto been run by a private company,

[7] The Alexandra, which still exists as a cinema, was then a place where working men could buy cheap meals and where the Coventry Trades Council already held its meetings.

and pressure from the Trades Council was largely responsible for the Corporation's decision to exercise its option to purchase in 1911. It worked long and admirably on the subject of housing, devoting attention to slum-clearance and working patiently and persistently to get the City Council to exercise its full powers under the Housing Act of 1909. It fought the efforts of the Governors of Bablake to increase their fees because it was felt that this would have the effect of penalising the intelligent working-class child, keeping him from this school which had a particular connection with industry. In all these campaigns the Trades Council worked closely with the first Labour councillors; but what particularly impresses the present day is the complete lack of dogmatism in their approach. There is no trace of any insistence that those joining in a campaign with them must be paid-up party members; on the contrary, when, on 22 August 1911, they mounted their great demonstration in the Corn Exchange upon the subject of working-class housing Canon Masterman, Vicar of St Michael's, was among the speakers and the organisations invited to send delegates included such non-political bodies as Allotment Associations and Pleasant Sunday Afternoons from the city churches and chapels.[8]

The call for a separate Labour Party had come first from two small socialist societies, the Social Democratic Federation,[9] founded in 1884, and the Independent Labour Party, formed in 1893. Both had branches in Coventry with premises of their own. The I.L.P. had rooms in Broadgate over a grocer's shop, in what had once been the Commercial Hotel where Charles Dickens had been presented with a Coventry gold-watch by admirers of his readings. There, portraits of William Morris and Robert Blatchford reminded visitors that this was a Socialist Club. Justice Hall, built near the

[8] The Trades Council was also interested in the protection of female labour. In 1913 a young woman trade-unionist, Sally Griffiths, brought to Coventry some of the Cradley Heath chain makers, who had been locked out because their employers had wanted them to defer for six months a wage increase granted by the Trade Board for the industry. She paraded them in the town with specimens of the chains they made and took a collection on their behalf.

[9] One of the leading members of the S.D.F. was Tom Mann (1852–1941), born at Longford, then a country village to the north of Coventry. After working as a boy in the Victoria Pit, the site of which is now marked by the Longford Power Station, he became an engineering worker in Birmingham and was one of the leaders of the London Dock Strike in 1899.

Swanswell for the S.D.F., was soon to become the headquarters of a separate party. Both societies were disappointed with the performance of the Labour Party, and the S.D.F. separated from it in 1909 to become the Social Democratic Party. This automatically made difficulties for Arthur Bannington, one of Coventry's two Labour councillors and a member of the S.D.F.

There appears to have been a very well-marked S.D.F. type, and Arthur Bannington (1879–1951) was a typical representative of it. Those who remember him recall a bitter, rather withdrawn man, who had certainly had his share of misfortune. His background was middle class, his father having been a moneylender whose fortunes were already declining when Arthur was born. His mother had married beneath her and he himself was to contract a marriage which did not give him the kind of intellectual companionship he sought. After attending Bablake School he became a carpenter, later turning to political organising. His actual time on the City Council was short and his most significant intervention in Coventry politics was disastrous. After the General Election of December 1918, when he stood as a Soldiers' and Sailors' candidate, he was accused of thwarting the election of R. C. Wallhead, the Labour candidate. Henceforth many Labour Party doors were closed to him and he had one job after another until, in 1937, he left the city. It is an unhappy story; he seems to have been an intensely lonely man, trying desperately to establish communication with his daughter in order to gain some of the intellectual contact his personal life had not hitherto given him, and failing in his attempt. He painted watercolours and wrote poetry, neither of which he did well, but had things gone differently with him he might have been a considerable figure.

The local I.L.P. appears to have been much gayer. It included two gifted propagandists, Rowland Barrett, a carpet-fitter at Anslows, and Tom Hutt, an employee of the local Public Library. They joined together to launch a brief venture in socialist journalism called the *Coventry Sentinel.* To this Hutt contributed such excellent cartoons that he lost his job and both he and Barrett soon left town. Rowland Barrett moved up and down the country editing and producing various socialist newspapers, including one at Leicester where he showed the strongest suspicion of Ramsay MacDonald, then one of the city's M.P.s. He died in 1951 in a bungalow in Devon which he had converted into a holiday camp where socialists from all over Europe could enjoy that pattern of living so common in the I.L.P., a mixture of politics, cycling and life in the open air. Among other socialists in the city mentioned by Rowland Barrett in his papers are Dr Karey, Jack Price, manager of the Swift Cycle Company, and several clergymen, of whom the most distinguished was P. E. T. Widdrington of Hillfields, but above all these were recognised the outstanding qualities of Stephen George Poole (1861–1924).

George Poole ranks high in the contribution which Coventry's two traditional industries have made to its public life. His father was a watchmaker in Earlsdon. When George was nine he had to leave school and for five years he worked as a part-timer in cotton mills in Lancashire, where his family had moved owing to bad trade in Coventry. When the family returned to Coventry he was apprenticed to a textile designer. After the end of his apprenticeship he began his own business, designed many of the Stevengraph pictures and got to know Tom Cash. He was a somewhat unsectarian Christian for, although he had attended the Holy Trinity Bible Class himself, he gave his children complete freedom of choice as to which Sunday School they went to, provided they attended something. He read enormously and at his death had a library which filled the walls of his drawing-room. A man of his temperament was bound to take the people's side in politics and he was one of the first members of the Coventry Liberal Club in the days when that was the most radical political centre in Coventry. He joined the S.D.F. on its inception but soon identified himself with the I.L.P. which he found much more congenial. He was forty-five, with many years of thought and the cares of a large family behind him, when he at last became the first Labour member of the City Council in 1905.

In the Parliamentary Labour Party of that time there were few who could equal Poole in character and quality of mind but in those days there was no salary for a Member of Parliament, and he had a large family whose welfare he always placed first. He never became bitter because of this limitation of his political career for he never regarded it merely as a career. A deeply emotional man, his eyes could fill with tears at the sight of poverty or of children in slums.

He could grow angry, but only with social injustice, and was never known to lose his temper inside his own home. Far too little is known today of the extent of his political work. On national issues, he was a friend of Sylvia Pankhurst and a worker for women's emancipation. Locally, he played his part in the campaign to obtain the city tramways for public-ownership. His long struggle for the municipal abattoir is remembered largely because of the generous words of Vincent Wyles, then Mayor, at its opening. George Poole had realised that it was impossible to guarantee by inspection the quality of meat sold in the city while animals were being slaughtered in forty private slaughterhouses all working at the same time. He fought for educational opportunities and against the imposition of increased fees at Bablake. He was intimately associated with projects for slum-clearance and had much to do with the first large Council house estate in Kingfield Road. He also joined with Tom Cash in building the Garden City, a private and non-profit-making venture in good housing which was intended to set the pace for a not over-diligent local authority.[10] He was so deeply and rightly respected that, towards the end of his Council service, no one wasted his time by opposing him at elections.

This fine man and the small, rather attractive group around him were destroyed as a result of the First World War. Speaking at George Poole's funeral in July 1924, Widdrington likened him to William Morris, but by that time he had been expelled from the Labour Party and was rapidly being forgotten. New men were emerging.

III

On 14 December 1918 the Coventry Labour movement at last had the opportunity of contesting the city's single Parliamentary seat. Since 1910 that seat had been held by a Radical Liberal, D. M. Mason, who had come out in favour of negotiations with Germany during the war and was not likely to be forgiven for this now that victory had been achieved. A second Liberal, Sir Courtney Mansell, had entered the contest as a supporter of Lloyd George, then head of a

[10] For a fuller treatment of Poole's work in housing see Chapter Eight.

coalition government of Liberals and Conservatives. The officially endorsed coalition candidate, however, was Sir Edward Manville, Chairman of Daimler and a Conservative. With the Liberals and Conservatives split three ways, there seemed an excellent chance for a Labour victory. R. C. Wallhead, a leading member of the I.L.P., had been in the field since 1911, when circumstances had compelled George Poole to abandon his Parliamentary hopes.

Unfortunately, there was also a split on the Labour side since, as well as Wallhead, there was a Soldiers' and Sailors' candidate, Arthur Bannington. The returned ex-servicemen represented a political force which no one could quite predict, particularly in view of the part played by soldiers in the recent Russian and German revolutions. Bannington, like his master, H. M. Hyndman, had supported the war and had volunteered to serve. Wallhead had been a conscientious objector, and Bannington might well prove a dangerous challenger. On the eve of the election, a public opinion poll forecast that the order of the candidates would be Manville, followed by Bannington, Mansell, Mason and Wallhead. With George Poole supporting Bannington it looked as if Wallhead would be heavily defeated. The poll probably indicates that there was a large Labour vote which had not made up its mind, but which might easily have gone to Bannington. In actual fact the result was: Manville, 17,380 votes; Wallhead, 10,298 votes; Mansell, 4128 votes; Bannington, 3806 votes; Mason, 3145 votes.

At this election the national Labour Party succeeded in obtaining only 73 seats. Its Parliamentary leader and virtual creator, James Ramsay MacDonald, was defeated by an electorate which had not forgiven his opposition to the war. Nor had membership of the Lloyd George War Cabinet preserved Arthur Henderson. Despite a new Constitution and Party Manifesto, both provided by Sidney Webb, the Party, at the end of 1918, resembled only too closely what it had been at the end of 1910. It seemed hardly likely, and it was certainly not inevitable, that this collection of respectable and ageing trade-union officials would have much success in laying claim to the loyalty of soldiers back from the trenches or young militants trained as shop-stewards in the wartime factories.

In the few years after the Armistice three dissident movements were developing. One was an attempt to create a British Socialist

Party on the Left by persuading the I.L.P. to move away from the Labour Party. There was also a movement among ex-servicemen, which, in fact, had little support. The third was a continuation among trade-unions of the syndicalist tradition that the less the workers had to do with politics the better. All three were represented in Coventry, the third being powerful at the time of the 1922 engineering strike. It is more surprising than is generally realised that, in 1922, the Labour Party was beginning to emerge as a respectable political force with an obvious future before it.

For this they had reason to be grateful to David Lloyd George. In December 1916 he had cut himself off from the official Liberal Party by ousting Asquith from the Premiership with the support of the Conservatives. Two years later he was to rub salt in those wounds by winning an election in which Asquith himself was defeated and the official Liberal Party almost wiped out. Genuine reconciliation between the followers of Asquith and Lloyd George was henceforth impossible and in 1922, with its national organisation still incomplete, its programme undecided and its national leadership still to be welded together, the Labour Party suddenly found itself the second largest party in the country.

In the Coventry elections of the early twenties the same curious fluctuations of fortune are visible. In 1922 Manville retained the seat, although a rather unsatisfactory Labour candidate polled 16,289 votes, more than the combined poll of Wallhead and Bannington four years earlier. In 1923 came the greatest surprise of all. In a three-cornered contest the Conservative and Liberal candidates polled an almost exactly equal number of votes each and the Labour candidate, Alfred Purcell, was returned by a narrow majority as the first Labour member for Coventry.[11] He was not to stay in Parliament for long; in the 1924 election the seat was regained for the Conservatives by Sir Archibald Boyd-Carpenter, father of John Boyd-Carpenter, with a majority of 4824.

Then, in 1926, a most important change occurred. Hitherto, the Coventry Borough Labour Party had preferred its Parliamentary candidates to be strong trade-unionists. Purcell himself, together with A. J. Cook and Fred Bramley, had been one of that generation

[11] Purcell (Labour), 16,346; Manville (Conservative), 15,720; Gisborne (Liberal), 15,714.

1. 'Middlemarch' – Great Butcher Row, drawn by Nathaniel Troughton

2. The homes of craftsmen – Cash's Kingfield factory, founded in 1857

3. The watchmaking district of Chapelfields

4. The technology of the 1970s – the assembly line for the Jaguar V12 engine, 1971

5. Allesley Village – a conservation area

6. Coombe Abbey

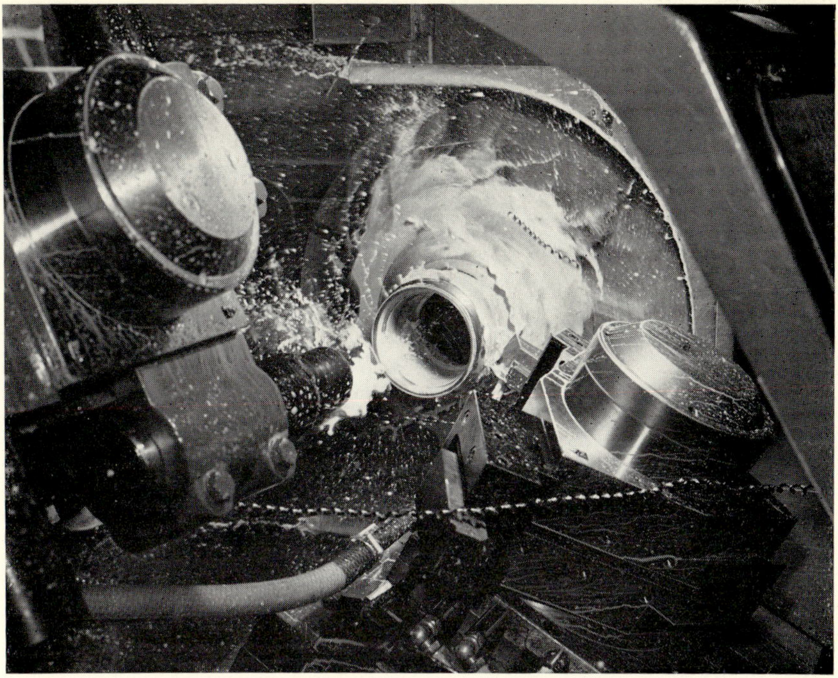

7. A Wickman CSA 600 producing wheel hubs for British Leyland

8. A Herbert/Devlieg jigmil with a tape control system machining parts for Rolls-Royce engines

9. Standard 'Flying Twenty' saloon, 1936

10. Jack Brabham in a Brabham-Climax at the Brands Hatch Race of Champions, 1965

11. W. A. Weaver in his Ornithoplane, 1906

12. The Armstrong-Whitworth Argosy, 1927

13. The Armstrong-Whitworth Whitley bomber, 1936

14. G.E.C.–A.E.I. Telecommunications – a microwave radio station in the Chilean High Andes

15. Faith and ruin – the crosses of charred wood and nails in the old Cathedral

16. Ecumenism in the new Cathedral – the liturgy of the Eastern Orthodox Church is celebrated at the High Altar

17. The biggest tractor plant in the Western world – the Massey-Ferguson factory at Banner Lane

18. The birthplace of 'Courtelle' – Courtaulds Synthetic Fibres Laboratory

19. Broadgate in 1931

20. Broadgate in 1971

21. Court 38, Spon Street, 1957

22. Comprehensive redevelopment at Spon End, 1971

23. The first large post-war estate, Tile Hill, begun 1953

24. Corinthian Place, Manor Park Estate, 1969

25. The old Bablake School a sixteenth-century building

26. President Kennedy Comprehensive Secondary School

27. Bull Yard, completed in 1969

28. The University of Warwick – the East Site, designed by Grey, Goodman and Associates

29. The Great Fair on Pool Meadow, about 1920

30. The Central Swimming Baths

of trade-union leaders produced by the great strikes before the First World War. In 1926 the local party chose Philip Noel-Baker (b. 1889), a distinguished amateur athlete and a don of King's College, Cambridge, at the same time as E. M. Forster and J. M. Keynes. He was exactly the type of man MacDonald wished to encourage and after the Labour victory of 1929 he became Parliamentary Secretary to Arthur Henderson at the Foreign Office. There he began those years of work for international peace which eventually brought him the respect of the international community and the award of the Nobel Peace Prize in 1959. He worked unavailingly for the success of the Disarmament Conference, wrote a classic work on the private manufacture of armaments and held office in the post-war Attlee governments. He brought into the House of Commons something of the moral stature of Gladstone until ill health forced him to retire in 1970.

Unfortunately, this great work had not been done as member for Coventry. In 1931 he had been defeated by Captain Strickland, a local engineering employer, and his attempt to regain the seat in 1935 was unsuccessful so he had to look elsewhere. A vacancy was found for him in Derby in 1936 but he had done much to set the pattern for the type of candidate which the Coventry Labour Party would adopt in the future. In 1938 its Selection Committee had a choice of two candidates only, both of them middle-class intellectuals. One was T. P. Garratt, author of *Mussolini's Roman Empire*, a best-selling attack on the Italian invasion of Abyssinia.[12] Garratt, although a gifted man, was not a gifted speaker. He was, therefore, at an obvious disadvantage when compared with his successful rival, R. H. S. Crossman.

Richard Crossman (b. 1907) had spoken in support of the General Strike while head boy at Winchester in 1926. By a natural process he had gone from Winchester to New College, Oxford, had done brilliantly and had been drawn under the influence of its Warden, H. A. L. Fisher, who had entered Lloyd George's government as Minister of Education after the war. He was a classics don, but Fisher encouraged him to place his great gifts at the service of the

[12] Also joint author with the elder Edward Thompson of *The Rise and Fulfilment of British Rule in India*, probably the best history of the British occupation of India ever produced.

State by entering politics. This he did in the traditional way, by first acquiring experience on the Oxford City Council, of which he was leader between 1934 and 1940, and then trying for a Parliamentary nomination. West Birmingham rejected him in a by-election but the Coventry Labour Party took him as its candidate soon afterwards. He, like many others, confidently expected to be fighting an election in 1939. He was, in fact, fighting a war instead, having become an expert on psychological warfare, a job which took him to London and elsewhere, but never to Coventry. There his name meant nothing to the thousands of war workers who had not been in the city when he was first selected. Communist influence seemed to be growing and his Parliamentary future looked a little precarious.

The election finally came in July 1945, six years later than had been anticipated and under very different conditions. The city was now to return two members for the new constituencies of Coventry East and Coventry West and the two major parties had to find an extra candidate in a hurry. For the Conservatives, Captain Strickland, the sitting member, decided to fight in Coventry West, leaving to another local industrialist, Harry Weston, the task of trying to contain Richard Crossman in Coventry East. For the Labour Party the problems were not solved so easily. A candidate for Coventry West was found rather late in the day in Maurice Edelman, a Cambridge intellectual and left-wing journalist. George Hodgkinson, the only full-time secretary the Labour Party in Coventry had ever had, was widely nominated for the seat but found at the last moment that he was unable to become a candidate.[13] The principal dangers, however, seemed present in Coventry East. E. A. C. Roberts, then Chairman of the A.E.U. District Committee and a man to be reckoned with, made great efforts to get the nomination for the seat and, even after he had been debarred, Richard Crossman found himself faced with competition of unknown dimensions from William Alexander, a Communist candidate. The Communist Party had wanted Crossman to fight Coventry West in order to give Alexander a clear run against the Conservatives in Coventry East. This had been refused and the damage the Communists might

[13] Rather late in the day the Party's National Executive had introduced a rule that no agent could fight an election in a constituency for which he had acted unless he had resigned his agency at least six months previously.

do in return could well be considerable, but in fact the two results, when they came, were a triumph:

Coventry West		*Coventry East*	
Edelman (Lab.)	38,249	Crossman (Lab.)	34,379
Strickland (Con.)	23,236	Weston (Con.)	15,630
		Alexander (Com.)	3,987
		Payne (Lib.)	2,820

The Attlee Government, formed after this election, ran for its full term and by 1950 Coventry had three constituencies and the two sitting members had to decide which they would contest. Richard Crossman would obviously be the candidate for Coventry East, Maurice Edelman decided that he would go to Coventry North, and in Coventry South, covering many of the residential areas on the Kenilworth side of the city, both parties would have to put forward new candidates. The Conservatives decided that here should be mounted their principal counterattack. They chose for the constituency an agent who was himself a page out of the political history of the West Midlands. Like many of the best Conservative Party professionals, Arthur Walker was of working-class origin. He had begun his political career as a lad by standing on a platform holding the two loaves, one large and one small, used by Joseph Chamberlain to illustrate the benefit of Tariff Reform for the British people. Later Walker had been Neville Chamberlain's election agent and had never lost an election. His candidate in Coventry South was Leslie Hore-Belisha, a contemporary of Harold Macmillan at Oxford in the golden days before the First World War. He had entered Parliament as a Liberal in the twenties, seen his hopes of a Radical revival under Lloyd George fade and became a minister in the National Government during the following decade. His record of achievement was not inconsiderable; as Minister of Transport he had tried to tackle the traffic problem, he had been sympathetic to Eleanor Rathbone's campaign for family allowances and had been a successful and intelligent reformer while at the War Office. He had lost his seat at Devonport in 1945 and now wanted to return to Parliament as a Conservative. He was handsomely defeated by Elaine Burton, now Lady Burton of Coventry, a young Yorkshire schoolteacher who had been doing social work in South Wales.[14]

[14] Coventry South – Burton (Labour), 27,977; Hore-Belisha (Conservative), 21,885; Soper (Liberal), 3239.

Labour's triumph of 1950 was repeated in the following year but one thing pointed to trouble ahead. A great deal of Labour's impetus in the previous two elections had depended upon the shop-steward organisation in the factories and the most striking demonstration of this had been a march by the Standard workers into the centre of the city with the candidates at their head. In 1951 the three Labour candidates were left standing on Hearsall Common waiting for a procession which never came; and it has never marched since. Four years later, when the election of 1955 came in the wake of the agitation caused by the City Council's action over its Civil Defence Committee, all Labour majorities were seriously down. Richard Crossman's majority fell from 12,671 to 6104, Maurice Edelman's from 9588 to 3173 and Elaine Burton's from 5468 to 1688.

Elaine Burton had given the representation of Coventry South a stamp which it had not lost, even today. She had been a very good constituency M.P., giving a great deal of her time to such issues as consumer protection and local employment trouble and being more than assiduous in dealing with constituents' problems. In 1959 she was defeated by Philip Hocking, the son of a local builder and a member of the City Council. Philip Hocking was, in 1964, defeated in his turn by another local candidate, William Wilson (b. 1913), who is still the sitting member (1971). William Wilson's parents had been pioneers of the Coventry Labour movement in the years when the cause itself had to be the reward. After serving in the forces during the war he qualified as a solicitor and became a member of the County Council, a member of Coventry City Football Club and a man with irons in many different local fires. Over the years he has proved himself very much more than a local politician, having a deep interest in disarmament and peace, in the problems of undeveloped countries and in the reform of the divorce laws in which he played a major part.

IV

The fortunes of the Coventry Labour Party in municipal elections improved significantly during 1928 and 1929, years which saw the extension of the city's boundaries and a national swing towards radicalism reflected in the Noel-Baker victory in Coventry in May 1929. At the beginning of the 1920s about eleven members of the Council had Labour sympathies. It is impossible to be more precise since Arthur Bannington, who was a councillor until 1920, had, as has been said, opposed the official Labour Party candidate at the 1918 General Election, Alice Arnold, first woman member of the Council, had actually stood as a trade-union, not a Labour Party, candidate and the railwaymen's unions had officially sponsored several Labour councillors, including Jack Moseley and Jack Peutrell. There appears to have been no organised Labour Party Council group and, in any case, by 1926 the number of 'Labour' members had fallen to three.

Employers were not obliged to give people paid release for public service in those days and this undoubtedly faced many men on the Labour side with serious personal difficulties. The man who had an industrial life insurance book had an advantage here as he had some control over how he arranged his time. So did Sidney Stringer as a Trading Club collector for the Coventry Co-operative Society. Trade union officials were available during the day for public work if their members would permit it and this they proved reluctant to do. George Hodgkinson, a veteran of local elections since 1921 and paid secretary of the Coventry Borough Labour Party since 1923, got their permission to stand for election but only after some time, and before 1939 the number of men coming forward was insufficient for the opportunities that offered themselves and, therefore, housewives had to step in.

Some of these women, including Emily Smith, had served an apprenticeship on the Board of Guardians before going on the Council; Emily Allen is the last survivor of this early group of pioneers. Annie Corrie was probably the oldest Labour woman on the Council. The record says, rather mysteriously, that she was born abroad, educated at boarding-school and privately and that her father was in the Army. When she came to Coventry she was elected to the Board of Guardians and passed on to the Council in the 1930s. Sally Griffiths, helper of the Cradley Heath women chain makers before the First World War, had been a part-timer from the age of seven and two years later became a full-time wage-earner for wages of 1*s* 3*d* a week and her food. She joined the Labour Party in

1906 and was a keen trade-unionist and a member of the Board of Guardians in the very early days of Labour representation. After the abolition of the Board of Guardians she was elected to the Council in 1933 and remained there until her retirement only a month before her death. There were other working-class women on the Council, such as Jeannie Cant and Henrietta Givens, but only Alice Arnold (1881–1955) appears to have exceeded Sally Griffiths in the poverty of her upbringing and the zeal for social justice which this inspired.

Alice Arnold herself was a peasant at heart, admirably equipped to be the voice of the general workers, the men brought into the city by the cycle trade, unskilled and ill at ease with town ideas. Her father appears to have been a blacksmith. When times were bad he kept the family fed by poaching in Stoneleigh Park, and it was the young Alice's job to work the forge while he was away so that the police, who kept a special watch on him, would be convinced that he was hard at work. She left school at the age of eleven to work in one factory after another, soon becoming an active trade-unionist. She was, for a long time, suspicious of the Labour Party and, when she first stood for election to the Council in 1920, she was a trade-union candidate. She probably never had much in the way of political ideas but her natural class instinct and honesty of purpose gave her a curious dignity and a capacity to inspire an affectionate respect which is still not quite forgotten.

In 1929 she faced a personal tragedy when the Workers' Union, of which she was an official, amalgamated with the Transport and General Workers which had the great Ernest Bevin as its General Secretary. He was one of the first to put some idea of cost effectiveness into the running of trade unions and to decide that there was such a thing as having too many union officials. The General Workers' Union in Coventry had three full-time officials and this was two too many. He offered Alice Arnold a job in Birmingham which she refused to take. Friends in the movement raised the money to set her up in a greengrocers' shop but Alice Arnold was no businesswoman.

Her republican views probably cost her the Mayoralty in the year of the coronation of King George VI but in 1937/8 she became the first woman Mayor of the city. After the Second World War she grew more and more estranged from the Labour Party, attacked it in public and bitterly felt that the movement was losing its edge and quality. Her later years were in many ways a tragedy. There is a persistent legend, impossible either to prove or disprove, that she received some help from Sir Alfred Herbert and help she certainly needed towards her end. She was opinionated, difficult to handle, impossible to contradict; she had no sense of dress, no interest in outward show; she was a lover of humanity who hated men, and a convinced believer in spiritualism. To the eye that could not see within she was disreputable and a little sad, but Joan of Arc was probably more than a little like Alice Arnold.

Among the men who joined the Council as Labour members in the thirties two sections of opinion should be noted. George Briggs, a Methodist lay preacher, the Reverend Richard Lee, the city's Unitarian minister, and John Fennel from Longford represented the Non-Conformist influence which remained important. Another group, some of whom were not on the Council until the forties or fifties, represented the influence from the Minority Movement and the industrial struggles of the early 1920s. This group included H. B. W. (Bertie) Cresswell, W. I. Thomson and that veteran member of the S.D.F. – W. U. (Billie) Binks. Robert Thomson, who had been chairman of the Coventry Lockout Committee in the engineering lockout of 1922, might have been a contender for the leadership of the Council in the days of the Labour majority if his vanity and other weaknesses had not clearly shown that he was much inferior in stature to three other men; William Halliwell, George Hodgkinson and Sidney Stringer, all of whom joined the Council between 1928 and 1929.

William Halliwell (1888–1963) had walked to Coventry from Stoke-on-Trent to find work. After 1937 he was the moving spirit behind the drive to form a Policy Advisory Committee and, when that Committee was inaugurated in the summer of 1938, he was its first chairman. During the war he was the first chairman of the National Emergency Committee, the central link between the city and central government. As such, he acted with conspicuous success as leader of the Council throughout the raid of 14/15 November 1940. William Halliwell probably expressed the secret of his own character when he once told a friend and colleague that he had to be always fighting. He was a difficult man, certainly dictatorial by instinct and inclined to be a bully to those who were too sensitive to stand up to him. One very senior officer of the Corporation came to dislike him so much that he avoided being in the same room. Halliwell had some friends and there were many who respected him. Among these was the Earl of Dudley, the Regional Commissioner, but among his enemies were many in his own Party. These cannot have received with much pleasure the announcement on 27 December 1940 that the Ministry of Home Security had recognised his services during the great raid by inviting him, at the suggestion of the Artists' Wartime Committee of the Ministry of Information, to have his portrait painted. On 24 March 1941 it was announced that this seasoned Labour leader, one of those who had joined the Council in 1929, had resigned from the party, and that his resignation had been accepted by the delegate meeting by a majority of eighteen to eight. His friends' battle to secure his reinstatement did not end until, in 1949, he was removed from the aldermanic bench by his former colleagues, after refusing to subscribe to the Labour Whip.

George Edward Hodgkinson (b. 1893), first paid secretary of Coventry Borough Labour Party, had seen his own family life shaken while he was still a boy. His father had been a worker in the lace trade of Beeston and he himself had started work at the age of ten scraping the flues of the Lancashire boilers at the firm of Goddard and Humber. Beeston was badly hit by the decline in the lace trade and the Humber cycle factory's move to Coventry, and George spent some time as an engineering worker in Lancashire before coming to Coventry in September 1914. During the First World War he worked as a skilled man at Daimler where lay the heart of the shop-steward movement. He himself became a steward and took part in the 1917 strike about dilution of labour and the recognition of shop-stewards. He was then junior to such well-known leaders as Tom Dingley, but his qualities of judgement and leadership were far greater than theirs and something of this was already beginning to come through.

After the war he spent a year at Ruskin College, Oxford. Over a long political career in the city he was to prove himself a great civic statesman. Much is owed to him in the way of reconstruction in the period after the war, when Coventry moved forward with a vigour that was not always visible elsewhere. In his earlier years he had a raw edge to him which he has now lost. He was so much more forceful than those around him that it was inevitable that he should come to the top, for he had a terrible intensity of purpose. Those who know him now must find it difficult to comprehend the authentic George Hodgkinson of earlier years; they have never known the spell of the magician, never known his poise and skill as a chairman, never known his force in stating a case to an audience; they have never heard the lion roar, seen the chin jutting forward, seen him hold a meeting in the hollow of his hand.

The quiet, modest and unassuming Sidney Stringer (1889–1969) had become chairman of Coventry Borough Labour Party in 1932. In the same year those qualities of moderation and willingness to take account of other points of view took him to the presidency of the local Co-operative Society. He had joined the Labour group on the Council at the municipal election of 1929 but he was by no means its most prominent member. Few people could then have realised that he would be leader of a Labour majority on the Council by 1938 until that majority disappeared in 1967. He was never the first with any great idea but he always knew with an unerring instinct which of other people's ideas would ultimately command the greatest possible support. He was never a great orator but at his best could speak with resounding commonsense, which would bring most people of goodwill to his side. By avoiding extremes and always remembering that he had to think of his city as well as of his party he gave the Council a long period of steady and progressive government.

The Stringer family was one of those exceptional homes which produced so many of the pioneers of the Labour and trade-union movements in the days when sacrifice was often called for and hardship to be expected. His father was a baker with a shop near the Cook Street Gate. He was a Radical and a reader of *Reynolds News*, a paper founded by one of the last of the Chartists. He followed his paper in opposing the Boer War and held fierce political arguments with his customers, a habit which cannot have done his business much good. Besides being a keen radical politician he read Dickens and Shakespeare, used to give his customers nicknames from his favourite authors and when ill in bed asked the young Sidney to read to him. He was obviously a remarkable man, bringing up his children to love books and to be diligent attenders at the excellent classes provided by the local Co-operative Society on winter evenings. His large family had cause to be grateful for the comfortable home and careful beginnings which he and his wife gave all their children. Sidney early became a Socialist, joined the I.L.P., was a shop-steward during the First World War and afterwards suffered a great many hardships during the lean post-war years. He had a part in the 1922 strike, although not a very prominent one, and was admirably prepared for public service when the opportunity came. He would no doubt have been astonished by it, but he was the true representative of the tradition of George Poole, himself born in the city and himself a moderate man.

V

During its thirty years of control of the City Council from 1937 the Labour Party was to bring about a significant change in the quality of local government in Coventry. This is not to say that they made it either better or worse, but simply that they brought it one stage nearer than it had been to the lives of the ordinary citizens. There had been good councillors before Sidney Stringer and George Hodgkinson, men who had often favoured particular acts of municipal enterprise, such as the municipal abattoir and Isolation Hospital of 1932, or the construction of Trinity Street, the Bill for which went to Parliament in 1930. Nor, early in 1937, was the Labour party left as unsupported as is sometimes supposed in pressing for a minimum wage of £3 a week for all Corporation employees. Nevertheless, it remains true that, in November 1937, as a result of the municipal elections, the Council passed under the control of men who believed that they were the representatives of the people in a way in which their predecessors had not. They had faced struggle and hardship and had found wisdom the hard way. Now they had to exercise power on behalf of their fellow citizens. This was to be done by a new and unprecedented emphasis on party in the conduct of the city's local government.

It happened that 1937 was a year in which half the aldermen on the Council were due for re-election. These elections had been largely a matter of form, since aldermen had been created according to their length of service on the Council, but now it was shown that times had changed. Of the seven retiring aldermen, only Colonel Wyley was left undisturbed. The other six, including Vincent Wyles of the Conservatives and Charles Payne of the Liberals, were replaced by Labour members. This dramatic break with the past involved yet another. Among the dispossessed aldermen was Arthur Barnacle, who had been Mayor in 1936–7 and, according to custom, should now have been appointed Deputy Mayor. The Labour councillors refused to follow this tradition and appointed Sidney Stringer instead. Party politics had arrived in Coventry municipal government. There were cheers and counter-cheers as the retired aldermen walked out of the annual meeting of the Council at St Mary's Hall on 9 November 1937. It was not so easy then as it is now to see that what was really beginning was a new attempt to solve an old problem, that of securing the co-ordination of all sections of a large local authority. The Labour Party was about to do this by giving its party group on the City Council a power and coherence which had not previously been seen in Coventry.

It was to prove fortunate that the three principal administrative posts had all changed hands in the early 1920s and were occupied by able men of about the same age whose partnership was to be unbroken until the worst of the Second World War was over. Frederick Smith became Town Clerk in 1924 and remained such until 1946; Sydney Larkin became City Treasurer in 1922 and retired in 1944, while Ernest Hone Ford was City Engineer between 1924 and 1947.

When Frederick Smith (1881–1956) became Town Clerk of Coventry he had successfully completed a journey which had always been difficult and sometimes precarious. His father had been born at Fillongley in the country near the city, but had moved into Coventry to keep a small general shop in New Buildings near the centre and to supply milk to the neighbouring shopkeepers. At one time after leaving Bablake, this quiet, rather melancholy young man appears to have wanted to become a clergyman. He decided instead to work for the City Council, first in the City Engineer's Department and later transferring to that of the Town Clerk, because he wanted to become a solicitor. There he met with no help from

George Sutton, Coventry's second full-time Town Clerk,[15] and himself a former charity-schoolboy. Sutton refused to give Frederick Smith his articles, kept him as a Committee Clerk and raised no opposition when he departed for service in the First World War. There he did well, became a captain and returned to his old office in 1919.

Smith became Deputy Town Clerk to Sutton, whom he succeeded in 1924. A decent, liberal-minded man, he played the game according to the rules, and was not always at his best in dealing with those who did not, such as the Earl of Dudley and Alderman William Halliwell. His deep love of the city's history, particularly that of the rich trading community of the Middle Ages, gave him a real sense of his own obligation towards the planning of the new Coventry which was rising around him. When Labour representation increased significantly after 1928 and became a majority in 1937, his quiet manner and obvious civic patriotism conquered most of the new men and earned their respect; he was indeed a very good Town Clerk.

When Sydney Larkin (1884–1948) came to Coventry in 1919 as Assistant Treasurer he had already laid the foundations of a distinguished career. Born in Lichfield and educated at the Grammar School there and later at King Edward VI School at Birmingham, he had taken a degree and been classified first in his year for the examinations of the professional institute. After he became Treasurer in 1922 he showed himself a reformer and pioneer. He was well ahead of his time in the use of office machinery, responsible for the issue of Coventry local bonds and the creator of the capital fund. He and his successor, A. H. Marshall, played a great part in ensuring a high standard of efficiency in local finance departments today. He was a breaker of images, ruthless in his criticism, a stimulating companion to those for whom he had respect, a biting and witty opponent of those for whom he did not. Sydney Larkin might seem to be the last man able to establish an understanding with working-class Labour representatives but many of them liked him very much

[15] When the City Council decided to appoint a full-time Town Clerk in 1893 it first appointed Lewis Beard, who had been employed in the office of Frederick Browett, solicitor and part-time Town Clerk. Sutton had come to the Council House with Beard.

and owed more than they would admit to the advice of this wise, mordant and rather fastidious intellectual.

Ernest Hone Ford (1884–1955) was a Black Country man, born at Bloxwich, near Walsall, where his father seems to have had a share in one of the small coal-mines which abounded in that part of the world. With this industrial background it was perhaps natural that Ford should turn to engineering and for a long time he worked in the office of the Borough Surveyor at Walsall where he had been articled. When it came to dealing with old buildings, of which there were many in Coventry during his time, he showed the sensitivity and understanding of an artist and his enthusiasm for the city's history rivalled that of Frederick Smith. This was particularly illustrated by the loving care with which he arranged for the restoration of St Mary's Hall after it had been damaged during the Second World War. As City Engineer he was in charge of the department which had the greatest opportunity of leaving its mark on the development of the growing city as the planning, construction and maintenance of the city's roads, with its drainage and sewers, were all his responsibility. Until the appointment of a City Architect in 1938 he had some share in the design of council houses and, until that same important date, was unchallenged in his control of whatever planning legislation then existed. The latter part of his tenure is mentioned more fully elsewhere, but among his earlier monuments are Corporation Street, Trinity Street and the great by-pass to the south of the city which links the London and Birmingham roads.

Sydney Larkin and Frederick Smith were both succeeded by their deputies when the time came for a further change of chief officers. Dr A. H. Marshall (b. 1904) had been Deputy City Treasurer since 1935 and had formed a firm friendship with his gifted chief, whose progressive administrative outlook he shared and whose work in building up the reputation of the Coventry office he was to continue. While City Treasurer he was invited by the British Government to visit the Sudan and later British Guiana, Kenya and Uganda to give advice to these countries on the development of their machinery of local government. He is now (1971) at the University of Birmingham as Associate Director of Local Government Studies and has served on the Maude Commission which reported in 1969.

Charles, later Sir Charles, Barratt (1910–71) had arrived as Deputy to Frederick Smith in 1941. Five years later he succeeded him as Town Clerk and was from the very beginning deeply immersed in problems of civic reconstruction. The Coventry Plan was a particularly ambitious one, involving great use of powers of compulsory purchase, and there were many personal and other difficulties to be ironed out. The city owed a lot to this quiet, talented Yorkshireman with his special gift for acting as moderator and chairman. Towards the end of his period of office he was much concerned with the creation of the University of Warwick and between 1961 and 1965 he acted as Secretary to both its Promotion Committee and Academic Planning Board. Throughout this period he was also steadily encouraging the development of general management within the rapidly growing city administration.

In the theory of traditional local government each department was independent, responsible to its own Committee, recruiting its own staff and pursuing its own policy. In practice, however, a high degree of coherence had already been achieved in Coventry before 1937, simply because Frederick Smith, Sydney Larkin and Ernest Ford were men of similar outlook who worked together very well. The importance of the Town Clerk in achieving co-ordination between departments had long been recognised, partly because such co-ordination had in fact already been occurring. Charles Barratt became Town Clerk at a time when this would have to be formalised because issues which involved more than one department were growing in both size and number. His work in civic reconstruction gave him invaluable experience in bringing together the work of various departments and further developments came after a Treasury Organisation and Methods team examined the workings of the city administration and published its reports at the end of 1953. In February 1954 the Council declared that the Town Clerk was also to be the Chief Administrative Officer and set up an Establishment Committee which was to take over the recruitment of most staff, as well as providing method services to watch over the efficiency of other Corporation departments.

For the next few years the story was one of gradual development as the Chief Administrative Officer learned what tools he would need in order to make his new appointment a reality. In 1966 came a further step forward when the traditional statutory duties of the Town Clerk were made the province of his deputy, now given the title of Associate Town Clerk. This left the Town Clerk himself free for the general co-ordination implied in his new title of Chief Executive Officer. In 1967 the Policy Advisory Committee, which had tended to deal mainly with disputes between Committees, was given greater powers and became the Policy Committee. The Town Clerk was given the right to take any matter having policy implications direct to the Policy Committee before it had been dealt with by the Committee immediately concerned. A year later came a further step. Sir Charles Barratt was shortly to retire and those concerned realised that his successor need not necessarily be a lawyer. In October 1969 he was succeeded as Chief Executive Officer by J. D. Hender, the former City Treasurer.

CHAPTER EIGHT

Housing and other Services

The housing problem in Coventry, before and after the war. The squatters. The caravan sites. Size of the problem. The magnitude of the effort. The large new estates and their problems. Tower blocks. Rents. Other services, such as water, drainage, transport, markets and airports.

I

In the last thirty years of the nineteenth century the business and professional men of the great industrial cities began to move more rapidly towards solving the problems of urban living which industrial development and the rising population had bequeathed to them. Instruments to their hand were two; the elective town councils which they had been allowed to set up under the Municipal Corporations Act of 1835, and the private Act of Parliament which they could use to give themselves additional powers. Many new councils had, at first, been very little more than police authorities. Now, such was the strength of this new wave of interest in the community, they began to administer water undertakings, gasworks and street lighting and cleansing. Undoubtedly the greatest single monument of this period was Joseph Chamberlain's term of office as Liberal Mayor of Birmingham between 1873 and 1878 but even in smaller authorities such as Coventry enthusiastic new men such as William Wyley were touched by the reforming spirit.

As early as 1870 sixty-nine local authorities were in control of their own waterworks and forty-nine of their own gas undertakings; but it was in the twentieth century that municipal enterprise rose to its height of complexity and daring. Great English cities such as

Birmingham, Manchester, and Sheffield reached into the valleys of Wales, Cumberland, and Derbyshire in order to create large artificial lakes which would furnish their factories and homes with water, and burrowed into their own soil to lay down a regular pattern of mains and cables which would guarantee them power and light and dispose of the waste products of industry and the home. Coventry was, in some ways, more fortunate than other large cities in that its great burst of industrial development came later than most. The earlier experiences and mistakes of other authorities were there to be drawn upon, and the machinery for securing guidance and advice from central government was more developed. It, nevertheless, remained true that responsibilities in this expanding community would, of necessity, fall upon the City Council.

Of all the needs which drove enlightened men to action, that of providing each home in our cities with a supply of pure water was perhaps the most important. Coventry was a small city in the early nineteenth century, but it had no less than thirty wells[1] and other points, all in the custody of the Corporation, from which water could be obtained free. Danger to health was by no means absent, but at least there was no private water company to be bought out. Even the waterworks which existed at the Swanswell to supply Hillfields was on lease from the Corporation. When the pressure of rising population in the first half of the last century brought a demand for piped water, further wells were sunk in the western part of the city. These wells are still active, and the water they produce is among the best which Coventry uses, but they could not keep pace with the increasing demand. By 1847 a small pumping-station was already needed and this was established beside the river Sherbourne, in the district of Spon End.

By the end of the nineteenth century the population was already beginning to press hard upon these available sources of water. In 1895, therefore, a new pumping-station was opened at Whitley, but it was clearly necessary to look a good deal further ahead. Charles Hawksley, an eminent consulting engineer, was employed to forecast the city's growth and future needs. He reported in 1905 that, by 1951, the city's population would be 98,800 and its daily consumption

[1] The memory of some of these has been preserved in such street names as Well Street and Jordan Well.

of water, 2,667,600 gallons. Since, in 1908, the Corporation concluded an agreement with Birmingham which gave it a guarantee of nearly four millions a day, the future seemed to present no problems. However, the Hawksley estimate of the city's population in 1951 was actually exceeded by 1911, and his estimate of the 1951 daily consumption by 1918. A serious crisis was prevented by drawing more heavily on Birmingham than had originally been intended, but it was obvious that something would have to be done to enable Coventry to stand on its own feet.

In 1921 the city used 1068 million gallons and in 1931, 1671 million. A new and comprehensive scheme was obviously called for and, in 1938, the city presented a Bill in Parliament which would give it authority to take up to ten million gallons a day from the river Severn. In September of that year, however, the outbreak of war halted the scheme. During the war years the city had to make emergency arrangements, and in 1941 it began taking and treating water from the river Avon. The Severn Scheme was taken up again after the war, but it was not until April 1953 that the new waterworks at Strensham was actually opened with an initial capacity of six million gallons a day. Further extensions have taken place since, so that, in 1965, Strensham was handling fifteen million gallons a day at a time when the city's consumption was reaching an annual total of 6360 million gallons.

The Water Undertaking still remains the responsibility of the City Council, although its work is now carefully co-ordinated with that of neighbouring undertakings as part of a national attempt to provide all parts of the country with a piped water supply. One of the reasons which has brought this about has been the need to meet the increasingly heavy demands of industry. Another has been the steady rise of consumption per head of population, due to an increase in personal and domestic cleanliness and the use of water for new purposes such as the washing of cars.[2]

A scheme such as that for obtaining Severn water, with its initial capital cost of £2 million, would have been impossible without the spun cast iron pipe, steam and electrical pumping equipment and the isolation of bacteria. Science and industry came to supply the

[2] In 1951 the daily domestic consumption of water per head in Coventry was 19·36 gallons. By 1967 this had risen to 26·55 gallons.

answers to problems which they themselves had helped to create, and to furnish the means of securing a steady improvement in standards of public health. In some cities progress was held back by the dead hand of the past. London, for centuries our only large city, had made its sewers by the simple process of bricking over the tributaries of the Thames and, although this practice soon came to be regarded as primitive, it was not so easy to eliminate its effects. Coventry was more fortunate in that the principal developments in its main drainage and sewage-disposal schemes were to come well within the twentieth century.

In 1853 the city had driven its first main sewer from west to east with an outfall at Whitley into the river Sherbourne leaving all treatment to safeguard health in the hands of nature, where, in the last resort, it still rests. Thirty years later the first sewage works was built near by by a private company which intended to sell the treated product as agricultural fertiliser. The Whitley scheme failed, but many local authorities attempted to develop sewage farms until well into the 1920s. Coventry itself bought a farm at Baginton at the beginning of the twentieth century and was still using parts of it for broad irrigation treatment in 1932. But the increasingly dangerous qualities of industrial effluent have caused practically all local authorities to abandon the idea that their sewage works could, in any way, yield a profit.[3]

Oil, grease, cyanides and the by-products of electro-plating are obvious dangers, but an equal danger to public health might be presented by the effects of storm water. At one time it was felt necessary to provide every street with one sewer only into which could flow rainwater as well as the products of the kitchen and the bathroom. It was soon found that this could be highly dangerous to public health, since a sudden rush of storm water might easily exceed the capacity of the sewers and cause dangerous flooding. At present Coventry is working towards a complete separation between the water which is drained from the front gutters of the house and that which is drained from the back. The first is combined with

[3] Under the Public Health (Drainage of Trade Premises) Acts of 1937 and 1961 Coventry, like every large local authority, has extensive powers to guard against dangers arising from industrial effluents. Many of the larger factories have their own pre-treatment plants, and the city's inspectors keep a careful check upon what is discharged into the main sewers.

the rainwater which falls into the streets and empties into the adjacent brooks, the second is conveyed through a series of foul sewers into one of the three great trunk sewers which follow the valleys of the Sherbourne, the Sowe and the Canley Brook. The Canley Brook sewer was completed in 1934 and that along the Sowe valley in 1937.

All three are now being duplicated, and each has been provided with a storm balancing station intended to divert an excess of storm water into storage tanks, where it can be held until the pressure on the sewer subsides and no dangerous overflowing can result. These sewers each become ten feet wide as they converge on the Finham Sewage Works which the city first occupied in 1929. In 1932 it had a capacity of three million gallons per day. By 1951 this had increased fourfold. As the result of further development the treatment capacity of Finham is now twenty-four million gallons a day, slightly more than the present dry weather flow from the city.

In 1884 Coventry became one of the local authorities controlling its own gas undertaking. The little works in Gas Street, which had been operated by a private company since 1820, had become increasingly unable to supply the city which was then moving towards the height of the cycle boom. In 1898 the Corporation bought a site at Foleshill for a much larger works, which they opened in 1909 and which was to prove invaluable during the First World War when consumption rose to 1800 million cubic feet per year. This output was to be greatly exceeded during the Second World War when, in 1944, 4213 million cubic feet were produced. In both wars industry was the greatest customer, taking 50 per cent of output in the First and 60 per cent in the Second. Many of the new factories were situated around the edge of the city and the Coventry undertaking was one of the first to lay a ring main with gas at high pressure to supply these industries.

When the undertaking was nationalised under the Gas Act of 1948 street and household lighting by gas had not entirely ceased. Both tended to be found in the poorer areas of the city and the Corporation had, for many years, lit half its council houses by gas and half by electricity, since it ran both undertakings. Where gas has had an ascendancy, which it still maintains, was in its use for domestic cooking. Attempts were made, with some success, to increase the sale of gas fires and heaters for hot water, but in 1936, of 62,968 consumers, 42,649 were renting cookers. In 1947 the number of consumers had risen to 75,195 but the number of ovens on hire had fallen to 40,312. By that time electricity was becoming a serious competitor.

The Corporation no longer owns the power station which generates the current to light the city's roads and streets, but it must erect the lamp standards and plan the lighting. The Corporation first established a generating station in Sandy Lane in 1895 under an Order made by the Board of Trade within the terms of the Electricity Acts of 1882 and 1888. The first use of electricity in Coventry was to provide street lighting along the road from the railway station to Broadgate, while leaving the rest of the streets still lit by gas. Private customers came along gradually, and probably the first shop to be lit by electricity was that of T. H. Welton, one of the long-established local chemists, in the High Street. In those days factories were powered by steam or gas engines and homes used a gas-stove or open range for cooking. It was between the wars that new factories began to use electricity and that the central government gave increasing attention to the problem of providing British industry with this most up to date of all forms of power. In 1928 Coventry Corporation established a large new electricity power station at Longford and this became one of the designated stations under the national grid which was created by the Electricity Supply Act of 1926. The city's consumption of electricity had been 26,134,570 units in 1922. This figure had almost quadrupled by 1933. Then came a tremendous expansion in order to meet the needs of rearmament; the station's total capacity, which had been 38,500 kilowatts in 1928, was dramatically raised to 100,000 in 1938. After the war this rise was to continue unimpeded until the responsibility for providing the service passed to the East Midlands Electricity Board in 1948.

The Coventry Electric Tramways Company, which was purchased by the Corporation in 1912, had begun in 1882 by operating a steam tramway from the station on the south side of the city to Bedworth in the north. Some people still alive can remember those trams and the difficulties they had in climbing hills. By 1912 steam trams had long ceased, and the company had turned to electricity for power. They had opened up several new routes and this policy was continued by the Corporation. In 1935 a fleet of 55 tramcars and 95 petrol-driven buses transported about 37 million fare-paying passengers throughout the city. The numbers of vehicles show that Coventry was already sharing in the nationwide reaction against trams. The complete destruction of tracks in the air raid of 14 November 1940 meant that trams were completely abandoned. By 1949/50 the number of petrol-driven buses had risen to 304 and the number of fare-paying passengers was over 110 million. Since then, public transport has suffered more and more in all great cities from the competition of the private motor-car, but the number of fare-paying passengers conveyed in 1969/70 still stood at the considerable total of 74,260,168.

II

All these people travelling daily within the city had to live somewhere, and by 1970 nearly 27,000 families had found a home on one of the estates or in one of the blocks of flats owned and administered by Coventry Corporation. During the first three months of 1970 four out of every five houses being built in Coventry were being constructed for the Housing Committee of the City Council. This was a far cry from the days at the beginning of the century when the Council had reluctantly decided to build, as an experiment, seventy houses and flats in Short Street and Narrow Lane, to be let cheaply to families who had been moved out of slums but were unable to afford the few extra shillings demanded by private builders for better conditions.

This Council decision, taken in 1907, followed more than ten years of agitation in Coventry led by a number of middle-class philanthropists such as George Heaviside, the Unitarian Minister, and Malcolm Pridmore, a solicitor and member of the Council. They had been joined by Labour Party pioneers, such as George Poole and Hugh Farren. Coventry had been fortunate in missing most of the rapid industrialisation of the early nineteenth century which had transformed in a few years villages such as Birmingham and Manchester into cities with soaring population figures and closely packed, quickly built rows of houses which soon became overcrowded, unhealthy slums. Despite this, some of the homes described by Joseph Gutteridge[4] in the 1860s must have approached, if on a smaller scale, the conditions of the larger cities. It was, however, the bicycle boom which brought the real problem of inadequate housing to Coventry. Thousands of people pouring into the city were forced to live in the small, dark, overcrowded courts which had earlier been built on the gardens of the houses of a more spacious age.

This development of new slums in Coventry coincided with a national reawakening of concern about the effect of overcrowding and lack of sanitation on public health and, therefore, upon the industrial production of the country, and in 1890 a Housing Act was passed by Parliament. This permitted local authorities, if they so chose, to build houses to let to families who had lost their homes due to slum-clearance schemes. Within a few years of the passing of this Act meetings were being held in Coventry and resolutions passed asking that the Council take some action to provide houses for the working classes. Little resulted from all this, despite a report drawn up by a Special Committee of the Council in May 1899 recommending that 'as soon as the Council becomes possessed of a suitable plot of land at a reasonable cost an experiment be made by erecting dwellings of from two to three rooms to be let at rents of about 2/6*d.* and 3/6*d.* a week under regulations to secure their proper and legitimate use'.

In 1901 the Coventry Housing Reform Council led by Hugh Farren and George Poole laid two resolutions before the City Council drawing its attention to the need for an improvement in living conditions and unsuccessfully urging an official inquiry into the extent of overcrowding and lack of sanitation in the city. It was five years after this, however, that George Poole finally carried a motion in the Council pledging it to definite action, and only in 1907 that the Council put aside its fear of increased rates sufficiently to agree to the building of twenty-two tenements in Short Street and forty-eight houses in Narrow Lane. In an attempt to justify this rash move an editorial in the *Coventry Herald*

[4] See Chapter One, page 4.

emphasised that the Committee 'believe that there will be no charge on the rates'.[5]

George Poole's activity in the field of housing was not confined to his work on the City Council. In 1911 he joined with Tom Cash, a member of the silk weaving family, to set up an organisation to build a garden city at Radford. Seven years earlier Ebenezer Howard and Raymond Unwin had embarked on a new way of building a housing estate at Letchworth. Coventry was growing and seemed likely to go on growing and a garden suburb on the lines proposed by Howard and Unwin seemed an excellent idea. In 1911, however, it proved impossible to find enough money to enable a start to be made on the scheme and only when Coventry Co-operative Society offered to back the idea by giving the founders £8000 just before the beginning of the First World War could work begin.

As the First World War brought more and more people crowding into Coventry for war work, central government was forced to step in to help finance and build row upon row of cottages and hostels near the new factories to the north of the city. The coming of peace in 1918 brought no easing of the problem and it soon became clear that local government would have to continue to help to provide houses in large numbers for those who could not afford, or even find, houses to buy or rent from private landlords. During the years of economic depression the scope of local authority housing was greatly extended. Under the 1923 Housing Act, with support from central government subsidies, they were empowered to make loans to private builders and to give guarantees to building societies on behalf of both individuals and groups of people who wanted to buy their own homes.[6] Armed with these wider powers the Council began to build its first great housing estate. In 1924 over 138 acres

[5] These two estates proved so successful that only three years later it was decided to extend the estate at Narrow Lane. It was fitting that one of the roads in this extension should be called after Malcolm Pridmore, who had been first Chairman of the Housing Committee and a tireless worker alongside the Labour Party and Trades Council in attempts to foster Corporation housing in Coventry.

[6] One such organisation in Coventry was the Workmen's Housing Association which wanted to build 406 houses at Rowley's Green in Foleshill in the early 1930s. It seems to have run into difficulties, however, and little is known of the results of this venture.

of land was set aside for housing at Radford and before the beginning of the Second World War nearly 2500 terraced houses had been built on the estate. By the end of March 1926 the Corporation owned over 2000 houses, had guaranteed over £10,600 to building societies on behalf of people buying their own homes and had subsidised nearly 700 houses built by private builders.

In 1927, however, there were still 5500 people on the waiting list for a Corporation house and it was estimated that 15,000 houses would be needed over the next ten years if Coventry's supply of homes was to be adequate for her needs. The problem was made worse in 1930 when the Labour Government passed a Housing Act which required every local housing authority to draw up a five-year programme of slum-clearance. During the twenties little had been done in this field, perhaps because it was considered that during this period of shortage any house, however bad, was better than none. The Act also made it necessary for a local authority, with government help, to provide alternative accommodation at a rent which could be afforded by families moved out of these slums.

Coventry was no exception to the need for slum-clearance, especially in the city centre. In St John's Street, for instance, the death-rate from tuberculosis was more than eight times the figure for Coventry as a whole, and in Much Park Street the infant mortality rate was more than four times that for the city. There were over 1000 slum houses to be demolished in Coventry before 1938 according to the city's five-year programme, which meant that large estates would have to be built to provide for the people made homeless. The first of the slum rehousing schemes was at Stoke Aldermoor, but before the Second World War an even larger slum-clearance rehousing area was begun at Canley, very near the site of an ordinary housing scheme at Charter Avenue.[7]

Between 1933 and 1936 private builders and building societies made remarkable efforts to provide workers with houses for sale on easy terms.[8] As war drew nearer manufacturers who had workers to

[7] These slum rehousing estates were under the control, not of the Housing Committee, but of the Public Health Committee.

[8] In 1936, 3841 houses were completed in the city. See also Chapter Two, page 61.

accommodate felt that this was not enough. They told the Housing Committee that they regarded it as essential that the Council should provide yet more houses for letting. Private enterprise, although providing about 3000 houses a year, was building mainly for selling, and the number of those able to buy their own house was limited as the building boom of the mid-thirties came to an end. However, as early as 1936, the Corporation had found that, if they were only to keep pace with their slum-clearance programme, 300 houses would have to be built each year; a further 200 homes were needed to re-house those living in overcrowded conditions and on top of this an ordinary housing programme had to be fulfilled. In 1937 the Medical Officer of Health reported that the city's population had increased by about 14,000 in the previous year, representing a demand for about 4000 houses, with the rate of increase growing every year. On the basis of this report the Housing Committee concluded that, despite rising costs and Coventry's perennial shortage of building labour, the Corporation should try to build a thousand homes a year. With the Radford scheme completed, attention was turned to the west of the city near the new factories of Coventry Gauge and Tool, Wickman's and Standard. Here at Canley it was planned to build an estate of 1000 houses.[9]

This great spate of activity was brought to a sudden halt in the first days of war. House-building throughout the country was immediately stopped and, although Coventry Corporation was allowed to continue and later tried to produce its own hostels for war workers, the situation was soon made drastically worse by the enemy air raids of the last few months of 1940. By January 1941 it was estimated that two out of three properties in the city had been damaged and nearly 8500 houses had been demolished or too seriously damaged to be repaired. Slaters and bricklayers were rushed into the city and an emergency housing programme was quickly drawn up. By the end of 1941 even this was being held up because of lack of labour, and the amount of house-building being done had to be drastically cut; hostels[10] and houses were abandoned with only the foundations dug, other houses which had already reached first-

[9] This number was later cut by the Council to 500.

[10] From 1941 onwards the housing of war workers depended largely on the National Service Hostels Corporation. See Chapter Three, page 93.

floor level had flat concrete roofs put on and were used as bungalows with a staircase leading nowhere in the hallway, and others nearly finished were merely covered over and left.

As it became clear that the war would soon come to an end the Government embarked on the building of thousands of bungalows made very often from sheets of aluminium in factories no longer needed for war production. These prefabricated sections would then merely be fitted together on the site. In 1948 Coventry Corporation had 1096 of these dwellings which were often compact, well fitted and surprisingly warm. They were let to families who would otherwise have been homeless. For those who were not so lucky the only solution was to take possession of a hut on a disused army site or to live in a caravan on one of the bombed sites in the city centre and this they did in their hundreds. On 13 August 1946 seven families chalked their names on the doors of huts at an old army camp at Fillongley and began to arrange for their furniture to arrive. Within a few hours a baker and a milkman had called at the camp seeking trade. A few days later a party of about forty families with every conceivable furniture-carrying vehicle took possession of a former anti-aircraft gun site on Tile Hill Lane. The tenants there soon formed an association with an elected chairman and secretary and arrangements were made for sums of money to be set aside every week to help in the organisation of the camp. By 23 August it was estimated that there were about 250 squatters on military sites around the city and about 400 more in hostels.

The squatters fell into two categories. There were those who had tried but had been unable to find anywhere else in which they could afford to live, but there were also those who had heard that there was free accommodation to be had and had come to the camps merely because of this. The conditions in which some were living were appalling. Cecil Dodson, who came to the city as Housing Officer in 1946, has described leaving Wyken Croft camp one evening when he saw smoke coming from the middle of a field on the edge of the site. Going closer he saw that it came from a stove pipe poking up from the middle of a grass-covered mound, which turned out to have been one of the air-raid shelters for gun crews. It was in fact little more than a hole in the ground, yet here were living husband, wife and eleven children. Dodson was able to send them to rooms in the NAAFI where they could stay until something better could be found for them.

At first the Government refused to recognise the squatters but by the end of 1946, when there were about 50,000 scattered all over the country, the Ministry of Health suggested that local authorities should take over the sites in order to reduce the risk of epidemics and to provide some of the basic necessities such as fuel and water. Electricity had been cut off as bills were not paid and, because squatting was illegal, fuel permits had been refused. With the take-over of the camps by local authorities conditions improved. They were able to put in squatters they knew to be genuine cases of hardship, reducing the numbers of those who had come merely to take advantage of the camps. Fuel and electricity supplies and charges for these were organised so that heating and hot meals were possible, and, with the Government supplying the materials, the men living in the camps dug drains and trenches, laid pipes and fitted sinks in the huts. An army hut divided into a bedroom and living-room by a wooden partition and surrounded by a sea of mud was no place for a family to live for long, but it was not until 1950 that the worst two camps, Howes Lane and the Memorial Park, were cleared. The 'Shanty Town' which had grown up on Little Park Street still had people living in it in caravans and railway carriages in 1953, and the last family was not rehoused from the last (Cheylesmore) hostel until the late 1950s.

III

The existence of the squatters was a reminder that the housing situation after the war was desperate. Three and a half million houses had been damaged and of these about 250,000 were uninhabitable, while 200,000 had been completely destroyed. Few private builders wanted to provide houses for letting and local authorities would certainly have to do most of the work in tackling the problem. Even they, however, could not create labour or materials which did not exist and had to accept wartime controls. Progress was, therefore, bound to be slow. A number of experimental houses using steel and concrete were erected in Coventry but the Housing Committee favoured brick-built houses with two or three bedrooms as permanent homes. Local builders were linked together in groups and each group was assigned an area for building. But, despite this, the problem remained formidable and progress desperately slow. By 1947 the number of those on the waiting list was 13,300 and a year later it had reached 14,200 but, between 1945 and October 1947, only 1000 'prefabs' and 147 permanent houses had been completed.

It was at this time that three men came together who were to revolutionise the Corporation's house building programme over the next ten years. The first was Councillor William Thomson, who became Chairman of the Housing Committee in 1949. He was a man ready to take risks and full of concern for those for whom he was determined to find homes as quickly as possible. He found a similar enthusiasm and determination in William Sheridan, his Vice-Chairman, and Cecil Dodson, the Housing Officer, who had come to Coventry three years earlier from a similar job in his home town of Leyton in Essex. Together these three men were able to fire their Committee and the Council with their own conviction that, despite all the obstacles, the problem could be solved. They saw that the two great difficulties holding back the building programme were lack of materials and lack of men. In an attempt to solve them, members of the Committee travelled all over the country looking at houses built in non-traditional ways by different authorities. They returned to Coventry with two systems of building which they thought would be worth trying out. After experimenting with both, it was decided to give a much larger contract to one of the firms, George Wimpey's, a large national concern able to import into the city enough men accustomed to using their 'no-fines' system to enable large numbers of houses to be built quickly and cheaply but to a high standard.[11]

The Housing Committee soon realised that, if this one firm could be given really large orders for houses, they could be built at even lower cost. Since time was the all-important factor, Wimpeys agreed to pay the rent of any house which was not ready by the promised

[11] The 'no-fines' system is a method of mixing concrete and aggregate rock to create a mixture filled with pockets of air to provide insulation. It was poured between wooden shutters which were left for twenty-four hours before being removed. This made possible the construction of the shell of a house in three days.

delivery date, a penalty clause which has not yet had to be put into effect. The company started work at Stonebridge Highway early in 1950 and here the friendly relations which had already been built up between the Housing Committee and the company were deepened by the hard work and special interest taken in the job by the site foreman, Dan Jardine. Jardine was a big, but shy Scot. He was a man who rarely spoke but he was capable of getting that extra ounce of effort from the men who worked under him. He could always be depended upon when the situation was really desperate to somehow have one or two houses ready before time. The affection in which he was held by the people whose houses he built and the Council for whom he built them is shown in the naming after him of a crescent on the Tile Hill estate, the second of the Corporation estates on which he worked.

The 350-acre estate at Tile Hill to the west of the city centre was the first to be built in Coventry on the principle of the neighbourhood unit. Before the Second World War large council estates had been built at Radford and Canley, but little provision had been made for those things which, it was hoped, would turn a housing estate into a community. A neighbourhood unit would be an estate large enough to support a community centre, shops, a primary school, public houses and churches and would contain houses and flats sufficiently varied to provide homes for single people, large families with children and old people living alone or in old people's homes. By the mid-fifties doubts were beginning to be raised as to whether or not this sort of planning really led to the development of any special sense of community. Most of the families on these early estates had moved from different parts of the city within a few months of each other so that it was not possible gradually to absorb newcomers into an already established community. Few of the promised amenities were actually built until long after most of the houses had been occupied, so that for their social activities and shopping people had to go outside the unit. Of course, in the early 1950s, the all-important thing had been to get families into houses away from the dirt, damp and overcrowding of camps, hostels and slums and people were moved into each house as soon as it was ready, regardless of whether or not pavements and roads were surfaced or shops and community centres built.

The Tile Hill estate had another feature which was absolutely new at the time. When its layout was being considered, the whole emphasis from the Ministry and throughout the country was on the building of family-type houses only. Coventry was advised that this was wrong, partly because many of the most desperate cases had only one child, did not need 1000 square feet of accommodation and could not afford to furnish it anyway, but, more important, it was adding to the imbalance of housing in the city which already consisted largely of three-bedroom terraced houses. Dodson had calculated what were the ideal proportions of dwellings needed by a community such as Coventry and the regional Ministry officials raised no objections. Tile Hill, therefore, provided, for the first time in a reasonably defined geographical area, dwellings of every kind, enabling families to move according to their needs without leaving their neighbourhood. At the same time the types of houses were properly distributed to give a spread of children over the estate so that, although it had a density of twenty-two dwellings per acre, the highest outside London at that time, it gave no sign of being overcrowded. The estate soon won national acclaim. In 1953 the *Architects' Journal* hailed it as having 'quite exceptional qualities in layout and design', adding that 'when completed (it) will surely be recognised as being second to none in the whole of England'. A year later the Ministry of Housing and Local Government gave it their Midland Area Housing Medal Award.[12]

The layout and appearance of the later estates differed widely as housing theory changed over the years. Willenhall Wood is one example of this, Woodway Lane another. Willenhall Wood, an estate of over 1000 houses built in the late fifties and early sixties, was the first of the Council estates in Coventry to use the Radburn layout, a system of building houses to face green spaces and footpaths with roadways and garages in cul-de-sacs at the back,[13] quite different from the more traditional layout at Tile Hill. As one of the early examples of this theory in Britain, Willenhall Wood aroused

[12] This was the second such award won by the Corporation since the war. The first was for part of the Monks Park estate.

[13] The name comes from the town of Radburn in New Jersey, U.S.A., where this idea was first put into practice in the 1930s. Willenhall Wood is, in fact, one variation of the principle.

a great deal of interest in planning circles and won a Civic Trust Amenity Design Award in 1960.

Willenhall Wood was the last of the really large estates to be built in Coventry and since the early 1960s housing design has concentrated on building smaller groups of dwellings where it may well be easier for new tenants to become part of the community. This has happened for instance at Whoberley and at Cheylesmore where about two hundred new houses have replaced post-war 'pre-fabs'. The open spaces in front of the houses of earlier estates have gone, to be replaced by high brick walls with narrow pavements between them. Family privacy has become as important a concern as was earlier the attempt to foster a community spirit.

As well as indicating a change in concepts of estate design this policy is also a reflection of the attempt to put more and more people into a smaller area without losing the privacy of the individual family and without giving a sense of overcrowding. It is as yet too early to assess whether or not the recent estates built at very high densities will achieve this purpose. One of these is Woodway Lane where 132 houses were built at a density of eighty people per acre. This was a pilot scheme for the Midland Housing Consortium which had been set up in 1963 in an attempt to cut local authority building costs by making possible bulk buying and designing on a really large scale. There are now ten authorities in the Consortium and the Woodway Lane scheme has been copied in many of them.

At the same time as Woodway Lane was being built other attempts were being made to conserve space by erecting tower blocks of flats. As early as 1953 three eleven-storey blocks had been constructed at Tile Hill, but the building of really tall flats began in earnest when, in 1960, the Ministry of Housing gave local authorities the advice to 'build upwards'. In order to encourage this, government subsidies for tower blocks were increased and Coventry eagerly developed its programme. By 1963 it had been decided to build what proved to be the first of many seventeen-storey blocks, Alpha House, at Barras Heath. It was thought that the bed-sitter and one-bedroom flats would appeal to old people and with this in mind an old-age pensioners' club was incorporated into the building to be run by the W.R.V.S. and financed by the Stoke Philanthropic

Society. Although an old people's club room has been included in many later blocks of flats, nowhere is the idea so highly developed as at Alpha House where lunch is provided every day and there are socials and concerts on most evenings.

Alpha House was the first tower block in the world to be built on the jack-block principle which enables the working conditions of a factory to be brought to a building site, thus preventing loss of building time through bad weather.[14] Other blocks of flats were later built on other principles. Naul's Mill House on the Radford Road was the tallest building in Europe to be completed by the lift slab system when it was finished in October 1964 and Longfield House on Bell Green Road was the first in the city to use the Trus-con method two years later.

Towards the end of the sixties national policy changed. Tower blocks were very expensive to build and, it had been found, saved very little land as they needed a certain amount of open space around them. In Coventry it was proving so difficult to let high flats that, in 1968, the residential waiting qualification was reduced from three years to one for those willing to live above the sixth floor. The Ronan Point disaster of 1969[15] did little to encourage people to live high above the city, although none of the Coventry blocks were built on the Ronan Point principle.

It seemed that the traditional British dislike of living in high flats was reasserting itself. Old people often tend to feel lonely in a huge block after a lifetime in a street of terraced houses, and mothers with young children find the height worrying when children have to travel down several storeys to get to a play area at ground level. Building costs were proving so high that, in order to make it possible to charge reasonable rents, interior finishes were sometimes skimped resulting in dingy entrance halls and draughty rooms. However spectacular such blocks appeared, it was decided when the generous national subsidies were cut, that no more tall flats should, for the time being, be included in the Coventry programme.

[14] By this system the roof and top storey are first built under cover at ground level and then raised into position by hydraulic jacks. The rest of the building follows in the same way.

[15] In 1969 part of a tower block in East London collapsed due, probably, to a gas explosion.

IV

By the end of the 1950s all the really large estates which were to be built in the city had at least been started and the housing situation presented a very different picture from that of the 1940s. The waiting list had dropped from over 14,000 in 1949 to 4700 in 1959 and, of these, few were cases of immediate hardship. The difficulties of building experienced immediately after the war had also disappeared, new materials were readily available and many prefabricated parts could be obtained from factories thus cutting down on the need for labour actually on the building site. The standards of local authority housing were improving all the time and the pattern of those coming to the Council to be housed was gradually changing.

In 1907 the level of Corporation rents had been kept down to about the same as that which people would expect to pay for rooms in slums, since those houses were designed to cater only for families which could afford nothing else. Wartime destruction in the forties had made it necessary to increase the scope of Corporation housing as local authorities were the only organisations large enough and backed by sufficient government funds to undertake the vast task of rebuilding. With the advent of a Labour Government in 1945 public housing became, under Aneurin Bevan, one of the most important parts of government policy. In 1949 the words 'for the working classes' were removed for the first time from the provisions of a Housing Act and authorities were encouraged to build homes for all types of people. Bevan's dream of housing estates in which both rich and poor would live side by side did not in fact come into being but more recent changes in pay structures and standards of housing have, perhaps, gone some way to bringing his dream nearer reality.

Of the families who had moved into council houses in the late 1940s many by the 1950s had grown-up children who were bringing additional money into the home. Many wives were working and wages in Coventry were booming. Living standards were rising rapidly and, like everyone else, many council tenants were able to afford things which would have been unheard of ten years before. In 1950 a survey of part of the Tile Hill Estate was done on behalf of the Council. It was discovered that, as early as this, the wages of those interviewed on the estate varied considerably from £6 a week to over £15 which would be among the highest weekly wages in the city at the time. Later social surveys showed the percentage of car-ownership increasing from 25 per cent in Tile Hill in the mid-fifties to 50 per cent at Willenhall in 1963. In the same year Woodway Lane became the first estate to be built for the Corporation with one garage and one parking space to each house.

Despite this apparent affluence, however, many families worked on a very tight budget and any increase in rent hit the well-off with their hire-purchase commitments and their higher standard of living as much as the poorer tenants. Between 1945 and 1959 the net cost to the Corporation of its housing rose from £29,000 to £139,000. As early as 1946 the higher rents made necessary by this huge increase in costs were causing anxiety in the Housing Committee. It was pointed out that families living in post-war houses were paying rents far higher than those living in pre-war houses of the same type because rent was based on construction costs. In February 1948 fears were expressed that rents based on costs would be so high that it would become 'impossible to let houses to those with low income'. Despite this, it was not until 1953 that costs had begun to fall and numbers of houses had grown sufficiently for the Council to consider equalising rents for houses with the same sort of amenities and of a similar size regardless of the cost involved in their building.

Rents were gradually raised by the Corporation in attempts to offset to some extent the increases in costs. But these increases in rent raised storms of protest from tenants. By 1967 the Council was losing £8000 a week on the housing account and, in order to eliminate this deficit, it was decided to raise rents yet again, some by as much as 50 per cent. At the same time a rent rebate scheme was to be introduced.[16] In retaliation, rent rise boycotts were organised on some estates although few met with much success. Coventry's rent increase was, however, referred to the Prices and Incomes Board in November 1967 and five months later the Board reported that 'no rent should rise by more than 7*s*.6*d*. per week in any twelve months' period'.

16 This was a scheme whereby those with only a low income could have their rent reduced but only to a certain level.

Although many people could, in fact, afford an increase in their rent, others could not and, despite the rent rebate scheme, fears have recently been expressed that council rents are far above the pockets of those who are at present living in older and much cheaper accommodation near the centre of the city. As replanning proceeds so these people, many of whom pay not much more than £1 a week in rent, will find it increasingly difficult to find a home as cheap. In a housing survey made by the Department of Architecture and Planning in 1969 it was found that in some parts of the city, 48·25 per cent of the privately rented accommodation surveyed was let for less than £1·50p whereas only 9·7 per cent of the Corporation tenants were paying rents as low as this. On one estate, Wood End, 35·7 per cent of tenants were, in the period 1967–70, paying more than a quarter of their income in rent. Of course, much of the privately rented accommodation is in a much worse state of repair than any Corporation house, but, nevertheless, it is still fulfilling a need which as yet is not completely met by the Corporation.

At about the same time as the most recent rent increases were being discussed, the Corporation introduced a scheme whereby tenants would be able to buy their homes with the aid of 100 per cent mortgages from the Housing Committee. This scheme came into operation in December 1967, and by July 1968 306 houses had been sold to their tenants. Since then the numbers sold have fluctuated considerably, reaching the high total of 631 in 1968–9. This scheme, however, was not the first time the Council had sold the houses they had built. Before the war some Corporation houses had been built for sale and in 1950 the Housing Superintendent had suggested selling some houses to their occupants in order to reduce the cost of housing to the rates and taxes. The Minister of Health refused to agree to the suggestion and it was not until 1958 that the Corporation decided once again to build houses specifically for sale. By March 1960 the first houses on the Belgrave estate at Wyken were ready to be sold and three years later the estate was completed, winning a Ministry of Housing and Local Government award for good design in that year. When the final costs were assessed, however, in 1966, it was shown that the scheme had in fact made a loss of over £15,000. It was an experiment which was not repeated.

The change in the type of people who were coming forward for council houses in the late 1950s necessitated a change in attitudes on the part of the Corporation. No longer was the Housing Department dealing with people who could not afford any other accommodation, but with a group of people who knew exactly what were their rights and obligations and who demanded to be treated as people rather than merely numbers on a housing list. Since the war the number of houses controlled by the Corporation had risen from 8000 in 1947 to 19,000 ten years later, on estates scattered all over the city. The Housing Officers were, therefore, becoming increasingly remote from the people who were their tenants. In an attempt to make landlord–tenant relations more personal it was decided to alter the administrative structure of the Department. The city was divided into five areas with about 5000 houses in each under the direct supervision of an Area Housing Officer who would thus have a better chance of getting to know the special problems and needs of his area. Despite the fact that these areas are still large and no one man can be expected to know all the tenants the introduction of the more personal element may well prove to be of advantage in giving tenants a small office which they can get to know and where their complaints and difficulties can be ironed out.[17]

It cannot be expected, however, that this administrative change alone could solve all the problems of the Corporation's tenants. When a family with young children gets into arrears of rent the Children's Officer is notified. In 1957 there were fifty such cases but in 1961 there were 300, and rent arrears is only one of the many problems facing the Housing Officers. Once it is accepted that council housing must be available for all, it follows that those who cannot find homes elsewhere will come to the local authority. Not all are stable families able to get on well with neighbours. Often a large number of children can cause annoyance without intending to, teenagers with few social facilities near by to catch their interest can cause more malicious damage and one family with more than ordinary problems can create an environment which others find difficult to tolerate. These problems are heightened in areas where housing has been built to a very high density and where play spaces

[17] At the same time the Housing Department gained its independence from the City Treasurer under whose ultimate control it had been since its inception over fifty years before.

are few and far between. To some extent, each new council estate with hundreds of people moved on to it all at the same time, many from bad housing conditions, has had these difficulties, but most have, within a few years, settled down and become pleasant, respectable residential areas. This has, however, not been true of all estates. One of these exceptions is Wood End.

Wood End, to the north of the city centre, is part of the Bell Green Estate and was built between 1954 and 1957. It seems to have been the estate in the city which suffered most from the effects of Harold Macmillan's promise in 1952 that within a few years the country would be building 300,000 houses a year. In order to achieve this as quickly as possible and without raising government subsidies too drastically standards of local authority housing were cut. The size of the average three-bedroomed council house, for instance, fell from 1050 square feet to 909 square feet between 1950 and 1954. Ebenezer Howard's idea of bringing country and town together was no longer in vogue; instead it was thought that building at really high densities preserved an exciting urban environment and this, together with a higher subsidy for four-storey development, led to the building of a considerable number of four-storey maisonettes at, among other places, Wood End. This led to concentrations of child population.[18]

When Wood End was being built the desperate cases on the housing waiting list arising from illness and war separation had, in the main, been dealt with and the families then being housed were those whose need arose almost entirely from overcrowding. They were often young couples with small children who were among the more feckless and improvident families on the waiting list. It is not income differences which create tensions between people, but differences of behaviour standards and aspirations. People with good standards of behaviour will readily sacrifice other things in order to live with people of the same standards. Where small estates were originally populated by the transfer of tenants willing to pay a much higher rent for a more modern house the tenants have remained almost constant, but, in areas like Wood End, where families were moving in, sometimes at the rate of fifty a week, these

[18] In 1966, 43·8 per cent of the population at Wood End was under ten years of age.

standards could not be maintained and those with high aspirations tended to move quickly out of the area.

In 1970 21 per cent of the 1800 tenants at Wood End were on the transfer list in order to move off the estate. This figure is kept as low as this because transfer can only be obtained after three years' residence or thirteen weeks free from arrears, conditions which many families in Wood End do not fulfil. In the same year 25 per cent of the tenants at Wood End were in arrears of rent. Recently, however, the local authority has begun to realise that this is merely an indication of the deeper difficulties of the estate and several studies have been made in order to try to find a way of improving the area. None of the studies have come up with a convincing answer. Altering the physical layout of the estate might be an improvement, but it will do nothing to help women left alone with a family of small children or those who, earning high wages, are unable to budget properly for their household expenses or parents who go out or work in the evenings leaving their children to do as they will. It is consideration of this type of problem which is now making the Housing Department more aware that its function is much wider than merely the construction of houses.

V

As well as developing large new estates a local authority can do much to improve the older parts of its city and in recent years the emphasis in Coventry has come to rest more and more on the concept of urban renewal. One of the ways in which this can be achieved is through improvement grants which will bring the living standards of the seventies into houses built in the early part of the century. Improvement grants had been available for some houses since 1948 but it was only in 1959 that a new Act simplified the scheme and, by 1970, over 12,400 such grants had been given in Coventry, ranging from providing a food store to converting a large house into flats.

Many of the local authority's own houses were, by the late 1960s, also falling far behind the standards of the new council houses and in some of the older areas, such as Stoke, house improvements were gradually made. A rather more ambitious scheme began in 1968 when Binley Village was declared to be one of three pilot schemes under the Government White Paper, *Old Houses into New Homes*. Five years earlier Binley Colliery had been closed and the 302 houses which had provided homes for many of the miners and their families since the 1920s were sold to the Corporation. Urgent repairs and modernisation were obviously necessary but, under the White Paper, it was decided to try to do something rather more extensive.

Instead of confining repairs to individual houses it was decided to try to improve the area as a whole by closing some roads to provide children's play areas, building garages and access roads behind the houses, planting trees and providing new employment on the site of the old colliery workings. People who had lived in the old village all their lives were naturally attached to their homes which were still structurally sound and perfectly habitable and it was hoped that this rehabilitation would be less unsettling than the destruction of the old village in order to build new blocks of flats or houses. Despite fears of rent increases beyond what most residents could well afford, the scheme appears to be going forward with their full co-operation, although it is, as yet, incomplete.

The Binley Village Scheme is one way in which older areas can be made attractive once more. Another is through the declaration of Areas of Comprehensive Development. Under the Town and Country Planning Act of 1944, the Minister could allow local authorities special powers to develop areas which had either been badly bombed or had been allowed to fall into decay. The development plan prepared in the late 1940s contained three such areas, the city centre, Hillfields and Spon End.[19] Although the Hillfields C.D.A. is over three times as large as that at Spon End, both areas have many things in common. Both were old industrial villages, Hillfields the centre of the silk weaving industry in the early nineteenth century, and Spon End the centre of watch- and later bicycle-making, and both had suffered severely through wartime bombing which had led to derelict bomb sites and neglected houses.

Work began in earnest on Hillfields and Spon End at the beginning of the 1960s. Possibly because the fact of imminent develop-

[19] For central redevelopment, see Chapter Ten.

ment was so widely known so long beforehand, few owners bothered to make improvements to their houses which were likely soon to be demolished. By 1961, therefore, it was estimated that 53 per cent of the houses in Hillfields and 75 per cent of those in Spon End were likely to be declared unfit within the next five years. At Spon End the developments of the early 1960s, the tower block of seventeen storeys and the smaller ten-storey blocks with their wide windows and balconies, now contrast sharply with the four-storey maisonettes built nearly ten years later around small squares on the other side of the river Sherbourne.

Neither Spon End nor Hillfields is yet complete. At Spon End there are still small pockets of old houses and shops and at Hillfields blocks of flats rise from the remnants of terraces of weavers' three-storey houses and the beginnings of attempts to landscape the ground around them. In Hillfields a community, which may have been disappearing in any case, seems to have been destroyed by the long process of planning, demolition and reconstruction and there have been several recent attempts to create something new to take its place. Towards the middle of 1969 Coventry Council of Churches decided to employ a full-time community development officer in Hillfields. His job would be to bring into being groups of local people who, after a time, should take over the organisation of their own activities.

A few months after this the Minister for Health and Social Security, Richard Crossman, announced that Hillfields was to become an area of social experiment. A family advice centre and research and action teams were set up closely co-ordinating their work with that of the officer of the Council of Churches. These teams tried to find out what was needed in the area and then stimulate the setting up and organisation of groups to tackle the problems. The number of multiracial playgroups was increased, old peoples' luncheon clubs started, young peoples' groups organised and, in June 1970, a neighbourhood newspaper was launched. Called the *Hillfields Voice*, it was aimed at giving local people an opportunity to air their own views and read articles which would inform them of future plans for the area.

By the spring of 1971 the community officers were beginning to work themselves out of a job. The residents' associations which they had begun were now able to organise their own activities. The *Hillfields Voice* was being run by local people and the Hillfields Community Association no longer consisted of a group of five or six professional people from outside the area but of representatives of the Indian and Pakistani communities who were living in the older houses, as well as Corporation tenants from the blocks of flats. The Association began to run its own meetings and employ its own staff to run nursery play-groups and adventure playgrounds. Despite the fact that Hillfields is an area of high social mobility and continuous physical change, a sense of identity with a group, if not with the community as a whole, may now be slowly emerging.

Since the 1950s the concept of Comprehensive Development Areas has been extended and Coventry now has twelve. Their size varies widely from only five acres along Queen Victoria Road near the city centre to ninety-five at Longford on the northern edge of the city. Most C.D.A.s are near, or to the north of the city centre where new road patterns and the reorganisation of industry away from residential areas means demolition and redevelopment of streets of houses, many of which are now growing old and falling into decay. This again means extensive new plans which, it is hoped, will provide a better environment for those living in the city.

VI

In 1867, when great Victorian towns were building great market halls, Coventry built a small one and adorned it with a market clock made by E. T. Loseby, a Leicester clockmaker who had served his apprenticeship in Coventry and who accepted a penalty clause of Draconian severity. He agreed to pay those who had commissioned him £1 for every second over one which the clock varied in any given day. It was in active working order until the Second World War.[20] By then the growth of the city had already caused considerable changes in its markets. At one time or another we hear of cattle, sheep and pigs being sold in Spon End and Gosford Street, horses in

[20] When the tower was taken down in 1942 because it was said no longer to be safe, the mechanism was carefully stored and is housed in the Godiva clock at the top of Hertford Street today.

Fleet Street, cheeses in Broadgate and crocks in the porch of St Michael's. From 1853 the sale of live animals was concentrated in an open-air market, the Smithfield, the site of which is commemorated in the name of a near-by hotel. Cattle and corn sales alike were bound to diminish as Coventry drew further from the country and the Smithfield finally closed in 1933 long after the Corn Exchange had become a cinema. A new municipal enterprise in this field was the abattoir which was opened in 1932.

The fruit and vegetable market was given a new home in 1922 when the City Council took over the Barracks from which, in 1792, the Dragoons had ridden away to the war with France. Retail trade was accommodated in open-sided stalls in the centre of the old parade ground and the Barracks buildings, such as the orderly room and the old military hospital, became quarters for wholesale firms. There retailers and wholesalers remained in cheerful confusion, often with over 500 lorries going in and out between six and nine in the morning, until 1955 when the Corporation's plans for rebuilding began to take effect.

The city's markets had begun to present a problem even before the war when it had been recognised that the wholesale and retail sides of the Barracks Market would have to be separated. After the war it was decided to build a new wholesale market on the edge of the city, with good road and rail communication in order to supply the city with fruit, vegetables and fish. A site was found at Barras Heath, to the north-east of the city centre, near a railway line which would allow banana and fish trains to deliver direct. Here were created six steel-framed ranges of standings, with warehouses and lorry parks grouped around a central clock tower and offices. The new market was opened for business by the then Lord Mayor, Alderman T. H. Dewis, on 29 June 1955.

The next stage was to be the building of a new retail market which would merge the West Orchard and Barracks Markets under one roof. Most Victorian market halls had owed something to the design of the Crystal Palace, and there are signs that something of this kind was intended in Coventry. Later a more revolutionary design was substituted and built in eighteen months. The market is circular and one-storeyed, with parking for 200 cars on the roof. Inside the building, the stalls are arranged in concentric circles with the name boards of the traders brightly coloured. From the six entrances which lead into the market from the open air, broad gangways run to a central open space where seats are provided for weary shoppers under a lantern which admits the daylight.

It is all very striking as well as profitable. In both wholesale and retail markets complaints have been heard that rents are too high, but the place of anyone who drops out is easily filled from the waiting list and nobody disputes that, although the rents are much greater than they were in the old markets, the facilities provided are incomparably better. The present central retail market is not what the old Market Hall used to be, and many of those who used to sell there have inevitably disappeared. The Ollerenshaws of Rugby no longer bring their eggs, nor the Dadsworthys their cheeses. Piper's Penny Bazaar has gone and so has William Luckman, the antique dealer, but the Coopers are still there with their pottery and china, as are Arthur Harper and Albert Norman, market trader for forty-six years, owner of two pickle factories and a leading personality in Coventry art circles.

VII

On 16 November 1967 G. S. N. Richards, Leader of the City Council, announced that Coventry's municipal airport at Baginton would, in future, be allowed to grow only within the limits of its existing facilities, since the Board of Trade had made it clear that no government help would be available for further expansion. He was ending one phase and opening another in the thirty-year-old history of the airport. In July 1935, at a time when interest in flight was rapidly growing, the City Council had decided to establish a municipal flying ground at Baginton, to the south of the city, on land which they had held since 1897. Many other local authorities, such as Nottingham, Leicester and Birmingham, were doing the same. Probably all of them had the development of private flying uppermost in their minds and the Coventry Aeroplane Club had played an important part in the talks which had been going on locally for the previous two years. So had John Siddeley, who was building aircraft at Whitley in a factory which the technical revolution in aviation was making obsolete. He needed a new building with a safe testing ground next to it, and he got both in July 1935. He was to build a factory at Baginton on Corporation land and to use the municipal flying ground for flight tests.

The Baginton site certainly was and is an excellent one. Situated on a plateau in a low-lying district, it is almost free of fog throughout the year. Its subsoil is so firm that, during the war, the heaviest bombers could land safely on grass. Its main runway is aligned along the direction of the prevailing wind and its area of 387 acres allows room for expansion. It could accommodate 6100 feet of concrete runways which could be further extended to take the largest international aircraft, and it would be easy to distribute arriving passengers through the system of near-by motorways. Nobody has ever denied that Baginton has many merits, but it happens to be very near the Birmingham municipal airport at Elmdon. This also has excellent communications, with the Coventry to Birmingham road on one side and the London to Birmingham main-line railway on the other. From the first, Elmdon was intended to be the airport for the undoubted regional capital of the West Midlands. This was bound to give it a tremendous advantage after the war when central government began to decide which airports should be assisted in order to develop the passenger air services which were then beginning. The fact that the Ministry of Transport ran Elmdon for the ten years before 1958 was helpful, since it secured concrete runways in 1948 shortly after Coventry had failed to get them at Baginton.

Coventry City Council could derive little encouragement from the results of their running of Baginton Airport after the war. Some aircraft were still landing for servicing at A.W.A., a certain amount of private flying took place and there was a two-day Air Pageant in July. Passenger services were not developing to any appreciable extent since customs facilities did not exist and terminal buildings were negligible. In December 1958, therefore, the City Council took a bold decision. Despite obvious government support for Elmdon, they produced a comprehensive plan to develop Baginton as a major airport with large terminal buildings, concrete runways and a heliport. In October 1960 Lord Brabazon opened the first mile of concrete runway which the Corporation had provided out of its own resources as the Ministry of Transport had refused a grant.

Objections to the proposed development came rapidly from near-by villages, but they had less cause for worry than they imagined. The actual amount of traffic attracted to Baginton was small and, early in 1969, the West Midlands Economic Planning Council came out firmly in favour of Elmdon as the international airport for the region. Its chairman, Adrian Cadbury, welcomed the news that the local authorities of Birmingham and Coventry were in agreement. The running of Elmdon, even with generous government assistance, was not so profitable that Birmingham was likely to object to sharing the cost with a near neighbour. The two authorities may shortly be part of a great metropolitan county and it may well be that the two airports will then be under the same control.

CHAPTER NINE

Education, Libraries and Health

The Technical College. The slow growth of Coventry's educational services between the wars. Wartime problems. The post-war effort. Comprehensive schools. The ancient grammar schools. The development of higher education. The University of Warwick and the Lanchester Polytechnic. Libraries and other cultural services. Hospitals in an expanding city.

I

Much of the industrial development of the first quarter of the twentieth century had actually taken place within the parishes of Radford, Foleshill, Wyken and Stoke which were then part of the area of the Foleshill Rural District Council. Corporation installations such as the Foleshill Gas Works and the Baginton Sewage Farm, together with a number of factories which included Courtaulds Main Works, a National Shell Filling Factory in Holbrook Lane and a Humber factory at Stoke had all been built outside the city. Around them had grown streets of working-class houses creating an economic unit which was much larger than the actual area within the city boundary. Sooner or later these boundaries would have to be adjusted to conform to the new economic pattern and this was to come in the boundary extensions of 1928 and 1932. This delay in making administration conform to fact may well be largely responsible for the slow progress which had been made before the 1930s in giving this expanded and vital city the social services which it needed.

As a result of these two boundary extensions the city's population rose from 139,000 in 1928 to 182,000 in 1932. The area, 4147 acres in the first of these years, was 19,167 in the second. At the same time the rateable value rose from £651,000 to £1,000,000. In an attempt to enable industry to catch any fair wind of prosperity which might be about, central government substantially de-rated factory property, so that the city's new acquisitions were not as profitable as they might have been; nor were the years immediately after the great depression favourable for vigorous social planning. Nevertheless, Coventry was in a better economic position than most cities, with a more pronounced building boom in the early thirties and the onset of rearmament later.

This was by no means the whole story, as the refounding of the City Guild in 1936 shows. There was a new quickening of civic interest, much of it due to the increasing influence of the Labour Party which became an important factor in municipal politics after 1929. In 1933 the Council formed a sub-committee to consider the building of a new civic centre worthy of a growing city and a few people were even beginning to think of a university. It was a pity that the hopes of people like Frederick Smith, the Town Clerk, went far beyond the amount of money then available. A Council could do little about the city's shortage of hospital beds and doctors, but even in education there seemed never to be enough school places, never enough room on the educational ladder for all those who wanted to climb it. In a city where men loved precision workmanship above everything else it was perhaps natural that the greatest actual achievement to emerge from this period of stress and hope should be a new Technical College which was opened in 1935.

II

In June 1883 a number of Coventry employers, including John and Alexander Rotherham, started the movement which was to lead to the creation of a Technical Institute.[1] They gained the support of survivors from the early Radical days such as John Gulson and Albert Tomson, Mayor of the city at the time. Tomson called a Town's Meeting in the following November in response to a requi-

[1] A reading room was provided for the remaining members of the Coventry Institute, formed in 1855 from an amalgamation of two earlier bodies, the Mechanics Institute and the Religious and Useful Knowledge Society.

sition signed by forty manufacturers and at least three hundred skilled workers. More money was then promised towards the Technical Institute than was later actually forthcoming and it was largely owing to the gift of a disused warehouse in Earl Street from David Spencer that the Institute was able to open its doors in 1887. It had its own weaving shed and science laboratory, but it was small and began with no full-time staff.

The work of the early textile and horological departments was supervised by committees of interested employers who had the right to come round in the evenings to see which of their young men were applying themselves to work in their own time for the examinations of the new City and Guilds of London Institute. Charles and Rowland Hill, Alfred Fridlander, Philip Cohen and Joseph Player were all on the Horological Committee, with Joseph Cash, Arthur Bill and Carey Franklin among the Committee members for the Textile Department. The Horological Department was near to extinction in 1910 when the prospectus stated that its classes would be formed only if there were enough students available. The most important work in the Institute had by then already become that of the Mechanical Engineering Department, the only department with a full-time head and with the list of its classes covering eighteen of the thirty-two pages in the prospectus.

The little building in Earl Street, at the back of Palace Yard, was to house the Technical Institute until the new college opened its doors to students in the autumn term of 1935. Plans to build a new college had been halted by the outbreak of war in 1914 and the post-war economic depression was to slow down the development of the new site in the Butts, chosen in 1919. The architect of the 1914 scheme was asked to submit a revised design in 1930 but three more years were to go by before building could actually begin. It is said that the then Principal, a careful Scot, was rather distressed by the opulence of the new building and thought that at least the staff would not require desks in their staff rooms. They could do their marking perfectly well at broad shelving placed around the walls.

The Technical College building, with its superfluous pediment and pillars and façade of stone, is not to the taste of our generation, but its provision of accommodation for the staff was far more generous than was usual at the time, its theatre played a great part in keeping drama alive in the city and its broad corridors, far wider than would be sanctioned nowadays, have been able to cope with numbers of students at least four times as large as anything envisaged when the building was first erected. With all its many defects, it is a worthy monument to a tradition which is still not entirely forgotten in Coventry, that of the working-class student who has left school earlier than he might have done and is working hard to improve his qualifications for a better and more responsible job.

In accordance with this tradition the Technical Institute had started a junior school for boys as early as 1919. Entrants came in at thirteen and were given a two-year course which prepared them for an apprenticeship with special emphasis on mathematics, engineering drawing and training in the use of hand and machine tools. Numbers at the school were increased to over 300 boys when the new building opened, and a junior commercial school was also started. Many of the Technical School's old boys came back as apprentices to study part-time, and between 1931 and 1936 the numbers taking the ordinary and higher National Certificates in Mechanical Engineering rose from fifty-one to seventy-four. A steadily expanding number of day release students helped to swell the total numbers enrolled in October 1936 to 3998, and a year later to 4575.

It was a considerable achievement at a time when the general picture in Coventry education was one of hope frustrated and expectations unrealised. The creation of new school places kept pace with an expanding population and the growth of new estates only with the acceptance of overcrowding and the renting of temporary premises. In 1931 2235 pupils were crowded into the new Barkers' Butts and Radford schools, although the number of places provided was supposed to be only 1980, including classes in a rented parish hall. A number of National Society schools which were becoming very old had to be maintained in service. Holy Trinity, opened in 1854 and still remembered for Ernest Cooke, head teacher there for twenty years, was closed only in 1915.[2] The undenominational

[2] Ernest Cooke (1861–1964) was the son of a watchmaker and a foundation scholar at Bablake. He was trained as a pupil teacher at Holy Trinity and was headmaster there until 1908. A strict disciplinarian, he gave all latecomers two on each hand with the cane whether or not they had a valid excuse.

school in Thomas Street, opened in 1835 and, once owned by the Cashs, had been at last taken out of service in 1922, but St Peter's National school, opened originally in 1848, was still being used as late as 1930. The St Michael's school building dated from 1855 and was not finally abandoned until 1958. St Mark's school, which opened in 1836, entered a new building in 1884, which was being repaired for further use in 1953.

During this same difficult period progress in the reduction of the size of classes was disappointingly slow. In September 1925, of the 446 junior classes existing in the city, no less than 238 contained fifty or more pupils. This position was perhaps slightly better than it had been two years earlier, when 133 classes out of 436 had contained more than fifty-six pupils. Progress was slow simply because pupil accommodation could not be sacrificed in the then prevailing financial climate. As late as March 1934 11 per cent of Coventry classes contained over fifty pupils, compared with the national average of 6·2 per cent. This disparity between the local and national figures had grown worse since March 1933 when the corresponding figures had been 11·2 per cent and 9 per cent. In March 1936 Coventry was twenty-third in the list of County Boroughs for the number of children in attendance at its elementary schools, fifty-fourth in net expenditure per child, sixtieth in net expenditure on salaries for teachers, sixty-fifth for administration and inspection and sixty-sixth for special services. The total number of County Boroughs at that time was eighty-three. Between 1932 and 1936 Coventry's expenditure on each child in its elementary schools had remained below the national average.

Throughout this period the Board of Education had its objectives, although it had to be content to move very slowly towards them. It wished to increase the number of teachers and improve their quality by abolishing the pupil teacher system and introducing a two-year course of training. It did not actually succeed in securing the raising of the school-leaving age to fifteen, although a first attempt was made in the Trevelyan Bill of 1930 and a second in the Halifax Act of 1936. This cautious measure, which provided that the school-leaving age should be raised in September 1939, with wide provisions for exemption, was nullified by the outbreak of war. Rather more success came in its attempts to break up the old elementary school pattern by implementing the recommendations of the Hadow Committee's report on *The Education of the Adolescent*, published in 1926.

In 1927 Coventry Education Committee found itself faced with the Hadow Report at a particularly unfortunate time. The city's boundaries were soon to be extended and a lot of preparatory work might then have to be done all over again. With the prevailing shortage of school accommodation in the city it was going to take a great deal of time to carry out one of the principal recommendations of the Hadow Committee, that of providing a break in education at the age of eleven, so that the pupil would pass from a primary school to some kind of secondary school at that age. It had been evident for some time that Coventry Education Committee's policy towards secondary education was certainly not generous and not even very clear. The Balfour Education Act of 1902 had permitted local education authorities, if they so wished, to establish secondary schools which should give a five-year course between the ages of eleven and sixteen, charge fees and tend towards the academic rather than the practical in their curricula. Sir Robert Morant, the real inspirer of this Act, had been to Winchester and wanted to give the new schools something of the liberal tradition which he himself had known. It is safe to say that his views were not shared by Coventry Education Committee. In 1905, when they asked the Secretary to the Sub-Committee for Higher Education for his advice on what provision they should make for secondary schooling, his reply was to the effect that Coventry would probably want very little since it had only a small middle class.[3]

In order to make a start on secondary education for girls, it was suggested in 1905 that the city's ancient grammar school of King Henry VIII should become co-educational. The idea was in advance of its time and did not prosper, but there was another way in which a girls' secondary school could be founded. One of the new careers then opening up for young women of education was that of elementary school-teacher and Coventry, like many other places, had al-

[3] The Board of Education had estimated that Coventry would need 1716 secondary school places 'but as Coventry, so far as I can gather, does not contain a large proportion of what, for want of a better term, may be called middle-class population, the numbers are doubtless much in excess of the real requirements of the city . . .'.

ready set up a small pupil teacher-training centre. It admitted seventy girls a year for a two-year course and, in order to provide them with opportunities for practical classroom experience, it was housed in buildings within the grounds of Wheatley Street School. Its staff, women of good family and deep idealism, including the sister of Sir Stafford Cripps, tended to be members of the Women's Social and Political Union, firm, if not extreme, supporters of women's rights. At their head was a young graduate of Bedford College London, Grace Howell. She was to become the first headmistress of the new secondary school when, in 1908, the students of the pupil teachers' centre were transferred to Barr's Hill House, a former residence of J. K. Starley, on the Radford Road. Pupils were to be admitted from the age of eleven, uniforms adopted and a new girls' secondary school was born.

Barr's Hill House, built on a slope overlooking the pleasant valley of the Radford brook, is not as far from the centre of the city now as it was when Miss Howell and her colleagues took it over. In many ways their spirit is still very much about the place; the school's tradition of seriousness, interest in good causes and love of music all spring from the work of that gifted and forceful woman who remained its headmistress until her retirement in 1932. She left behind her a school which had already reached 400 pupils in 1920 and which had a strong, sternly selective sixth form by the time she departed. She was the true creator of Barr's Hill and her successor, Winifred Barrow (1893–1957), continued where she left off. Miss Barrow came from one of those Liverpool families which had made their money in trade across the oceans of the world. Her father was a shipowner and she was one of the members of the family who contributed to the learned professions. She took over a school which was already established on sure foundations and her own contribution came mainly in building a larger sixth form. Her quiet, composed dignity played a great part in keeping Barr's Hill out of many later controversies.

In January 1919 a number of girls from Barr's Hill went across the city to start a new secondary school in Stoke Park. Harefield, the house in which the school began, was a Victorian mansion in large and shady grounds and there the school was to remain until at last the move to a new building started in 1946. Its first library was in an attic with a book grant of £7 a year, and it soon had to acquire a number of extensions and outside classrooms as numbers grew.

In 1911 London County Council had begun to establish a number of selective central schools which managed to build up a good record of achievement and attract a high quality of staff. When Coventry Education Committee became interested in this experiment they decided that Wheatley Street School should become a selective central school as soon as the juniors and infants could be moved out of the building. They also decided that, in a number of other schools, there should be established central advanced or 'higher top' classes giving a two-year course up to the age of fifteen. In order to allocate the very small number of free places at King Henry VIII and Bablake and the slightly larger number at the two girls' secondary schools, together with the places in the higher top classes, the Education Committee established a double examination.

Overcrowding in Coventry elementary schools had been a permanent problem. In 1893, when Wheatley Street opened with Selina Dix as headmistress of the girls' department, 510 girls were admitted to occupy classrooms meant for 420.[4] A similar overcrowding had, by the 1920s, spread to the secondary schools. In October 1925 it was estimated that the two girls' schools, Barr's Hill and Stoke Park, contained 650 girls instead of 434. The shortage of places for boys was similarly acute. In 1925 Coventry Education Committee admitted that they would have to provide 1400 more places in order to reach the standard which the Board of Education was trying to achieve. The two ancient foundations provided secondary education for boys, but not many of their pupils came to them via the local authority. In 1925 it was paying for only five boys at King Henry VIII and eleven at Bablake. Such was the pressure of numbers that, in 1937, those at King Henry VIII had been raised to thirty. Nevertheless, there was an urgent need for new secondary schools for both boys and girls. The Caludon Castle estate had been acquired for a

[4] Selina Dix (1859–1942) was born at Beeston near Nottingham, and came to Coventry at the age of thirty. She was headmistress of South Street and Wheatley Street girls' schools and became such an unchallenged leader of her profession that, at one time, she was invited to stand for Parliament. She became increasingly crippled as she grew older but this did not stop her work on behalf of the city's children or prevent her from advocating the rights of women.

new secondary school in 1938 and a new building in Dane Road, Stoke, was actually in process of being built. Both these were intended for boys, but the then headmistress of Stoke Park, Winifred Michell drew so much public attention to the inadequacies of her own school buildings that the Education Committee changed its mind. She was expecting to move her school into brand new premises in September 1939.

III

The outbreak of war was to add tremendously to the difficulties of education in Coventry. For many years the Education Committee had done no more than keep abreast of some of its problems; now it was going to find it difficult not to be overwhelmed by them. A total of 8187 school places were removed altogether; civilian services took over school space for 2716 places and rooms which could provide 1284 places were converted into air-raid shelters. These would be easily retrievable at the end of the war, but by then 4187 further places had been so damaged by enemy action that they would require extensive rebuilding. Equally serious in its effects on teaching was the disturbance caused by evacuation, by frequent changes of teacher as the call-up intensified, and by broken education through parents moving about the country from job to job. It was revealed in one report published in October 1943, that one boy of seven had attended no less than seven schools in two years and that one class had had ten teachers in eighteen months. About 3000 children in the city were seriously backward owing to the process of evacuation, return, re-evacuation after a raid and transfer from one damaged school to another. Truancy and casual absences were problems all over the country and Coventry's experience was no better than that of other bombed towns.

A great effort would clearly be required to bring the Coventry education service back to the standard it had known before the war, and that standard itself was not now going to be acceptable. The pre-war overcrowding would no longer be tolerated and at least twenty school buildings required replacement on the grounds of age and unsuitability. Under the Butler Education Act of 1944 the

Ministry of Education, as it then was, gained victories in a number of battles it had been fighting for a long time. The word 'elementary' was abolished by statute and education was in future to be divided into the two stages of primary and secondary. The Act gave powers to the Minister to raise the school-leaving age to fifteen, and later to sixteen, when the necessary resources in teachers and buildings were available.

The promise that education for all pupils would be according to age, aptitude and abilities and the naming of all schools for pupils over eleven 'secondary', gave rise to a popular feeling that great advances in education were about to take place. The Act itself said nothing about different types of secondary schools, but the Ministry of Education paid much attention to the findings of the Norwood Committee, published in 1943. That Committee, set up to deal with the curriculum and examinations in secondary schools, had recommended the creation of three different types of schools to which it gave the names of grammar, technical and modern. These corresponded, it claimed, to three distinct types of pupil, and selection procedures should be established in order to place all pupils in the school for which they were best fitted.

All this lay in the future when, in May 1944, Coventry Education Committee had a first look at its post-war plans and decided, under the influence of the Norwood Report, that it would need four grammar schools, eight technical schools and eighteen modern schools, each with 450 places. The relatively high number of technical schools is interesting, considering the background of the city. Then, in October 1944, came a second Education Committee report, prepared after the passing of the Butler Act. This represented a complete reversal of the Committee's views and proposed the building on thirty-acre sites of ten or eleven multilateral schools of 1200 pupils each. A multilateral school would offer a wide variety of courses for different types of pupils drawn from a given area without any preliminary entrance examination. The multilateral concept was later developed into that of the comprehensive school which has come to play a dominant part in Coventry's secondary education. The preference for such schools was maintained in 1946 when Coventry submitted to the Ministry of Education its first education development plan drawn up under the new Act.

The future shape of Coventry's secondary education, however, could not expect to get much attention in the difficult years immediately after the war. The age distribution of the school population and its increasing numbers demanded that the Education Committee should give its main attention to the urgent problem of providing primary school places, even if other things had to go by the board. Between 1946 and 1954 the primary school population in Coventry rose by nearly 10,000, from 19,941 to 29,753. Damaged and badly needed accommodation had to be brought back into use as quickly as scarce building labour and materials would allow. Parts of war-time hostels were hastily brought into service as temporary schools and were to remain so for a long time. Huts on the Fletchampstead Highway, which had originally been built to accommodate police brought into the city during air raids, were commandeered for educational use but, before they could be used, a group of squatters had to be removed. In 1952 1540 places were being provided in schools made out of old hostels and 6820 more school places were provided in rented halls, 'pre-fab' huts and similar makeshift premises. In September 1956 a third of secondary modern places were still provided in various kinds of temporary accommodation and the attempt to create selective secondary schools out of unsatisfactory buildings such as John Gulson and Wheatley Street could hardly be more than a short-term expedient.

This multitude of problems could hardly fail to tax the energy and challenge the foresight of the new Director of Education, Walter Chinn, appointed in 1947. Born in Birmingham in 1904, he came from a family with a strong tradition of social work for the handicapped and underprivileged.[5] His sympathies coincided with those of many leading members of the Education Committee such as William Callow, Sidney Stringer, Emily Smith and Emily Allen, who worked with him to give Coventry a range of schools for the physically handicapped, the educationally subnormal and the delicate which may well be their most enduring monuments. Schools such as Alice Stevens' for the educationally subnormal, Corley, a residential school for the delicate, Wainbody Wood for the

[5] His father was probably the first Probation Officer in the country, having been appointed in 1905 under a Birmingham scheme which preceded the establishment of the national Probation Service.

maladjusted, Baginton Fields and Sherbourne Fields for the physically handicapped and Town Thorns for the slow learners, have gained such a reputation for the quality of their work that Coventry has now been selected as the home for the Hereward College, the national technical college for the physically handicapped.

The Education Committee's decision to implement its policy for comprehensive secondary schools could not be realised immediately in the difficult years that followed the end of the war. Priority had to be given to the erection of new primary schools to meet the needs of the rapidly rising population.[6] In 1949 Coventry assessed its school building needs for the period 1950 to 1952. These included eight new primary schools and the first instalments of three new secondary schools. Their requirements were to be cut, but the new secondary schools were at last on the way. Caludon Castle and Woodlands, the first of them, were opened in September 1954.

IV

The comprehensive schools are now such an established part of the Coventry landscape that it is becoming increasingly difficult to remember the great efforts in school building which the city has had to make over the last fifteen years. There are now sixteen comprehensive schools, four of them Roman Catholic, and one Church of England representing the continuation of the old Blue Coat Charity.[7] The other eleven are directly maintained by the local education authority and stand on large sites around the edge of the city, from Tile Hill Wood and Woodlands in the west to Caludon Castle and Woodway Park in the east, from President Kennedy in the north to Finham Park in the south. All are purpose-built and some of the buildings, such as those of President Kennedy, one of the most recent schools, are very pleasing in appearance. On many

[6] Eighty per cent of the city's primary school population is now accommodated in buildings erected since 1950. Coventry has fully shared in the astonishing revolution in primary school teaching which has been one of the most hopeful features of post-war education.

[7] The Blue Coat School was founded as a small charity school for girls in 1714 and was rebuilt on the same site in 1856–7. That building still stands in Priory Row, close to the church of Holy Trinity with which the charity has always been connected.

sites old buildings and natural beauty have been carefully guarded; Coundon Court has the florid mansion in which George Singer, the motor-car magnate, once lived; the Lyng Hall farmhouse, with its orchard and walnut trees, is still preserved; the mansion at Whitley Abbey has gone, but the lake is still cared for and swans have sometimes been tempted on to it; and the great trees which once adorned this former nobleman's park remain, as do those which are part of the beauty of Tile Hill Wood.

The comprehensive school won increasing support in the late forties when it became clear that the new pattern of secondary education was not working out as the Norwood Committee had intended. That Committee specifically said that equal resources should be available to the three different types of school without discrimination, but this was not being achieved. Some parents were already beginning to speak of the selection procedure as a scholarship examination and to regard a place in a secondary modern school as equivalent to failure.[8] The supporters of the comprehensive school, therefore, argued that this process of selection should be done away with so that all children living in a particular area should be sent to one secondary school, where all pupils, after being kept under close observation for two years, could be allocated to the courses best suited to their abilities.

These comprehensive schools, it was felt, would have to be large in order to maintain a viable sixth form, although Coventry did not originally wish to adopt the ten-form entry which the Ministry insisted was the minimum. Since this very size would make it difficult for the head teacher to know individual pupils the schools were divided into sub-units called houses. Coventry's distinctive contribution to the house system was the creation of houses as physical entities with house masters or mistresses and house staff. Each house would be a cross-section of the school with about 150 pupils to each.

[8] Some of these secondary modern schools had at one time been 'higher tops' and have their own special traditions behind them. Hearsall Secondary Modern School, formerly Centaur Road, has produced Sir George Harriman, now (1971) President of British Leyland, and Phillip Callow, the novelist; Broad Heath has a long and distinguished record in the field of rugby football; and Stoke Secondary Modern School for Girls achieved a remarkably high academic standard under the headship of Dorothy Parncutt between 1956 and 1963.

Comprehensive schools in Coventry, however, are still not able to operate as their founders had hoped. The two boys' direct grant schools of King Henry VIII and Bablake take large numbers of pupils from the local authority, and the two girls' grammar schools still exist. When the Minister of Education was first approached about the building of comprehensive schools in Coventry she raised no objection, provided that the percentage of selective places did not fall. Each comprehensive school has, therefore, a selective intake and the process of selection at eleven plus continues. The Coventry pattern of secondary education is clearly some distance from its final form, particularly since the last of the secondary modern schools, all of them in relatively old buildings, have not yet been eliminated.

If the test of a good school is that its pupils should be happy and interested, then Coventry's comprehensive schools are very good indeed. Early controversies in which their defenders and opponents made the most of a number of hardly tenable arguments have now been largely forgotten and this is not the place to try to assess their educational achievements when they are still very young. At first they were too much aware that there were grammar schools in the same town and perhaps they were over-preoccupied in claiming that anything the grammar schools could do, they could do better. They are gradually becoming aware of the great cultural changes of our time and of the need to make applied knowledge far more respectable than it has been in the past. Caludon Castle and Woodlands have always had large and well-organised practical courses which have produced a high percentage of apprentices for local engineering.[9] In order to emphasise that all pupils, even the most intellectually gifted, should be able to think with their hands, President Kennedy school has provided that everyone should, in the first five years, spend the same amount of time on practical subjects.

The development of applied studies to which the comprehensive schools are beginning to contribute has long been part of the his-

[9] In 1966 44 per cent of all school-leavers using the Youth Employment Service had entered into some kind of engineering employment by 30 September of that year and 39 per cent had signed articles of apprenticeship. In 1970 the corresponding figures had risen to 51 per cent and 41 per cent. Coventry's interest in the practical forms of education which began with the foundation of Bablake seems to be still continuing.

toric purpose of Bablake.[10] This ancient foundation was regarded at the beginning of this century as a school which gave an excellent, though rather narrow, science and trade training. Two successive headmasters between 1918 and 1962 broadened the school's outlook while preserving its essential tradition. Dr Frankland, an Anglican clergyman, increased the importance of the arts side within the school and was the virtual creator of the sixth form with its large number of university entrants.[11] After his retirement in 1937 his work was continued by Edward Seaborne, a product of Bristol Grammar School, who had read mathematics and English at Magdalen College, Oxford. He was to prove himself a belated Victorian headmaster, the last of the line of Arnold, Thring and the Temples, the self-confident men who had created the public schools of the latter part of the last century and early part of this.

Bablake has never had any reason to doubt the importance of its contribution to the life of the city. Sir Stanley Harley of Coventry Gauge and Tool and George Turnbull of British Leyland are two recent examples of the quality which it has contributed to Midland industry, and there will be many more to come. An analysis, published in 1956, of the careers adopted by Bablake school-leavers during a five-year period showed that 19 per cent went to university (all on scholarships); 17 per cent went as chemists into local laboratories; 16 per cent embarked upon engineering, 4 per cent upon aeronautical, 4 per cent upon electrical and 6 per cent on automobile engineering; 5 per cent were destined for architecture; 5 per cent for various forms of clerical work; 4 per cent entered various banks; another 4 per cent took up civil or municipal service and 3 per cent chose surveying. In 1955 40 per cent of all leavers went to university.

Bablake has never been lacking in either money or pupils and in both respects its history during the twentieth century has contrasted sharply with that of the grammar school of King Henry VIII. In 1916 when Bablake, with 300 places, had 353 boys on its books, King Henry VIII had 133 boys, but 190 places. As late as 1931 the numbers had risen to only 250 and the governors had reintroduced the Preparatory Department because the annual intake was so

[10] See Chapter One, page 6.

[11] A small, active man, he was an excellent soccer player and occasionally turned out for the school team.

small.[12] This was in the time of John Lupton, a Cambridge classics first, who had taught at Shrewsbury, Marlborough and Uppingham before he became headmaster in 1910.[13] In some respects his twenty-one years as headmaster can be looked back upon as a golden age. From his time came such old boys as Vaughan Reynolds, later editor of the *Birmingham Post* and G. L. Allen, who became a University Professor, but was best known in the school as Captain of Cricket. One of those who played under his leadership was R. E. S. Wyatt, later to captain Warwickshire and England. It was a small rather attractive grammar school with Sir William Wyley as its Chairman of Governors, but it had no money. It was on the direct grant list of the Board of Education, but unless the school could achieve a great increase in numbers there would have to be an increase in fees which might be self-defeating. A. A. C. Burton, the headmaster who followed Lupton, had many serious problems with which to cope.

The phase of the school's history which continues to the present day can be said to have begun with Burton. His predecessors, from Sweet-Escott to Lupton, had all been public school men. They had looked for their educational ideal to such places as Shrewsbury and Rugby and had tried to make King Henry VIII part of that world. Their aims were the same as those of other headmasters who were taking small grammar schools and making them into public schools, but their policy did not succeed in Coventry. Something else would have to be tried and Burton tried it. He developed the Preparatory Class into a Junior School with a staff of seven, expanded the science side and took many more pupils from the local authority, changing the character of the school, increasing its numbers and probably saving its life.

Academically Burton lacked much of the quality and public school background of his predecessor but was far superior to him in business sense, with a touch of ruthlessness which was probably very useful in the difficult years with which he had to deal. Evacuation, air-raid damage and re-evacuation all came his way and he

[12] In 1905 the Governors had rejected the interesting idea that the school should become co-educational.

[13] Lupton was the first layman to become headmaster of the school. When he took over, he was told by his predecessor that the school was generally referred to as 'that bankrupt concern at the top of the hill'.

perhaps lacked the gift of making life easy for himself. In 1950 he departed after an open breach with his governors but he continued to be active in education until his death. He was a farmer's son who had worked hard for what he had achieved, taking two degrees and earning respect as an excellent teacher before his organising ability and force of character won him the headship of King Henry VIII. He always remained a farmer at heart, kept Middle White pigs and grew cabbages. One of the men appointed by him remembers the mild surprise with which, on his first day in the staff room, he read a notice stating that the headmaster had tomatoes for sale.

Burton's firm friends were counterbalanced by the number of his enemies, for many people found him a very disquieting man. The same thing cannot be said of his successor, Herbert Walker, who came to the school after working as deputy to Robert, now Sir Robert, Bierley in the Allied Control Commission in Germany. This quiet, soft-spoken Yorkshireman, now (1971) one of the senior statesmen among headmasters of direct grant schools, has continued Burton's policy by very different methods. In 1971 the main school had 840 pupils, the same number as Bablake, with 90 places paid for each year by the local education authority. The school's science side is strong and expanding, its mathematics is among the best in the city and its doors are open wider than ever before to talent from any background.

In 1922 both King Henry VIII and Bablake were offered the choice of receiving state assistance from either the local authority or the Board of Education. Since they could no longer receive aid from both these sources, the governors of the two schools saw which would give the greater independence and chose to be added to the direct grant list. The existence of direct grant schools as such began to be criticised after the Second World War. As early as 17 May 1944 Coventry Education Committee stated that, unless the two ancient foundations came under their control and abolished fees, it would be necessary for them to build at least one more boys' grammar school. A meeting of Bablake parents in the Central Hall carried a resolution in favour of local authority control, but the governors had a very different intention. On 9 January 1946 it was reported that they had decided to apply to the Ministry of Education for recognition as an independent school. In due course the governors of King Henry VIII were to follow their example but the period of independence did not last long. The headmasters of the two schools are still members of the Headmasters' Conference but they have returned to their direct grant status.

Whatever their status, the two schools were every year taking a large number of pupils from the local authority, thus reducing the city's difficulties as well as their own. It was not, perhaps, a logical arrangement, but it worked although there were signs that the comprehensive schools, as they grew in number, were casting their eyes enviously upon the gifted pupils denied to them. Voices were heard in 1955 and 1961 advocating some change in the existing arrangements but widespread controversy did not break out until the publication of Circular 10/65 by the Ministry of Education.

This circular, produced by the Wilson government which had taken office in November 1964, directed all local education authorities to submit plans within a given period for the reorganisation of their secondary schools on fully comprehensive lines. This reorganisation might take any one of several forms and would undoubtedly have to be spread over a number of years. It would eventually lead to the abolition of the selection procedure and with it the abolition of grammar and all other kinds of selective schools. The two boys' foundations, therefore, found themselves exposed to a twofold onslaught as the Public Schools Committee appointed by the Government was expected to recommend the abolition of the direct grant list at the time when their position inside the city was being questioned as a result of Circular 10/65.

In September 1966 Coventry's Education Committee adopted the plan which had been drawn up for carrying out the intentions of Circular 10/65. Its members and officers had long wished to get rid of the secondary modern schools which were still carrying on in out-of-date buildings in the older areas. They decided that the whole city could be covered by a system of comprehensive schools by 1971, provided that the age of entry was raised to twelve plus and that secondary modern buildings were still used as annexes.[14] The

[14] King Henry VIII and Bablake were both offered places within this all-embracing comprehensive system. The proposals made to them were interesting, including one for the amalgamation of Bablake and Barr's Hill, the nearby girl's grammar school. The governors of the two schools did not, however, feel that this was acceptable.

city had previously created comprehensive schools only when it could give them new buildings and a proper start in life. They were now proposing, with the best of intentions, to build something very different. Existing grammar and secondary modern schools were to be linked together despite the fact that they might be some distance from each other. The resulting product would be called a comprehensive school which would one day have a fine new building, but no one could guarantee when that day would be. Postponements are frequent in education and the temporary can last for a very long time. The plan looked bureaucratic and was criticised far more than it was defended. Two changes in government, in the city during 1967, and in the country three years later, brought an end to the immediate controversy but left the problem unsolved.

V

The new comprehensive schools were only one of the signs that education in Coventry was beginning to move forward again after the long period of stagnation before the war and the difficulties during and immediately after it. A further sign has been a steady growth in the number and size of the establishments for higher education within the city. Coventry is in the centre of England, easily accessible from all directions, and after the war it contained a number of empty hostels which were available for any purpose the central government might have in mind over the next few years. One of them, in Charter Avenue, Canley, was converted into a training college for men teachers under an emergency scheme which the Ministry of Education began after the end of the war. Those selected received full-time training for just over a year and were expected to attend further part-time classes in the two years following their engagement as teachers. Before it was closed at the end of 1948 Canley College had produced 880 teachers, but that was not to be the end.

Before the last emergency course finished, it had been decided that the buildings should be used for a permanent teacher-training college providing a two-year course for 180 women students. It has had only one Principal, Miss J. D. Browne, who came to Coventry after being Vice-Principal at Furzedown. By March 1954, the date which saw the opening of its first hall of residence, it had become the largest training college in the country with places for 350 students. In February 1959 it was included in the expansion programme announced by the Ministry of Education. It was to become a mixed college with 520 students, a total which has now (1971) risen to 1350. In accordance with the recommendations of the Robbins Committee on Higher Education its name was, in 1964, changed to the City of Coventry College of Education. It has long since replaced the two-year course by a three-year one which leads to a Certificate granted by the University of Warwick, just across the road, and the status of a qualified teacher. Recently it has added a fourth year for students selected for the B.Ed. Degree at Warwick. The Coventry College of Education, like all others, will be affected by the recommendations which will be put forward by the James Committee on the training of teachers which is now (1971) sitting. Some people are already thinking that it is, perhaps, not a good idea to train teachers apart from other professions such as social workers, and the future will certainly see changes.

In 1948, when Coventry Education Committee submitted its Development Plan for Further Education to the Minister under the 1944 Education Act, the idea of a permanent training college in the city was still relatively new. Two further education establishments only were in existence in the city, the Technical College, which would be able to continue the expansion which had begun before the war, and the School of Art, which would not.[15] Since a new School of Art would be required in any case, the plan provided for the building of a group of three associated colleges in the centre of the city. There was to be a College of Art, a College of Technology, which would take over some of the work of the Technical College, and a College of General Education, which would expand the adult education classes which the Technical College was already developing. The Plan considered and rejected the idea of developing the

[15] The School of Art had been opened in 1843 as part of the extension to the provinces of the work of the School of Design started five years earlier at Somerset House. This school, under the control of the Board of Trade, was intended to extend opportunities for proficiency in art and design to the industrious classes and as such it received the support of Albert, the Prince Consort.

Technical College into a University College since this would not enable the needs of industry to be satisfied with flexibility and speed. The plan reads very strangely today since what it rejected and what it advocated have both come about in different forms. The first students of the University of Warwick were admitted in the autumn of 1964 and the area proposed for the three colleges, which many people never expected to see, has been covered by the Lanchester Polytechnic which includes the College of Art as one of its faculties.

In Coventry and many other places a mystique had long surrounded the figure of the part-time student. After his day's work was over he would go to the Technical College on two or three evenings a week in order to attend classes which would last for two or perhaps three hours. He would give up other evenings and part of his week-end to prepare written work and study his textbooks. All this might go on for five years and it would certainly require of him a real self-discipline and dedication. Those qualities are still called for although things are easier now with the increase of day release. The part-time student is still an excellent recruit to the army of learning but in the mid-fifties some people began to wonder if the system was doing its best for him. Coventry Technical College was full to capacity but it was falling behind the times.[16] The growing complexity and efficiency of industry was beginning to require that part-time training should be supplemented by full-time courses. A new wind was beginning to blow and Coventry was going to be affected by it.

As early as 1943 that gifted man, Dr Neville Gorton, newly appointed Bishop of Coventry, put forward the idea that this great engineering centre should be the home of a new technological university. He placed the idea before the Association of Technical Institutions, as it was then, spoke on the subject in the House of Lords in June 1952 and made contact with a wide range of notables in industry and research associations.[17] Nevertheless, when he put forward the idea in Coventry itself, he found that leading members

[16] In 1947/8 the total number of students at the Technical College had been 6555 but this had risen to 8652 by 1953/4.

[17] Dr Gorton was not alone. In December 1951 the *Financial Times* had suggested that a new University with a scientific bias should be built 'at Coventry (which) might be described as the mechanical centre of England'.

of the City Council were curiously unreceptive. Then, in the middle fifties, came a series of shocks which were to make the local authority a little less complacent. The Ministry of Education began to favour technical colleges having their own independent governing bodies and many people in touch with the needs of industry began advocating advanced colleges to cover age ranges roughly corresponding to those at universities. For a long time Coventry wanted none of this until suddenly the Ministry published a list of colleges which were to get an increased grant because they had done what the Ministry had required of them. Coventry was not on it, but Rugby was. This was followed in 1956 by the designation of certain colleges as Colleges of Advanced Technology and again Coventry was not on the list.

One of the ladders for the good part-timer to climb had always been the external degree in engineering awarded by the University of London but its syllabuses were becoming increasingly difficult and were getting further away from the day-to-day needs of industry. A number of the younger men teaching in what were then the London Polytechnics gave enthusiastic support to the idea of a Diploma in Technology. Leading industrialists, such as Sir Walter Puckey and Lord Hives, then Chairman of Rolls-Royce, were also strong supporters of this proposed award. It would be a degree level qualification to be granted by an independent body on which both universities and industry would be represented. Lord Hives became the first chairman of this National Council for Technological Awards and it was expected that the new Colleges of Advanced Technology would give most of their time to such courses. Other colleges would, nevertheless, not be debarred, provided that their facilities matched the high standards set by the Council. Here, it seemed, was hope for Coventry. It was fortunate that a new Principal was required at the Technical College in 1958 and that the Committee were able to appoint Dr, now Sir Alan, Richmond who had already been actively concerned with the creation of the Diploma in Technology. The College of Technology in the centre of the city, first projected in 1948, now began to take shape with great speed. Buildings originally intended for the College of Art were adapted and new ones planned so that in September 1960, the Lanchester College of Technology was able to open its doors.

Progress was being made in one direction just when it was beginning to seem possible in another. In the autumn of 1958 Arthur Ling, then City Architect, began to prepare a pamphlet containing sketches of what a new university in Coventry could look like. It was to be situated on the southern edge of the city to the north of Gibbet Hill Road, where the Corporation already owned pleasant green farmland which gave a distant view of the three spires. Near-by streams were to be used to produce an ornamental lake close to the buildings where almost 700 students would live and work. Since tower blocks were fashionable in those days, there was to be a Tower of Learning containing most of the teaching departments. Other buildings, including a theatre and art gallery, were grouped around two piazzas. The whole composition looked a little Mexican and was certainly pleasant and interesting. It was, perhaps, the most permanent result arising out of the work of the Council for the Establishment of a University in Coventry which, between 1954 and 1956, had tried to create a public opinion in favour of the idea.

In December 1958 Coventry City Council at last accepted the idea of establishing a university in the city. At about the same time, Tom Chapman, then Managing Director of Armstrong-Siddeley, was becoming convinced, together with many others, that the Technical College was not suited to the highest needs of industry and that the city needed a university of its own. That fine civic patriot, Charles Barratt, the Town Clerk, was beginning to think along the same lines. In February 1960 Sir Arnold Hall, then Managing Director of Bristol Siddeley, invited many leading local industrialists to a private dinner party at which Charles Barratt was given an opportunity of stating his case. He got such a cool reception that he was extremely disheartened but a month later he began to see the situation in a new light. When, together with Sir Arnold Hall, he addressed a meeting at the Council House which contained representatives of both City and County Councils, the volume of opinion in favour was so considerable that it was possible to make an early approach to the University Grants Committee.

Universities were, and are, independent Corporations created by Royal Charter with the consequent right to receive and administer endowments of their own. In practice, they cannot maintain their activities without government help and the University Grants

Committee was created in 1919 so that they might receive that help directly from the Exchequer. The impending spate of new universities in the early 1960s was about to transform the Committee's organisation but it had already developed criteria to guide it in recognising where new universities should be created. It required strong evidence of local interest and was certainly influenced by the fact that Coventry City Council offered a 200-acre site and an annual contribution equal to the product of a penny rate when it submitted its formal case in April 1960. Warwickshire County Council could do no less and with such generous backing, including the largest site in the country for a new university, the application was assured of success. The new creation, to be known as the University of Warwick, was one of the six new universities to be authorised by the Macmillan Government.

The next step was to be the formation of an Appeals Committee to build up an endowment and an Academic Planning Board to plan the range of courses which the University would offer. Chairmanship of the Appeals Committee was taken by the first Lord Rootes, who made it one of his last and greatest successes. Sir Arnold Hall, who had come to the world of industry from Cambridge and the University of London, became a member of the Academic Planning Board and threw his considerable influence behind the idea that the University of Warwick should be broadly based and cover a wide range of studies. It would include technological subjects, since it was within the boundaries of one of the greatest engineering centres in the country, and business studies, since these were coming to be accepted as proper work for an academic establishment, but it would not be simply a copy of the Massachusetts Institute of Technology and should have no point of overlap with the Lanchester College of Technology.

The situation was dramatically changed in October 1963 by the publication of the Robbins Report on Higher Education which forecast that the number of home and overseas students requiring full-time higher education would double between 1962 and 1975, rising from 216,000 to 433,000. This expansion should be met by the creation of new universities, partly by giving university status to the Colleges of Advanced Technology. Regional colleges, of which the Lanchester College of Technology was one, might also hope to become universities in due course of time. A new body, the Council for National Academic Awards, would enable them to offer full-time degree courses. This Council, which received a Royal Charter, took over the work of the old National Council for Technological Awards and remained under the Presidency of Lord Kings Norton.

There was now an obvious danger of the University of Warwick and the Lanchester coming into conflict which would be in the interests of neither. An attempt was, therefore, made to secure the integration of both, with the consent of Coventry City Council. From the University side the inspiration appears to have come from Sir Arnold Hall. On the Lanchester side it was taken up by the man who was then Chairman both of the Governors and of the Education Committee, T. L. K. Locksley. He had displayed a rare energy and foresight in helping to get the Lanchester off the ground and might have been expected to regard the University as a dangerous rival. He accepted, early in 1964, that an attempt should be made to integrate the two but the move was rejected by the Department of Education and Science in September 1965. It was later revealed that the Lanchester was intended to follow a different course.

For many years steady pressure has been applied from central government in order to bring some kind of system into the national pattern of technical colleges and colleges of art. They had originally arisen in response to local needs and local initiative, often providing duplicated courses within a comparatively short distance. This had, perhaps, not mattered at one time, but with an increasing number of students and an increasing burden of cost something had to be done about it. The result was a plan to group the regional colleges of technology and colleges of art together into a number of establishments which could offer a wide range of courses, both part-time and full-time. In May 1966 these were given the name of polytechnics. The process of producing them was a slow one, since many local obstacles had to be overcome and cherished prejudices put on one side. It was eventually decided to designate thirty polytechnics, which would have a considerable degree of independence, but not be completely free from the final control of local authorities. Lanchester naturally became one of them and, since it was amalgamated in the process with the Coventry College of Art and the Rugby College of Technology, it became one of the largest. Though lacking a Royal Charter and the name of a university, it emerged as an establishment containing 3200 full-time and sandwich-course students taking degrees of the Council for National Academic Awards.

Meanwhile the University of Warwick was having troubles of its own. There had been a change of personalities at the top. The first Lord Rootes, its Chancellor-designate who had done so much to amass its endowment, died before he could be installed and was succeeded by Lord Radcliffe, a distinguished lawyer statesman who lived in the county. Problems of buildings and finance were emerging. The daring and imaginative mind of Arthur Ling had devised a majestic layout for the new site which proved to be sadly at variance with the resources which the University had at its disposal in its first five years. Money had to be spent very carefully and the students on the site, which is some distance outside the city centre, soon began to complain that the social amenities provided for them were inadequate. These complaints were to merge with others which were to attract considerable national attention in 1970.

A great number of local industrialists had supported the University very generously and had accepted places on its Council. This intimate link between the University and local industry, although it conformed with the wishes of the government of the time, was not developed without protest from some of the University staff. A university is traditionally a loose federation of schools or faculties, with the vice-chancellor as a chairman of committee rather than an administrative director. The amount of actual control which he possesses can be exaggerated and this probably explains why the disputes within the University in 1970 appeared to be so intense. Throughout this difficult period the normal work of the University went on and all classes were held.

The University's school of pure mathematics has acquired an international reputation and its Centre for Industrial and Business Studies has carried out valuable work in industrial relations and manpower planning, but the best efforts of the late Lord Rootes failed to get for Warwick one of the two government-sponsored management schools. The University seems, however, to have been more successful with the Todd Commission on Medical Education. In January 1969 it was announced that Sir Brian Windeyer, Dean of the Faculty of Medicine in the University of London, had been appointed chairman of a committee to consider plans for a medical school at the University of Warwick. These things can, however, take a great deal of time and it seems probable that, over the next five years, most students at Warwick will still be studying the arts and social sciences, the departments of which were among the first to be launched by the University, partly because of a genuine desire by interested industrialists that it should not be dominated by the demands of science and technology. In October 1970 it was announced that the University was preparing for an expansion of the student body to 5000 by 1976 with 2000 studying science and technology and 3000 arts and social science.

VI

Horizons seemed to be widening in many directions at the time of Charles Barratt's support for the idea of establishing a university in the city. The new Cathedral was already being built and was to be consecrated in May 1962, the Belgrade Theatre, the first in the country to be built with the direct backing of a local authority, had been opened in 1958 and the relatively modest layout of the central Colleges of Art and Technology was shortly to be expanded into what was to become the Lanchester Polytechnic. In October 1963 work began on the first instalment of the great hospital complex at Walsgrave. The city was indeed acquiring a new stature during this period but there were some things which could not be done. A large swimming baths and indoor sports centre was completed in 1965 but it has so far proved impossible to find resources for either a concert hall or a new central lending library.

The Museums and Art Gallery, which are administered as part of the library service, owe a great deal to the generosity of Sir Alfred Herbert both before and after the war. Among its many exhibitions the Art Gallery gives hospitality to the three local societies, the Coventry and Warwickshire Society of Artists, the Art Circle and the Art Guild. The museum staff have shown a lively interest in the work of the Archaeological Society and helped with valuable excavation work on the site of Coventry's first Cathedral and the Lunt fort at Baginton. They were encouraged in July 1970 by the opening of the Whitefriars, with its cloister and dormitory, as an additional museum. There is some record that the Corporation began to accumulate a museum in the 1890s but this collection was somehow dispersed and it was only in 1930 that the city agreed to take over the Folk Museum which had been assembled by the City Guild and Museum Society in old Bablake, and the five interesting old schoolboy uniforms which it then inherited have now been expanded into a sizeable costume collection. In 1937 the Bartleet collection of bicycles was acquired and by 1969 a hundred bicycles and thirty-five vintage cars were stored away because there was nowhere for them to be shown to the public. A new industrial museum is certainly called for since few cities have more to offer to the visitor in this field.

In 1791 a Coventry Library Society was formed among the families of the professional and employing classes and for many years it maintained itself in what had once been a Nonconformist chapel in Hertford Street. When, in the 1860s, its affairs were in a bad way owing to the local economic depression it was agreed that the city should take over its stock as the nucleus of a public library. This happened in 1867, but it was not until 1873 that the present Derby Lane premises were opened, largely owing to the generosity of the revered John Gulson. This appears to have been a very hesitant step towards civic enterprise since, in 1874, the Coventry Book Club was founded to continue the old Library Society's work under another name. The members of the Club bought the books first and only after they had finished with them were they sold to the Public Library at a nominal rate.

In the first half of the twentieth century two chief librarians were responsible for improvements which kept the service abreast of the times. Septimus Pitt, later to go to Glasgow and Librarian in Coventry between 1908 and 1914, introduced the open access system which allowed borrowers to take their own books from the shelves. The number of borrowers' tickets had risen from 5000 when he came, to 20,000 when he left. Charles Nowell, who had been Pitt's Chief Assistant, returned after the war and remained City Librarian until 1931. He established the Reference Library, the Coventry and Warwickshire Collection, the Schools' Library Service and six new branches. He aimed throughout at making the libraries general centres of culture and was particularly interested in the development of radio discussion groups. His successor, Austin Hinton, continued this policy of steady expansion. He established a gramophone society, built up contacts with the repertory theatre and opened special sections of the library for children. But, in 1941, the record of steady progress ended. The Derby Lane premises were destroyed by enemy action and, when Hinton left, what remained of the library had to be kept in temporary premises under an acting Librarian until the end of the war.

Coventry always seems to have been reluctant to spend its money on its public libraries. When a new library building was first thought of in 1868 local newspapers were against it, one saying that the money could be much better spent on a good soup kitchen. The first three branch libraries, built before 1914, were paid for by Andrew Carnegie, the Scottish-American steel king, and in 1936 a proposal to reconstruct the Shire Hall for use as a library and art gallery did not get very far. The two post-war Librarians, Ernest Simpson and Alexander Wilson, found that they had to reconstruct a shattered service without a new central building. When at last it seemed possible that Coventry might become a university town, a new Central Library was designed by Arthur Ling and the first stage was actually finished in January 1967. Excellent and wide-ranging cultural activities, including a record library, have been organised in what accommodation there is, but the completion of the new premises is still awaited.

It has been frequently suggested that, in the post-war period, the people of Coventry do not read very much. In 1959 a government committee reported that no local authority could be regarded as providing a satisfactory library service if it did not spend at least 24*d* per head on books. Coventry's spending had been 10·6*d* per head in 1957/8, less than the amount spent by any other town with a population of more than 100,000. Newcastle, with a similar population, had spent 26·9*d*. In 1966/7, expenditure on new library books in county boroughs averaged £172 per thousand of the population. The figure for Wolverhampton was £182, that for Coventry, the lowest but one for any county borough, was £122. In 1970 Coventry came at the bottom of the list of county boroughs for the number of books in stock and books out per thousand of the population.

VII

The beginning of widespread medical care in Coventry is connected with the two Dispensaries, the General and the Provident, both established in the 1830s. The Provident, where the patient was expected to make a weekly contribution towards the cost of his treatment, remained at work until 1936 and its Victorian building disappeared very much later. It employed a staff of three doctors and Dr St Lawrence Burke, larger than life with a vast family tree on one of his surgery walls, is still remembered. The General gave free treatment and was the origin of the Coventry and Warwickshire Hospital which was officially opened in 1838 and moved to Stoney Stanton Road twenty-nine years later. There it remained as the city's one voluntary hospital, receiving contributions from, among others, neighbouring landowners who presided over its governing body until 1922. By this time the hospital's income was coming more and more from industry, much of it through the Hospital Saturday Fund,[18] and it was time for leading industrialists to take over the government of the hospital.

Close to the Coventry and Warwickshire was the city's isolation hospital, first the so-called Iron Hospital, established in 1872, and ten years later a more permanent building which was sold to the Coventry and Warwickshire in 1930. In 1934 the isolation hospital, which was owned by the City Council, moved to its present building at Whitley near the old eighteen-bed smallpox ward at Pinley. The City Council acquired a second hospital in 1929 when the Board of Guardians was dissolved and the Poor Law Infirmary in Gulson Road was transferred to the Corporation.

Many doctors were well aware that these arrangements were not perfect and that many people who needed medical care could not get it because they were too poor. In 1893 a number of the leading practitioners in the city bearing respected names such as Soden, Webb-Fowler and Iliffe came together to form the Coventry Public Medical Service which was open to all with a maximum weekly income of £2 (later £1 10*s*).[19] Collectors were employed to collect

[18] As early as 1938 the Fund was enjoying an income of £50,000 and still maintains its convalescent homes.

[19] Among doctors who later joined the scheme we find the names of Collington, Kenderdine and Ballantyne.

1*d* per week from each contributing member, and this small payment entitled them to free medical treatment. The Service had its own list of chemists who were paid for their prescriptions from the central fund and at the end of the year the doctors shared any profit there was among themselves as a return for their services. Similar schemes were to be found elsewhere and Coventry doctors who were not in the Public Medical Service tended to operate in the same way within their own practices, employing their own collectors. The 1911 Health Insurance Act, which protected only the breadwinner in each family, did not affect the success of these schemes, and the Public Medical Service, which had 15,000 members in 1916, did not finally cease until the beginning of the National Health Service in 1948.

The Coventry doctors of those days were by no means lacking in social concern, but one of the reasons why they operated a scheme such as the Public Medical Service was that they needed the guaranteed income it provided. Some general practitioners also gave their services to the various hospitals but voluntary hospitals in particular could not afford much in the way of fees, nor could they afford large, full-time medical establishments. A new doctor, on arriving at the Coventry and Warwickshire, found that he was one of the two resident medical staff. These two young men also did most of the emergency operations, a fact which did not surprise one of them who had just come from a Salford hospital where he had not set foot outside the door for three months.

The National Health scheme was to achieve many objectives, one of the most important being the co-ordination of the many different types of hospital into a common service. This was an ideal which had widespread support but, unfortunately, there was no agreement on how to carry it out. Many felt that municipalisation was the answer, but the medical profession had enormous objections to this, and it was seen when the National Health Service Act was introduced that they had been successful. Coventry City Council, like every other local authority, was to lose control over its hospitals; Birmingham was to be the centre of one of the new Regional Hospital Boards and for the Coventry area there was to be a Hospital Management Committee.

Some of the property being used for hospital purposes in 1948 was so obviously unsuitable that it was either not taken over at all or was certain to have a very short life. The beds in the old smallpox hospital at Pinley came into the first category but the wards built in the grounds of Keresley Hall during the war, with their thick concrete roofs and blast-proof walls, in the second. Whitley Hospital had a new building, Gulson Road was not very convenient but had stood the test of war and the Coventry and Warwickshire had been badly damaged but could be rebuilt. When everything was added up the total number of hospital beds in the city was 892. It was not enough, the deficiency was of long standing and the new hospital authority would have to do its best to eliminate it.

The task was not made any easier by the shortages of the immediate post-war period but by 1953 the first talks were being held on the subject of the site of a new general hospital. Two were considered and rejected, the first at Pinley and the second at Tile Hill, to the west of the city. The final choice fell upon the grounds of Walsgrave Hall, to the east of the city along the Leicester road. The Wakefield family had left the Hall in 1952 and the Hospital Board was coming to favour the Walsgrave site by 1953. However, it was not until November 1955 that the Ministry of Housing and Local Government allocated forty-seven acres of the Park for a hospital and open space. English planning procedure is so magnificently fair to all the interests concerned that time was inevitably consumed while the medical needs of an expanding city were growing.

Then came the longest delay of all. It was not until January 1962 that the Macmillan Government announced a great programme of hospital expansion which would include the Walsgrave scheme, and work began there a year later. The city had many medical needs which were crying out for attention but there was no doubt which came first on the list. The maternity and child welfare services had long been dependent on the wartime buildings at Keresley, and new maternity wards were the first to be opened at Walsgrave in 1966. From that date progress has been steady; the new acute block was handed over for hospital use in 1968 and psychiatric accommodation has been built since. All this enabled the temporary premises at Keresley to be closed down and the load on some of the older buildings still in use to be lightened.

The major reorganisation of the hospitals has been accompanied by widespread changes in the local authority's health and welfare services. The care of children, the provision of clinics and the employment of midwives and health visitors have all been local authority responsibilities for many years. They have been developed in the post-war period when the public conscience has become more ready to see its responsibilities and public expectations have become higher. An increasing awareness of the problems of mental health and old age have also meant that the local authority's commitment in this field is bound to remain large although the services provided may not stay the same.

NOTE: *The Family Health Club*

The success of the National Health Service was unfortunately accompanied by the failure of a most interesting unofficial scheme. One of the outstanding social experiments of the 1930s had been the Peckham Health Centre, created in a working-class district of London. There, in 1934, had been erected a large, well-designed building containing a theatre, swimming-pool and gymnasia, as well as doctors' consulting rooms. It was a great experiment in preventive medicine, in getting people to keep themselves healthy instead of going to a doctor only when they were ill. The Centre was the creation of two doctors, Scott Williamson and Innes Pierce, and one of those interested in it was Kenneth Barlow who later came to Coventry as a general practitioner and anaesthetist at the Coventry and Warwickshire Hospital.

In the enthusiasm for social reconstruction towards the end of the war one of the founders of the Peckham experiment suggested to Barlow that he might try something even more ambitious in Coventry by creating an entirely new community with its own farms and based on a health centre. The Coventry Family Health Club, in which a number of people, such as Kenneth Bell, friend of Neville Gorton, were to lose money they could ill afford, purchased about 300 acres of land at Binley outside the city. There they proposed to build an estate of 2000 houses and flats with its own schools, shopping centre and cinema. The scheme was, in fact, defeated by the friends of social progress; Warwickshire County Council was in favour, but Coventry City Council was not. Its objections were powerful and decisive and the scheme was beaten, although that good and shrewd man, Sidney Stringer, then Leader of the Council, appears to have had some doubts about what his colleagues were doing.

CHAPTER TEN

Planning

The difficulties of the 1930s and attempts to resolve them. E. H. Ford. The appointment of a City Architect. War. The Gibson Plan. The Development Plan of 1951. The early building. The coming of Arthur Ling. Shopping in Coventry. Roads.

I

'In the centre of the city I found ample remains of the cutlery, cloth, button, clock and ribbon periods scattered about, now oddly mixed up with Lyons, cheap tailors, Ronald Colman, cut-price shops, berets and loudspeakers' (J. B. Priestley, *English Journey*).

It was this sharp contrast between old and new which most impressed J. B. Priestley when he visited Coventry in the autumn of 1933. The number of half-timbered and gabled houses, the soaring stone and carved wood surprised him, but he also noticed the thick ring of 'motor-car and cycle factories, the machine tool makers, the magneto manufacturers and the electrical companies ... [beyond which] ... are whole new quarters where the mechanics and fitters, and turners and furnace men live in neat brick rows, and drink their beer in gigantic new public houses and take their wives to gigantic new picture theatres.' It was these industries and the people who worked in them which had been gradually changing the face of Coventry since the beginning of the twentieth century.

In 1901 the City Council had controlled an area of about 4000 acres and a population of less than 70,000; by the time of Priestley's visit it was estimated that 184,000 people lived within the city, which had been extended in 1928 and 1932 to cover an area of over 19,000 acres. Between 1921 and 1937 Coventry's population rose at a rate seven times that of the country as a whole, after allowing for the boundary extensions. Thus, by the end of the 1930s, Coventry had a population far greater than that with which its still largely mediaeval central area and road system could cope. Its inadequacy was made even more obvious by its relative prosperity at a time when many goods which had previously been considered luxuries were coming within the reach of many ordinary people. People were buying their own homes on the new housing estates and services had to be provided for them by the local authority. Some were buying cars, making the problem of providing an adequate road system equally urgent. The problem was especially acute in Coventry where in 1938 there were 68 cars per 1000 of the population, nearly double the national average of 39 per 1000. The narrow streets of the city centre had to carry not only these local cars but also trams and buses bringing people from the suburbs and through traffic travelling from London to Birmingham and the north. Since there were few car parks the congestion in these central streets was made worse by parked cars and vans loading and unloading on either side of many roads.

The provision of new services and the extension of the old meant a great deal of work for the Corporation and the large imposing Council House which was opened in 1920 soon proved insufficient to contain all the Corporation Departments, which were therefore scattered throughout the city in old and unsatisfactory buildings. A new and larger police station, a fire station and law courts were all needed. The Technical College was housed in an old factory in Earl Street and this was rapidly proving inadequate for the needs of the 1930s. Coventry had no civic hall, no art gallery and no museum; and local organisations began to urge the provision of these amenities which they felt were essential if the new Coventry was to develop any worthwhile cultural life or corporate spirit.

It was the increasing urgency of these needs which faced the Council and its chief officers in the 1920s and 1930s. It soon became clear that the only adequate answer to the chaos in the city centre would be extensive reconstruction, but there was neither the legislation nor the finance available to make this a practical proposition. Until the Town Planning Act of 1944 the only way to achieve radical change over a large area of built-up land was through a private Act of Parliament, a long and expensive business. Even the Town Planning Act of 1932 which, in theory, gave an authority power to plan any part of the area under its control made none of the financial provisions which alone could have made extensive re-development by a city or county council a feasible proposition.

In 1924, therefore, when Ernest Ford, the newly-arrived City Engineer, was asked by the Council to prepare a Town Planning map of the city he had to omit from the plan the city centre which was the most densely built-up area and therefore that which was most in need of attention. However, the plan could be used to control the development of the city's suburbs. It included much of the land outside the city boundary as it then was, land controlled by the urban and rural district councils of Meriden, Bedworth and Foleshill in the north and west and Kenilworth and Warwick in the south. In all, Ford wished to include in the plan nearly 30,000 acres; and the Ministry of Health, which was at that time the Ministry concerned with town planning matters, gave approval to the inclusion of most of this area in the Coventry Plan. During the twenties and thirties a beginning was made on working out detailed plans for the five districts into which the area was divided but the process of Ministry approval was so slow that by 1938 only one of these district plans had been completed.

Despite the lack of an overall plan for the city centre something obviously had to be done to deal with the problems presented by the increase in motor traffic. As early as 1920 the Corporation had promoted a local Act of Parliament which would enable them to make six improvements to the central road pattern.[1] It was left to Ernest Ford to complete the detailed planning of these road schemes. The four planned improvements to roads such as High Street and Parkside were less important than the building of two completely new roads. The first, called Corporation Street and stretching from Fleet Street to the Burges, was opened in 1931, and the second, Trinity Street, from Hales Street to Broadgate, was finished in 1937.[2]

[1] In 1914, largely due to the persistence of Vincent Wyles, the Council decided to produce a plan of the entire city and carry out far-reaching street improvements. It was this idea which was revived after the war.

[2] Unfortunately the construction of Trinity Street involved the destruction of Butcher Row, Little Butcher Row and the Bull Ring, a collection of picturesque, half-timbered buildings, known as the Shambles. However, the demolition of this area was not regretted as much as might have been expected since the buildings had long been in a bad state of disrepair.

As the volume of traffic increased so it became clear that even these two new wide roads did little to help to ease the traffic situation in the narrow crowded streets and it also became clear that some effort should be made to keep traffic not actually meant for the city centre away from the main shopping streets. In order to do this, Ford adopted an idea which had already been widely used in many towns in the 1930s; the idea of ring roads. Ford seems to have thought that Coventry needed a series of three of which only one, the outer, was anything more than an idea by 1939. As early as July 1924 Warwickshire County Council had informed Coventry City Council that the Ministry of Transport favoured the idea of a by-pass to the south of the city from the London Road at Willenhall to the Birmingham Road at Allesley. On 20 February 1925 the City Engineer met representatives of the County Council and a few days later reported to his Committee. In this report Ford suggested that the County Council's scheme be accepted as 'Coventry is fairly well served with radial roads but ring roads to connect these are very desirable'. He said that it was to be hoped that the bypass road would eventually act as a section of an outer ring road to encircle the city centre at a distance of about three miles. As control of the land on which the by-pass was to be built passed from county to city, so the City Council took a more active part in preparing the plans for the road and in 1930 it was Coventry which was granted powers by Parliament to begin work on part of this dual carriage-way near Allesley. Economic restrictions brought about by the Depression meant that work was slow and the six-miles-long road was not finished until 1939.

It was while these new roads were being considered that the Council decided to investigate the possibility of redeveloping part of the city as a civic centre where a civic hall, art gallery, museum, library and college could be planned as a group of buildings worthy of the status of the growing city. In November 1934 the Council set up a Sub-Committee to examine proposals for the building of such a centre. The Sub-Committee reported during the following year suggesting that the Council should begin buying land around the Council House in Earl Street and Little Park Street and gradually construct in this area the buildings needed.

A renewal of public interest in the subject of planning the central area coincided with this Council report. In 1934 the Coventry and Warwickshire Society of Artists impressed upon the Council the need for an art gallery and two years later the City Guild was revived under the leadership of some of the city's younger architects, Claude Redgrave, Rolf Hellberg and Alfred Gardner. The City Guild and Museum Society had originally been founded as an antiquarian society in 1914 under the leadership of the Brazil family and Mary Dormer Harris.[3] The Guild of the 1930s was a very different body. Its aim was not only to preserve old buildings but to create a wider concern for the beauty of the city and to instil in it a new spirit. It held lectures given by people involved in many different aspects of the city's life, such as the Provost of the Cathedral and the City Engineer; it made plans for the remodelling of parts of the city such as Greyfriars Green and, in 1937, it made a survey of traffic and car parking in an attempt to assess the city's needs and how to cater for them. The Guild also helped to promote interest in the building of a civic centre. They held an exhibition on this subject in the Technical College during the winter of 1936/7 and in February 1939 their Civic Centre Sub-Committee, which had been set up three years before produced four different plans, three based on land near the Council House and the fourth on Greyfriars Green.

The interest in the replanning of the city aroused by the action of City Council and City Guild was at its height when, in November 1937, the Labour Party gained control of the City Council for the first time.

II

One of the first acts of the new City Council was to set up a Policy Advisory Committee and, early in 1938, this Committee came to the decision that Coventry needed an Architectural Department. As yet, very few cities had such a department but those which did, such as Bristol, were consulted so that by July the Policy Advisory Committee was able to set out a summary of the duties to be expected of a City Architect. The Committee was careful to point out that his duties should in no way encroach upon those of the City Engineer,

[3] See Chapter One, page 19.

who remained 'the responsible officer . . . for the preparation of town planning schemes ... and other town planning matters'.

Of the sixty-nine applicants for the post, the Committee chose a young man of twenty-nine who was then Deputy County Architect of the Isle of Ely. But their choice of Donald, now Sir Donald, Gibson was not as unexpected as might first appear as he was filled with the same spirit of enthusiasm, willingness to experiment and care for the way people should live as many of the men who gave him the job. The appointment of this relatively unknown young man to the responsible position of chief officer in a large authority led to increasing professional interest in Coventry's new department. The *Architects' Journal* late in 1938 praised Coventry for its foresight in appointing a young man of ideals to such a post. This publicity meant that, for some of the posts in the new department, there were as many as 700 applicants, and when Coventry City Architect's Department began work in January 1939, its staff consisted almost entirely of young men who were to prove themselves both enthusiastic and able.

In the few months which remained before the outbreak of war most of the Department's work was confined to the designing of necessary but commonplace articles such as public conveniences and lamp-posts. Of the large and exciting tasks which Frederick Smith had outlined when talking to Gibson after his appointment there was as yet little sign. The one project which was begun at this time was one for which Donald Gibson felt the deepest disapproval. This was the plan for an art gallery to be built with money provided by Sir Alfred Herbert to a design of his own choosing. To Gibson, the white Portland stone building with its green cupola was far from being in harmony with the more domestic red brick and stone buildings around it, but despite the doubts which he voiced in no uncertain manner the building of the art gallery went ahead.

Progress within the Department was slow despite the request from the Policy Advisory Committee in February 1939 that it collaborate with the City Engineer's Department on the preparation of a plan for a civic centre. A joint team from both Departments was set up and began work but here again little seemed to be achieved. Gibson and some of the members of his team, therefore, began meeting each other in their own homes to talk about their ideas of what form a civic centre should take. These evening talks led to the holding of an exhibition and series of lectures to stimulate public interest in town planning. This exhibition was duly held in St Mary's Hall during May and June 1939 and lectures were given by such well-known authorities on various aspects of town planning as Thomas Sharp and Clough Williams-Ellis. The exhibition and lectures were officially run by the local branch of the A.A.S.T.A. (the Association of Architects, Surveyors and Technical Assistants) which, in effect, meant the City Architect's Department. The centre piece of the exhibition was their model of the ideal civic centre for Coventry. It showed a large civic park spreading down from the hill on which stood St Michael's Cathedral and the Church of the Holy Trinity to Pool Meadow. Within the park and following the lines of its contours were three-storeyed curved buildings which would house the municipal offices, art gallery, library, and college.

Ernest Ford, as the officer directly responsible for town planning, had already put his ideas before the Civic Centre Sub-Committee and there is in existence a map bearing his name and dated 1938 showing possible future zoning, not only of the civic area but of the entire city centre, including new roads and open spaces. In his hands the city emerges as a quieter and more intimate place with a number of squares in the civic area. Only between Broadgate and the Cathedral did he envisage the broad vistas and grand spaciousness of Donald Gibson's plan. In 1938 he summed up his attitude to the planning of a city centre as having two main aims; the first to make the city work, and the second to make it noble. Although in many ways he showed himself to be very much the traditionalist, in others he was prepared to use ideas as advanced as Gibson's. In a paper written before the war he had already emphasised the need to get away from the idea that motor traffic and pedestrians must mix together in a shopping street. Instead, he said, there was a great need for areas where pedestrians could move about freely and safely in precincts or arcades. Despite this, the interests and views of the two chief officers involved in planning did not coincide and co-operation on the drawing up of a civic centre scheme did little to ease the situation.

All these ideas seem to have encouraged the public to put

forward their own views on redevelopment in the centre. The local newspaper supported the efforts of the City Council to interest people in replanning by organising a competition in connection with the rebuilding of parts of the central area and at least one man, Charles Payne, did himself produce a plan for a civic centre. However, only nine months after the new Architect's Department had begun work the whole situation was drastically changed by the coming of war.

III

With the beginning of the war in September 1939, the possibility of any actual building seemed so remote that in Coventry the Architect's Department soon found its existence being questioned in the Council Chamber. In January 1940 Alderman Charles Payne asked in a Council meeting if the estimated cost of the Department for that year (£10,000) could be justified in view of the fact that most of the architects would soon be called up, and that there would be very little work for those who remained until the end of the war. Gibson and his Committee fought hard to ensure the retention of the Department. Air-raid shelters and houses had to be designed and built, and it was work like this which occupied them throughout the spring and summer of 1940. During this time the joint planning group of architects and engineers continued its work, although it was becoming increasingly obvious that the views of City Architect and City Engineer were as different as could be expected from two men of different generations, different temperaments and different skills.

Bodies interested in planning, such as the National Housing and Town Planning Council, formed in the late nineteenth century to press for planning legislation, urged local planning authorities to continue their activities, so that they might make adequate provision for the situation which would arise at the end of the war in a country which was already in need of urban planning. This concern for the post-war situation was shared by the Government. In January 1940 the Barlow Report (*The Report of the Royal Commission on the Distribution of Industrial Population*) had been published. This was the first comprehensive look at the basic problems facing large cities and their future development. In the Report the Commission pointed out that, after the war, government intervention in such spheres as the distribution of industry would have to be very much greater than it had been previously. This would mean the active involvement of the Government in town planning. In the atmosphere of wartime when government was taking action in many fields in which it had not previously been concerned, the Barlow Report caused a great deal of discussion. As a result the Cabinet, in October 1940, asked Lord Reith to report to them upon the laws which would be required to help forward the post-war reconstruction of British cities.

Only a month later much of Coventry's shopping and commercial centre was destroyed by enemy bombs and the real task of the local planning authority had begun. The most immediate jobs of the men concerned in planning were the emergency repair of houses which had escaped serious damage and the giving of help in the planning and building of the hostels and camps needed to accommodate the temporary workers who were flooding into the city. While this essential work was going on the decision was taken by the Council to proceed immediately with plans for the rebuilding of the post-war city. At their first meeting after the blitz the General Purposes Committee recommended that a City Redevelopment Committee should be set up to consider 'the steps which it will be desirable for the municipality to take to secure a worthy replanning and redevelopment of the city'. On 8 December the City Redevelopment Committee held its first meeting under the chairmanship of Jack Moseley. Its first action was to request the City Engineer and City Architect to collaborate in the preparation of a plan for the city centre.

Coventry, while being among the first, was certainly not the only city to be devastated during the winter of 1940/1. It shared with others the huge problems which this largely unprepared for eventuality brought about. There was no national legal framework within which the vast programmes of rebuilding could fit and compensation be paid to those who had lost home and livelihood. It became part of Lord Reith's job to assess just what would be needed for this task. He decided to make a detailed study of two or three cities in order to try to establish points which could later be used in drawing up national legislation. Coventry was chosen as one of the cities to be included in this study and, early in January 1941, Lord Reith met representatives of the Corporation in London in order to discuss the city's future. At this meeting he seems to have emphasised the need for the rapid production of an outline plan, a plan which should be concerned with the best which could be built, rather than with the most economical; a plan which could inspire, rather than one which could be easily costed. At about the same time, he sent a senior official of the Ministry of Health to Coventry to attend Council and Committee meetings and to report back to him. This the official did in March 1941, when he returned to London with a plan which had been agreed upon by the Redevelopment Committee.

The speed with which this plan was produced gives no indication of the bitter conflict which preceded its presentation to the Minister. Even before the blitz gave Coventry the opportunity for radical changes within the city centre, the City Engineer and City Architect had shown very different attitudes to the nature of town planning. It had quickly become clear that the Committee's instructions that the two officers should co-operate in the drawing up of a plan could not be carried out. Each department, therefore, concentrated on its own ideas, and both Ford and Gibson presented their different plans to the Committee in February 1941. Under the leadership of George Hodgkinson, the Committee chose Gibson's plan and resolved that, in future, the primary responsibility in town planning matters should be placed upon the City Architect. In May 1941 this decision was confirmed by the Council, although it was agreed that, until Ford's retirement, the two men should act together as officers jointly in charge of town planning.

It is important, however, not to see E. H. Ford as a man merely trying to put the clock back, to rebuild the old city around its services. In a report to Lord Reith, representatives of the Ministry of Works and Buildings said that Ford's plan was certainly not to be regarded as conservative in the light of previous planning, although it did aim at the retention of most of the lines of the old medieval lanes. Ford himself said that his prime purpose was to rebuild the city so that it would work without costing the authority too much money by disturbing rateable values unnecessarily. A plan bearing his name and dated January 1941 shows just how far he was prepared to go in changing the city. He accepted the pedestrian precinct contained in the Gibson plan, but the rest of his design was on a much less monumental scale than that envisaged by the young City Architect. He retained his idea of small squares around the Cathedral and civic offices to the east of the central hill-top. However, the basis of his plan was certainly the widening of streets already in existence rather than the substitution of a completely new street pattern. His ideas did not have the wide and radical vision of Donald Gibson, and it was this which appealed to Hodgkinson and his fellow members of the City Redevelopment Committee and which fitted most closely into Lord Reith's idea that the plan should be as much an ideal to boost morale as anything else. Once the Council had made its decision Ford loyally carried out his duties as Joint Town Planning Officer and occasionally gave lectures explaining the plan to national bodies such as the Institute of Municipal and County Engineers and the Royal Sanitary Institute.

By March 1941, therefore, the citizens of Coventry were able to look at sketches and plans of how it was thought their new city should appear. As soon as it was published the plan was hailed as a great pioneering effort. It must be remembered that most of the theoretical work which has since been done in Britain on modern town planning had then not been produced. Alker Tripp's book on town planning and road traffic, for instance, which first impressed the idea of the separation of pedestrians and motor traffic on urban planners, did not appear until 1942, and the Ministry of Town and Country Planning's handbook on the redevelopment of central areas was not produced until 1947. Of the cities forced to rebuild their central areas after the war, Coventry was undoubtedly the leader in daring from the first to accept a plan which was radically different from anything which had previously been envisaged on any scale in Britain. Bristol, for instance, remained faithful on the whole to its old street lines and Plymouth decided to adopt dual carriageways and a grid pattern on the lines of many American towns.

The central theme of this, Donald Gibson's first post-blitz plan, was the precinct of shops to which there would be motor access for service vehicles only at the back. The idea behind this was to bring back the comfortable, more spacious days when wandering from shop to shop was not done at the mercy of cars, lorries and buses. The front of the shops, to be built near the line of the old Smithford Street, Coventry's main pre-war shopping street, would face two squares linked with banks of plants, bushes and water cascades, looking up to the spire of the old Cathedral across a stretch of green, Broadgate Square. The pedestrian precinct was designed on two levels, an idea based upon the Rows at Chester. One of the architects working with Gibson at this time has described a visit he made with the City Architect to London when Gibson, oblivious of the traffic, stood in the middle of Lower Regent Street and pointed out to his startled friend the proportions of that street as the example Coventry should follow. Wide, straight roads would give people approaching Broadgate long views of this focal point. Gibson retained from his earlier plan the large park stretching from Trinity Street to Pool Meadow and Cox Street, in which to set civic offices, art gallery, college and museum.

In line with the ideas of the times the centre was strictly zoned. Commerce retained what was largely its old area to the south of Smithford Street, around Greyfriars Green and the railway station, while entertainment was centred upon Corporation Street. A green parkway encircled an inner ring road (more or less on the line of the inner circulatory road today). This would keep through traffic out of the centre while providing an attractive line around it. There were later many changes in the detail of the plan, but the basic ideas have in general remained and can still be seen in the plan of today.

No other blitzed British city rivalled Coventry in the speed with which the plans were published, but the general public did not see the drawbacks caused by this very speed. The plans of February 1941 were really little more than sketches of the ideas of a small group of men and women centred on Donald Gibson. There were many problems in their way. Several of the members of the Department had been called up for active service leaving the office understaffed. The most urgent work which had been assigned to the City Architect's Department in November 1940 was the planning of accommodation for incoming workers, the inspection and repair of houses and the building of emergency houses and temporary shops. This left the Department with little time to devote to the detailed planning of over 200 acres of land in the centre of the city.

The main problem was the fact that the plan was prepared in an atmosphere of uncertainty generated by the lack of a legal framework which would provide for the large scale buying of land, changing of property boundaries and compensation for property owners. All this was essential if rapid rebuilding was to be a viable proposition. The Ministry of Town and Country Planning, set up in 1943,[4] could not officially approve the plan just as the Corporation did not, at this time, have sufficient power actually to impose the plan on existing owners. Until the 1944 Town and Country Planning Act, very little information as to how redevelopment on such a vast scale would be financed was forthcoming from the Ministry, and the circle was completed by the fact that, until the Minister had information borne out by the results of carefully worked out surveys, he had no clear idea of exactly what towns such as Coventry needed in the way of legislation. At times relations between Ministry and local government officials became very strained, each waiting for action by the other, and complaining bitterly when this was not forthcoming. The fact, that, by the end of the war, a practical plan was being worked out with the agreement of all was largely due to the sympathetic relationship of two men, E. H. Doubleday, the Regional Officer of the Ministry stationed in Birmingham, and Frederick Smith, the Town Clerk.

The Ministry of Town and Country Planning was not the only place where misgivings about the plan were voiced. Many people in Coventry itself felt that vision had been put before practicability. Letters in the press expressed great bitterness over the proposed demolition by the Council of the few of the old city's landmarks which still remained. The most vociferous critics, however, were the Coventry traders. They adhered firmly to the traditional idea that people would not shop if they had to walk to the shops from car parks. It was, therefore, regarded as essential that shops should face a street where people could pull up and park for a short time. Members of the Chamber of Commerce had produced their own plan for a city centre in which they accepted a small extent of pedestrian area but wanted it encircled by wide shopping roads. In the face of this

[4] This Ministry was replaced seven years later by, firstly, the Ministry of Local Government and Planning and later in the same year by the Ministry of Housing and Local Government.

volume of criticism the Planning Officers, towards the end of 1945, were forced to accept the idea of a road bisecting their planned precinct. They saw this as the negation of their attempt to provide quiet and traffic-free shopping, and in an endeavour to avoid this, they proposed a traffic bridge which would take traffic flowing along the intercepting road over the precinct. This was later rejected in favour of pedestrian subways, and the idea remained in the Coventry plan until the coming of a new architect in 1955 made a reversal of the decision possible.

For Donald Gibson and his Department these years of war consisted of emergency work, routine surveying and the fight to preserve the principles and details of their plans. Throughout this rather unhappy period Gibson was given full and unstinting support by the City Redevelopment Committee led by George Hodgkinson, whose faith in the plan equalled that of its authors. Gradually, the detailed work on the plan was done and by the end of the war it was coming to completion with the certainty of the 1944 Town and Country Planning Act behind it. Under this Act compulsory purchase was made a lot easier for local authorities in areas which had been declared Areas of Extensive War Damage by the Ministry.

In the winter of 1945–6 the centre of Coventry was still a grey, unpainted waste with cellars and temporary corrugated-iron buildings where once prosperous shops had stood; but something more than shops, cinemas and public houses had gone. The life of a whole community had been dislocated and those who could remember the cheerful, friendly pre-war shopping crowds were painfully aware of the change. It seemed to many that the Gibson plan, prepared by a young and daring architect without regard to cost, was calling them to do something far more important than to merely rebuild the city centre; the best of them felt that they would be remaking the city's soul.

The purchase of land and the rebuilding of whole areas by an enlightened local authority was nothing new; Joseph Chamberlain had built Corporation Street while he was mayor of Birmingham and Coventry City Council itself had created its own Corporation Street and Trinity Street in the 1930s at a time when it already owned part of the land in the city centre. The difference now lay in the huge scale of the problem and the new means of tackling it provided by the Acts of 1944 and 1947. The general planning provision of the 1944 Act was sufficient for many cities, but it did not wholly satisfy Coventry. Compulsory powers were invoked to enable the Corporation itself to carry out the rebuilding with the tenants of shops and offices paying it rent. One day, it was intended, after the rebuilding had been paid for, a great annual revenue should come in to the Corporation from these rents and be available for the use of the community. This policy did not involve the redistribution of income as between classes; it made the present pay for the future. Like all ideals, it has not always worked out as expected but this idealistic side should never be forgotten.

Liberals and others had long felt that it was unjust for property-owners to have the value of their property increased by the action of the community and attempts to tax such values had been made in Lloyd George's People's Budget of 1909. Coventry Corporation Acts before the war had included provisions which enabled owners to be charged when the value of their property was enhanced by the laying of sewers or the building of roads. Frederick Smith, when Town Clerk, was particularly interested in this and gave evidence to the Uthwatt Committee on Compensation and Betterment which reported in 1942. Under the Town and Country Planning Act of 1947 it seemed that a new opportunity was being presented for each community to regain part of the increase in property values for which its actions had been partly responsible.

Meanwhile, Gibson was using every opportunity presented to him to establish the basic principles of his design. One of his first chances was the official Victory Celebrations of June 1946. Instead of a fireworks display, Gibson suggested that more suitable would be the laying of a levelling stone near the head of what was to be the pedestrian precinct. This was agreed to by the City Council. Gibson got in touch with a sculptor friend of his, Trevor Tennant, and together they drove one evening to Westmorland, chose a suitable stone and worked out the design of the Phoenix rising from the flames. The stone was ready to be laid in place in time for Victory Day, 8 June 1946.

The building of the large Broadgate Square would have to be first in the establishment of the plan and a beginning was made possible in 1946 when the Dutch people sent a gift of bulbs and plants to Coventry. This meant that somewhere had to be found in the city centre for the gift to be planted before the autumn of 1947. The proposed Broadgate island was the obvious place. The owners of all save one of the plots of land which would be needed if Broadgate was to be established as in the plan agreed to sell. The one remaining eventually sold the land to the Corporation after work had already begun and a Compulsory Purchase Order submitted. A reluctant Ministry of Transport, whose authority would be needed for the construction of the road around the garden, agreed that it should be constructed and gave permission for the work to begin. The same sort of use was made of the Savings for Reconstruction Exhibition held in March 1948 in two marquees on the derelict land where Broadgate House and the Leofric Hotel now stand. As a focal point of the Exhibition a mast with a gilded elephant and castle (Coventry's symbol) on top was erected and this was later retained as a marking point for the top of the Precinct.

IV

In January 1946 the Public Enquiry into the city's application for a Declaratory Order under the 1944 Act began. This would make it possible for the Corporation to purchase compulsorily 452 acres of land in the city centre. In July of the following year the Ministry of Town and Country Planning declared 274 acres of this area to be an Area of Extensive War Damage and a way was opened for the beginning of actual rebuilding in the centre of the city. A month later the Town and Country Planning Act of 1947 came into force giving local planning authorities even wider powers to regulate the use of land. It also laid upon them the responsibility for producing a development plan which would give guidelines for as far ahead as ten or twenty years while leaving the detailed planning flexible as ideas and needs changed over this period. The plan was to be produced if possible within five years. Coventry City Council presented their Development Plan to the Ministry in 1951 after public inquiries, discussions and meetings and it was officially approved by the Minister in 1957.

When compared with the Review of the Plan made in 1966 the original Development Plan of 1951 is a much shorter and simpler work. The elaborate systems of survey and projection used in 1966 were not so widespread in the immediate post-war years. Despite this, the problems raised by both often appear similar, although many are intensified; diversification of industry, improvement of the road system and of shopping facilities in the centre of the city and the provision of adequate housing and other services all loom large in both plans. Again, both have had to fit into the larger plan for the West Midlands region.

The first Regional Plan for the West Midlands was prepared by Sir Patrick Abercrombie and Herbert Jackson immediately after the war. One of their aims was to try to reduce the magnet effect of the Birmingham conurbation by introducing new industries into near-by towns which could then take overspill population. Coventry was one of the cities considered for this and the 1951 Plan allowed for 40,000 people from Birmingham to move into Coventry over an unspecified period. The regional planners proposed two motor roads, one from London to the north-east and one from South Wales to Yorkshire. These would cross to the west of Coventry taking much traffic away from the city's roads and, therefore, they had to be taken into consideration by the City Engineer.

Much of the first plan has changed over nearly twenty years; the unexpectedly rapid increase in traffic and the vastly developed national programme of motorways has made alterations in the planned road pattern necessary, and the rigid zoning which caused much discussion at the 1953 Enquiry into the Development Plan has now been modified. However, many of the central ideas of the Plan remain; all but light industry is gradually being moved away from the centre to the edge of the city, the centre is still delineated by a ring road and the dominant fact within this area is the pedestrian precinct.

V

Broadgate House, the first building to be begun in the city centre, was developed by the Corporation, a policy previously followed in the construction of the Drinkwater Arcade.[5] This development brought additional problems for the weekly meetings of chief officers held with Charles Barratt in the chair. At these, each part of the city's development was carefully co-ordinated and the detailed timing of each operation worked out against a background of continual shortages of materials and labour. Essential materials, such as steel, were strictly controlled by the Government and in Coventry only a small proportion of the city's share could be diverted to central redevelopment. The problem was particularly grave here because the city also had an extremely large programme of housing and school building to fulfil. One of the greatest problems was the fact that only 1·5 per cent of its labour-force was employed in the building and civil engineering trades compared with the national average of 6·5 per cent. The question of using prisoner-of-war labour was raised early in 1947 but this was not pursued and the problem remained.

Throughout these years there was an atmosphere of excitement in Coventry. People who were then in the city described it as rather like being in a gold-rush town. There were the same high rewards to be won in the factories of this modern boom town and everywhere there were temporary homes and shops of wood and tin, built often in the shells of buildings bombed a few years before. The excitement of such a place transformed the redevelopment of Coventry into something to be argued about and fought for. Even one of the major stores which intended to rebuild in the city centre produced its own plan for the city centre. Exhibitions of plans and sketches of the new centre were held and models made and shown to the public. The local newspaper in conjunction with the City Council sponsored a competition for ideas and essays on what people would like to see in the city, and for this there were 2500 entries. There was a feeling that Coventry was attracting the attention of the world and all this helped to maintain interest at a time when there was very little actually to see on the ground. The new city, it was hoped, would be a showpiece of modern architecture and an example of the most daring and radical planning in the country.

This attitude was in sharp contrast with that of the people who

[5] In 1932 the city built the Drinkwater Arcade at a cost of £41,545. The twenty-four premises in the Arcade were clear of debt within six years.

felt a deep attachment to the old Coventry and found themselves strangers in this new city which they neither liked nor understood. From them came a great deal of opposition to the plan itself and to many of its details. Sir Giles Gilbert Scott's plans for the new cathedral provoked letters in the local newspaper from both Helen Rotherham, a member of the old Coventry watchmaking family, and Sir Alfred Herbert, who had himself helped to make the city what it was. Both wanted to see the old St Michael's rebuilt as it had been before the blitz. In 1947 Sir Alfred acted as chairman of a meeting held to discuss the cathedral rebuilding proposals and later he helped to organise a petition for the restoration of the old church.[6] Violent objections were also raised against the wooden figures of Lady Godiva and Peeping Tom beneath the clock to be built on the side of the three-storey bridge spanning Hertford Street. They were regarded as suitable for a fairground but not in keeping with the dignity of Coventry.

In May 1948, Broadgate was officially opened by Princess Elizabeth and in December of the same year the Ministry of Works announced that £1½ million had been allocated to Coventry for the first phase of its rebuilding. In the following March the foundations of Broadgate House were laid but it was not until May 1953, nearly thirteen years after the beginning of the raids on Coventry that this, the first of the new buildings in the 'Dream City', was opened. Three months later Woolworths, the first of the large multiples, was also opened to the public. The design of their building had been closely supervised by the City Architect's Department and the firm was in fact asked to modify its original design to make sure that it fitted into the development plan satisfactorily. Other large stores also started building at the beginning of the 1950s, but even before the first shops were open, it was clear that progress was slow and in May the Council decided to grant a lease to a large development company for the building of an hotel block facing Broadgate and matching Broadgate House on the other side of the Precinct.

A year previously the Council had come to the conclusion that the building of an hotel would be too expensive for their limited resources and a modified plan for this block had been recommended by the Redevelopment Committee. The use of a development

[6] See Chapter Six, page 164.

company would make a reversion to the original project possible. The company employed one of the largest contractors in the country, a firm able both to import as much labour as necessary and to make full use of the most advanced techniques. In November, when work on the hotel was beginning, the developers offered to build two link blocks, one between Broadgate House and the British Home Stores, and the other from the hotel to Marks and Spencer's, thus completing the Upper Precinct. At a stormy meeting of the Council in December 1953, the Labour majority rejected the Redevelopment Committee's recommendation to accept the offer. Sidney Stringer argued that the benefits accruing to the city from municipal development would be far greater than the short-term benefits of rapid rebuilding, despite the mood of impatience growing among the people. These views carried the day, but two months later the Ministry of Housing and Local Government refused loan sanction for the municipal development of these blocks and the City Council granted the development company the lease. The Hotel was finished within fourteen months and the building of the Upper Precinct was finished by the end of 1955. By this time building controls had been lifted, materials and labour were more plentiful and new techniques were being developed to make building quicker and easier.[7]

The Council had early decided, largely on the inspiration of Donald Gibson, that the modern buildings of the new city should, as had happened in the great cities of early centuries, be used to provide a background for works of art. The statue of Lady Godiva by Sir William Reid-Dick in the centre of Broadgate Garden was a gift from William Bassett-Green,[8] but other features were commissioned by the Council itself acting as patron of both local and international artists. One of the most interesting of these works is the mosaic of the Coventry Martyrs[9] under the Hertford Street Bridge. This shows the brightly-coloured, stylised figures of the

[7] The first of the huge cranes, now so commonplace, was used in Coventry in the construction of the link blocks in the Upper Precinct.

[8] William Bassett-Green (1870–1960) was an estate developer and grandson of Eli Green, the silk manufacturer, who has been mentioned in Chapter One, page 12.

[9] The Coventry Martyrs were burned at the stake for heresy during the reign of Queen Mary.

eleven martyrs surrounded by red and gold tongues of flame. It was designed by Hugh Hosking, who was at the time Principal of Coventry College of Art, and executed by a Genevan mosaicist, René Antonietti.

This use of art, like so many other features of Coventry's central redevelopment, was hailed at the time as being a breakthrough in existing concepts of urban design, but recently this early redevelopment has been looked at anew by architectural critics. One of these is Leslie Ginsburg who, in an article in the *Architectural Review* of January 1969 has described the Upper Precinct as 'correct, seemly, yet dull'. The sharp contrast between this view and descriptions written by the enthusiastic commentators of the 1950s shows clearly how much concepts of architecture have changed over the past twenty years. However, in the very divergence of these views it is possible to see the success of one of Gibson's hopes, namely that his buildings would be expressions of the world of the 1950s. Indeed one of the aims of the Architect's Department in designing Broadgate House was to create a building completely of 1953. Many of the criticisms levelled at Coventry's Precinct today are in fact comments upon the circumstances in which it was built as much as upon the buildings themselves. Financial and material restrictions immediately after the war made redevelopment difficult and the prefabricated blocks of artificial materials now in existence were not available in those early years. For most of his building Gibson used the local red brick, retaining for Coventry the homeliness of a West Midlands market town, but also making possible an end to the policy which he described as 'Queen Anne fronts and Mary Ann backs', since he used the same brick for every side of the buildings.

The Coventry plan was the first in Britain on such a large scale to separate the motor-car from the fronts of shops. Being the first in the field obviously has its disadvantages. There was very little theory to work on at the time and no significant practical examples before the planners. It was Coventry, therefore, which made the mistakes by which later cities and towns have been able to benefit. One of the least successful aspects of the Upper Precinct in Coventry has proved to be the two-level shopping. Unlike the Rows in Chester, upon which it is based, the only access to first-floor level is up a steep flight of steps. It proved difficult to let premises horizontally on this level and instead shops have leased vertical blocks. The idea, therefore, of having a lively terrace looking down upon the square of the Upper Precinct has not come to reality. The lesson has been learnt in the Lower Precinct where use of gentle slopes to both upper and lower levels has made access easier. Nevertheless, despite criticism, Donald Gibson's own contribution to the architectural ideas of his generation has been compared with that made by Roger Fry to the art of the 1920s.

By 1955 the first part of the new shopping centre was complete and the Corporation began the laying out of the first block of the intercepting traffic road. In the civic area the College of Art was open, the first stage of new civic offices was ready for use and a start had been made on the second of the buildings which had been intended for use as an Art Gallery. In accordance with Sir Alfred Herbert's wish, work on the first art gallery had begun in 1939 to a plan which Donald Gibson had felt was totally out of harmony with its surroundings. After the war Sir Alfred had not only doubled his original gift but instructed his architect to alter his design in order to bring it into line with Corporation policy. Thus order was slowly emerging from the temporary streets and tin shops when an unexpected and unsought for change occurred.

Donald Gibson resigned from his post in Coventry at the end of 1954. Despite attempts to keep in the city this man who had become so identified with Coventry's rebirth after 1940, Gibson left to become County Architect of Nottinghamshire in January 1955. Three years later he left the Midlands for the post of Director-General of Works at the War Office from which he moved in 1962 to the Ministry of Public Buildings and Works.

VI

The man who took Donald Gibson's place had already been working in town planning for the London County Council for fifteen years and was accustomed to dealing with far-reaching civic redevelopment. Arthur Ling had been trained at London University and had later worked for two years in the office of that brilliant partnership, Maxwell Fry and Walter Gropius. There he showed conspicuous promise and he is still remembered by the surviving partner. His ideas as to what Coventry needed were as decided as had been those of his predecessor. He was not a man to accept the established ideas of his time, and many of his suggestions caused the same sort of controversy as had Gibson's before him. With his coming the plan caught a fresh impetus and regained its capacity to arouse the feelings of the citizens of Coventry. The late 1950s and early 1960s were years in which Coventry again became very often the focus of what was new in the world of town planning and architecture, helped of course by the building of Sir Basil Spence's Cathedral.

In many ways Ling was in tune with the idea of earlier planners in the city. One of his first acts was very much in line with Donald Gibson's policy. With one part of the pedestrian area completed, opposition to the extension of the Precinct had diminished. The City Council, therefore, accepted the idea that the intercepting traffic road was unnecessary and should instead be used to extend the pedestrian area; the centre was thus brought back to a more faithful fulfilment of the original plan. Like Ernest Ford, Ling favoured the development of small, intimate squares where people could sit quietly. The Lower Precinct was the first area to be developed on these lines. The buildings in the Upper Precinct have five or six storeys, those in the Lower Precinct have only three. Access to shops on both levels is very much easier, the range of shopping wider and the individual shop units smaller. In consequence both levels are more freely used. The idea of a small square was also adopted to give the civic theatre much more prominence than had originally been intended. The façade of the Belgrade had been designed as part of a row of shops along Corporation Street. Ling redesigned it so that the main entrance was set in a wall of glass facing not a traffic street, but a small grassed space with bushes and a fountain.

On the other hand, Ling was prepared to use architecture in a way which would not have occurred to Ernest Ford and which was quite different from Donald Gibson's homely style. Gibson had been against the idea of tall buildings in the centre of the city, but under Ling this policy was reversed. The skyline of Coventry had long been dominated by the three spires of Christchurch, Holy Trinity and St Michael's and for many reasons Ling wanted to add to these a number of tall blocks of flats actually within the shopping area. They would add variety to the skyline and would serve to make the terminal points of the pedestrian precincts much more dramatic than had hitherto been planned. Two of these tower blocks were built, one at the end of the Lower Precinct and the other at the end of Smithford Way, the name given to the northern part of what had been the intercepting road.[10] These flats meant that there would be people actually living within the city centre, replacing those who, before the war, had lived inside the line of the city's medieval walls but who had been forced by enemy action and redevelopment to move out to the suburbs. It was intended that they, together with the lights and glass walls of both the circular café in the Lower Precinct and the Belgrade Theatre, should help to introduce some liveliness into the city centre after the shops were closed.

Lights and glass may help to give the impression of liveliness, but there must be something to bring people from their homes into the city centre in the evening. Cinemas were already in existence, but the plan also allowed for a dance hall and a new central swimming baths as extra attractions. The dance hall was constructed on the corner of Smithford Way and the Lower Precinct. It was built of red brick, but the window spaces form a glass mosaic of abstract patterns in red, orange and yellow and the entrance to the dance floor takes the form of a glass tower in which the movement of the lift and people on the staircase break up the long wide expanse of Smithford Way.

The new swimming baths was completed in 1965. It is seen by many as one of the most spectacular buildings in the city centre and is certainly one of the most impressive swimming baths in the country. Again glass has been used for a large proportion of the walls but the structure is dominated by the high long sweeps of roofs at angles and stretching out far beyond the walls and concrete columns which support it. Grant Lewison and Rosalind Billingham

[10] A third, planned for land to the east of Market Way (the southern part of the cross-road) as a second central hotel has now been replaced by a twin-tower project for shops, offices and entertainment.

in their book, *Coventry New Architecture*,[11] say that 'Coventry has been provided with one of the finest swimming pools in the world... this enormous bird-like form has an imaginative and dramatic elegance which outclasses any of the other recently erected buildings in central Coventry and constitutes an exciting addition to the rebuilt city'. The original development plan had allowed for several baths in different parts of the city, but in 1956 it was decided to abandon this idea in favour of one large central baths which would provide three swimming pools, restaurants, rooms for meetings and a games area. Much of this was based upon German experience, for there was probably no such building in Britain at the time. Coventry Baths are now used as the international swimming pool for the West Midlands and the idea has been copied and developed in many other places.

In 1964 Arthur Ling, the man who had inspired these buildings, left Coventry to become Professor of Architecture and Civic Planning at the University of Nottingham and his place was taken by Terence Gregory, who had been his deputy for four years.

VII

As the reconstruction of shops continued and new premises were gradually allocated to shopkeepers who had been bombed out of their old buildings, so the problem of what sort of shops would be needed to provide a balanced city centre came to the fore. The Corporation as far as possible retained control of the allocation of shops and, despite pressures to let to the highest bidder, tried to introduce variety with some success in, for example, the Lower Precinct, but the problem of providing quality shopping was not new in the 1950s, for Coventry had long suffered from a lack of small, more expensive shops.

In the twenties and thirties workers moving into Coventry, earning high wages and wanting to spend them on the mass-produced goods available for the first time, created a demand for a new sort of shop. The small local man was no longer able to provide for their needs and, with the increasing population, came a decline in the

[11] Published by the editors, 1969.

number of local shops, as J. B. Priestley had noticed in 1933. By 1938 only about one-third of the shops in Broadgate, one of the major shopping streets, appear to have been run by local families; the others were branches of national multiples. Before the Second World War, Leamington, London or, to a lesser extent, Birmingham, had offered more attractive and better-quality goods and it was there that Coventry's middle class had gone to shop. One of those who knew the city at this time tells of food for special occasions being brought to Coventry by train from Fortnum and Mason's, shoes being handmade in Rugby, guns bought in Birmingham and clothes made or bought in London or Leamington – one or two shops in Coventry were used but only if absolutely necessary. After the war it was hoped that the new shopping centre would be able to remedy these deficiencies by providing an area where quality shops could be grouped together. One of the first suggestions was to put such shops into the Burges and Bishop Street, an area which had, in fact, never been an area of quality shopping, and this idea was soon dropped.

After the blitz the retail section of the Chamber of Commerce had urged upon the City Council the necessity for rapid rebuilding which, they felt, could alone prevent trade from going to the undamaged towns near by, but even when new premises were available there were many reasons why the small shopkeeper found it impossible to take a lease. The difference between the rent of the temporary prefabricated huts in which many shops had been housed after 1940 and that of a new shop in a rebuilt block was very considerable and often prohibitive. Another factor was the size of shop being built. As late as 1963 the study on shopping made for the Review of the Development Plan in 1966 gives, as one of the shopowners' complaints, the fact that many premises, especially in the early development, are too large for the small man. Another of the traders' complaints was the high cost of car parking for their customers in the city centre and the insufficiency of such facilities for themselves. On busy shopping mornings, customers may find that they not only have to pay for a car parking space but that there is a long wait for one to become available. It is often as easy for people to go to near-by smaller towns where parking is often easily available and cheap.

The first attempt to make suitable shops available for high quality businesses was the building of the City Arcade, a narrow, colourful street, which, together with Shelton Square, won a Civic Trust Award in 1963. The premises are small and the setting attractive but subsequent lettings have raised the question of whether Coventry can provide sufficient trade to enable such shops to survive. A more recent attempt has been made possible by the extension of the pedestrian area into Bull Yard and Hertford Street. Before the war such quality shops as there were in Coventry were to be found in the latter; Curtis's bookshop, Hanson's music shop and Lomas' fruit shop, for example. The new pedestrian Hertford Street has been built by a number of different developers including the Corporation. Like the City Arcade, it is in parts narrow and arcaded with small premises on one side and, on the other, shops, many of them long established in the street, now rehoused in new buildings. The architects have achieved an attractive variety in the street by the use of changing levels and different materials.

VIII

The problem of car parking, which was cited by Coventry traders as one of the reasons why shopping in the city is less attractive than it should be, is part of the problem which has recently come to dominate all others in most British cities; the problem of providing adequate roads and parking facilities for the rapidly increasing number of motor-cars. Most town plans, including Coventry's, had, immediately after the war, vastly underestimated the way in which the number of motor vehicles would increase once the immediate post-war shortages had disappeared and Coventry regained the position it had before the war with a much higher proportion of motor vehicles to population than the national average. In 1965, for instance, Coventry had 146 cars per 1000 of the population while the national average was only 107 per 1000.

The road plan envisaged in the 1951 Development Plan was very like that devised by Ernest Ford in the 1930s. It consisted of three ring roads, of which the outer would be a continuation of the pre-war by-pass on the south of the city. In the Enquiry into the

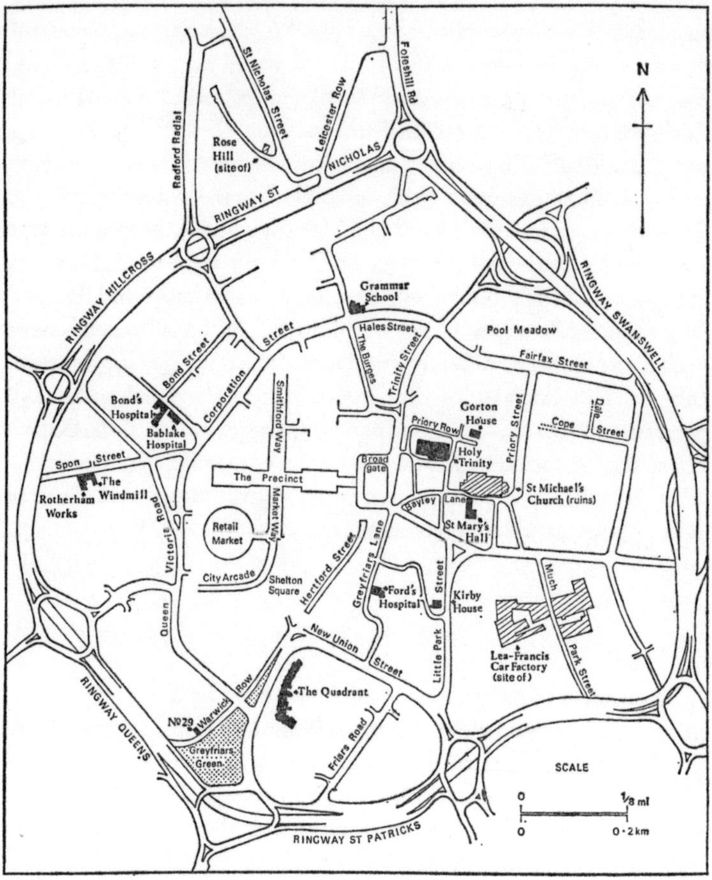

IV The City Centre, 1970

Development Plan held in 1949 Gibson said that he hoped that the inner ring road would be completed by 1964 as congestion on the roads across the city was increasing year by year. There were, however, many other demands on the resources of both the Corporation and the Ministry of Transport which would be responsible for 75 per cent of the cost, and many years passed before work began. In May 1957 the City Engineer warned the Council of the likelihood of a traffic breakdown in the centre of the city if a start was not soon made on the road. Seven months later the building of the first section from London Road to Quinton Road was approved by the Ministry and in December 1959 it was open to traffic for the first time. Construction of the rest of the inner ring road followed, and work on the final section began in 1971.

Together with the diversion of traffic from central streets the original plan had included the widening of the radial roads which would feed traffic on to the inner ring road. This idea was accepted by most people until plans were announced for the building of an eighty-feet-wide dual carriageway along the line of Warwick Road in April 1961. This created an immediate response since it would mean the destruction of forty-seven lime and plane trees. Forty-seven thousand people signed a petition asking for the retention of the trees and after a Public Enquiry in November 1963, the Ministry of Transport refused permission for compulsory purchase.

In the late 1950s, when Coventry's traffic problem was becoming grave, the situation was being reconsidered at national level. In 1947 two motor roads had been planned to cross close to Coventry, but nothing was done about the construction of those roads until March 1958 when work began on the M1 from London to Birmingham. Three years later a working group under the leadership of Colin Buchanan was set up by the Ministry of Transport to study the problem of traffic in towns. At about the same time it was decided in Coventry that detailed studies would have to be made of the difficulties peculiar to this city.

In 1960 a survey was made of the inner ring road which provided the City Engineer with the sort of detail necessary for planning multi-level intersections, since large roundabouts would no longer be sufficient to cope with the traffic entering and leaving the ring road. A year later a joint roads team was formed from the Architectural and Planning, Engineers' and Transport Departments to study the problem of traffic more closely. This group made surveys of journeys to work, starting-points and destinations in order to try to discover an ideal as close as possible to reality. The Buchanan report had developed the idea of the need for categories of roads, each catering for a different type of traffic and the Coventry team were able to use this when planning their revised road pattern. Rather than use the simple pattern of three ring roads as devised for the 1951 plan, it was decided that it would be best to construct, on the lines of Buchanan, a system of different roads designed to carry neighbourhood, local and through traffic. The latter would be urban motor roads, fast and with four or six lanes with as few junctions as possible, carrying people from their own district to their place of work, the national motorway network or the city centre.

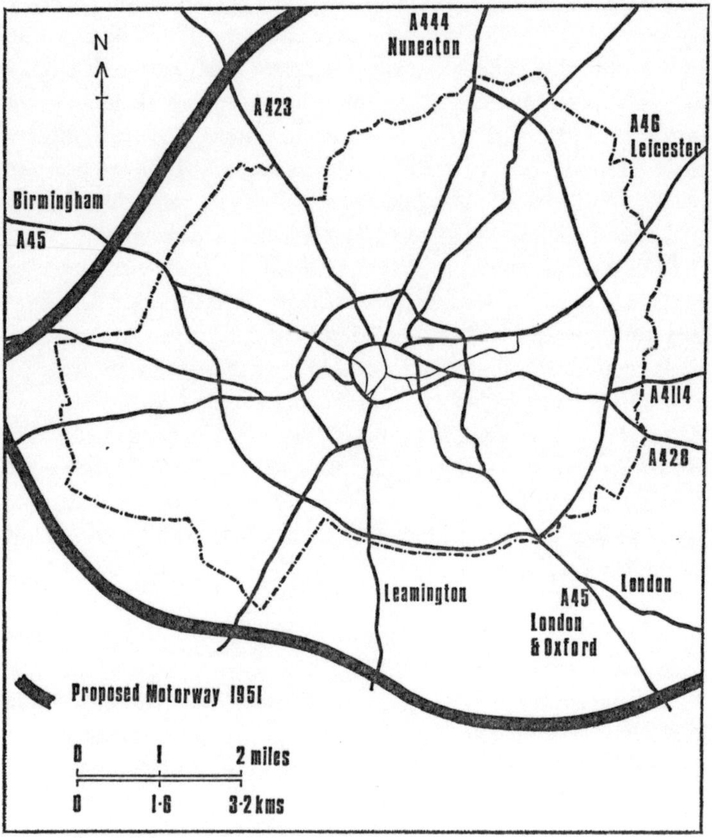

V Changing ideas on Coventry's road pattern
(*a*) The 1951 map from the Development Plan

Together with the pre-war by-pass to the south the urban motor-roads would form a triangle around the city centre. One would go from south-west to north where it would join the other, which would run from the M6 down the eastern side of the city centre to join the by-pass at Whitley. It might be possible for part of this road to use the old eastern loop of the railway line. Opposition to this eastern road was mild compared with that aroused by the road to the west of the city centre, which was to be included in the programme for the 1980s. Petitions were raised protesting against it and one was

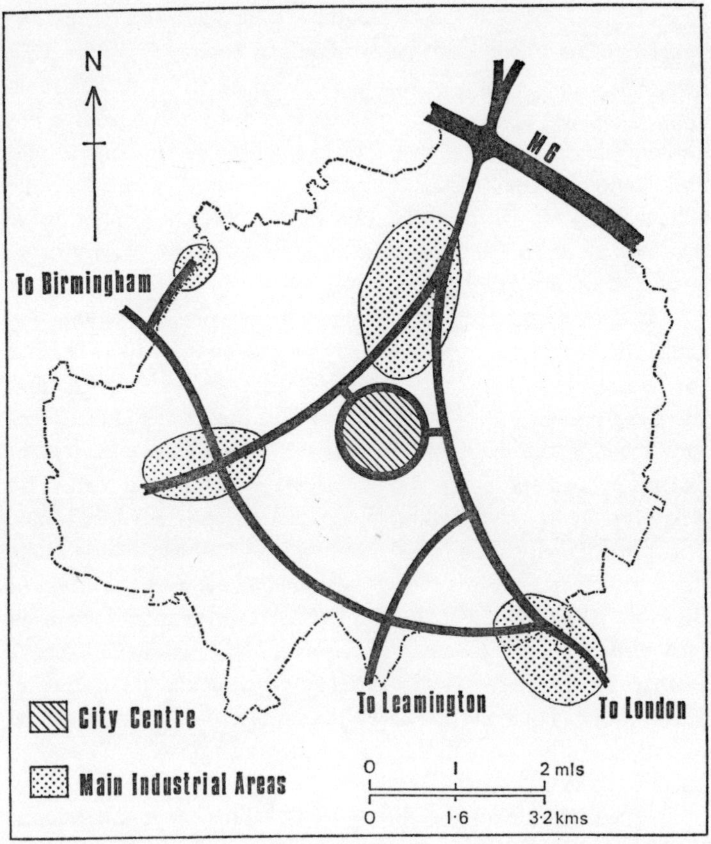

(*b*) Diagram of proposed road pattern from 1966 Review of the Development Plan

sent to the M.P. for Coventry East, Richard Crossman, who was at that time Minister of Housing and Local Government. Despite the protests, the City Council accepted the road proposals in July 1966, but this did not stop the fight to have the plans changed, for in

August of the same year various local protest committees joined together to form a joint organisation to fight the roads plan. In 1968 they were rewarded with a measure of success when some details of the Development Plan Review as it affected roads were reconsidered by the Council.

Coventry's road pattern, therefore, has separated different types of traffic but the Plan also includes the separation of traffic and pedestrians to a far greater extent than was envisaged by the early planners. The adoption of multi-level road junctions on the Inner Ring Road has offered new opportunities for both extending the area of pedestrian movement and making possible a more interesting use of land near the Road. For instance, it is hoped eventually to be able to link Lady Herbert's Garden and the Swanswell Park under the Ring Road to the north thus providing a much larger area of open space near the city centre.

A parallel to the shopping precinct is now planned around the Cathedral so that it should eventually become possible to walk from the Lanchester Polytechnic in the east through the Cathedral and shopping precincts to Greyfriars Green in the south, Queen Victoria Road in the west and Corporation Street, Pool Meadow or Hales Street in the north without crossing one motor road. The redevelopment of Hertford Street as a pedestrian area is part of this plan. Broadgate poses a rather more difficult problem as it is at the moment part of the inner road pattern and, while being the centre of the city, in fact divides it. At one time or another there have been many different plans for this traffic island. Ideas have included converting the area between the shopping precinct and the Cathedral into a stretch of green or, alternatively, a green space bounded on the east or west only by a motor road with traffic possibly limited to buses and service vehicles.

With such limitations on the use of the motor-car it is important that car parking facilities are adequate. The original plan provided central area car parking for only 7000 cars and in the 1966 plan this number was increased to 10,000. This has been made possible by two factors; the development of the idea of multi-storey parks and the use of the flat roofs of part of the precinct area. When the design of the retail market to the west of Market Way was changed from its traditional, parabolic shape to a circular, flat-roofed building it became possible to link its roof with others at a similar level in Market Way and the City Arcade. A ramp with electric elements set in it to prevent icing in winter was built up at the side of the market to lead to the car parks. Behind the pedestrian areas the original ground-level parking has become three-storey car parks built and controlled by the City Council. It is hoped eventually that these parks can be linked by overhead roads to the inner ring road.

Since the expectation of traffic in the future has risen so considerably it is now thought that it will be impossible to provide enough spaces for all the cars which will want to come into the centre at peak periods, and instead some people must have alternative means of transport. In the early plan it had been considered that there would probably be an increase in the use of the helicopter within twenty or thirty years and provisions were to be made for a heliport on the roof of Broadgate House or the Pool Meadow Bus Station. Later the use of a monorail within the city region was investigated, but it was decided that Coventry had neither the right size nor the right layout to make this a viable proposition. Coventry, therefore, is dependent on the more normal means of local transport and a great expansion in the service is envisaged in an attempt to control congestion and limit the use of private cars in the city centre to the capacity of the road network.

CHAPTER ELEVEN

The Maturing of a Community

Working-class life in the bicycle boom. The first theatres. The amateur societies. The Belgrade. International understanding. Immigration. The Coventry sub-region. Working-men's clubs and sport. The arts.

I

At the beginning of this century the young men of the Holy Trinity Bible Class used to engage in an interesting piece of social rescue every Sunday morning. Starting from their headquarters at the old Grammar School, they worked through long-vanished slum streets, such as the Rope Walk and the Chauntries, looking for drunks who were still stupefied from the previous night in those days of unrestricted licensing hours. They found them lying in the gutters or on the stone floors of their lodgings and took them back to their headquarters to give them cocoa, a little food and some warmth. Then they exhorted them, probably without success, wrote letters for them, since these were illiterate and lonely men, and sent them on their way. By such means did young men with prospects and a stable home background look over the edge into the pit where dwelt some of those who had been attracted to the city by the work and wages offered in the bicycle boom.

In those days before 1914 a young man found it easier and more pleasant to build a purposeful life if he belonged to a Bible class or had some other religious connection. George Poole, born in Coventry and later the first and much respected Labour member of the City Council, was a member of the Holy Trinity Bible Class. George Hodgkinson, soon after he first came to the city, taught in the Junior Adult School in the Friends' Meeting House. When W. H. Oliver went from Bible class work to become a lay-reader, he was much influenced by Everard Digby, curate at St Michael's, who ran a gymnasium as part of his work among the poor of the parish. Oliver ran his own gymnasium in Spon End, as well as working untiringly on the education side of the Co-operative Society. The young Walter Hadley also found that his life was bounded by the classes of the Co-operative Society and the activities of his chapel. There was not much else to do. Like many others he attended a very respectable dancing class on Saturday evenings at the Liberal Club, but on other weekday evenings classes had to be attended at the Co-operative Institute, and on Sunday there was the Bible class and services at West Orchard Chapel.

These young men, hard-worked and with a life which we should find rather narrow, were the contemporaries of H. G. Wells' 'Mr Kipps' and 'Mr Polly'. They were separate on the one hand from the old manufacturing and professional families of Coundon Green and the Drapers' Club, and on the other from the immigrant workers attracted to the bicycle factories. These latter were simple men, driven from the land by the depression in agriculture. They were now living in a city which rewarded them well for their labour but seemed to offer them very little else. In the evening there was always the public house, with the resplendent glitter of the Sydenham Palace, reopened and licensed as a music hall in 1891, and the Britannia Tavern and Music Hall in Smithford Street which closed in 1892.[1]

There were other occasional attractions, such as the periodic visits of Sequah, a travelling medicine man who came dressed as a Red Indian, and who rode about the city in a coach followed by a brass band similarly dressed. After he had attracted a crowd to the old Bull Fields, now covered by Queen Victoria Road and its factories, he sold bottles of Sequah's Elixir and Prairie Flower. This

[1] The needs of the more abstemious among the poor were met by the Alexandra Coffee Tavern in Ford Street, opened in the 1890s by Samuel Allchurch. It had a bar with sawdust on the floor but served cups of tea, coffee and cocoa with pieces of cake. Local tradesmen sent in meat, bones and vegetables which were made into soup and anyone could buy a can of this for a penny. On the first floor the Alexandra provided a lunch at *2s 6d* for a very different clientele.

was such a guaranteed cure that on the last night of his visit he always collected together the sticks and crutches of his patients and burned them. He also extracted teeth free, and the band played while he was doing it in order to drown the screams.

Every Whitsun came the steam roundabouts and the acetylene flares of the Great Fair and sometimes a visit from Wombwell's Menagerie or Sangster's Circus. In 1903 there was something which could only happen once in a lifetime, a visit from the circus owned by the great Buffalo Bill, Colonel William Cody himself. So large was the company which he brought with him that five special trains were required to bring it from Stafford, where it had last performed. Pool Meadow, which easily took the Great Fair, was too small for this enormous attraction, which had to be housed on a site in the open country along the Birmingham Road. There it presented its great spectacle of mounted warriors of the world with cowboys, Indians, South American gauchos, Cuban revolutionaries, Teddy Roosevelt's Rough Riders, Bedouins and Cossacks in glorious profusion.

Pool Meadow was the site used for the visits of the Bennett and Patch travelling theatre. It was also to become the home of the first Coventry Hippodrome, a circular, corrugated-iron, rat-ridden building with a plan which owed far more to the circus than the legitimate theatre. Its seats ranged in price from 1*s*6*d* for the most luxurious stalls to 2*d* for the most inconvenient and uncomfortable gallery. It was opened in 1903 by Captain H. H. D. FitzGerald, to provide entertainment for a public which was more interested in colour and movement than in the life of the intellect. With his manager, T. M. Sylvester, who came from Barnum and Bailey's circus, he gave them sometimes variety programmes and sometimes spectacles with horses, such as Dick Turpin's 'Ride to York'. His success attracted the attention of Samuel Theo Newsome, head of a local watchmaking family, who was already interested in the theatre as part-owner of the Empire, formerly the Corn Exchange, in Hertford Street. In 1907 a new Coventry Hippodrome was opened in Hales Street, not far from the old, and FitzGerald disappeared from the scene. Newsome and other local men looking for a good investment took over.

The first showing in Coventry of that exciting new novelty, the motion picture, came to the Corn Exchange in 1901. By 1905 motion pictures were to be found at the Hippodrome, taking the place of one live turn on the variety bill. The first building permanently in business as a cinema was the Star in Hertford Street, in what had formerly been a sales room. Four more, including the Continentale in Earlsdon Street, were opened in 1912, and the Crown, still surviving as the Paris, came a little later. Most of them appealed to a working-class audience, but the evolution of popular taste in Coventry is probably more clearly illustrated by the development of the Coventry Hippodrome than anything else. The little theatre in Hales Street prospered. The young Charlie Chaplin appeared there, so did George Robey and Harry Lauder, and later Gracie Fields. By the mid-1930s it appeared to be insufficient to meet the popular demand for variety. It was, therefore, demolished, and a new Hippodrome, which still survives as the Coventry Theatre, was opened in 1937.

It was one of the largest variety houses in the provinces, seating over 2000 people and giving every seat-holder a clear view of the stage, a very unusual thing in older theatres. It was no place for subtleties, but its stage and lighting were the most up to date of the time, and the artists who worked there found that they had spacious dressing rooms, showers and hot food.

Samuel H. Newsome, son and successor of Samuel Theo, felt that he had a responsibility for the cultural life of the city. After the war he realised that popular taste was improving and did his best to cater for the new public in opera and ballet, but he found himself imprisoned by the sheer size of the new building. Whatever he might have wanted to do the Coventry Theatre had to make its profit and pay its wages and this it could do only if it were full for most of the year. He managed to find space for visits from the Royal Ballet, the Covent Garden Opera and D'Oyly Carte Opera companies. He also opened his theatre for two more ambitious ventures, the Coventry Music Festival and the Midlands Festival of Ballet sponsored by Anton Dolin and John Gilpin. Usually he had to play safe with big bands such as Ambrose, or London musicals such as Ivor Novello's *Perchance to Dream*. Months had to be given to shows which were bound to make money such as the Pantomime and Birthday Show, with front-rank variety stars attracting a sure audience based on coach parties coming from all over the West Midlands.

Probably the Empire was also dominated by its own size during the years between 1906 and 1933 when it operated as a theatre. It opened with Zena Dare in *Catch of the Season*, a light comedy by Seymour Hicks. Others who appeared ranged from Pavlova to George Robey, and from Dame Clara Butt to Julia Neilson and Phyllis Neilson Terry. Against these great names should be set such entertainments as a bill of 1910 which included two comedies, *He Stubs his Toes* and *Mother-in-Law*, and two dramas, *A Special Agent* and *The Sailor's Sacrifice*.

The Theatre Royal in Smithford Street appears to have aimed a little higher. It closed in 1889 when William Bennett, its owner, moved to the Opera House in Hales Street, which he opened with Frank Benson's production of *A Midsummer Night's Dream*. Straight theatre did not prosper in small provincial cities in those days. Competition from the talkies was becoming acute in the late twenties and the Opera House, which was rebuilt in 1928, might well have seemed destined for conversion into a cinema. What happened was quite different. In 1931 it entered upon its richest period as a theatre. Redvers Leech, a local accountant with a keen love of theatre, took a decisive step forward in creating a theatre-going public in Coventry by forming the Coventry Repertory Company. It included, at one time or another, Phyllis Calvert, Ann Casson, James Hayter and Raymond Francis.[2] It must have been hard work for everyone concerned. Redvers Leech was the administrator of the theatre on behalf of its creditors, and he had to make things pay. Front-of-house and backstage staff were cut to a minimum, seats in the gallery cost as little as fourpence and the actors gave two shows a night. While performing one play for one or two weeks, they were also rehearsing a second. Productions ranged from *Dracula* and Edgar Wallace's *The Squeaker* on the one hand, to Priestley, Shaw and Galsworthy on the other. They put on Laurence Housman's *Victoria Regina* as well as *Daddy Longlegs*; *Charley's Aunt* as well as *Gallows Glorious*.

[2] Also Howieson Culff, Ann Titheridge, Richard Hurndall and Hamilton Dyce.

II

The contribution of Leonard Turner to the theatre in Coventry was equally important and somewhat wider than that of Redvers Leech, since it covered the amateur as well as the professional stage. He was a local man, coming from one of those magnificent, large watch-making families which had been such an essential part of the city's social fabric. After becoming a teacher, he left the city but soon returned, and was on the staff of the Technical College when the new building opened in 1936. That building contained an assembly hall with over 800 seats, which became a very passable theatre at a time when the city had nothing else. It became the home of the professional Midland Theatre Company as well as of the annual amateur drama festival and Leonard Turner was admirably equipped to be a helpful influence on both. He was an excellent businessman of the theatre, an experienced producer of pageants and plays and no one knew better than he what the West Midland public would take.

The plays produced by militia officers at the old Theatre Royal in Smithford Street cannot be called part of an amateur drama movement in Coventry; that came much later, later even than that select society, 'The Thespians', drawn from the Twists, the Browetts and others of the best Coventry families and producing plays in the first part of this century. Shortly before the outbreak of the Second World War the growth of amateur dramatic societies in the city encouraged an attempt at a festival but there were only six entrants and it was not a success. Then came the war, the black-out and a hunger for social contact, particularly among people who felt themselves to be strangers without roots in their new community. In 1943 a drama festival was again attempted and this time there were twenty-one entries, mainly from churches and works societies, virtually all of them very new. It was a competitive festival of one-act plays and no one in 1943 could expect these plays to be new, but authors represented included Harold Brighouse, Stanley Houghton and Ronald Gow. The festival became an annual event, moved to the Technical College and was supported by the local Education Committee. It has now disappeared, but in 1948 it had thirty-three entrants and undoubtedly helped the best local societies to improve their standards of performance and choice of plays.

The decline of the drama festival was a consequence of the success achieved by the best of the new societies such as the Wheatsheaf, the Talisman at Kenilworth, the Little Theatre and the Criterion. Their very success and the quality of the people who were attracted to them had itself created problems. Those dedicated young men and women had usually no intention of going on the professional stage, but they soon came to want something more ambitious than the one-act plays offered by the Drama Festival, which gradually lost its attraction. The best of them began to want their own premises, in which they could probably meet every night of the week and certainly produce full-length plays. Some societies which did not acquire premises went out of existence, while those which did, such as the Talisman at Kenilworth and the Criterion, which built an excellent little theatre in Earlsdon, soon found that, like the professional theatre, they had their bills to pay. This might make their choice of plays a little less adventurous, but they soon found, nevertheless, that their premises were indispensable, since the amateur theatre in the city did not receive the welcome it had expected from the Belgrade, the new civic theatre which was opened in March 1958.

Typical of such societies was the Criterion which began in association with Warwick Road Church and moved rapidly from a one act entry for the Drama Festival in April 1955 to its first full-length production the same year. Early in 1961 its members took a daring decision. With a great deal of courage and little ready money they created their own theatre within an old Sunday School building in Earlsdon. A lot of the work of conversion they had to do with their own hands, but in this new home they were able to produce interesting and intelligent plays, from *Inherit the Wind* by Jerome Lawrence and Robert E. Lee to *The Ballad of the Sad Café* by Edward Albee, from *The Italian Straw Hat* to Aristophanes.

During the war and after it Coventry had been an obvious centre for the pioneering work of C.E.M.A., later to become the Arts Council.[3] The city lacked a permanent professional theatre and was surrounded by towns in a similar position. The Technical College Theatre was not perfect, but it was there, and during the war there were plenty of hostels which could accommodate a touring company of actors who would use Coventry as a base and perform sometimes

[3] See Chapter Three, page 93.

in the city and sometimes in the small towns around. After the war the Arts Council made Coventry the centre of its Midland Theatre Company, which produced new plays, ran them for a week and toured them around near-by places, such as Nuneaton, Redditch and Loughborough. The Company continued a brave pioneering existence for eleven years under three able directors, Beatrix Lehmann, Michael Langham[4] and Anthony John. Some of those it trained, such as Gwen Watford, Graham Stark, Michael Aldridge and Roger Delgado, were to become considerable names elsewhere. The members of the Company lived in Coventry and travelled to out of town dates in their own bus. Scenery was carried in an enormous pantechnicon with a cabin for the backstage staff built over the driver's seat.

Its choice of plays had many similarities with the pre-war Repertory Company and was aimed at the same intelligent, largely middle-class public. There was a yearly production of Shakespeare, including *Othello*, *Hamlet* and *Macbeth* as well as the comedies, and plenty of Shaw. Occasionally a thriller such as Patrick Hamilton's *Rope* came into the programme and there was a great deal of J. B. Priestley, Ronald MacKenzie and Terence Rattigan. In the fifties the Company responded to new tendencies and produced Christopher Fry and T. S. Eliot. Ugo Betti's *The Queen and the Rebels*, and Sartre's *Crime Passionnel* were among the more daring choices. It was the success of this Company which helped to persuade Coventry City Council that the time was fast approaching for the creation of a full-time civic theatre in the city.

III

The mental climate of the great new English cities of the nineteenth century was not really favourable for the communal encouragement of the arts. Many of their richer inhabitants were intelligent men, perhaps with excellent libraries and art collections of their own. They were often willing to promote voluntary societies such as the Hallé Concert Society founded in Manchester in 1858, or the arts

[4] Michael Langham was later the Director of the Shakespeare Theatre, Stratford, Ontario.

societies which existed in practically every large town. The general body of ratepayers, the shopkeepers and others, tended to be much more under the influence of evangelical Christianity, which made them feel that the theatre and the arts were, at best, a waste of valuable time. They were certainly not things upon which ratepayers' money should be wasted after it had been acquired by individual frugality and care. It was only in the twentieth century that this general attitude began to show signs of weakening and only in 1948, as a modest beginning, that local authorities were permitted to spend up to the product of a sixpenny rate on entertainment, which could include a dance hall or concert party. It might also include a civic theatre.

There were many who felt that something very heroic would be required to save the provincial theatre from extinction, since it had been steadily declining in the years before 1939, owing to the growing popularity of the cinema. They welcomed the decision taken by Coventry City Council in the spring of 1953 to build a civic theatre which was to be named the Belgrade. Five years were to elapse before it was opened by the Duchess of Kent and during this period the details of its administration were settled. The possibility of leasing it to a commercial repertory company was never seriously considered and it was decided to form a non-profit-making Belgrade Theatre Trust consisting of ten Council representatives and five members of the public with special interest and experience. It was intended to give the theatre the greatest possible amount of independence, and this was a good idea. Whether the right people have always been chosen to make this independence a reality is a different matter. It is, perhaps, a pity that members of the Trust with theatrical experience have never been appointed from outside the city.

In many ways the Belgrade seemed to foreshadow a new age. The rich red of the seating, the large restaurant and ample circulating space, the handsome situation, all pointed to the emergence of a theatre which could become an active and creative force in the life of the community. Owing to the skill with which its auditorium was constructed, those in the stalls could imagine that they were in a small intimate theatre, although the actual seating capacity is over 900. This very size was to create a problem of cost which was to bring disappointment to amateur societies. They had expected that this new civic theatre would become the home of the Drama Festival and a centre to which they could turn for help and advice. The Belgrade was so large and so new that its letting charge was bound to be considerable and most amateur societies simply could not afford it. The Drama Festival was held there for one year only, in 1959, and only the musical play societies which have large casts and a still larger supporting public have been able to take it on with success.

There was a time when young men and women of exceptional talent had to spend years in the provinces before their opportunity came in London. It was this which made the Liverpool Playhouse the beginning for Robert Donat and Eric Portman, gave Sybil Thorndike to Miss Horniman's Repertory Company at the Gaiety in Manchester, and enabled Sir Barry Jackson to give lustre to the Birmingham Repertory. No one who became the director of the Belgrade could be expected to equal these earlier triumphs in other cities and no one with an established national reputation would be likely to want to try. At best, the Trustees would have to look for a young man with much of his road before him and they could not expect to detain him for long. He would have to have infinite energy, breadth of vision and determination, and after the appointment of Bryan Bailey in 1957, they felt that they had found such a man. Bailey had been drawn to the theatre while at Oxford, and had been a successful member of the University Dramatic Society. Later he had been an outstanding student at the Royal Academy of Dramatic Art, and had then entered the professional theatre. He had been manager of the Guildford Repertory Company since 1953 until his acceptance of the Coventry appointment.

Bailey was to launch the theatre with a bang in March 1958 with a production of *Half in Earnest*, a musical version of Oscar Wilde's *The Importance of Being Ernest*, with Marie Lohr as Lady Bracknell. He also created a resident company, among whose leading members were Frank Finlay, Richard Briers and Patsy Byrne. In his choice of plays Bailey did not depart very widely from the policy which had already proved successful in the city. There was Shakespeare, Shaw and Restoration comedy, together with Eugene O'Neill's *The Iceman Cometh*. He produced two thrillers by Edgar Wallace as well as work by Agatha Christie. The Cambridge Arts

Theatre visited the Belgrade twice, and it was Bailey who drew to Coventry the company which had produced James Elroy Flecker's *Hassan* at the Dublin Festival. As a gesture to the country which had given a name to the theatre he brought to the Belgrade Marin Drzic's *Uncle Dundo*, a comedy of the Croatian Renaissance. It was probably Bailey who arranged for the first production of N. F. Simpson's *One Way Pendulum* in November 1960, but his greatest discovery was undoubtedly Arnold Wesker. *Chicken Soup with Barley* and *Roots* had both been staged for the first time at the Belgrade and the third play in the trilogy, *I'm Talking about Jerusalem*, was about to be presented when Bailey was killed.

This man of the great world, with his drive and restless energy, his urge to cram two lives into the space of one, loved the speed and power of fast sports cars. He was frequently on the M1 between Coventry and London, and on 25 March 1960 he must simply have fallen asleep at the wheel. He was killed, and a bright star of the English theatre was suddenly extinguished. Had he lived, Bryan Bailey might well have become a great man, but it would not have been in Coventry. He had already let it be known that he thought it was a mistake for any man to stay in a job for more than three years. The Trustees, men of very different backgrounds from his own, had fallen under his spell; it would not have been easy to find a second Bryan Bailey and they were wise not to try.

The new Director, Anthony Richardson, was to hold the post for six years. He had been educated at Blundell's under Neville Gorton, later Bishop of Coventry, and went into the professional theatre after taking a degree at Oxford. When appointed to the Belgrade he was Director of the Queen's Theatre in Hornchurch, another repertory company on the outskirts of London. His personality was entirely different from that of Bryan Bailey. A quiet man, devoted to his family and with a real sense of social purpose, he once spoke to an interviewer about the importance of the part played by the theatre director in social administration. It would, nevertheless, be difficult to find any policy initiated by Bryan Bailey which Anthony Richardson did not develop. He gave the same opportunities to David Turner which Bailey had given to Arnold Wesker. In June 1962 *Semi-Detached*, a comedy about the snobberies of the lower middle class of the Midlands, was produced at the Belgrade with Ian McKellan. It had a successful run in London with Sir Laurence Olivier, but did not survive the journey very well when taken to New York.[5] Three other plays by David Turner were performed at the Belgrade. The most recent was *Bottomley*, first performed on 31 March 1965 and a serious study of Horatio Bottomley's career to his eventual ruin.

Bailey had already started to make the theatre a cultural centre with Sunday evening concerts and lunchtime poetry readings. He had also tried to form an Under Twenty Club from which the Young Stagers has grown. The Young Stagers were formed in April 1960 and had a membership of 1000 within six weeks, although this figure has not been maintained. An even more ambitious venture came in November 1964, when Anthony Richardson announced that the Belgrade would form a special company to work in the city's schools in order to encourage teachers to help the children to create their own theatre. The project, later known as the Theatre in Education, was given £50,000 by the local authority in its first year.

The third Director, appointed after Richardson's resignation in March 1966, was a very different type of man again. His two predecessors had been Oxford men and young. Warren Jenkins was sixty, and knew all that there was to know about the rough and tumble of the theatre. His great experience included thirteen years in repertory, work with the Bristol Old Vic and a period as director of the Ipswich Arts Theatre. He had worked in television and had been director of the Welsh (now Welsh National) Theatre Company for the four years immediately preceding his appointment to Coventry.

In July 1968 he inaugurated the tradition of an annual musical with an excellent production of *No, No, Nanette!*, which was first produced in London in 1925, and has now become as much a classic as *The Belle of New York*. At Christmas in the same year he took an even bolder step. The Belgrade had always recognised Christmas, and had produced a Christmas Show which was always good, usually colourful and sometimes funny. *Believe it or not*, by David

[5] The Belgrade Company opened at the Music Box Theatre on 7 October 1963, the first time an English repertory company had transferred to Broadway.

Turner and Edward J. Mason, had come remarkably near pantomime in 1962, as had the production of *Oh, My Papa* in 1966. It was left to Warren Jenkins to realise that the pantomime stood at the heart of the English theatrical tradition, and fully deserved its place in a civic theatre backed by the Arts Council. The spectacle of Dick Whittington's cat conducting community singing in the circle may not have been what some people expected of a civic theatre, but the most ardent intellectual purist could not have failed to notice that all the seats were full.

When Warren Jenkins came to the Belgrade many people had already begun to be aware that the theatre was not perfect and that, for some plays, it was too large. A new building to contain workshops, storage space, green room and an experimental theatre with seating for up to 300 people had been approved in the middle of 1964. This building has not yet come about, but Warren Jenkins created a studio in existing office premises near by. He put on eight plays there in 1969 and nine in 1970, running them for between three nights and two weeks. The Studio only holds about seventy people and perhaps some of those productions should have been tried in the main theatre. Plays by Ibsen, Samuel Beckett and Harold Pinter might run at a loss there, but that is what the Arts Council subsidy is for and it would be a pity if Warren Jenkins's name were to be associated only with musical plays and pantomimes.

The design of the Belgrade was begun in the early 1950s when wartime austerity was still more than just a memory. Post-war tendencies in stage design, such as the theatre in the round, had yet to assert themselves and if the building of the Belgrade had been delayed for another ten years the professional advice received on the designing of its stage would have been quite different. It is sometimes said that too much money had been spent on the front of the house, but the Belgrade is a comfortable and attractive theatre for which there is no need to apologise. It has 910 seats compared with 450 in the old Birmingham Repertory and 700 in the new one; the Nottingham Playhouse has 700 seats, the Leicester Phoenix 250. In the Arts Council Report of 1969/70 it was revealed that the Belgrade sold more seats than any other provincial theatre with the exception of Stratford and sold them at the lowest Arts Council subsidy per seat of seven comparable provincial theatres.

The financing of the Belgrade has been a happy blend of national and local initiative. From the Arts Council has come an annual subsidy which is now running at the rate of £45,000 and the City Council also make a large yearly grant. This is still apt to leave an annual deficit which is extinguished by further help from the two bodies concerned. Owing to this first initiative in Coventry the principle of civic aid to the arts is now firmly established and the position of the theatre in the provinces is now far less precarious than it was. It would not take much to make the Belgrade an assured success; all that is required is a smaller theatre of about 200 seats to take productions which would perhaps be too venturesome for the large one. The need for this has long been realised, plans for it have long been made, but so far it has not come about. When it has finally been created, the Belgrade will become something more than just a theatre, it will be a cultural centre; but that is precisely what three gifted directors have worked to try to make it and it would be a pity if their efforts were not to be crowned with success.

IV

In 1953, when the Yugoslav Ambassador visited Coventry, he heard with interest that some members of the City Council were thinking of establishing a civic theatre. He offered a gift of timber from his native country to help with the interior finish of the building and further details were discussed when a civic delegation from Coventry visited Belgrade and Sarajevo in the following year. A Coventry-made car was presented to the Mayor of Belgrade, other gifts were made to Sarajevo and in 1955 a delegation from these two cities visited Coventry. On 9 May they unveiled a plaque to mark the site of the proposed theatre which was to be given the name of the Belgrade as an expression of friendship between the peoples of Coventry and Yugoslavia.

The damage caused by enemy air raids during the war appears to have given Coventry a new significance. Many people in Europe and elsewhere regarded it as a symbol of the victory achieved over Nazism, and the City Council understood Coventry's new importance. The city's international contacts had begun before the war was actually over, and a more recent report names no less than twenty-two links with foreign cities, although they do not all have the same degree of intensity. That with Coventry, in the American state of Connecticut, became active in the early 1960s when Dennis Berry of the City Council went there and arranged for a number of parties to pay reciprocal visits. Messages of goodwill have been exchanged with the township of Parkes in New South Wales, named after Sir Henry Parkes, Premier of the state and one of the leading founders of the present Commonwealth of Australia. In 1839 he had left Moat House Farm at Canley to emigrate to Australia like many other disappointed Chartists. In 1956 Coventry City Council commissioned a painting of his birthplace and made a donation to the National Fund which had been raised in Australia to commemorate his name.

In 1963 a joint delegation from the two Canadian cities of Granby and Windsor inaugurated a link of friendship which was revived in 1970. A party of twenty citizens of Granby headed by the Mayor then visited Coventry for two days as part of a tour of western Europe and North Africa. Coventry also has international links in Europe: with Warsaw in Poland, the two towns of Dunaujvaros and Kecskemet in Hungary and Lidice and Ostrava in Czechoslovakia. From 1942 onwards much was heard of the mining village of Lidice which had been destroyed during the war by the Germans as a reprisal for partisan activity. An international project to rebuild it was set on foot in 1945, and in 1954 Coventry gave 1000 rose trees. Coventry's other link in Czechoslovakia is with the industrial city of Ostrava where a projected 'Coventry Week' had to be postponed in 1968 owing to circumstances beyond the control of its organisers. The Week was actually held in May 1969 and was, in some sense, a reply to the two 'Meet Czechoslovakia' Weeks held in Coventry in 1959 and 1967.

Coventry's connection with St Etienne, which began in 1955, is one of the liveliest and friendliest which it possesses. Personal friendships and even marriages have developed between citizens of the two towns. Youth football matches have been played and every summer schoolchildren go from one city to spend a few weeks with a family in the other. When, in September 1970, a party of young people from Coventry toured Europe in a converted Corporation bus they spent five days in St Etienne where they were received with great friendliness. They then made for Graz in Austria, another of Coventry's twinned towns. Of all Coventry's links, however, those established with Kiel in Germany and Volgograd (formerly Stalingrad) in the Soviet Union are the most longstanding.

Towards the end of 1942 it seemed that the fate of Britain, as well as that of the Soviet Union, depended on the resistance to the German advance at Stalingrad on the River Volga. The city was never completely captured, but almost all of it was totally destroyed.[6] In 1943 Coventry paid for the rebuilding of two wards in the Stalingrad Hospital, and a Coventry–Stalingrad Bond of Friendship Committee was formed by Coventry City Council in June 1944. Official visits were exchanged even in the darkest days of the cold war. In 1951 the Deputy Mayor of Stalingrad spent two days in Coventry, and three years later Coventry City Council invited Stalingrad to join it in an appeal for the banning of the hydrogen bomb. As a result a delegation from Coventry visited Stalingrad and the visit was returned in 1955. The Lord Mayor of Coventry was again in Volgograd in 1965, and a delegation from Coventry Trades Council went there in 1970. Civic visits are not likely at the present time but there have been exchanges of students and lecturers between the Lanchester Polytechnic on the one hand and similar establishments in Volgograd on the other. There are also other cultural links such as a regular exchange of correspondence between schoolchildren of the two cities.

Coventry's link with Kiel was forged in a very different manner. This German seaport had also suffered in war and had endured over 200 air raids. After the war it had come under Allied military occupation and one of the most respected officials of the Allied Control Commission locally had been a Coventrian, Gwillyn Williams. It was partly as a tribute to him that, early in 1947, the Burgomaster of Kiel proposed the formation in the town of a Friends of Coventry Society which soon had a membership of 800. A corresponding move seemed to be required from Coventry, and the then Mayor, George Briggs, called a meeting in the Council House to form an Association of Friends of Kiel. In 1948, when an invitation came

[6] Something has already been said about the assistance sent from this country in Chapter Three.

from Kiel that he should visit the town, he did not feel that he was able to go in more than a personal capacity, but Provost Richard Howard's visit in the same year, as part of the Cathedral's efforts for international reconciliation, has already been mentioned.[7] Coventry's friendship with Kiel has remained remarkably fresh and alive. There have been regular exchanges of official parties and the establishment of a Coventry Room in Kiel University. There are annual youth football and swimming matches and a regular exchange of visits by musicians which is not as one-sided as might be supposed.

On Christmas Day 1946 the B.B.C. arranged an international radio exchange programme between the cities of Coventry, Caen, Arnhem, Stalingrad and Warsaw. This led to an exchange of visits between the Mayors of Coventry, Arnhem and Caen over the next two years and also began to attract the attention of governments who wished to develop ties between different parts of western Europe. The idea of a Western European union was in the air and a Congress at The Hague decided, in May 1948, to establish a consultative Council of Europe to meet at Strasbourg. This Council began to encourage friendship between cities, and in 1955 one of its committees selected Coventry as the city which most exemplified the European idea. In the following year a delegation led by Georges Chaban-Delmas, now (1970) Prime Minister of France, visited Coventry, and in 1959 the city decided to commemorate this honour by giving the name of Unity Way to one of its remodelled streets.[8]

This growing movement towards fraternal relations between cities in western Europe had a great deal to do with the establishment of a United Towns Organisation by a Congress held at Aix-les-Bains in April 1957. Representatives of French, British, American and Canadian towns were at this Congress and five years later the Organisation had 580 members in forty-three different countries. In September 1962 its Fourth World Congress was held in Coventry at the Belgrade Theatre under the chairmanship of the then Lord Mayor, Alderman Arthur Waugh, who was at the time President of the Organisation. Three hundred delegates attended from 140 cities and towns.

[7] See Chapter Six, page 172.
[8] The renaming has, in fact, not yet taken place.

Some ratepayers were inclined to think that international friendship of this kind was really no part of a city council's business. In actual fact the movement has never cost very much, and it has played an important part in making the life of the city a little broader, a little more mature than it had been before the war. This was the intention of Charles Barratt, Town Clerk throughout this period and advisor to successive Lord Mayors. Mrs Pearl Hyde, Lord Mayor in 1957/58, was very enthusiastic about this part of her work, but the most substantial steps forward were perhaps achieved under William Callow (d. 1967), Lord Mayor from 1961 to 1962.

William Callow had been one of the most promising recruits to the Labour Party in the city before the war. Formerly a vehicle builder, he was enthusiastic, intelligent, and more widely read than most. After serving on Council Committees before the war he had entered the Council in October 1942 during the days of unopposed returns. During the war he had become a full-time Civil Defence worker and showed gallantry far beyond the bounds of duty, and powers of leadership much greater than average. After the war he became the local Labour Party's specialist in education and probably longed for positions of leadership which were in the hands of others. When he became Lord Mayor he was no longer under Party control and nobody could say him nay.

Callow brought great sincerity to the development of the city's international links. He was responsible for establishing a voluntary committee, the Coventry Committee for International Understanding, to handle the detailed work of cultural visits and exchanges under the Lord Mayor's patronage. In August 1961, during the crisis which led to the building of the Berlin Wall, he issued an appeal for international peace which was supported by the International Friendship Committee of the City Council. A conference was called with cities with which Coventry had friendly relations and, on 25 September, the Mayors of Aosta, Caen, Graz, Lidice, Parkes, St-Etienne, Volgograd and Warsaw met at the Council House under his chairmanship to issue a second declaration.

The strength of the link between Coventry and the city of Dresden in East Germany also owes a great deal to William Callow. Visits between individuals in the two cities had been exchanged for a number of years, and Pearl Hyde had visited Dresden as Lord Mayor in 1958. More impact appears to have been made when William Callow paid a later visit in April 1962 in order to attend a further international peace conference. This was followed two years later by a formal Bond of Friendship between the two cities and there have been many exchanges since despite the problems presented by visas. A delegation from Dresden visited Coventry in April 1969 and exhibits have been loaned to the Herbert Art Gallery.[9] William Callow also visited East Berlin, and came back very enthusiastic about what he had seen. His views on the democracy of the East German State, acquired after a very short visit, were sharply criticised by those who had never been there at all, and so he ended a controversial but vigorous and useful year. The Council's work for international understanding which he did so much to stimulate has continued to this day. A great city, particularly a great exporting city, must have its international contacts and most people in Coventry realise this.

V

The men who drank at the Sydenham, watched the Bennett and Patch travelling theatre and eagerly crowded to see Buffalo Bill or Sequah, had been drawn from the fields of Warwickshire and neighbouring counties in order to provide labour for the bicycle boom, that significant landmark in the creation of modern Coventry. Other waves of immigration were to follow as the city became a great arsenal of war and a centre of engineering. Since the employment situation in Coventry between the wars was much better than that in other parts of the country, people tended to come from further and further afield; from Ireland, Scotland, County Durham and South Wales. Among them was Harry Urwin, later to become a trade-union official and now (1970) Assistant General Secretary of the Transport and General Workers' Union. Also among their number were William Parfitt, now an Alderman of the City Council, and George Park, the Leader of its Labour Group. A difference

[9] At least six delegations of Coventry teachers have visited Dresden under the auspices of the Coventry Committee for International Understanding.

in religion and the survival of old enmities did not make the assimilation of the Irish easy, but there was little or no difficulty with those who came from other parts of the British Isles. The Scots and the Welsh, like their brothers all over the world, remembered their homeland but soon ceased seriously to want to return to it.

After the Second World War a new social problem emerged for the Government. During the war the country had been the base of a small Polish Army and Air Force which had fought from the West on the Allied side. Many of the Poles had displayed conspicuous gallantry, and it seemed unthinkable that they should be forced to return to their native country after it had come under Russian control. They were bitterly anti-Communist, and Poland would certainly never be free from Russian influence in the future. Something had to be done, therefore, to resettle these Poles in this country in order to enable them to find a useful and happy life. In addition, allied armies had captured a large number of Ukranians, Latvians and others, who had been conscripted into the German Army. The three tiny Baltic states of Lithuania, Latvia and Estonia had been independent for a time until Stalin had taken them over to forestall any possible future German invasion. The Ukraine had enjoyed a brief period of independence after 1918, and had suffered under parts of Stalin's policy in the 1930s. The people of these communities who were now in Allied hands felt that the Soviet Union would show them no mercy if they returned, and to these also the British Government decided to extend its help and protection.

Those who refused repatriation were, therefore, given the status of European Voluntary Workers. In 1946 a camp in Wyken Croft, to the east of the city, was allocated to the Polish Resettlement Corps and Poles were drafted into Coventry to become part of its industrial working force. They could not be given work for which British labour was available and tended to be sent into the building industry where the repair of bomb damage had provided more work than native building workers could cope with. They were very highly thought of, and their numbers rose steadily until, in 1968, the Polish community in Coventry was estimated at about 1500. The other eastern European communities were very much smaller, the Latvians numbering about 260 in 1971. Most of the Latvians were recruited into the Courtaulds plant at Little Heath, and it was this same firm which later brought into Coventry a small group of Italians.

All these communities have diversified the pattern of life in Coventry by making creditable efforts to retain something of their old national identity. Their children go to English-speaking schools, but many are still sent on Saturday mornings to classes in which they learn the language of the country from which their parents came, and to which, perhaps, all hope of returning has not been entirely abandoned. In 1968 170 children were attending the Polish school and seven years before fifty-six had been attending Ukrainian classes. It was reported in 1965, however, that the Polish books available in the Central Library were no longer used as much as they had been a few years before. This is perhaps evidence of a silent process of assimilation, but the existence of separate places of worship naturally helps to keep old memories alive.

The Aliens Order of 1960, which exempted European Voluntary Workers from all restrictions on employment and the need to register with the police, was itself a proof of the ease with which the process of assimilation has taken place. National costumes are still worn by these exiles from another land, folk memories are still kept bright and festivals celebrated, but no one would dream of denying to the Poles and Latvians a degree of tolerance which is not very different from that which has always been afforded to the Scots and Welsh. A very different problem was to be presented nationally by the steady influx of immigrants from the new Commonwealth which, beginning as a trickle in the 1950s, was to mount to a flood in the first part of the following decade.

In the islands of the West Indies, in Pakistan and India, people have always been plentiful and they have always been poor. The land itself could not feed all who were born on to it and the death of children was nature's way of making sure that dire poverty did not become sheer starvation. The Second World War brought many changes. Some West Indians enlisted in the R.A.F. and others came to Britain to work in munition factories. These saw the British standard of living for themselves, and some remained. When, after the war, British industry needed all the labour it could get, many more arrived. They had the right of free entry which then belonged to every Commonwealth citizen, and the first attempt to limit this did not come until 1962. This attempt in itself appears to have increased the flow of immigrants, a flow in which people from other Commonwealth countries were beginning to join and Indians and Pakistanis coming from a cultural background very different from that of Britain were to add to the problem.

The Act of 1962, which had precipitated an increase in Commonwealth immigration, was followed by further Acts at intervals of three years. That of 1965 endeavoured to improve community relations by setting up a National Committee for Commonwealth Immigrants of which the Archbishop of Canterbury agreed to be Chairman. The National Committee encouraged the establishment of Community Relations Councils in areas where there had been considerable immigration from the Commonwealth, and such a body was set up in Coventry in 1967. It began with a small grant from the City Council and was largely dependent on the work of Peter Berry, the Bishop's Chaplain for Community Relations, who acted as its Secretary and had already begun work in this field. In 1968 a further Act replaced the National Committee by a national Community Relations Council with increased resources. This allowed for the appointment of paid officers to the various local bodies.

Like all such bodies, the Coventry Community Relations Council does not exist to deal with specific complaints about racial discrimination. When it receives such complaints, they are forwarded to the Race Relations Board, an entirely separate body. Its own purpose is that of promoting goodwill between immigrants and the host community. Its first chairman was J. B. Butterworth, Vice-Chancellor of the University of Warwick, and he has now been succeeded by Walter Chinn, formerly Director of Education and a respected figure in the Quaker community. Many religious bodies, employers' organisations and trade unions are represented on the Council which also receives a great deal of help from chief officers of the Corporation, teachers, and representatives of the immigrant communities themselves.

The Council operates through a number of panels, such as one on housing which has an estate agent as chairman. This panel can give specialist advice in order to check and overcome the various housing difficulties with which immigrants are liable to be faced in a large English city. At one time it intended to establish a housing society which would build fifty dwellings near the centre of the city and rent them to members of different races and communities. The accommodation had to be rented because it could not otherwise have been controlled and the multiracial purpose might soon have been lost. The panel would still like to proceed with a suitable housing scheme but has had to give up this particular idea because immigrants who were approached did not seem to be interested.

The industrial panel has had to proceed very slowly. Immigrants have found it difficult to enter many fields. As late as 1961 only one was employed on the buses although this picture has now changed considerably. The Council's officers have visited many firms and their main aim has always been to build up goodwill so that wider opportunities for immigrants might be given in time. Its education panel has had no difficulty in persuading the local authority to take special steps to teach English to immigrant children. Work in this was already beginning before the Council was established, and now there exists the Priory Centre for Supplementary Education to which immigrant children with particular difficulties in the English language can be sent for special attention. The panel has also had success in the establishment of multiracial play-groups. There is a long haul ahead before all problems connected with the peaceful assimilation of immigrant communities into the life of Coventry have been settled. Perhaps the real testing time will come when gifted children wish to break out of the Stoney Stanton Road and the Foleshill Road to enter the professions and join in the battle of life on equal terms with English people who are no more clever than they.

In the meantime, the communities concerned are doing what they can to preserve their own cultural traditions. The Sikhs, who, it was estimated, numbered 5000 in 1971, have established two temples in the city, and have already formed links with Christian churches. In 1969, when the Sikhs of Coventry celebrated the five-hundredth anniversary of the birth of Guru Nanak, the congregation of St John's, Willenhall, held a combined service with them. In August 1961 the Pakistani community became the first in the Midlands to build its own mosque and since then the building has been twice extended under the leadership of a resident Imam. The Hindus, said to be about 2000 in 1970, hold their meetings in the old St Mark's schoolroom in the Stoney Stanton Road, which, during the week, acts as a social centre for all immigrant communities.

VI

The father of one Coventry doctor in practice today used to do his rounds on horseback along country lanes in Foleshill and Wyken, parishes which are now covered by factories and housing estates. Some people can still remember the Misses Verrall, who gave up their house at Hove to live in Coventry because they liked the hunting. They eventually settled in the village of Walsgrave with its Hall, church, manor-house and schoolhouse. There are others who can recall the time when the little church of Styvechale, with the Hall behind it, was reached by a footpath which led up to the knoll and through a wicket-gate. Others have been told how Earlsdon Street ended by old Earlsdon House, at a field gate with meadows beyond, and housewives from this isolated village had to come to Coventry in a brake along the winding Earlsdon Lane. It is, however, now no longer possible for a man to go into Broadgate on Saturday morning and be surprised to see a stranger. In such a short space of time has a great manufacturing city come to absorb not only other races but other communities as well.

The process had already gone so far by the 1930s that some people were coming to dread the prospect of ribbon development joining Coventry to neighbouring towns including Birmingham. As early as May 1938 the Birmingham and Coventry City Councils had begun to confer with Warwickshire on steps which should be taken to preserve a rural zone, or green belt, around the city and this policy has been maintained ever since. More recently the motor-car has combined with planning legislation to give a new character to the growth of Coventry. The population within the city boundary appears at present to be declining slightly as more people take advantage of the gift of mobility which the private motor-car has placed in their hands. They are moving out, not simply to Leamington and Kenilworth, but to the surrounding villages from which thousands of people now come into Coventry to work every day.

It is this which is the principal, although by no means the only, factor which makes Coventry the centre of a definable sub-region.

Planners in the West Midlands have long been aware that the region can be divided into three sub-regions, one based on Birmingham, another on Wolverhampton and the third on Coventry. For many people the Coventry sub-region extends from Hinckley and Nuneaton in the north to Leamington in the south. In the east it swings far out to include Rugby, while on the west the pull of Coventry soon meets and conflicts with the counter pull of Birmingham. The total population of this sub-region has been estimated at 650,000 of which rather more than half is within the boundaries of the city. The days of the small, closely-knit community are over; mobility is here to stay, the only question is the effect which it will have on the pattern on our local government, a pattern determined nearly a century ago. Two recent attempts have been made to re-draw the local government map in order to make it correspond more closely to contemporary social realities. Under the first, the report of the Maude Commission published in June 1969, Coventry was to find itself merged with most of Warwickshire to form a new county. Under the White Paper published by the succeeding government in February 1971, this is to be superseded and Coventry will, in 1974, find itself part of a Greater Birmingham Authority.

It will be interesting to see how all this works out in practice. Since the days of the bicycle industry, the social patterns of Birmingham and Coventry have had more in common than perhaps either would like to admit. Both have been great engineering centres with a powerful, self-conscious and independent-minded working class. If Birmingham looks with affection towards the traditions of the small masters in the gun and jewellery trade, Coventry appears to have inherited the spirit of the ribbon weavers and watchmakers. Both cities are last citadels of piecework, with the opportunities for bargaining and speaking one's mind that this gives. No one can tell for certain what the future may hold for Coventry; it has met economic disaster before and could do so again but it has a remarkable talent for overcoming difficulties and we can speculate with some confidence on its future quality of life. Permanent and growing features of this will certainly be its working-men's clubs and its sports.

The Coventry Working Men's Club, still in existence, began in 1860 with one room in Little Park Street, at the very centre of the old city. It provided newspapers and other means of social contact for abstemious and intelligent working men and so was a welcome member of the Club and Institute Union formed two years later under the inspiration of the Reverend Henry Solly. That movement now has a national membership of about four million and, in the same way, the Coventry clubs have also grown in numbers and strength. In the 1870s a second club, the West End, was formed in the watchmaking district of Spon End, and after the First World War came a number of foundations, mainly for ex-Servicemen. The present Stoke Club was, at first, connected with the British Legion, the Howitzer was for old gunners and the present 1925 Club grew out of one originally formed by shop-stewards and others on the extreme left of the Labour movement. Rearmament and the prosperity it brought caused the foundation of others such as the Wyken Club, originally started in a miner's cottage in 1936. Then, after the war, with long spells of full employment and high wages in Coventry, the movement grew and there are now forty-two clubs in the city affiliated to the C.I.U. with an average membership of 1500 each.

The Coventry clubs are not the richest of their kind in the country; that honour belongs to those in one area where the clubs own their own brewery and often find the disposal of their profits quite a problem, nor do they have as many concerts given by stars who had earlier been popular in London as do some areas. But they are prosperous, self-governing communities, run under approved rules by elected committees of intelligent and careful men who value the good name of their clubs, exert discipline to expel undesirables and cherish the fact that the police cannot enter their premises at will. Their value to community life, particularly on the great new housing estates, is so accepted that the Corporation will grant advances on mortgage in order to enable clubs to extend their premises. Since the largest club in the city has annual receipts averaging slightly less than a quarter of a million pounds and employs a full and part-time staff of forty-six, finances have not been a great problem in recent years. The large clubs now have far more to offer than a bar. They have games rooms, with tables for billiards, snooker and a particularly skilful form of bagatelle known only in Coventry and district. It is played with cues on a green baize table and involves such intricate calculations of angle that only men with a feeling for precise work can become really adept at it. All have lounges, televisions (usually coloured) and halls for concerts and dances; many have well-equipped stages and all have electric organs, valued at four figures. They are generous to pensioners and good to their members' children. Their educational activity has never come near what their more enlightened officials would like to see, but, through their angling sections and their football, boxing and cricket teams, they share to the full in the vigorous and successful sporting life of the city.

VII

George Singer, the cycle king, left his mark on the life of the city in many ways. He took a personal interest in his workers, helped to provide them with decent housing and created a works band which used to go to out-of-town engagements on a thirteen-seater bicycle with a pannier on the back to take the big drum. He also established a works football team in 1883 and it was this club which, in 1898, changed its name to Coventry City. Between 1908 and 1914 the team was in the Southern League, and in 1910 they were among the giant-killers of the F.A. Cup, reaching the quarter-finals. A further step forward came in 1919 when they were elected to the Football League.

Since then the fortunes of the Club have tended to mirror those of the city. In 1935, when good times were coming again for Coventry, the Club moved into the Second Division, but it was back in the Third by 1951. Seven years later City dropped to the newly-formed Fourth Division, although it stayed there for one season only. This was a worrying time for everyone concerned with the Club. They knew that a place in the First Division mattered very much for the prestige of the city as a whole, but they also knew that it was becoming more and more difficult to get there. It had long been impossible to keep the wages of the professional players to the low pre-war level and the standard of accommodation provided at the grounds of many clubs was beginning to be criticised by those who had seen the new stadiums on the Continent. Great financial resources were becoming necessary to make a great football club and the question was whether Coventry had enough. Club managers came and went as they tried to solve the problem, and Billy Frith acquired the distinction of being dismissed twice, once in 1947 and later in 1961. When he left for the second time the Club was still in the Third Division and the Board of Directors appointed Jimmy Hill to succeed him.

Jimmy Hill now (1971) head of Sport at London Weekend Television, had himself been a professional footballer for Fulham. A former Chairman of the Professional Footballers' Association, he understood and inspired players, but he understood many other things as well. From 1964 money began to be spent on improving the amenities and capacity of the ground, with new stands, bars, a restaurant and suites which business firms could rent. As early as 1963, while still in the Third Division, the Club reached the last eight in the F.A. Cup competition. In 1964 it was promoted to the Second, and three years later to the First Division. Immediately afterwards Jimmy Hill left, but the Club has never fallen from the pinnacle on which he placed it.

This great professional club is constantly seeking talent among the young who play in the many amateur clubs in the city. Their number exceeds 200; about thirty in the Service of Youth League, which is connected with the various youth centres maintained by the Corporation; the Combination and Coventry and District Leagues together contain over eighty teams and the Works League has another sixty-three. A further forty or more are in the Coventry and North Warwickshire League which bears the same name as the group of sports clubs which have their headquarters at the pleasant cricket grounds on the Binley Road.

The Coventry and North Warwickshire Cricket Club, which has now attracted to itself tennis, hockey and squash clubs, was originally founded in 1851. It cannot claim to have produced every fine cricketer born within the city. Tom Cartwright, now (1971) with Somerset and earlier a Warwickshire and England player, came from the Courtaulds works team, but the Coventry and North Warwickshire record is a very distinguished one and includes many sporting achievements of old Coventry families which have now moved out of the city. Particularly prominent have been the Rotherhams. The two brothers, John and Alex,[10] were in the side soon after the Club began and the tradition was maintained until just before the Second World War when Gerald Rotherham captained. Warwickshire. Two Ratcliffes were among the earliest players in the side but the most distinguished member of recent times has undoubtedly been R. E. S. Wyatt, old boy of King Henry VIII School, captain of Warwickshire and sixteen times captain of England.

Before moving to their present Stoke ground in 1900, the Club had played in the Butts and had actually begun in the old Bull Fields in 1851. Coventry Football Club also began there and for a long time the two Clubs were to depend upon many of the same people. When Coventry Football Club first began in 1873 it owed much to the sons of families who had been sent to the new public schools. Harry Ratcliffe was its first captain and at one time he had three brothers in the side. Other families represented were those of Newsome, Cash, Waters, Rotherham and Loveitt. Following in the tradition of such players have been Peter Robbins, who captained Warwickshire in 1956 and Oxford University in 1957, and John Owen, member of the Cambridge pack, who was capped fourteen times for England. Although the game began in the city among the young sons of upper middle-class families it has come to acquire such a firm hold in works and school teams that those days are long since over. The broadening of the game's appeal is reflected most clearly in the sporting record of the school which used to be Broad Street Elementary School for boys.

Broad Street, now a secondary modern school, was built early in this century to serve one of the working-class districts produced by the bicycle boom. Today it has four houses, each of them named after a front-rank sportsman produced by the school. Stan Ashby ran for England in the Amsterdam Olympics of 1928 and Bobby Lord swam in the Tokyo Olympics of 1964. Jim Stewart played cricket for Warwickshire and Ivor Preece captained the England Boys' Rugby team twice, in 1935 and 1936. He was capped twelve

[10] Also leading founders of the Technical Institute, see Chapter Nine, page 244.

times for England and captained the side in 1948 and 1949. Two others, Bert Godwin and Phil Judd, who once attended Broad Heath School, as it is now, played for England in 1963 and 1967, when Judd was captain. It is a remarkable record for a school which has never enjoyed many advantages and a lot of it is due to that remarkable sporting headmaster, Harold Suddens.

Coventry Football Club has produced twenty-seven England players, and four Coventry men were in the British Lions team which toured Australia and New Zealand in 1959 while five went to New Zealand in 1963. In the immortal year of 1962/3 five members of the Coventry team, Peter Jackson, John Owen, Tom Pargetter, Phil Judd and Bert Godwin, were capped for England. In 1967 this astonishing success was improved upon. Ron Jones captained Wales and Phil Judd, Bert Godwin, Rodney Webb, John Owen and Bill Gittings turned out for England. In the six years between 1958 and 1963 the Warwickshire County side, which has always contained a high proportion of Coventry players, won the County Championship five times.

In many fields the sporting and athletic life of Coventry reaches a very high standard and much of it has been helped by the excellent facilities provided at the larger factories. It was G.E.C. which first gave an opportunity to Tony Mottram, member of the Davis Cup team after the war and now (1971) national coach for the Lawn Tennis Association. Cycling as a sport has a long history in Coventry, where it has grown out of the testing of bicycles after manufacture. The happenings at the Butts Stadium, including contests between the penny-farthing and the safety bicycle, are part of the city's folklore and such present-day cyclists as John Atkins and Carl Barton continue a long tradition. Carl Barton of the Coventry Road Club won a silver medal in the Commonwealth Games of 1962 and John Atkins was twice National Cyclocross Champion. The lack of an Olympic-style swimming pool before 1965 hampered the development of the city's swimming, but Graham Sykes, an old boy of King Henry VIII School, captained the British Olympic Swimming Team in Rome in 1960 and gained a gold medal at the Commonwealth Games of 1962. Bill Adcocks, Sheila Taylor and Dick Taylor, all of Coventry's Godiva Harriers, were members of the British Olympic Athletics team in Mexico in 1968 where Sheila

Taylor was fourth in the 800 metres and Bill Adcocks, who came sixth in the 26-mile marathon, was the first European home in this punishing contest at high altitude.

VII

All this is good, but it is not enough to make a great city. That must be the work of time, which alone can produce a mature intellectual and social life out of leisure, prosperity and a sense of corporate identity. This has not yet happened in Coventry, but it will not be prevented from happening merely because Coventry is an engineering city. Walter Elliot once described precision workmanship as the greatest aesthetic discovery of the nineteenth century and a city in which so many love precision workmanship may not be far from developing a love of art.

There are, nevertheless, real difficulties; the country is better educated than ever before and the cultural life which satisfied a few in the great cities of the last century would certainly not be acceptable to the much greater numbers who want such a life today. That great gift of mobility which is shaping our age has also brought its problems. Like everyone else, the artist has a thoroughly healthy desire to be well paid for what he does. Once they had found a patron, the great ones of the Italian Renaissance tended to stay in one place for a long time; if they moved, they moved rarely. Nowadays their successors need never be still. The cultural life of a provincial city, therefore, tends to be continually decapitated, as many of its best people tend to go somewhere else. Even if they do not actually live there, they are often attracted to London, where are concentrated the major publishing houses, the great galleries, the leading theatres and the television services.

One of those with his interest centred on the capital is John Siddeley, son of the second Lord Kenilworth. He was born in Earlsdon and appears to have regarded Coventry as his home until he reached the age of twenty-one. At one time he was attracted by the theatre and worked with the Liverpool Repertory, but in 1953 he became a full-time professional interior decorator. His work includes designs for the Swedish Embassy and the Rootes Group's

Linwood factory, but he also joined with John Piper in the preparation of the new vestments for Coventry Cathedral. From a very different background came David Tindle, now one of the most considerable of British painters with works in two Oxford colleges and a long run of successful exhibitions since 1952. Coming to Coventry as a child, he was trained at the local College of Art where William Parkinson advised him to go to London. The Herbert Art Gallery now holds a number of his sombre studies of the Thames and the sea. Derek Southam, an old boy of John Gulson School, had at one time taught art at Broad Heath School and now works in London. He is a painter with his own distinctive technique which includes the use of marble dust, wood chippings, powdered slate and sand. William Chattaway has moved further afield and now lives in Paris. He is recognised as a professional sculptor of importance. The quality of his work is probably well represented by his bust of Jean Albertini, the first of his works to be bought for the Herbert Art Gallery at Coventry.

Paul Jennings, grandson of a Coventry watchmaker and at one time head boy at Douai, showed great promise as a poet when he was in the Army during the war. He has since given a new direction to his talents and become a witty and urbane essayist. Philip Callow, who was born in Birmingham, came to Coventry as a boy and served an apprenticeship with the Gauge and Tool Company after some years at Centaur Road School. He has written several novels, many of them based upon life in Midland cities. Philip Larkin, son of that highly intelligent City Treasurer of Coventry, Sydney Larkin, has acquired a considerable standing in contemporary literature. He has three novels to his credit and several volumes of poetry. Susan Hill, who wrote her first novel at the age of sixteen and had it published two years later, was awarded in 1971 the Somerset Maugham prize for literature with *I am the King of the Castle*.[11]

James Kessell, who has found it possible to live in Coventry and receive commissions for paintings from three continents, has

[11] Many, although not all, of those named were helped on their way by the Spencer Travelling Scholarship for residents within the city. The Scholarship was first awarded in 1948 to Alan Barlow, now head of design at the National Theatre School of Canada. It represents an earlier charity established in 1888 by the will of David Spencer, who had originally wanted to establish a fund to help skilled artisans to improve their proficiency in the industrial arts.

established his own independent school in order to satisfy the longing to practice the visual arts which is so widespread in the city. He has had as many as 130 students at one time. Those who are spectators in the arts are catered for, together with practitioners, in the Umbrella Club, which began in a comfortable little seventeenth century house in the centre of the city. That house is there no longer and the Club is at present based in a Victorian house not far from Greyfriars Green. In its time it has organised exhibitions of paintings and glassware, run seasons of Continental films at a cinema long since demolished, encouraged the practice and appreciation of music with lectures and recitals and triumphantly survived those personal differences which must be expected in any voluntary organisation. At least one similar club, the Greyfriars Arts and Recreation Club, has been formed from it, but the ambitions of the parent body are still undiminished. Interest in the arts has never been greater, the crying need is for suitable buildings in which they can be practised.

In the middle of the last century, when merchant and manufacturing families in the new cities were creating their opulent town halls, Coventry was still not a very large place. For small gatherings there was St Mary's Hall, for large ones the Corn Exchange. The city did not need anything like Sir Charles Barry's great Town Hall at Birmingham, could not have afforded it, and probably never felt the lack. The Huddersfield Choral Society is not entirely explained by the fact that it has a large town hall in which to sing, but the possession of a specialist building can help forward the musical life of a community, just as its absence can retard it. Only a local authority can nowadays provide such buildings and we have already mentioned the Belgrade Theatre built and maintained by Coventry City Council. It also intends to develop the Charterhouse along the London Road, the former gatehouse of a Carthusian monastery. Here will be created an arts centre which may well give greatly increased scope to the enthusiasm of the Umbrella Club and perhaps provide local arts societies with the studio space which they badly need. The recent perceptible advances in Coventry's musical life have, nevertheless, been achieved with the use of two buildings, neither of which was specially designed for secular music. The new Cathedral opens its doors to symphony concerts and the successful

Orchestral and Chamber Music Society meets in the large lecture theatre of the Lanchester Polytechnic opposite.

For a long time the city's musical life was dependent upon the chapels. Then, during the war, two engineers at G.E.C. formed an organisation which held a very successful series of concerts at the Central Hall. From this venture came the Coventry Philharmonic Society, founded in 1943 and now a seasoned veteran with a long record of successes behind it. At about the same time two officers in the Air Training Corps, J. F. Parbury and J. R. Major, were engaged in a piece of social service which was to have important consequences for music in the city. Because a large number of adolescents were running loose at night in the blacked-out streets, these two men got as many as possible into the A.T.C. and formed a Corps of Drums in order to keep them occupied. The inspecting officers of the A.T.C. liked the idea but suggested that it should not be done under their auspices. In 1944, therefore, the Corps of Drums became the solid core of a new Coventry School of Music which later began to develop other activities, among which are the Fairfax Choir and a Youth Opera Club.

This creditable voluntary enterprise asked Charles Barratt to be its president. His love of music was to suffer many disappointments in the next few years, such as the failure of the annual Coventry Music Festival, which began in 1957 but was not held after 1963. He was not to see a concert hall built in the city before he died but, in September 1964, together with Walter Chinn, then Director of Education, he brought about an agreement between the School of Music and the local authority which may prove to be equally important. The School was to have both a full-time Director, who would also be adviser to the city's schools, and a refitted building to act as its base. That agreement is now working and the School has day and evening students, a full-time two-year course and a whole range of additional activities, including a Coventry Symphony Orchestra. There is always much to hope for from the future in Coventry and not in music alone.

Appendix: The Early Motor-car Industry in Coventry

The point has already been made that a satisfactory list of car manufacturers in Coventry will probably never be made. How many of the cars on the following list were actually manufactured, and manufactured in any great quantity, it is virtually impossible to say. It is equally impossible to decide how much of the process of manufacture was actually done by some of the firms named.

The following abbreviations have been used to indicate periods of manufacture as far as they are known:

A – between 1901 and 1905
B – between 1906 and 1910
C – between 1911 and 1915
D – between 1919 and 1925
E – between 1926 and 1930

Cars and their Manufacturers

Academy – E. J. West, Foleshill Road	1906–8
Aircraft, Motor and Engineering Works, Shackleton Road	E
Albatros – Albatros Motors, Croft Road	1923–4
Allard – Allard and Co., Earlsdon Works	1899–1906
Alpha – Johnston, Hurley and Martin, Gosford Street	B – 1914 and E
Alvis – T. G. John Ltd., Alvis Car & Engineering Co. Ltd., Holyhead Road	1920–67
Arden – Arden Motor Co. Ltd., Balsall Common, near Coventry	1912–16
Armstrong-Siddeley – Armstrong-Siddeley Motors Ltd., Parkside	1919–60
Arno Motor Co., Gosford Street	1908

Autovia – Autovia Cars Ltd., Ordnance Works, Midland Road	1936–8
Awson Motor Carriage Co., Awson Street	F
Barnet and Co., High Street	E
T. Bayliss, Excelsior Works, Stoney Stanton Road	E
Bramco, St. Nicholas Street	E
British Motor Traction Co. Ltd., Fleet Street	B
Brooks – Brooks Motor Co. Ltd., Holbrook Lane	1902
Buckingham – Buckingham Engineering Co. Ltd., Holyhead Road	1914–23
Calcott – Calcott Bros. Ltd., Far Gosford Street	1913–26
Carlton – Carlton Motor Co., Lockhurst Lane	1901–2
Centaur – Centaur Cycle Co. Ltd.	1900–1
Challenge Motor Co., Foleshill Road	D
Clarendon – Clarendon Motor Car and Bicycle Co. Ltd., Earlsdon	1902–3
Clement – Clement Motor Co. Ltd.	1908–14
Climax – White & Poppe, New George Street	1905–7
Cluley – Clarke, Cluley & Co., Globe Works, Well Street	1922–8
Cooper – Cooper Car Co. Ltd., 78 Ampthill Road, Bedford; Lythall's Lane, Coventry	1923
Coronet – Coronet Motor Co. Ltd., Far Gosford Street	1903–6
Coventry Premier – Coventry Premier Co., Read Street	1919–23
Coventry-Victor – Coventry-Victor Motor Co. Ltd., Cox Street	1926–38
Crawford – Crawford Gear Co. Ltd., Holbrook Lane	1901
Crouch – Crouch Cars Ltd., Tower Gate Works, Cook Street	1912–28
Cunard Motor & Engineering Co., Chauntry Place	B
Daimler – Daimler Motor Co. Ltd., Cotton Mills, Sandy Lane	1897 to date

Daisy Motor Works, Far Gosford Street	E
Dalton & Wade, Spon Street	B
Davidson Car Co., Clay Lane	E
Dawson – Dawson Car Co. Ltd.	1920–1
Deasy – Deasy Motor Car Mfg. Co. Ltd., Parkside	1906–11
Doherty Motor Co., Upper Well Street	B
Duryea, Widdrington Road	B
Dutson, Ward & Co., Gosford Street	B
Emms – Emms Motors Co., Walsgrave Road	1922–3
Endurance – Endurance Motor Co. Ltd.	1899–1901
Forman – Forman Motor Manufacturing Co. Ltd., Day's Lane and Payne's Lane	1904–6
Garrard & Blumfield – Raglan Cycle Co.	1894
Godiva – Payne & Bates, Foleshill	1900 1
Grovenor A., Melville Street	B
Hamilton Motor Co., Dale Street	B
Hill S. & Co. Motors Ltd., Godiva Street	E
Hillman – Hillman-Coatalen – Hillman Coatalen, Hillman Motor Co. Ltd., Pinley and Ryton-on-Dunsmore	1907 to date
Hobart – Bird & Co., St. Patrick's Road	B
Hotchkiss – Hotchkiss & Co.	1920
Hubbard Motor & Engineering Co., Much Park Street	B
Humber – Humber Ltd., Beeston, Notts–Coventry–Ryton-on-Dunsmore	1898 to date
Hurley D., Far Gosford Street	B
Iden – Iden Motor Car Co. Ltd., Fleet Street, Parkside	1904–7
Jaguar (*vide* S.S.) – Jaguar Cars Ltd.	1934 to date

Lanchester – Lanchester Engine Co. Ltd., Lanchester Motor Co. Ltd., Sandy Lane, Coventry; Fallows Road, Armourer Mills, Montgomery Street, Birmingham — 1895–1956

Lee Eabb & Co., Queen's Road — F

Lea Francis – Lea Francis Ltd., Lower Ford Street, Much Park Street — 1903–12

Lotis – Sturmey Motors Ltd., Lotis Works, Widdrington Road — 1908–12

Marseal – Marseal Motors Ltd., Atlantic Works, Stoke — 1919–25

Maudslay – Maudslay Motor Co. Ltd., Parkside — 1901–26

M.M.C. – The Great Horseless Carriage Co. Ltd., Central Works Motor Mills, Coventry. The Motor Mfg. Co. Ltd., 157a Manor Street, High Street, Clapham, London S.W. — 1898–1910

Moore & Owen, Much Park Street — B

Morris – W. R. Morris, Morris Motors Ltd., Cowley, Oxford–Coventry — 1912 to date

Neville Sinclair & Co., Fleet Street — B

Noble A. & Co., Stoneleigh Works, Hill Street — D

Omega – W. J. Green Ltd., Omega Works, Swan Lane — 1926–7

Premier – Coventry-Premier Ltd. — 1912–23

Priory – Priory Motor Co. Ltd., Dale Street and Cope Street — B

Progress – Progress Cycle Co. Ltd., Progress Motor Co., Bishopsgate Green — 1899–1903

Ranger – Ranger Cyclecar Co., West Orchard — 1914–15

Remington Motor Co., Foleshill Road — E

Rex – Rex-Remo, Rexitte – Rex Motor Mfg. Co. Ltd., Earlsdon — 1902–14

Ridley – John Ridley, 18 Ellys Road; Ridley Autocar Co. Ltd., Upper Well Street — 1901–4

Riley – Riley Cycle Co. Ltd., City Works; Riley (Coventry) Ltd., Durbar Ave; Cunard Works, Foleshill–Abingdon	1898 to date
Rover – The Rover Co. Ltd., Meteor Works, West Orchard, Coventry; Hay Hall Road, Tyseley (and Solihull), Birmingham; New Meteor Works, Stoke, Coventry	1904 to date
Rudge – Rudge-Whitworth Ltd.	1912–13
Ryley – Ryley, Ward & Bradford	1901–2
Siddeley – Siddeley Autocar Co., Parkside	1902–4
Siddeley-Deasy (succeeding Deasy) – Siddeley-Deasy Motor Mfg. Co. Ltd.	1911–19
Singer – Singer & Co. Ltd., Canterbury Street, Coventry; Coventry Road, Birmingham	1900 to date
S.S. – S.S. Cars Ltd., Holbrook Lane	1932–6
Standard – Standard Motor Co. Ltd., Foleshill Road, Banner Lane and Canley	1903 to date
Sturmey – Sturmey Motors Ltd., 230–50 Widdrington Road	1909–12
Swift – Swift of Coventry Ltd., Cheylesmore and Quinton Works	1899–1931
Titan Co., Carmelite Road	D
Triumph – Triumph Motor Co. Ltd., Priory Street, Banner Lane	1923 to date
Velox – Velox Motor Co. Ltd.	1902–4
Vernon Cycle & Motor Co., Earl Street	B
Warwick – S. H. Newsome	E
West – West Ltd., Foleshill Road	1904–12
Whitley Motor & Engineering Co., Cow Lane	B
Wigan-Barlow – Wigan-Barlow Motors Ltd., Lowther Street	1922–3
Williamson – Williamson Motor Co. Ltd.	1913–16

Body Builders

1911

Charlesworth Bodies, Much Park Street
Coventry Motor Bodies, Cow Lane
Foleshill Motor & Carriage Works, 440 Stoney Stanton Road
Hewer's Car Bodies, Aldbourne Road
Thomas Hobley, 5 Chester Street
Albert Mason, Sir Thomas White Road
Hollick & Pratt, Mile Lane
Parkside Motor Body Works
T. Pass, Little Park Street
Standard, Bishopgate Green and Cash's Lane

1921–2

E. Bryant, North Street
Charlesworth, as above
Acme Motor Co., Osborn Road
Coventry Motor & Sundries, Spon End
Cross & Ellis, Clay Lane
Hancock & Warman, Walsgrave Road
Midland Light Bodies, Stoke Row
Midland Light Body, Byron Street
Midland Motor Body, Aldbourne Road
Motor Bodies (Cov), Holbrook Lane
Musson & Grindley, Spon End
Park Side, Motor Body Works
T. Pass, West Orchard and Little Park Street
Swift, as above
Tarver Bros, 39 Moor Street
W. E. Timms, 65 Butts
Viking Motor, Warwick Street, Earlsdon
Walsgrave Motor Body Co., Walsgrave Road

Motor Engine Makers

1911

Aero & Marine Engine Co., Stoney Stanton Road (also aeroplane fitters)
Condor Motor Co., Broad Street

Coventry Semplex Engine Co., Paynes Lane
Cromwell Engineering Co., Stoney Stanton Road
Forman, as above
Hillman, as above
Motor Accessories Co., Broad Street
Riley, as above
White & Poppe, as above

Sources and Method

Tapes

We have made over eighty tape-recordings during the course of our work. They were made during interviews with many people including Sir Arnold Hall, Jack Jones, the Honourable Ernest Siddeley, Lord Thomas of Remenham and others who have helped to shape the course of events in Coventry. They have proved invaluable in providing the supporting detail which makes a narrative live. We have, however, been able to confirm their accounts from the vast amount of written material which has been available to us. Among this material we have consulted the following:

Select Bibliography

We have drawn heavily on the files of the *Coventry Evening Telegraph* (previously the *Midland Daily Telegraph*), for the period between 1935 and the present day. Other newspapers consulted have been the *Coventry Standard*, *The Birmingham Post*, *The Times* and *The People*. The Committee and Council Minutes of Coventry City Council have been referred to from the year 1900, and particularly intensively from 1935 to the present day. The annual *Municipal Handbooks* of the same body have proved an invaluable source for the same period. The number of departmental publications dealing with particular undertakings or services is so large that they cannot all be mentioned. We have consulted the annual reports of the Medical Officer of Health and Chief Constable, and reports submitted by Chief Officers to their respective committees. The annual *Housing Reports*, which have been issued in printed form since 1962, have been most useful. The Town Clerk's correspondence on the promotion of the University of Warwick has also been consulted.

Central government departments have given us access to wartime files on both the reconstruction of Coventry's industry after the blitz and on official reactions to the early stages of the Gibson

Plan. The Coventry Office of the Department of Employment and Productivity has been most co-operative in the statistics it has placed at our disposal. We have consulted various social surveys, from the Tile Hill Social Survey undertaken in 1955 to a recent survey of three areas of Coventry Municipal Housing produced by John Holliday and Lisa Carter of the Lanchester Polytechnic. The Coventry and Warwickshire Street and Trade Directories for this century have proved very useful, as have the *Evening Telegraph*'s *Year Book* and *Who's Who* which began publication in 1966. We have also used Volumes II and VIII of the *Victoria County History of Warwickshire*. Many of the volumes of the official *History of the Second World War* have helped to put Coventry in its national perspective.

Earlier books have been written on various aspects of the history of Coventry. Probably the fullest of these is Benjamin Poole's *The History and Antiquities of Coventry*, published in 1870. Frederick Smith, Town Clerk of the city between 1924 and 1946, wrote *Six Hundred Years of Municipal Government*, concentrating mainly on the medieval city. Equally important is John Prest's book on *The Industrial Revolution in Coventry*. Rather more recent has been the study made in Coventry by J. K. Friend and W. N. Jessop on *Local Government and Strategic Choice*. Articles in journals such as *The Bicycle*, *The Cycling World Illustrated* and the *Indispensable Bicyclists' Handbook* have all added interesting pieces of information to our knowledge of the earlier industries in the city. This has been supplemented by such books as *The Craftsman in Textiles* by G. Clark, *Wheels Within Wheels* by G. Williamson, and *Early Days in British Motorcycle Industry* by E. W. Walford.

We have been allowed access to the private papers of the late Sir Alfred Herbert now in the custody of his grandson, Mr Brian Hollick of Fenny Compton, and have been provided with extracts from the unpublished autobiography of Siegfried Bettmann by courtesy of Mr George Moore, Mr William Maddocks has allowed us to see his own account of the Coventry air raid of 14 November 1940 and we have had access to the private papers of Rowland Barratt, now in the custody of his great nephew in Presteign. The four volumes of typescript left by Captain Thurston, Secretary to Coventry Cathedral Reconstruction Committee, have been made available to us by the Cathedral Archivist. The Unitarians have placed at our disposal valuable records from the early eighteenth century and the Salvation Army have lent us their Corps History.

For the chapters dealing with the city's industry we have referred to a large number of house journals past and present, including *The Armstrong-Siddeley Journal*, *Arrow* (Chrysler U.K.), *The Alfred Herbert Journal*, *Rayoneer* (Courtaulds) and the *Loudspeaker* (G.E.C.). Among house histories and related publications we have used *The Evening and the Morning* (Bristol Siddeley), *The History of Brico, 1909 to 1959*, *Aged in the Wood*, published by Burbridges, *Dunlop Wheels* and *The Dunlop Organisation* published by Dunlop, *Garlick's Limited*, *Bushills of Coventry* by E. Howe, *B.T.H. Reminiscences*, *The Products of the Jaguar Group of Companies* and *Case History*, both published by Jaguar, *The Leyland Motor Corporation*, *Seventy-five Years of Smith's Stamping Works* by A. Muir, *The Story of the Standard Pressed Steel Company*, *Umbrako Today* and a privately circulated typescript history of Armstrong Siddeley by R. Dean, lent to us by W. S. D. Lockwood, who also placed in our hands a most detailed record of employment and production at Hawker Siddeley's Baginton factory.

Both *Autocar* and *Motorsport* have, over the past fifty years, contained articles on Coventry cars and several books have been written on individual cars and the men who made them. P. Andrews and E. Bruner have written a *Life of Lord Nuffield.* Others have included *The Alvis Car from 1920 to 1926* by J. R. Day, *The Vintage Alvis* by P. Hull and R. Johnson, *Rover* by H. Light, *The Standard Car 1903 to 1966* by J. R. Davey and *Riley* by A. Birmingham. Lord Montagu of Beaulieu has written two very useful books, *Jaguar, a Biography* and *Lost Causes in Motoring.* Sir Miles, now Lord, Thomas's autobiography *Out on a Wing* has also been used. Other industries in Coventry have also attracted their biographers. Basil Tripp has written two books on the Renold Chain Company, *Renold Chains* and *Renold Limited 1956 to 1967.* D. C. Coleman has written a two-volume history of *Courtaulds* and E. B. Neufeld has written *Global Corporation* about Massey-Ferguson.

Both the Amalgamated Union of Engineers and the Transport and General Workers' Union have supplied us with handbooks and copies of national agreements. *The Humber Clarion*, a journal of shop-stewards at the Humber Works, has also proved useful. John Yates's *Pioneers to Power*, and George Tremlett's *The First Century*, a history of the Working Men's Clubs and Institutes Union, have been very useful in our study of working life in Coventry.

Many books have been written about the replanning of various cities after the war. Of the general books, we have relied heavily on Patrick Abercrombie's *Town and County Planning*, Wilfred Burns's two books, *British Shopping Centres* and *New Towns for Old*, and Percy Johnson Marshall's *Cities*. Articles in the *R.I.B.A. Journal*, the *Architects' Journal*, *Forum*, *The Chartered Surveyor*, *The Town Planning Review* and the *Architectural Review* have all proved invaluable, as has information sent from the City Council of Rotterdam and the Inter-Nationes of Germany.

Many aspects of religious life in Coventry are covered in F. R. Barrie's *Mervyn Haigh* and F. W. Moyles's *Neville Gorton*. Also used have been C. E. Binyon's *The Christian Socialist Movement in England*, R. Groves's *Conrad Noel and the Thaxted Movement*, Morris Reckett's *P. E. T. Widdrington*, R. T. Howard's *Ruined and Rebuilt*, S. Phipps's *God on Monday*, David Lepine's *Coventry Cathedral*, Basil Spence's account of the building of the Cathedral, *Phoenix at Coventry*, and the book on the work of the Cathedral, *Twentieth Century Cathedral*, by the present Provost, H. C. N. Williams.

Index